SELECTIONS FOR CONTRACTS

UNIFORM COMMERCIAL CODE, RESTATEMENT SECOND, UN SALES CONVENTION, UNIDROIT PRINCIPLES, FORMS

Compiled By

E. ALLAN FARNSWORTH
Alfred McCormack Professor of Law
Columbia University

WILLIAM F. YOUNG
James L. Dohr Professor of Law Emeritus
Columbia University

FOUNDATION PRESS
NEW YORK, NEW YORK
2004

Foundation Press, a Thomson business, has created this publication to provide you with accurate and authoritative information concerning the subject matter covered. However, this publication was not necessarily prepared by persons licensed to practice law in a particular jurisdiction. Foundation Press is not engaged in rendering legal or other professional advice, and this publication is not a substitute for the advice of an attorney. If you require legal or other expert advice, you should seek the services of a competent attorney or other professional.

© 1980, 1988, 1992, 1998, 2001 FOUNDATION PRESS
© 2003 By FOUNDATION PRESS
        395 Hudson Street
        New York, NY 10014
        Phone Toll Free 1–877–888–1330
        Fax (212) 367–6799
        fdpress.com
Printed in the United States of America

ISBN 1–58778–587–0

 *TEXT IS PRINTED ON 10% POST CONSUMER RECYCLED PAPER*

1st Reprint—2004

TABLE OF CONTENTS

*

SELECTIONS FOR CONTRACTS

UNIFORM COMMERCIAL CODE,
RESTATEMENT SECOND,
UN SALES CONVENTION, UNIDROIT
PRINCIPLES, FORMS

*

UNIFORM COMMERCIAL CODE

(Articles 1 and 2)[1]

COMPILERS' NOTE

The law of contracts has been much affected by the Uniform Commercial Code. Relevant parts of the Code, Article 1 (General Provisions), Article 2 (Sale of Goods), and an important section from Article 3 (Negotiable Instruments) are reproduced below, together with a few representative comments. A little background is important to an understanding of this unique piece of uniform legislation.[2]

History. Until the seventeenth century contracts dealing with commercial matters were governed largely by the law merchant, a specialized body of customs made and administered by merchants themselves. Thus courts of merchants decided controversies that developed—at the fairs that were the centers for much of early trade. Large bodies of mercantile practice were carried into the English common law of negotiable instruments and insurance. In substantial part this was the work of Lord Mansfield, who became Chief Justice of the King's Bench in 1756. In controversies between merchants, he made it a point to ascertain and apply the customs of the trade, sometimes using for this purpose a special merchants' jury to advise him on commercial practices. But as Professor Karl Llewellyn pointed out, it is one of the ironies of the law that mercantile custom was not fully imported into the law of sales.[3] Llewellyn contended that this was an accident: the decisive sales cases did not come to Mansfield but to judges of a different bent who were content to decide mercantile disputes on the basis of concepts developed for a static land economy. At any rate, a complex body of common-law doctrine developed to govern sales of goods.

The British law of sales was reduced to statutory form in the Sale of Goods Act of 1893. The National Conference of Commissioners on Uniform State Laws entrusted to Professor Samuel Williston the task of producing a similar statute for the American states. His draft, to be known as the Uniform Sales Act, was approved by the Commissioners in 1906 and was eventually adopted by more than thirty states. However, like its British cousin, it had relatively little to do with contractual problems arising out of the sale of goods and these remained largely

---

1. Along with UCC 3–311.
2. The following is adapted in part from E.A. Farnsworth, J. Honnold, S. Harris, C. Mooney & C. Reitz. Cases and Materials on Commercial Law 3–11 (5th ed. 1993).

3. Llewellyn, Across Sales on Horseback, 52 Harv.L.Rev. 725 (1939).

governed by common-law rules. During the half-century after the Uniform Sales Act, a number of proposals were made for change, and some states passed amendments to certain sections. A federal sales act was proposed in Congress in 1940, but the Commissioners succeeded in having it postponed. Work began in that year on a Uniform Revised Sales Act and in 1945 this project was expanded to concentrate upon a comprehensive Uniform Commercial Code, to replace not only the Uniform Sales Act but other uniform acts dealing with commercial matters as well. The American Law Institute joined forces with the National Conference of Commissioners in this effort, with Professor Llewellyn as Chief Reporter, and Soia Mentschikoff as Associate Chief Reporter. A final Official Draft with extensive comments was approved by the two sponsoring organizations in 1952, and was promptly enacted by Pennsylvania in April 1953, effective July 1, 1954.

In many areas the Code took an entirely new approach to problems. The most important of these for our purposes was the reduction to statutory text and inclusion of many rules of contract law relating to sale of goods that had previously been left largely to the common law. The New York Law Revision Commission began to study the Code in 1953 and, in response to criticism, the sponsors of the Code published a number of amendments in 1955. The Commission held public hearings and retained consultants to study the draft, and in February 1956, after three years, it reported to the state legislature that the Code was not satisfactory. Contemporaneous revision produced the 1956 Recommendations for the Uniform Commercial Code and these Recommendations became the 1957 Official Edition, which was published with Comments and minor revisions early in 1958.

By late 1961, thirteen states, including Pennsylvania, had adopted the 1958 Official Text of the Code, and the New York Law Revision Commission recommended its adoption in New York. It was enacted in 1962, to be effective on September 27, 1964. New York made, as had other states, a number of changes in the 1958 Official Text. In order to curb this tendency away from uniformity, a Permanent Editorial Board for the Uniform Commercial Code had been established in 1961. The Board passed upon the amendments made or proposed by each of the states and those of which it approved were incorporated in the 1962 Official Text. (It has since issued Commentaries on Code provisions that have proved troublesome.) The Code has now been adopted in all states except Louisiana, and in the District of Columbia. The Code is divided into the following substantive articles: Article 1, General Provisions; Article 2, Sales; Article 2A, Leases; Article 3, Negotiable Instruments; Article 4, Bank Deposits and Collections; Article 4A, Funds Transfers; Article 5, Letters of Credit; Article 6, Bulk Transfers[4]; Article 7, Ware-

---

4. The sponsors of the Code now recommend that Article 6 be repealed, and most states have repealed it.

house Receipts, Bills of Lading and Other Documents of Title; Article 8, Investment Securities; Article 9, Secured Transactions, Sales of Accounts and Chattel Paper.

Continuing Code Revision. As this list indicates, the original nine substantive articles have been significantly changed. In 1987 the sponsors of the Code promulgated a new Article 2A (Leases), and in 1990 amended it. A major purpose was to resolve "dissonances" between Article 2 (Sales) and Article 9 (Secured Transactions). The Article applies to a transaction in personal property that is a lease rather than either a sale or a security interest as such. Article 2A resembles Article 2 (Sales) in its structure and much of its text. Revisions of Articles 1 and 2 have been nearly completed as this book goes to press.

Use of the Code and Comments. The Code makes much less of an attempt than did the earlier codifications in Britain and the United States to follow existing formulations of the law. Very little of the language of the Uniform Sales Act was retained, and in some respects the Code takes a drastically new approach to the law. We shall have a chance to consider the soundness of some of the changes made by the Code.

One question in working with the Code is the extent to which recourse is to be had to prior drafts as an aid to interpretation. The 1952 edition of the Code attempted to close the door on such legislative history by providing: "Prior drafts of text and comments may not be used to ascertain legislative intent." This language was, however, deleted from the Code.

A comparable question is the extent to which, in interpreting the Code, recourse should be had to the Comments that follow each section. A hazard for the lazy mind, and a help for the responsible lawyer, the Comments raise troublesome problems about their place in the Code system. (Because of their bulk, only a few representative Comments have been reproduced here; the Comments run several times as long as the statutory text.)

The most obvious point about the Comments is often overlooked: The text to the Code was enacted by the legislature; the Comments were not. One is tempted to ignore this point because the Comments, written in an explanatory and non-statutory style, are easier to read. *Facilis est descensus Averno.* But the tempter will whisper: The drafters wrote these Comments, didn't they? If they say what the Code does, that's bound to be right, isn't it? Why bother then with this prickly statutory language?

The role of the Comments is discussed in the Comments themselves. Thus, the Comment to the Title of the Code (1962 Official Text, page 1) in part reads:

This Comment and those which follow are the Comments of the National Conference of Commissioners on Uniform State Laws and the American Law Institute. Uniformity throughout American jurisdictions is one of the main objectives of this Code; and that objective cannot be obtained without substantial uniformity of construction. To aid in uniform construction these Comments set forth the purpose of various provisions of this Act to promote uniformity, to aid in viewing the Act as an integrated whole, and to safeguard against misconstruction.

This Comment does not, however, indicate to what extent the revision of the Comments was brought before the sponsoring organizations or reviewed by the drafters. Apparently this revision of the Comments was considered part of the final editorial work and entrusted to the faithful few who were carrying the Code project to its conclusion. Furthermore, in some states the revised Comments had not yet been drafted at the time of the Code's adoption. In others it is highly doubtful that the Comments were laid before the legislators in the form of a committee report explaining the legislation that the legislators were asked to adopt.

It would be very wrong, however, to conclude that the Comments are without value to lawyers and to courts. Courts have repeatedly quoted the Comments in construing the Code. Surely the Comments may be given at least as much weight as an able article or treatise construing the Code. But if the statutory provisions adopted by the legislature contradict or fail to support the Comments, the Comments must be rejected. The point is significant, for there are instances, easily understood in light of the Comments' bulk and the many successive revisions of the Code, where the Comments contradict the statute. More frequent are instances of enthusiastic discussion of significant problems on which the statute is silent. (See, e.g., the Comment to the Title quoted above.)

A word of caution is also in order concerning the "Definitional Cross References" which are contained in the Comments and which are set out in these Selections. A careful lawyer will not rely on the completeness of these references in the Comments. For a thorough job, the lawyer will check Article 1, which contains important provisions applicable to the Code as a whole; UCC 1–201 contains the definitions of many terms used throughout the Code. In addition, the lawyer will check the definitions specially applicable to the article involved; nearly every article contains a helpful section, e.g., UCC 2–103, containing an "index of definitions."

Revision of Articles 1 and 2. In 2003, the Code's sponsors, the National Conference of Commissioners on Uniform State Laws and the American Law Institute, gave their approval, subject to stylistic changes, to a revised text of Article 2. This brought to an end a contentious effort that had lasted for over a decade and had been marked by the resignation in protest of the Reporter initially selected to draft the revised text. In the meantime, a revision of Article 1 had been completed. The texts of both revised Articles are set out below following the texts of original Articles 1 and 2. In the commentary by the compilers, sections of the original articles (the Official Text as it existed immediately prior to the revisions) are designated by "§" (e.g., § 2–201) while sections of the revised articles are designated by "R" (e.g., R 2–201).

Most sections of both Articles have undergone at least minor changes. Three types are pervasive. First, gender has been neutered by the elimination of all forms of the pronoun *he*. Second, the use of electronic means in contracting has been accommodated by the use of the term *record* in place of the term *writing*. Third, some special rules for consumers have been introduced.

The revision of Article 1 involved both substantive and organizational changes. A new Part 3 comprises ten new sections the substance of which was derived from sections of original Article 1.

The revision of Article 2 — much more modest than that envisaged by the initial drafting group—made substantive changes but retained the organization of original Article 2. It deleted six sections (§§ 2–319 to 2–324) as "inconsistent with modern commercial practices" and added two sections (R 2–313A and 2–313B). None of these changes is central to the subject of contract law. The final obstacle to approval of revised Article 2 was overcome by acceptance of a revised definition of *goods* in R 2–103(1)(k), under which the term "does not include information." The intention is that revised Article 2 will apply to a sale of "smart" goods such as an automobile that incorporates a computer program but will not apply to an electronic transfer of information not associated with goods.

The compilers have indicated significant changes, other than the ones just noted, by footnotes to original Articles 1 and 2, directing the reader to the sections of revised Articles 1 and 2 that incorporate those changes.

*

UNIFORM COMMERCIAL CODE

2000 OFFICIAL TEXT[1]

Table of Contents

ARTICLE 1. GENERAL PROVISIONS

ARTICLE 2. SALES

---

1. The original and revised texts of the Code are copyrighted by the American Law Institute and the National Conference of Commissioners on Uniform State Laws. Re- printed with permission of the Permanent Editorial Board of the Uniform Commercial Code.

ARTICLE 1.   GENERAL PROVISIONS

PART 1

SHORT TITLE, CONSTRUCTION, APPLICATION AND SUBJECT MATTER OF THE ACT

§ 1–101. Short Title

This Act shall be known and may be cited as Uniform Commercial Code.

§ 1–102. Purposes; Rules of Construction; Variation by Agreement[a]

(1) This Act shall be liberally construed and applied to promote its underlying purposes and policies.

(2) Underlying purposes and policies of this Act are

a. Parts of this section are recast and reassigned to R 1–103(a), R 1–106, and R 1–302. R 1–102 contains a brief new statement of the scope of the article.

(a) to simplify, clarify and modernize the law governing commercial transactions;

(b) to permit the continued expansion of commercial practices through custom, usage and agreement of the parties;

(c) to make uniform the law among the various jurisdictions.

(3) The effect of provisions of this Act may be varied by agreement, except as otherwise provided in this Act and except that the obligations of good faith, diligence, reasonableness and care prescribed by this Act may not be disclaimed by agreement but the parties may by agreement determine the standards by which the performance of such obligations is to be measured if such standards are not manifestly unreasonable.

(4) The presence in certain provisions of this Act of the words "unless otherwise agreed" or words of similar import does not imply that the effect of other provisions may not be varied by agreement under subsection (3).

(5) In this Act unless the context otherwise requires

(a) words in the singular number include the plural, and in the plural include the singular;

(b) words of the masculine gender include the feminine and the neuter, and when the sense so indicates words of the neuter gender may refer to any gender.

§ 1–103. Supplementary General Principles of Law Applicable[b]

Unless displaced by the particular provisions of this Act, the principles of law and equity, including the law merchant and the law relative to capacity to contract, principal and agent, estoppel, fraud, misrepresentation, duress, coercion, mistake, bankruptcy, or other validating or invalidating cause shall supplement its provisions.

§ 1–104. Construction Against Implicit Repeal[c]

This Act being a general act intended as a unified coverage of its subject matter, no part of it shall be deemed to be impliedly repealed by subsequent legislation if such construction can reasonably be avoided.

§ 1–105. Territorial Application of the Act; Parties' Power to Choose Applicable Law

(1) Except as provided hereafter in this section, when a transaction bears a reasonable relation to this state and also to another state or nation the parties may agree that the law either of this state or of such other state or nation shall govern their rights and duties. Failing such

b. Redesignated R 1–103(b).   **c.** Redesignated R 1–104.

agreement this Act applies to transactions bearing an appropriate relation to this state.

(2) Where one of the following provisions of this Act specifies the applicable law, that provision governs and a contrary agreement is effective only to the extent permitted by the law (including the conflict of laws rules) so specified:

Rights of creditors against sold goods. Section 2–402. . . .

§ **1–106.** Remedies to Be Liberally Administered[d]

(1) The remedies provided by this Act shall be liberally administered to the end that the aggrieved party may be put in as good a position as if the other party had fully performed but neither consequential or special nor penal damages may be had except as specifically provided in this Act or by other rule of law.

(2) Any right or obligation declared by this Act is enforceable by action unless the provision declaring it specifies a different and limited effect.

Definitional Cross References:

"Action". Section 1–201.

"Aggrieved party". Section 1–201.

"Party". Section 1–201.

"Remedy". Section 1–201.

"Rights". Section 1–201.

§ **1–107.** Waiver or Renunciation of Claim or Right After Breach[e]

Any claim or right arising out of an alleged breach can be discharged in whole or in part without consideration by a written waiver or renunciation signed and delivered by the aggrieved party.

Definitional Cross References:

"Aggrieved party". Section 1–201.

"Rights". Section 1–201.

"Signed". Section 1–201.

"Written". Section 1–201.

§ **1–108.** Severability[f]

If any provision or clause of this Act or application thereof to any person or circumstances is held invalid, such invalidity shall not affect other provisions or applications of the Act which can be given effect without the invalid provision or application, and to this end the provisions of this Act are declared to be severable.

Definitional Cross Reference:

"Person". Section 1–201.

d. Redesignated R 1–305, with stylistic changes.

e. Redesignated R 1–306, with a modification.

f. Redesignated R 1–105.

§ 1–109. Section Captions[g]

Section captions are parts of this Act.

PART 2

GENERAL DEFINITIONS AND PRINCIPLES OF INTERPRETATION

§ 1–201. General Definitions[h]

Subject to additional definitions contained in the subsequent Articles of this Act which are applicable to specific Articles or Parts thereof, and unless the context otherwise requires, in this Act:

(1) "Action" in the sense of a judicial proceeding includes recoupment, counterclaim, set-off, suit in equity and any other proceedings in which rights are determined.

(2) "Aggrieved party" means a party entitled to resort to a remedy.

(3) "Agreement" means the bargain of the parties in fact as found in their language or by implication from other circumstances including course of dealing or usage of trade or course of performance as provided in this Act (Sections 1–205 and 2–208). Whether an agreement has legal consequences is determined by the provisions of this Act, if applicable; otherwise by the law of contracts (Section 1–103). (Compare "Contract".)

(4) "Bank" means any person engaged in the business of banking.

(5) "Bearer" means the person in possession of an instrument, document of title, or certificated security payable to bearer or indorsed in blank.

(6) "Bill of lading" means a document evidencing the receipt of goods for shipment issued by a person engaged in the business of transporting or forwarding goods, and includes an airbill. "Airbill" means a document serving for air transportation as a bill of lading does for marine or rail transportation, and includes an air consignment note or air waybill.

(7) "Branch" includes a separately incorporated foreign branch of a bank.

(8) "Burden of establishing" a fact means the burden of persuading the triers of fact that the existence of the fact is more probable than its non-existence.

g. Redesignated R 1–107.

h. Most entries below appear in R 1–201(b), with some modifications. A few, as indicated by footnotes, are replaced with comparable provisions in new sections.

A few terms are newly defined in R 1–201(b). Two of these are "consumer" and "record".

(9) "Buyer in ordinary course of business" means a person who in good faith and without knowledge that the sale to him is in violation of the ownership rights or security interest of a third party in the goods buys in ordinary course from a person in the business of selling goods of that kind but does not include a pawnbroker. All persons who sell minerals or the like (including oil and gas) at wellhead or minehead shall be deemed to be persons in the business of selling goods of that kind. "Buying" may be for cash or by exchange of other property or on secured or unsecured credit and includes receiving goods or documents of title under a preexisting contract for sale but does not include a transfer in bulk or as security for or in total or partial satisfaction of a money debt.

(10) "Conspicuous": A term or clause is conspicuous when it is so written that a reasonable person against whom it is to operate ought to have noticed it. A printed heading in capitals (as: NON–NEGOTIABLE BILL OF LADING) is conspicuous. Language in the body of a form is "conspicuous" if it is in larger or other contrasting type or color. But in a telegram any stated term is "conspicuous". Whether a term or clause is "conspicuous" or not is for decision by the court.

(11) "Contract" means the total legal obligation which results from the parties' agreement as affected by this Act and any other applicable rules of law. (Compare "Agreement".)

(12) "Creditor" includes a general creditor, a secured creditor, a lien creditor and any representative of creditors, including an assignee for the benefit of creditors, a trustee in bankruptcy, a receiver in equity and an executor or administrator of an insolvent debtor's or assignor's estate.

(13) "Defendant" includes a person in the position of defendant in a cross-action or counterclaim.

(14) "Delivery" with respect to instruments, documents of title, chattel paper, or certificated securities means voluntary transfer of possession.

(15) "Document of title" includes bill of lading, dock warrant, dock receipt, warehouse receipt or order for the delivery of goods, and also any other document which in the regular course of business or financing is treated as adequately evidencing that the person in possession of it is entitled to receive, hold and dispose of the document and the goods it covers. To be a document of title a document must purport to be issued by or addressed to a bailee and purport to cover goods in the bailee's possession which are either identified or are fungible portions of an identified mass.

(16) "Fault" means wrongful act, omission or breach.

(17) "Fungible" with respect to goods or securities means goods or securities of which any unit is, by nature or usage of trade, the equiva-

lent of any other like unit. Goods which are not fungible shall be deemed fungible for the purposes of this Act to the extent that under a particular agreement or document unlike units are treated as equivalents.

(18) "Genuine" means free of forgery or counterfeiting.

(19) "Good faith" means honesty in fact in the conduct or transaction concerned.[i]

(20) "Holder," with respect to a negotiable instrument, means the person in possession if the instrument is payable to bearer or, in the case of an instrument payable to an identified person, if the identified person is in possession. "Holder" with respect to a document of title means the person in possession if the goods are deliverable to bearer or to the order of the person in possession.

(21) To "honor" is to pay or to accept and pay, or where a credit so engages to purchase or discount a draft complying with the terms of the credit.

(22) "Insolvency proceedings" includes any assignment for the benefit of creditors or other proceedings intended to liquidate or rehabilitate the estate of the person involved.

(23) A person is "insolvent" who either has ceased to pay his debts in the ordinary course of business or cannot pay his debts as they become due or is insolvent within the meaning of the federal bankruptcy law.

(24) "Money" means a medium of exchange authorized or adopted by a domestic or foreign government and includes a monetary unit of account established by an intergovernmental organization or by agreement between two or more nations.

(25) [j] A person has "notice" of a fact when

   (a) he has actual knowledge of it; or

   (b) he has received a notice or notification of it; or

   (c) from all the facts and circumstances known to him at the time in question he has reason to know that it exists.

A person "knows" or has "knowledge" of a fact when he has actual knowledge of it. "Discover" or "learn" or a word or phrase of similar import refers to knowledge rather than to reason to know. The time and circumstances under which a notice or notification may cease to be effective are not determined by this Act.

(26) [k] A person "notifies" or "gives" a notice or notification to another by taking such steps as may be reasonably required to inform

i. R 1–201(b)(20) modifies this definition materially by including "fair dealing".

j. Dealt with in R 1–202.

k. Dealt with in R 1–202.

the other in ordinary course whether or not such other actually comes to know of it. A person "receives" a notice or notification when

(a) it comes to his attention; or

(b) it is duly delivered at the place of business through which the contract was made or at any other place held out by him as the place for receipt of such communications.

(27) [1] Notice, knowledge or a notice or notification received by an organization is effective for a particular transaction from the time when it is brought to the attention of the individual conducting that transaction, and in any event from the time when it would have been brought to his attention if the organization had exercised due diligence. An organization exercises due diligence if it maintains reasonable routines for communicating significant information to the person conducting the transaction and there is reasonable compliance with the routines. Due diligence does not require an individual acting for the organization to communicate information unless such communication is part of his regular duties or unless he has reason to know of the transaction and that the transaction would be materially affected by the information.

(28) "Organization" includes a corporation, government or governmental subdivision or agency, business trust, estate, trust, partnership or association, two or more persons having a joint or common interest, or any other legal or commercial entity.

(29) "Party", as distinct from "third party", means a person who has engaged in a transaction or made an agreement within this Act.

(30) "Person" includes an individual or an organization (See Section 1–102).

(31) "Presumption" or "presumed" means that the trier of fact must find the existence of the fact presumed unless and until evidence is introduced which would support a finding of its non-existence.

(32) "Purchase" includes taking by sale, discount, negotiation, mortgage, pledge, lien, issue or re-issue, gift or any other voluntary transaction creating an interest in property.

(33) "Purchaser" means a person who takes by purchase.

(34) "Remedy" means any remedial right to which an aggrieved party is entitled with or without resort to a tribunal.

(35) "Representative" includes an agent, an officer of a corporation or association, and a trustee, executor or administrator of an estate, or any other person empowered to act for another.

(36) "Rights" includes remedies.

(37) "Security interest" means an interest in personal property or fixtures which secures payment or performance of an obligation. The

---

1. Dealt with in R 1–202.

term also includes any interest of a consignor and a buyer of accounts, chattel paper, a payment intangible, or a promissory note in a transaction that is subject to Article 9. . . . Whether a transaction creates a lease or security interest is determined by the facts of each case . . .[m]

(38) "Send" in connection with any writing or notice means to deposit in the mail or deliver for transmission by any other usual means of communication with postage or cost of transmission provided for and properly addressed and in the case of an instrument to an address specified thereon or otherwise agreed, or if there be none to any address reasonable under the circumstances. The receipt of any writing or notice within the time at which it would have arrived if properly sent has the effect of a proper sending.

(39) "Signed" includes any symbol executed or adopted by a party with present intention to authenticate a writing.

(40) "Surety" includes guarantor.

(41) "Telegram" includes a message transmitted by radio, teletype, cable, any mechanical method of transmission, or the like.

(42) "Term" means that portion of an agreement which relates to a particular matter.

(43) "Unauthorized" signature means one made without actual, implied, or apparent authority and includes a forgery.

(44) "Value".[n] Except as otherwise provided with respect to negotiable instruments and bank collections (Sections 3–303, 4–208 and 4–209) a person gives "value" for rights if he acquires them

> (a) in return for a binding commitment to extend credit or for the extension of immediately available credit whether or not drawn upon and whether or not a charge-back is provided for in the event of difficulties in collection; or
>
> (b) as security for or in total or partial satisfaction of a pre-existing claim; or
>
> (c) by accepting delivery pursuant to a pre-existing contract for purchase; or
>
> (d) generally, in return for any consideration sufficient to support a simple contract.

(45) "Warehouse receipt" means a receipt issued by a person engaged in the business of storing goods for hire.

(46) "Written" or "writing" includes printing, typewriting or any other intentional reduction to tangible form.

m. The definition continues with more than a dozen clauses bearing on the question whether or not a transaction designated as a lease generates instead a "security interest". These provisions affect Article 9 of the Code (Secured Transactions). In revised Article 1, the distinction is governed by R 1–203.

n. "Value" is dealt with in R 1–204.

§ 1–202. Prima Facie Evidence by Third Party Documents°

A document in due form purporting to be a bill of lading, policy or certificate of insurance, official weigher's or inspector's certificate, consular invoice, or any other document authorized or required by the contract to be issued by a third party shall be prima facie evidence of its own authenticity and genuineness and of the facts stated in the document by the third party.

Definitional Cross References:

"Bill of lading". Section 1–201.

"Contract". Section 1–201.

"Genuine". Section 1–201.

§ 1–203. Obligation of Good Faith°

Every contract or duty within this Act imposes an obligation of good faith in its performance or enforcement.

Definitional Cross References:

"Contract". Section 1–201.

"Good faith". Section 1–201; 2–103.

§ 1–204. Time; Reasonable Time; "Seasonably"°

(1) Whenever this Act requires any action to be taken within a reasonable time, any time which is not manifestly unreasonable may be fixed by agreement.

(2) What is a reasonable time for taking any action depends on the nature, purpose and circumstances of such action.

(3) An action is taken "seasonably" when it is taken at or within the time agreed or if no time is agreed at or within a reasonable time.

Definitional Cross Reference:

"Agreement". Section 1–201.

§ 1–205. Course of Dealing and Usage of Trade°

(1) A course of dealing is a sequence of previous conduct between the parties to a particular transaction which is fairly to be regarded as establishing a common basis of understanding for interpreting their expressions and other conduct.

(2) A usage of trade is any practice or method of dealing having such regularity of observance in a place, vocation or trade as to justify an expectation that it will be observed with respect to the transaction in

o. Redesignated R 1–307.

p. Redesignated R 1–304, with a minor modification.

q. The substance of this section is carried forward as R 1–302(b) and R 1–205.

r. Carried forward as R 1–303, with changes and additions. See note h, p. 32 below.

question. The existence and scope of such a usage are to be proved as facts. If it is established that such a usage is embodied in a written trade code or similar writing the interpretation of the writing is for the court.

(3) A course of dealing between parties and any usage of trade in the vocation or trade in which they are engaged or of which they are or should be aware give particular meaning to and supplement or qualify terms of an agreement.

(4) The express terms of an agreement and an applicable course of dealing or usage of trade shall be construed wherever reasonable as consistent with each other; but when such construction is unreasonable express terms control both course of dealing and usage of trade and course of dealing controls usage of trade.

(5) An applicable usage of trade in the place where any part of performance is to occur shall be used in interpreting the agreement as to that part of the performance.

(6) Evidence of a relevant usage of trade offered by one party is not admissible unless and until he has given the other party such notice as the court finds sufficient to prevent unfair surprise to the latter.

Definitional Cross References:

"Agreement". Section 1–201.

"Contract". Section 1–201

"Party". Section 1–201.

"Term". Section 1–201.

§ 1–206. Statute of Frauds for Kinds of Personal Property Not Otherwise Covered[s]

(1) Except in the cases described in subsection (2) of this section a contract for the sale of personal property is not enforceable by way of action or defense beyond five thousand dollars in amount or value of remedy unless there is some writing which indicates that a contract for sale has been made between the parties at a defined or stated price, reasonably identifies the subject matter, and is signed by the party against whom enforcement is sought or by his authorized agent.

(2) Subsection (1) of this section does not apply to contracts for the sale of goods (Section 2–201) nor of securities (Section 8–319) nor to security agreements (Section 9–203).

Definitional Cross References:

"Action". Section 1–201.

"Agreement". Section 1–201.

"Contract". Section 1–201.

"Contract for sale". Section 2–106.

"Goods". Section 2–105.

"Party". Section 1–201.

"Sale". Section 2–106.

"Signed". Section 1–201.

"Writing". Section 1–201.

s. Omitted from revised Article 1. See the Legislative Note following R 1–206.

§ 1–207. Performance or Acceptance Under Reservation of Rights[t]

(1) A party who with explicit reservation of rights performs or promises performance or assents to performance in a manner demanded or offered by the other party does not thereby prejudice the rights reserved. Such words as "without prejudice", "under protest" or the like are sufficient.

(2) Subsection (1) does not apply to an accord and satisfaction.

Definitional Cross References:

"Party". Section 1–201.

"Rights". Section 1–201.

§ 1–208. Option to Accelerate at Will[u]

A term providing that one party or his successor in interest may accelerate payment or performance or require collateral or additional collateral "at will" or "when he deems himself insecure" or in words of similar import shall be construed to mean that he shall have power to do so only if he in good faith believes that the prospect of payment or performance is impaired. The burden of establishing lack of good faith is on the party against whom the power has been exercised.

Definitional Cross References:

"Burden of establishing". Section 1–201.

"Good faith". Section 1–201.

"Party". Section 1–201.

"Term". Section 1–201.

§ 1–209. Subordinated Obligations[v]

[Optional provision. Omitted.]

t. Redesignated R 1–308.
u. Carried forward as R 1–309.

v. Carried forward as R 1–310 (not optional).

ARTICLE 2. SALES

PART 1

SHORT TITLE, GENERAL CONSTRUCTION AND SUBJECT MATTER

§ 2–101. Short Title

This Article shall be known and may be cited as Uniform Commercial Code—Sales.

§ 2–102. Scope; Certain Security and Other Transactions Excluded From This Article

Unless the context otherwise requires, this Article applies to transactions in goods; it does not apply to any transaction which although in the form of an unconditional contract to sell or present sale is intended to operate only as a security transaction nor does this Article impair or repeal any statute regulating sales to consumers, farmers or other specified classes of buyers.

Definitional Cross References:

"Contract". Section 1–201.

"Contract for sale". Section 2–106.

"Present sale". Section 2–106.

"Sale". Section 2–106.

§ 2–103. Definitions and Index of Definitions[a]

(1) In this Article unless the context otherwise requires

    (a) "Buyer" means a person who buys or contracts to buy goods.

    (b) "Good faith" in the case of a merchant means honesty in fact and the observance of reasonable commercial standards of fair dealing in the trade.

    (c) "Receipt" of goods means taking physical possession of them.

    (d) "Seller" means a person who sells or contracts to sell goods.

(2) Other definitions applying to this Article or to specified Parts thereof, and the sections in which they appear are:

"Acceptance". Section 2–606.

"Banker's credit". Section 2–325.

"Between merchants". Section 2–104.

---

a. R 2–103(1) contains a revised definition of "good faith" as an alternative to that in R 1–201(b)(20). The revised section includes a number of newly defined terms. Some of these relate specifically to electronic messages and records. Among the others, notable ones are "Conspicuous", "Consumer", and "Consumer contract".

Other additions, and some deletions, appear in R 2–103(2) and (3).

"Cancellation". Section 2–106(4).

"Commercial unit". Section 2–105.

"Confirmed credit". Section 2–325.

"Conforming to contract". Section 2–106.

"Contract for sale". Section 2–106.

"Cover". Section 2–712.

"Entrusting". Section 2–403.

"Financing agency". Section 2–104.

"Future goods". Section 2–105.

"Goods". Section 2–105.

"Identification". Section 2–501.

"Installment contract". Section 2–612.

"Letter of Credit". Section 2–325.

"Lot". Section 2–105.

"Merchant". Section 2–104.

"Overseas". Section 2–323.

"Person in position of seller". Section 2–707.

"Present sale". Section 2–106.

"Sale". Section 2–106.

"Sale on approval". Section 2–326.

"Sale or return". Section 2–326.

"Termination". Section 2–106.

(3) The following definitions in other Articles apply to this Article:

"Check". Section 3–104.

"Consignee". Section 7–102.

"Consignor". Section 7–102.

"Consumer goods". Section 9–102.

"Dishonor". Section 3–502.

"Draft". Section 3–104.

(4) In addition Article 1 contains general definitions and principles of construction and interpretation applicable throughout this Article.

Definitional Cross Reference:

"Person". Section 1–201.

§ 2–104. Definitions; "Merchant"; "Between Merchants"; "Financing Agency"

(1) "Merchant" means a person who deals in goods of the kind or otherwise by his occupation holds himself out as having knowledge or skill peculiar to the practices or goods involved in the transaction or to whom such knowledge or skill may be attributed by his employment of an agent or broker or other intermediary who by his occupation holds himself out as having such knowledge or skill.

(2) "Financing agency" means a bank, finance company or other person who in the ordinary course of business makes advances against goods or documents of title or who by arrangement with either the seller or the buyer intervenes in ordinary course to make or collect payment due or claimed under the contract for sale, as by purchasing or paying the seller's draft or making advances against it or by merely taking it for collection whether or not documents of title accompany the draft. "Financing agency" includes also a bank or other person who similarly intervenes between persons who are in the position of seller and buyer in respect to the goods (Section 2–707).

(3) "Between merchants" means in any transaction with respect to which both parties are chargeable with the knowledge or skill of merchants.

Definitional Cross References:

"Bank". Section 1–201.

"Buyer". Section 2–103.

§ 2–105. Definitions: Transferability; "Goods"; "Future" Goods; "Lot"; "Commercial Unit"[b]

(1) "Goods" means all things (including specially manufactured goods) which are movable at the time of identification to the contract for sale other than the money in which the price is to be paid, investment securities (Article 8) and things in action. "Goods" also includes the unborn young of animals and growing crops and other identified things attached to realty as described in the section on goods to be severed from realty (Section 2–107).

(2) Goods must be both existing and identified before any interest in them can pass. Goods which are not both existing and identified are "future" goods. A purported present sale of future goods or of any interest therein operates as a contract to sell.

(3) There may be a sale of a part interest in existing identified goods.

b. The definition of "goods" in subsection (1) is carried forward in R2–103(1)(k)—"information" being excluded.

(4) An undivided share in an identified bulk of fungible goods is sufficiently identified to be sold although the quantity of the bulk is not determined. Any agreed proportion of such a bulk or any quantity thereof agreed upon by number, weight or other measure may to the extent of the seller's interest in the bulk be sold to the buyer who then becomes an owner in common.

(5) "Lot" means a parcel or a single article which is the subject matter of a separate sale or delivery, whether or not it is sufficient to perform the contract.

(6) "Commercial unit" means such a unit of goods as by commercial usage is a single whole for purposes of sale and division of which materially impairs its character or value on the market or in use. A commercial unit may be a single article (as a machine) or a set of articles (as a suite of furniture or an assortment of sizes) or a quantity (as a bale, gross, or carload) or any other unit treated in use or in the relevant market as a single whole.

Definitional Cross References: "Contract for sale". Section 2–106.
   "Buyer". Section 2–103.
   "Contract". Section 1–201.

§ 2–106. Definitions: "Contract"; "Agreement"; "Contract for Sale"; "Sale"; "Present Sale"; "Conforming" to Contract; "Termination"; "Cancellation"

(1) In this Article unless the context otherwise requires "contract" and "agreement" are limited to those relating to the present or future sale of goods. "Contract for sale" includes both a present sale of goods and a contract to sell goods at a future time. A "sale" consists in the passing of title from the seller to the buyer for a price (Section 2–401). A "present sale" means a sale which is accomplished by the making of the contract.

(2) Goods or conduct including any part of a performance are "conforming" or conform to the contract when they are in accordance with the obligations under the contract.

(3) "Termination" occurs when either party pursuant to a power created by agreement or law puts an end to the contract otherwise than for its breach. On "termination" all obligations which are still executory on both sides are discharged but any right based on prior breach or performance survives.

(4) "Cancellation" occurs when either party puts an end to the contract for breach by the other and its effect is the same as that of "termination" except that the cancelling party also retains any remedy for breach of the whole contract or any unperformed balance.

Definitional Cross References:

"Agreement". Section 1–201.

"Buyer". Section 2–103.

"Contract". Section 1–201.

"Goods". Section 2–105.

"Party". Section 1–201.

"Remedy". Section 1–201.

"Rights". Section 1–201.

"Seller". Section 2–103.

§ 2–107. Goods to Be Severed From Realty: Recording

(1) A contract for the sale of minerals or the like (including oil and gas) or a structure or its materials to be removed from realty is a contract for the sale of goods within this Article if they are to be severed by the seller but until severance a purported present sale thereof which is not effective as a transfer of an interest in land is effective only as a contract to sell.

(2) A contract for the sale apart from the land of growing crops or other things attached to realty and capable of severance without material harm thereto but not described in subsection (1) or of timber to be cut is a contract for the sale of goods within this Article whether the subject matter is to be severed by the buyer or by the seller even though it forms part of the realty at the time of contracting, and the parties can by identification effect a present sale before severance.

(3) The provisions of this section are subject to any third party rights provided by the law relating to realty records, and the contract for sale may be executed and recorded as a document transferring an interest in land and shall then constitute notice to third parties of the buyer's rights under the contract for sale.

Definitional Cross References:

"Buyer". Section 2–103.

"Contract". Section 1–201.

"Contract for sale". Section 2–106.

"Goods". Section 2–105.

"Party". Section 1–201.

"Present sale". Section 2–106.

"Rights". Section 1–201.

"Seller". Section 2–103.

PART 2

FORM, FORMATION AND READJUSTMENT OF CONTRACT

§ 2–201. Formal Requirements; Statute of Frauds[c]

(1) Except as otherwise provided in this section a contract for the sale of goods for the price of $500 or more is not enforceable by way of

---

c. Among the alterations made in R 2–201, two notable ones are:

(i) The revised section begins—omitting the "Except" phrase—"A contract for the sale of goods . . ."; and

(ii) The price reference is changed from $500 to $5,000.

action or defense unless there is some writing sufficient to indicate that a contract for sale has been made between the parties and signed by the party against whom enforcement is sought or by his authorized agent or broker. A writing is not insufficient because it omits or incorrectly states a term agreed upon but the contract is not enforceable under this paragraph beyond the quantity of goods shown in such writing.

(2) Between merchants if within a reasonable time a writing in confirmation of the contract and sufficient against the sender is received and the party receiving it has reason to know its contents, it satisfies the requirements of subsection (1) against such party unless written notice of objection to its contents is given within ten days after it is received.

(3) A contract which does not satisfy the requirements of subsection (1) but which is valid in other respects is enforceable

    (a) if the goods are to be specially manufactured for the buyer and are not suitable for sale to others in the ordinary course of the seller's business and the seller, before notice of repudiation is received and under circumstances which reasonably indicate that the goods are for the buyer, has made either a substantial beginning of their manufacture or commitments for their procurement; or

    (b) if the party against whom enforcement is sought admits in his pleading, testimony or otherwise in court that a contract for sale was made, but the contract is not enforceable under this provision beyond the quantity of goods admitted; or

    (c) with respect to goods for which payment has been made and accepted or which have been received and accepted (Sec. 2–606).

Official Comment

Prior Uniform Statutory Provision: Section 4, Uniform Sales Act (which was based on Section 17 of the Statute of 29 Charles II).

Changes: Completely rephrased; restricted to sale of goods. See also Sections 1–206, 8–319 and 9–203.

Purposes of Changes: The changed phraseology of this section is intended to make it clear that:

1. The required writing need not contain all the material terms of the contract and such material terms as are stated need not be precisely stated. All that is required is that the writing afford a basis for believing that the offered oral evidence rests on a real transaction. It may be written in lead pencil on a scratch pad. It need not indicate which party is the buyer and which the seller. The only term which must appear is the quantity term which need not be accurately stated but recovery is limited to the amount stated. The price, time and place of payment or delivery, the general quality of the goods, or any particular warranties may all be omitted.

Special emphasis must be placed on the permissibility of omitting the price term in view of the insistence of some courts on the express inclusion of this term even where the parties have contracted on the basis of a published price list. In many valid contracts for sale the parties do not mention the price in express terms, the buyer being bound to pay and the seller to accept a reasonable price which the trier of the fact may well be trusted to determine. Again, frequently the price is not mentioned since the parties have based their agreement on a price list or catalogue known to both of them and this list serves as an efficient safeguard against perjury. Finally, "market" prices and valuations that are current in the vicinity constitute a similar check. Thus if the price is not stated in the memorandum it can normally be supplied without danger of fraud. Of course if the "price" consists of goods rather than money the quantity of goods must be stated.

Only three definite and invariable requirements as to the memorandum are made by this subsection. First, it must evidence a contract for the sale of goods; second, it must be "signed", a word which includes any authentication which identifies the party to be charged, and third, it must specify a quantity.

2. "Partial performance" as a substitute for the required memorandum can validate the contract only for the goods which have been accepted or for which payment has been made and accepted.

Receipt and acceptance either of goods or of the price constitutes an unambiguous overt admission by both parties that a contract actually exists. If the court can make a just apportionment, therefore, the agreed price of any goods actually delivered can be recovered without a writing or, if the price has been paid, the seller can be forced to deliver an apportionable part of the goods. The overt actions of the parties make admissible evidence of the other terms of the contract necessary to a just apportionment. This is true even though the actions of the parties are not in themselves inconsistent with a different transaction such as a consignment for resale or a mere loan of money.

Part performance by the buyer requires the delivery of something by him that is accepted by the seller as such performance. Thus, part payment may be made by money or check, accepted by the seller. If the agreed price consists of goods or services, then they must also have been delivered and accepted.

3. Between merchants, failure to answer a written confirmation of a contract within ten days of receipt is tantamount to a writing under subsection (2) and is sufficient against both parties under subsection (1). The only effect, however, is to take away from the party who fails to answer the defense of the Statute of Frauds; the burden of persuading the trier of fact that a contract was in fact made orally prior to the written confirmation is unaffected. Compare the effect of a failure to reply under Section 2–207.

4. Failure to satisfy the requirements of this section does not render the contract void for all purposes, but merely prevents it from being judicially enforced in favor of a party to the contract. For example, a buyer who takes possession of goods as provided in an oral contract which the seller has not meanwhile repudiated, is not a trespasser. Nor would the Statute of Frauds provisions of this section be a defense to a third person who wrongfully induces a party to refuse to perform an oral contract, even though the injured party cannot maintain an action for damages against the party so refusing to perform.

5. The requirement of "signing" is discussed in the comment to Section 1–201.

6. It is not necessary that the writing be delivered to anybody. It need not be signed or authenticated by both

parties but it is, of course, not sufficient against one who has not signed it. Prior to a dispute no one can determine which party's signing of the memorandum may be necessary but from the time of contracting each party should be aware that to him it is signing by the other which is important.

7.   If the making of a contract is admitted in court, either in a written pleading, by stipulation or by oral statement before the court, no additional writing is necessary for protection against fraud. Under this section it is no longer possible to admit the contract in court and still treat the Statute as a defense. However, the contract is not thus conclusively established. The admission so made by a party is itself evidential against him of the truth of the facts so admitted and of nothing more; as against the other party, it is not evidential at all.

Cross References:

See Sections 1–201, 2–202, 2–207, 2–209 and 2–304.

Definitional Cross References:

"Action". Section 1–201.

"Between merchants". Section 2–104.

"Buyer". Section 2–103.

"Contract". Section 1–201.

"Contract for sale". Section 2–106.

"Goods". Section 2–105.

"Notice". Section 1–201.

"Party". Section 1–201.

"Reasonable time". Section 1–204.

"Sale". Section 2–106.

"Seller". Section 2–103.

§ 2–202.   Final Written Expression: Parol or Extrinsic Evidence

Terms with respect to which the confirmatory memoranda of the parties agree or which are otherwise set forth in a writing intended by the parties as a <u>final expression</u> of their agreement with respect to such terms as are included therein may not be contradicted by evidence of any prior agreement or of a contemporaneous oral agreement but may be explained or supplemented

> (a) by course of dealing or usage of trade (Section 1–205) or by course of performance (Section 2–208); and

> (b) by evidence of consistent additional terms unless the court finds the writing to have been intended also as a complete and exclusive statement of the terms of the agreement.

Definitional Cross References:

"Agreed" and "agreement". Section 1–201.

"Course of dealing". Section 1–205.

"Parties". Section 1–201.

"Term". Section 1–201.

"Usage of trade". Section 1–205.

"Written" and "writing". Section 1–201.

§ 2–203.   Seals Inoperative

The affixing of a seal to a writing evidencing a contract for sale or an offer to buy or sell goods does not constitute the writing a sealed instrument and the law with respect to sealed instruments does not apply to such a contract or offer.

Definitional Cross References:

"Contract for sale". Section 2–106.

"Goods". Section 2–105.

"Writing". Section 1–201.

§ 2–204. Formation in General[d]

(1) A contract for sale of goods may be made in any manner sufficient to show agreement, including conduct by both parties which recognizes the existence of such a contract.

(2) An agreement sufficient to constitute a contract for sale may be found even though the moment of its making is undetermined.

(3) Even though one or more terms are left open a contract for sale does not fail for indefiniteness if the parties have intended to make a contract and there is a reasonably certain basis for giving an appropriate remedy.

Definitional Cross References:

"Agreement". Section 1–201.

"Contract". Section 1–201.

"Contract for sale". Section 2 106.

"Goods". Section 2–105.

"Party". Section 1–201.

"Remedy". Section 1–201.

"Term". Section 1–201.

§ 2–205. Firm Offers[e]

An offer by a merchant to buy or sell goods in a signed writing which by its terms gives assurance that it will be held open is not revocable, for lack of consideration, during the time stated or if no time is stated for a reasonable time, but in no event may such period of irrevocability exceed three months; but any such term of assurance on a form supplied by the offeree must be separately signed by the offeror.

Definitional Cross References:

"Goods". Section 2–105.

"Merchant". Section 2–104.

"Signed". Section 1–201.

"Writing". Section 1–201.

§ 2–206. Offer and Acceptance in Formation of Contract[f]

(1) Unless otherwise unambiguously indicated by the language or circumstances

    (a) an offer to make a contract shall be construed as inviting acceptance in any manner and by any medium reasonable in the circumstances;

    (b) an order or other offer to buy goods for prompt or current shipment shall be construed as inviting acceptance either by

d. R 2–204 alters subsection (1), and incorporates a new subsection (4) to deal with interactions with and between "electronic agents".

e. R 2–205 envisages firm offers in wholly electronic form.

f. R 2–206 includes a new subsection (3), derived from original § 2–207(1). See note g.

a prompt promise to ship or by the prompt or current shipment of conforming or non-conforming goods, but such a shipment of non-conforming goods does not constitute an acceptance if the seller seasonably notifies the buyer that the shipment is offered only as an accommodation to the buyer.

(2) Where the beginning of a requested performance is a reasonable mode of acceptance an offeror who is not notified of acceptance within a reasonable time may treat the offer as having lapsed before acceptance.

Definitional Cross References:

"Buyer". Section 2–103.

"Conforming". Section 2–106.

"Contract". Section 1–201.

"Goods". Section 2–105.

"Notifies". Section 1–201.

"Reasonable time". Section 1–204.

§ 2–207. Additional Terms in Acceptance or Confirmation[g]

(1) A definite and seasonable expression of acceptance or a written confirmation which is sent within a reasonable time operates as an acceptance even though it states terms additional to or different from those offered or agreed upon, unless acceptance is expressly made conditional on assent to the additional or different terms.

(2) The additional terms are to be construed as proposals for addition to the contract. Between merchants such terms become part of the contract unless:

(a) the offer expressly limits acceptance to the terms of the offer;

(b) they materially alter it; or

(c) notification of objection to them has already been given or is given within a reasonable time after notice of them is received.

(3) Conduct by both parties which recognizes the existence of a contract is sufficient to establish a contract for sale although the writings of the parties do not otherwise establish a contract. In such case the terms of the particular contract consist of those terms on which the writings of the parties agree, together with any supplementary terms incorporated under any other provisions of this Act.

Official Comment

Prior Uniform Statutory Provision: Sections 1 and 3, Uniform Sales Act.

Changes: Completely rewritten by this and other sections of this Article.

Purposes of Changes:

1. This section is intended to deal with two typical situations. The one is

g. R 2–207 eliminates some important elements of the original section, resulting in a text that is considerably abbreviated, even in conjunction with R 2–206(3).

the written confirmation, where an agreement has been reached either orally or by informal correspondence between the parties and is followed by one or both of the parties sending formal memoranda embodying the terms so far as agreed upon and adding terms not discussed. The other situation is offer and acceptance, in which a wire or letter expressed and intended as an acceptance or the closing of an agreement adds further minor suggestions or proposals such as "ship by Tuesday," "rush," "ship draft against bill of lading inspection allowed," or the like. A frequent example of the second situation is the exchange of printed purchase order and acceptance (sometimes called "acknowledgment") forms. Because the forms are oriented to the thinking of the respective drafting parties, the terms contained in them often do not correspond. Often the seller's form contains terms different from or additional to those set forth in the buyer's form. Nevertheless, the parties proceed with the transaction. [Comment 1 was amended in 1966.]

2. Under this Article a proposed deal which in commercial understanding has in fact been closed is recognized as a contract. Therefore, any additional matter contained in the confirmation or in the acceptance falls within subsection (2) and must be regarded as a proposal for an added term unless the acceptance is made conditional on the acceptance of the additional or different terms. [Comment 2 was amended in 1966.]

3. Whether or not additional or different terms will become part of the agreement depends upon the provisions of subsection (2). If they are such as materially to alter the original bargain, they will not be included unless expressly agreed to by the other party. If, however, they are terms which would not so change the bargain they will be incorporated unless notice of objection to them has already been given or is given within a reasonable time.

4. Examples of typical clauses which would normally "materially alter" the contract and so result in surprise or hardship if incorporated without express awareness by the other party are: a clause negating such standard warranties as that of merchantability or fitness for a particular purpose in circumstances in which either warranty normally attaches; a clause requiring a guaranty of 90% or 100% deliveries in a case such as a contract by cannery, where the usage of the trade allows greater quantity leeways; a clause reserving to the seller the power to cancel upon the buyer's failure to meet any invoice when due; a clause requiring that complaints be made in a time materially shorter than customary or reasonable.

5. Examples of clauses which involve no element of unreasonable surprise and which therefore are to be incorporated in the contract unless notice of objection is seasonably given are: a clause setting forth and perhaps enlarging slightly upon the seller's exemption due to supervening causes beyond his control, similar to those covered by the provision of this Article on merchant's excuse by failure of presupposed conditions or a clause fixing in advance any reasonable formula of proration under such circumstances; a clause fixing a reasonable time for complaints within customary limits, or in the case of a purchase for sub-sale, providing for inspection by the sub-purchaser; a clause providing for interest on overdue invoices or fixing the seller's standard credit terms where they are within the range of trade practice and do not limit any credit bargained for; a clause limiting the right of rejection for defects which fall within the customary trade tolerances

for acceptance "with adjustment" or otherwise limiting remedy in a reasonable manner (see Sections 2–718 and 2–719).

6. If no answer is received within a reasonable time after additional terms are proposed, it is both fair and commercially sound to assume that their inclusion has been assented to. Where clauses on confirming forms sent by both parties conflict each party must be assumed to object to a clause of the other conflicting with one on the confirmation sent by himself. As a result the requirement that there be notice of objection which is found in subsection (2) is satisfied and the conflicting terms do not become a part of the contract. The contract then consists of the terms originally expressly agreed to, terms on which the confirmations agree, and terms supplied by his Act, including subsection (2). The written confirmation is also subject to Section 2–201. Under that section a failure to respond permits enforcement of a prior oral agreement; under this section a failure to respond permits additional terms to become part of the agreement. [Comment 6 was amended in 1966.]

7. In many cases, as where goods are shipped, accepted and paid for before any dispute arises, there is no question whether a contract has been made. In such cases, where the writings of the parties do not establish a contract, it is not necessary to determine which act or document constituted the offer and which the acceptance. See Section 2–204. The only question is what terms are included in the contract, and subsection (3) furnishes the governing rule. [Comment 7 was added in 1966.]

Cross References:

See generally Section 2–302.

Point 5: Sections 2–513, 2–602, 2–607, 2–609, 2–612, 2–614, 2–615, 2–616, 2–718 and 2–719.

Point 6: Sections 1–102 and 2–104.

Definitional Cross References:

"Between merchants". Section 2–104.

"Contract". Section 1–201.

"Notification". Section 1–201.

"Reasonable time". Section 1–204.

"Seasonably". Section 1–204.

"Send". Section 1–201.

"Term". Section 1–201.

"Written". Section 1–201.

§ 2–208. Course of Performance or Practical Construction[h]

(1) Where the contract for sale involves repeated occasions for performance by either party with knowledge of the nature of the performance and opportunity for objection to it by the other, any course of performance accepted or acquiesced in without objection shall be relevant to determine the meaning of the agreement.

(2) The express terms of the agreement and any such course of performance, as well as any course of dealing and usage of trade, shall be construed whenever reasonable as consistent with each other; but when such construction is unreasonable, express terms shall control course of performance and course of performance shall control both course of dealing and usage of trade (Section 1–205).

h. Revised Article 2 proposes repeal of this section if the jurisdiction has adopted revised Article 1, in which R 1–303 treats the topic.

(3) Subject to the provisions of the next section on modification and waiver, such course of performance shall be relevant to show a waiver or modification of any term inconsistent with such course of performance.

Prior Uniform Statutory Provision: No such general provision but concept of this section recognized by terms such as "course of dealing", "the circumstances of the case," "the conduct of the parties," etc., in Uniform Sales Act.

§ 2–209. Modification, Rescission and Waiver

(1) An agreement modifying a contract within this Article needs no consideration to be binding.

(2) A signed agreement which excludes modification or rescission except by a signed writing cannot be otherwise modified or rescinded, but except as between merchants such a requirement on a form supplied by the merchant must be separately signed by the other party.

(3) The requirements of the statute of frauds section of this Article (Section 2–201) must be satisfied if the contract as modified is within its provisions.

(4) Although an attempt at modification or rescission does not satisfy the requirements of subsection (2) or (3) it can operate as a waiver.

(5) A party who has made a waiver affecting an executory portion of the contract may retract the waiver by reasonable notification received by the other party that strict performance will be required of any term waived, unless the retraction would be unjust in view of a material change of position in reliance on the waiver.

Definitional Cross References:

"Agreement". Section 1–201.

"Between merchants". Section 2–104.

"Contract". Section 1–201.

"Notification". Section 1–201.

"Signed". Section 1–201.

"Term". Section 1–201.

"Writing". Section 1–201.

§ 2–210. Delegation of Performance; Assignment of Rights[i]

(1) A party may perform his duty through a delegate unless otherwise agreed or unless the other party has a substantial interest in having his original promisor perform or control the acts required by the contract. No delegation of performance relieves the party delegating of any duty to perform or any liability for breach.

(2) Except as otherwise provided in Section 9–406, unless otherwise agreed all rights of either seller or buyer can be assigned except where the assignment would materially change the duty of the other party, or increase materially the burden or risk imposed on him by his contract, or

i. R 2–210 is a modified and reorganized treatment of these topics.

impair materially his chance of obtaining return performance. A right to damages for breach of the whole contract or a right arising out of the assignor's due performance of his entire obligation can be assigned despite agreement otherwise.

(3) The creation, attachment, perfection, or enforcement of a security interest in the seller's interest under a contract is not a transfer that materially changes the duty of or increases materially the burden or risk imposed on the buyer or impairs materially the buyer's chance of obtaining return performance within the purview of subsection (2) unless, and then only to the extent that, enforcement actually results in a delegation of material performance of the seller. Even in that event, the creation, attachment, perfection, and enforcement of the security interest remains effective, but (i) the seller is liable to the buyer for damages caused by the delegation to the extent that the damages could not reasonably be prevented by the buyer, and (ii) a court having jurisdiction may grant other appropriate relief, including cancellation of the contract for sale or an injunction against enforcement of the security interest or consummation of the enforcement.

(4) Unless the circumstances indicate the contrary a prohibition of assignment of "the contract" is to be construed as barring only the delegation to the assignee of the assignor's performance.

(5) An assignment of "the contract" or of "all my rights under the contract" or an assignment in similar general terms is an assignment of rights and unless the language or the circumstances (as in an assignment for security) indicate the contrary, it is a delegation of performance of the duties of the assignor and its acceptance by the assignee constitutes a promise by him to perform those duties. This promise is enforceable by either the assignor or the other party to the original contract.

(6) The other party may treat any assignment which delegates performance as creating reasonable grounds for insecurity and may without prejudice to his rights against the assignor demand assurances from the assignee (Section 2–609).

Definitional Cross References:

"Agreement". Section 1–201.

"Buyer". Section 2–103.

"Contract". Section 1–201.

"Party". Section 1–201.

"Rights". Section 1–201.

"Seller". Section 2–103.

"Term". Section 1–201.

PART 3

GENERAL OBLIGATION AND CONSTRUCTION OF CONTRACT

§ 2–301. General Obligations of Parties

The obligation of the seller is to transfer and deliver and that of the buyer is to accept and pay in accordance with the contract.

Definitional Cross References:

"Buyer". Section 2–103.

"Contract". Section 1–201.

"Party". Section 1–201.

"Seller". Section 2–103.

§ 2–302. Unconscionable Contract or Clause

(1) If the court as a matter of law finds the contract or any clause of the contract to have been unconscionable at the time it was made the court may refuse to enforce the contract, or it may enforce the remainder of the contract without the unconscionable clause, or it may so limit the application of any unconscionable clause as to avoid any unconscionable result.

(2) When it is claimed or appears to the court that the contract or any clause thereof may be unconscionable the parties shall be afforded a reasonable opportunity to present evidence as to its commercial setting, purpose and effect to aid the court in making the determination.

Official Comment

Prior Uniform Statutory Provision: None.

Purposes:

1. This section is intended to make it possible for the courts to police explicitly against the contracts or clauses which they find to be unconscionable. In the past such policing has been accomplished by adverse construction of language, by manipulation of the rules of offer and acceptance or by determinations that the clause is contrary to public policy or to the dominant purpose of the contract. This section is intended to allow the court to pass directly on the unconscionability of the contract or particular clause therein and to make a conclusion of law as to its unconscionability. The basic test is whether, in the light of the general commercial background and the commercial needs of the particular trade or case, the clauses involved are so one-sided as to be unconscionable under the circumstances existing at the time of the making of the contract. Subsection (2) makes it clear that it is proper for the court to hear evidence upon these questions. The principle is one of the prevention of oppression and unfair surprise (Cf. Campbell Soup Co. v. Wentz, 172 F.2d 80, 3d Cir.1948) and not of disturbance of allocation of risks because of superior bargaining power. The underlying basis of this section is illustrated by the results in cases such as the following:

Kansas City Wholesale Grocery Co. v. Weber Packing Corporation, 93 Utah 414, 73 P.2d 1272 (1937), where a clause limiting time for complaints was held inapplicable to latent defects in a shipment of catsup which could be discovered only by microscopic analysis; Hardy v. General Motors Acceptance Corporation, 38 Ga.App. 463, 144 S.E. 327 (1928), holding that a disclaimer of warranty clause applied only to express warranties, thus letting in a fair implied warranty; Andrews Bros. v. Singer & Co. (1934 CA) 1 K.B. 17, holding that where a car with substantial mileage was delivered instead of a "new" car, a disclaimer of warranties, including those "implied," left unaffected an "express obligation" on the description, even though the Sale of Goods Act called such an implied warranty; New Prague Flouring Mill Co. v. G.A. Spears, 194 Iowa 417, 189 N.W. 815 (1922), holding that a clause permitting the seller, upon the buyer's failure to supply shipping instructions, to cancel, ship, or allow delivery date to be indefinitely postponed 30 days at a time by the inaction, does not indefinitely postpone the date of measuring damages for the buyer's breach, to the seller's advantage; and Kansas Flour Mills Co. v. Dirks, 100 Kan. 376, 164 P. 273 (1917), where under a similar clause in a rising market the court permitted the buyer to measure his damages for non-delivery at the end of only one 30 day postponement; Green v. Arcos, Ltd. (1931 CA) 47 T.L.R. 336, where a blanket clause prohibiting rejection of shipments by the buyer was restricted to apply to shipments where discrepancies represented merely mercantile variations; Meyer v. Packard Cleveland Motor Co., 106 Ohio St. 328, 140 N.E. 118 (1922), in which the court held that a "waiver" of all agreements not specified did not preclude implied warranty of fitness of a rebuilt dump truck for ordinary use as a dump truck; Austin Co. v. J.H. Tillman Co., 104 Or. 541, 209 P. 131 (1922), where a clause limiting the buyer's remedy to return was held to be applicable only if the seller had delivered a machine needed for a construction job which reasonably met the contract description; Bekkevold v. Potts, 173 Minn. 87, 216 N.W. 790, 59 A.L.R. 1164 (1927),

refusing to allow warranty of fitness for purpose imposed by law to be negated by clause excluding all warranties "made" by the seller; Robert A. Munroe & Co. v. Meyer (1930) 2 K.B. 312, holding that the warranty of description overrides a clause reading "with all faults and defects" where adulterated meat not up to the contract description was delivered.

2. Under this section the court, in its discretion, may refuse to enforce the contract as a whole if it is permeated by the unconscionability, or it may strike any single clause or group of clauses which are so tainted or which are contrary to the essential purpose of the agreement, or it may simply limit unconscionable clauses so as to avoid unconscionable results.

3. The present section is addressed to the court, and the decision is to be made by it. The commercial evidence referred to in subsection (2) is for the court's consideration, not the jury's. Only the agreement which results from the court's action on these matters is to be submitted to the general triers of the facts.

Definitional Cross Reference:

"Contract". Section 1–201.

§ 2–303.　Allocation or Division of Risks

Where this Article allocates a risk or a burden as between the parties "unless otherwise agreed", the agreement may not only shift the allocation but may also divide the risk or burden.

Definitional Cross References:

"Agreement". Section 1–201.

"Party". Section 1–201.

§ 2–304.　Price Payable in Money, Goods, Realty, or Otherwise

(1) The price can be made payable in money or otherwise. If it is payable in whole or in part in goods each party is a seller of the goods which he is to transfer.

(2) Even though all or part of the price is payable in an interest in realty the transfer of the goods and the seller's obligations with reference to them are subject to this Article, but not the transfer of the interest in realty or the transferor's obligations in connection therewith.

§ 2–305. Open Price Term

(1) The parties if they so intend can conclude a contract for sale even though the price is not settled. In such a case the price is a reasonable price at the time for delivery if

(a) nothing is said as to price; or

(b) the price is left to be agreed by the parties and they fail to agree; or

(c) the price is to be fixed in terms of some agreed market or other standard as set or recorded by a third person or agency and it is not so set or recorded.

(2) A price to be fixed by the seller or by the buyer means a price for him to fix in good faith.

(3) When a price left to be fixed otherwise than by agreement of the parties fails to be fixed through fault of one party the other may at his option treat the contract as cancelled or himself fix a reasonable price.

(4) Where, however, the parties intend not to be bound unless the price be fixed or agreed and it is not fixed or agreed there is no contract. In such a case the buyer must return any goods already received or if unable so to do must pay their reasonable value at the time of delivery and the seller must return any portion of the price paid on account.

Definitional Cross References:

"Agreement". Section 1–201.

"Burden of establishing". Section 1–201.

"Buyer". Section 2–103.

"Cancellation". Section 2–106.

"Contract". Section 1–201.

"Contract for sale". Section 2–106.

"Fault". Section 1–201.

"Goods". Section 2–105.

"Party". Section 1–201.

"Receipt of goods". Section 2–103.

"Seller". Section 2–103.

"Term". Section 1–201.

§ 2–306. Output, Requirements and Exclusive Dealings

(1) A term which measures the quantity by the output of the seller or the requirements of the buyer means such actual output or requirements as may occur in good faith, except that no quantity unreasonably disproportionate to any stated estimate or in the absence of a stated estimate to any normal or otherwise comparable prior output or requirements may be tendered or demanded.

(2) A lawful agreement by either the seller or the buyer for exclusive dealing in the kind of goods concerned imposes unless otherwise

agreed an obligation by the seller to use best efforts to supply the goods and by the buyer to use best efforts to promote their sale.

Definitional Cross References:

"Agreement". Section 1–201.

"Buyer". Section 2–103.

"Contract for sale". Section 2–106.

"Good faith". Section 1–201.

"Goods". Section 2–105.

"Party". Section 1–201.

"Term". Section 1–201.

"Seller". Section 2–103.

§ 2–307. Delivery in Single Lot or Several Lots

Unless otherwise agreed all goods called for by a contract for sale must be tendered in a single delivery and payment is due only on such tender but where the circumstances give either party the right to make or demand delivery in lots the price if it can be apportioned may be demanded for each lot.

Definitional Cross References:

"Contract for sale". Section 2–106.

"Goods". Section 2–105.

"Lot". Section 2–105.

"Party". Section 1–201.

"Rights". Section 1–201.

§ 2–308. Absence of Specified Place for Delivery

Unless otherwise agreed

(a) the place for delivery of goods is the seller's place of business or if he has none his residence; but

(b) in a contract for sale of identified goods which to the knowledge of the parties at the time of contracting are in some other place, that place is the place for their delivery; and

(c) documents of title may be delivered through customary banking channels.

Definitional Cross References:

"Contract for sale". Section 2–106.

"Delivery". Section 1–201.

"Document of title". Section 1–201.

"Goods". Section 2–105.

"Party". Section 1–201.

"Seller". Section 2–103.

§ 2–309. Absence of Specific Time Provisions; Notice of Termination

(1) The time for shipment or delivery or any other action under a contract if not provided in this Article or agreed upon shall be a reasonable time.

(2) Where the contract provides for successive performances but is indefinite in duration it is valid for a reasonable time but unless otherwise agreed may be terminated at any time by either party.

(3) Termination of a contract by one party except on the happening of an agreed event requires that reasonable notification be received by the other party and an agreement dispensing with notification is invalid if its operation would be unconscionable.[j]

Definitional Cross References:

"Agreement". Section 1–201.

"Contract". Section 1–201.

"Notification". Section 1–201.

"Party". Section 1–201.

"Reasonable time". Section 1–204.

"Termination". Section 2–106.

§ 2–310. Open Time for Payment or Running of Credit; Authority to Ship Under Reservation

Unless otherwise agreed

 (a) payment is due at the time and place at which the buyer is to receive the goods even though the place of shipment is the place of delivery; and

 (b) if the seller is authorized to send the goods he may ship them under reservation, and may tender the documents of title, but the buyer may inspect the goods after their arrival before payment is due unless such inspection is inconsistent with the terms of the contract (Section 2–513); and

 (c) if delivery is authorized and made by way of documents of title otherwise than by subsection (b) then payment is due at the time and place at which the buyer is to receive the documents regardless of where the goods are to be received; and

 (d) where the seller is required or authorized to ship the goods on credit the credit period runs from the time of shipment but post-dating the invoice or delaying its dispatch will correspondingly delay the starting of the credit period.

Definitional Cross References:

"Buyer". Section 2–103.

"Delivery". Section 1–201.

"Document of title". Section 1–201.

"Goods". Section 2–105.

"Receipt of goods". Section 2–103.

"Seller". Section 2–103.

"Send". Section 1–201.

"Term". Section 1–201.

§ 2–311. Options and Cooperation Respecting Performance

(1) An agreement for sale which is otherwise sufficiently definite (subsection (3) of Section 2–204) to be a contract is not made invalid by the fact that it leaves particulars of performance to be specified by one of the parties. Any such specification must be made in good faith and within limits set by commercial reasonableness.

j. R 2–309 concludes with a new sentence about standards for the nature and timing of notice.

(2) Unless otherwise agreed specifications relating to assortment of the goods are at the buyer's option and except as otherwise provided in subsections (1)(c) and (3) of Section 2–319 specifications or arrangements relating to shipment are at the seller's option.

(3) Where such specification would materially affect the other party's performance but is not seasonably made or where one party's cooperation is necessary to the agreed performance of the other but is not seasonably forthcoming, the other party in addition to all other remedies

> (a) is excused for any resulting delay in his own performance; and
>
> (b) may also either proceed to perform in any reasonable manner or after the time for a material part of his own performance treat the failure to specify or to cooperate as a breach by failure to deliver or accept the goods.

Definitional Cross References:

"Agreement". Section 1–201.

"Buyer". Section 2–103.

"Contract for sale". Section 2–106.

"Goods". Section 2–105.

"Party". Section 1–201.

"Remedy". Section 1–201.

"Seasonably". Section 1–204.

"Seller". Section 2–103.

§ 2–312. Warranty of Title and Against Infringement; Buyer's Obligation Against Infringement[k]

(1) Subject to subsection (2) there is in a contract for sale a warranty by the seller that

> (a) the title conveyed shall be good, and its transfer rightful; and
>
> (b) the goods shall be delivered free from any security interest or other lien or encumbrance of which the buyer at the time of contracting has no knowledge.

(2) A warranty under subsection (1) will be excluded or modified only by specific language or by circumstances which give the buyer reason to know that the person selling does not claim title in himself or that he is purporting to sell only such right or title as he or a third person may have.

(3) Unless otherwise agreed a seller who is a merchant regularly dealing in goods of the kind warrants that the goods shall be delivered free of the rightful claim of any third person by way of infringement or the like but a buyer who furnishes specifications to the seller must hold the seller harmless against any such claim which arises out of compliance with the specifications.

---

k. R 2–312(1)(a) extends the seller's warranty, and makes other revisions.

§ 2–313. Express Warranties by Affirmation, Promise, Description, Sample

(1) Express warranties by the seller are created as follows:

    (a) Any affirmation of fact or promise made by the seller to the buyer which relates to the goods and becomes part of the basis of the bargain creates an express warranty that the goods shall conform to the affirmation or promise.

    (b) Any description of the goods which is made part of the basis of the bargain creates an express warranty that the goods shall conform to the description.

    (c) Any sample or model which is made part of the basis of the bargain creates an express warranty that the whole of the goods shall conform to the sample or model.

(2) It is not necessary to the creation of an express warranty that the seller use formal words such as "warrant" or "guarantee" or that he have a specific intention to make a warranty, but an affirmation merely of the value of the goods or a statement purporting to be merely the seller's opinion or commendation of the goods does not create a warranty.

§ 2–314. Implied Warranty: Merchantability; Usage of Trade

(1) Unless excluded or modified (Section 2–316), a warranty that the goods shall be merchantable is implied in a contract for their sale if the seller is a merchant with respect to goods of that kind. Under this section the serving for value of food or drink to be consumed either on the premises or elsewhere is a sale.

(2) Goods to be merchantable must be at least such as

    (a) pass without objection in the trade under the contract description; and

    (b) in the case of fungible goods, are of fair average quality within the description; and

    (c) are fit for the ordinary purposes for which such goods are used; and

    (d) run, within the variations permitted by the agreement, of even kind, quality and quantity within each unit and among all units involved; and

(e) are adequately contained, packaged, and labeled as the agreement may require; and

(f) conform to the promises or affirmations of fact made on the container or label if any.

(3) Unless excluded or modified (Section 2–316) other implied warranties may arise from course of dealing or usage of trade.

Definitional Cross References:

"Agreement". Section 1–201.

"Contract". Section 1–201.

"Contract for sale". Section 2–106.

"Goods". Section 2–105.

"Merchant". Section 2–104.

"Seller". Section 2–103.

§ 2–315. Implied Warranty: Fitness for Particular Purpose

Where the seller at the time of contracting has reason to know any particular purpose for which the goods are required and that the buyer is relying on the seller's skill or judgment to select or furnish suitable goods, there is unless excluded or modified under the next section an implied warranty that the goods shall be fit for such purpose.

Definitional Cross References:

"Buyer". Section 2–103.

"Goods". Section 2–105.

"Seller". Section 2–103.

§ 2–316. Exclusion or Modification of Warranties[1]

(1) Words or conduct relevant to the creation of an express warranty and words or conduct tending to negate or limit warranty shall be construed wherever reasonable as consistent with each other; but subject to the provisions of this Article on parol or extrinsic evidence (Section 2–202) negation or limitation is inoperative to the extent that such construction is unreasonable.

(2) Subject to subsection (3), to exclude or modify the implied warranty of merchantability or any part of it the language must mention merchantability and in case of a writing must be conspicuous, and to exclude or modify any implied warranty of fitness the exclusion must be by a writing and conspicuous. Language to exclude all implied warranties of fitness is sufficient if it states, for example, that "There are no warranties which extend beyond the description on the face hereof."

(3) Notwithstanding subsection (2)

(a) unless the circumstances indicate otherwise, all implied warranties are excluded by expressions like "as is", "with all faults" or other language which in common understanding calls the buyer's attention to the exclusion of warranties and makes plain that there is no implied warranty; and

1. R 2–316 introduces, for a "consumer contract", further requirements for the exclusion of implied warranties.

(b) when the buyer before entering into the contract has examined the goods or the sample or model as fully as he desired or has refused to examine the goods there is no implied warranty with regard to defects which an examination ought in the circumstances to have revealed to him; and

(c) an implied warranty can also be excluded or modified by course of dealing or course of performance or usage of trade.

(4) Remedies for breach of warranty can be limited in accordance with the provisions of this Article on liquidation or limitation of damages and on contractual modification of remedy (Sections 2–718 and 2–719).

Definitional Cross References:

"Agreement". Section 1–201.

"Buyer". Section 2–103.

"Contract". Section 1–201.

"Course of dealing". Section 1–205.

"Goods". Section 2–105.

"Remedy". Section 1–201.

"Seller". Section 2–103.

"Usage of trade". Section 1–205.

§ 2–317. Cumulation and Conflict of Warranties Express or Implied

Warranties whether express or implied shall be construed as consistent with each other and as cumulative, but if such construction is unreasonable the intention of the parties shall determine which warranty is dominant. In ascertaining that intention the following rules apply:

(a) Exact or technical specifications displace an inconsistent sample or model or general language of description.

(b) A sample from an existing bulk displaces inconsistent general language of description.

(c) Express warranties displace inconsistent implied warranties other than an implied warranty of fitness for a particular purpose.

Definitional Cross Reference:

"Party". Section 1–201.

§ 2–318. Third Party Beneficiaries of Warranties Express or Implied[m]

Note: *If this Act is introduced in the Congress of the United States this section should be omitted. (States to select one alternative.)*

Alternative A

A seller's warranty whether express or implied extends to any natural person who is in the family or household of his buyer or who is a

m. R 2–318 introduces a distinction between "immediate buyer" and "remote purchaser", each as defined. Each of the three alternatives is restated using those terms.

43

guest in his home if it is reasonable to expect that such person may use, consume or be affected by the goods and who is injured in person by breach of the warranty. A seller may not exclude or limit the operation of this section.

Alternative B

A seller's warranty whether express or implied extends to any natural person who may reasonably be expected to use, consume or be affected by the goods and who is injured in person by breach of the warranty. A seller may not exclude or limit the operation of this section.

Alternative C

A seller's warranty whether express or implied extends to any person who may reasonably be expected to use, consume or be affected by the goods and who is injured by breach of the warranty.

A seller may not exclude or limit the operation of this section with respect to injury to the person of an individual to whom the warranty extends.

§ 2–319. F.O.B. and F.A.S. Terms

(1) Unless otherwise agreed the term F.O.B. (which means "free on board") at a named place, even though used only in connection with the stated price, is a delivery term under which

>   (a) when the term is F.O.B. the place of shipment, the seller must at that place ship the goods in the manner provided in this Article (Section 2–504) and bear the expense and risk of putting them into the possession of the carrier; or

>   (b) when the term is F.O.B. the place of destination, the seller must at his own expense and risk transport the goods to that place and there tender delivery of them in the manner provided in this Article (Section 2–503);

>   (c) when under either (a) or (b) the term is also F.O.B. vessel, car or other vehicle, the seller must in addition at his own expense and risk load the goods on board. If the term is F.O.B. vessel the buyer must name the vessel and in an appropriate case the seller must comply with the provisions of this Article on the form of bill of lading (Section 2–323).

(2) Unless otherwise agreed the term F.A.S. vessel (which means "free alongside") at a named port, even though used only in connection with the stated price, is a delivery term under which the seller must

>   (a) at his own expense and risk deliver the goods alongside the vessel in the manner usual in that port or on a dock designated and provided by the buyer; and

(b) obtain and tender a receipt for the goods in exchange for which the carrier is under a duty to issue a bill of lading.

(3) Unless otherwise agreed in any case falling within subsection (1)(a) or (c) or subsection (2) the buyer must seasonably give any needed instructions for making delivery, including when the term is F.A.S. or F.O.B. the loading berth of the vessel and in an appropriate case its name and sailing date. The seller may treat the failure of needed instructions as a failure of cooperation under this Article (Section 2–311). He may also at his option move the goods in any reasonable manner preparatory to delivery or shipment.

(4) Under the term F.O.B. vessel or F.A.S. unless otherwise agreed the buyer must make payment against tender of the required documents and the seller may not tender nor the buyer demand delivery of the goods in substitution for the documents.

Definitional Cross References:

"Goods". Section 2–105.

"Agreed". Section 1–201.

"Seasonably". Section 1–204.

"Bill of lading". Section 1–201.

"Seller". Section 2–103.

"Buyer". Section 2–103.

"Term". Section 1–201.

§ 2–320. C.I.F. and C. & F. Terms

(1) The term C.I.F. means that the price includes in a lump sum the cost of the goods and the insurance and freight to the named destination. The term C. & F. or C.F. means that the price so includes cost and freight to the named destination.

(2) Unless otherwise agreed and even though used only in connection with the stated price and destination, the term C.I.F. destination or its equivalent requires the seller at his own expense and risk to

(a) put the goods into the possession of a carrier at the port for shipment and obtain a negotiable bill or bills of lading covering the entire transportation to the named destination; and

(b) load the goods and obtain a receipt from the carrier (which may be contained in the bill of lading) showing that the freight has been paid or provided for; and

(c) obtain a policy or certificate of insurance, including any war risk insurance, of a kind and on terms then current at the port of shipment in the usual amount, in the currency of the contract, shown to cover the same goods covered by the bill of lading and providing for payment of loss to the order of the buyer or for the account of whom it may concern; but the seller may add to the price the amount of the premium for any such war risk insurance; and

(d) prepare an invoice of the goods and procure any other documents required to effect shipment or to comply with the contract; and

(e) forward and tender with commercial promptness all the documents in due form and with any indorsement necessary to perfect the buyer's rights.

(3) Unless otherwise agreed the term C. & F. or its equivalent has the same effect and imposes upon the seller the same obligations and risks as a C.I.F. term except the obligation as to insurance.

(4) Under the term C.I.F. or C. & F. unless otherwise agreed the buyer must make payment against tender of the required documents and the seller may not tender nor the buyer demand delivery of the goods in substitution for the documents.

Definitional Cross References:

"Bill of lading". Section 1–201.

"Buyer". Section 2–103.

"Contract". Section 1–201.

"Goods". Section 2–105.

"Rights". Section 1–201.

"Seller". Section 2–103.

"Term". Section 1–201.

§ 2–321. C.I.F. or C. & F.: "Net Landed Weights"; "Payment on Arrival"; Warranty of Condition on Arrival

Under a contract containing a term C.I.F. or C. & F.

(1) Where the price is based on or is to be adjusted according to "net landed weights", "delivered weights", "out turn" quantity or quality or the like, unless otherwise agreed the seller must reasonably estimate the price. The payment due on tender of the documents called for by the contract is the amount so estimated, but after final adjustment of the price a settlement must be made with commercial promptness.

(2) An agreement described in subsection (1) or any warranty of quality or condition of the goods on arrival places upon the seller the risk of ordinary deterioration, shrinkage and the like in transportation but has no effect on the place or time of identification to the contract for sale or delivery or on the passing of the risk of loss.

(3) Unless otherwise agreed where the contract provides for payment on or after arrival of the goods the seller must before payment allow such preliminary inspection as is feasible; but if the goods are lost delivery of the documents and payment are due when the goods should have arrived.

Definitional Cross References:

"Agreement". Section 1–201.

"Contract". Section 1–201.

"Delivery". Section 1–201.

"Goods". Section 2–105.

"Seller". Section 2–103.

"Term". Section 1–201.

§ 2–322. Delivery "Ex–Ship"

(1) Unless otherwise agreed a term for delivery of goods "ex-ship" (which means from the carrying vessel) or in equivalent language is not restricted to a particular ship and requires delivery from a ship which has reached a place at the named port of destination where goods of the kind are usually discharged.

(2) Under such a term unless otherwise agreed

  (a) the seller must discharge all liens arising out of the carriage and furnish the buyer with a direction which puts the carrier under a duty to delivery the goods; and

  (b) the risk of loss does not pass to the buyer until the goods leave the ship's tackle or are otherwise properly unloaded.

Definitional Cross References:

"Buyer". Section 1–103.

"Goods". Section 2–105.

"Seller". Section 2–103.

"Term". Section 1–201.

§ 2–323. Form of Bill of Lading Required in Overseas Shipment; "Overseas"

(1) Where the contract contemplates overseas shipment and contains a term C.I.F. or C. & F. or F.O.B. vessel, the seller unless otherwise agreed must obtain a negotiable bill of lading stating that the goods have been loaded on board or, in the case of a term C.I.F. or C. & F., received for shipment.

(2) Where in a case within subsection (1) a bill of lading has been issued in a set of parts, unless otherwise agreed if the documents are not to be sent from abroad the buyer may demand tender of the full set; otherwise only one part of the bill of lading need be tendered. Even if the agreement expressly requires a full set

  (a) due tender of a single part is acceptable within the provisions of this Article on cure of improper delivery (subsection (1) of Section 2–508); and

  (b) even though the full set is demanded, if the documents are sent from abroad the person tendering an incomplete set may nevertheless require payment upon furnishing an indemnity which the buyer in good faith deems adequate.

(3) A shipment by water or by air or a contract contemplating such shipment is "overseas" insofar as by usage of trade or agreement it is subject to the commercial, financing or shipping practices characteristic of international deep water commerce.

Definitional Cross References:

"Bill of lading". Section 1–201.

"Buyer". Section 2–103.

"Contract". Section 1–201.

"Delivery". Section 1–201.

"Financing agency". Section 2–104.

"Person". Section 1–201.

"Seller". Section 2–103.

"Send". Section 1–201.

"Term". Section 1–201.

§ 2–324. "No Arrival, No Sale" Term

Under a term "no arrival, no sale" or terms of like meaning, unless otherwise agreed,

>   (a) the seller must properly ship conforming goods and if they arrive by any means he must tender them on arrival but he assumes no obligation that the goods will arrive unless he has caused the non-arrival; and

>   (b) where without fault of the seller the goods are in part lost or have so deteriorated as no longer to conform to the contract or arrive after the contract time, the buyer may proceed as if there had been casualty to identified goods (Section 2–613).

Definitional Cross References:

"Buyer". Section 2–103.

"Conforming". Section 2–106.

"Contract". Section 1–201.

"Fault". Section 1–201.

"Goods". Section 2–105.

"Sale". Section 2–106.

"Seller". Section 2–103.

"Term". Section 1–201.

§ 2–325. "Letter of Credit" Term; "Confirmed Credit"[n]

(1) Failure of the buyer seasonably to furnish an agreed letter of credit is a breach of the contract for sale.

(2) The delivery to seller of a proper letter of credit suspends the buyer's obligation to pay. If the letter of credit is dishonored, the seller may on seasonable notification to the buyer require payment directly from him.

(3) Unless otherwise agreed the term "letter of credit" or "banker's credit" in a contract for sale means an irrevocable credit issued by a financing agency of good repute and, where the shipment is overseas, of good international repute. The term "confirmed credit" means that the credit must also carry the direct obligation of such an agency which does business in the seller's financial market.

Definitional Cross References:

"Buyer". Section 2–103.

"Contract for sale". Section 2–106.

"Draft". Section 3–104.

"Financing agency". Section 2–104.

"Notifies". Section 1–201.

"Overseas". Section 2–323.

"Purchaser". Section 1–201.

n. R 2–325 deals, instead, with the subject "Failure to Pay by Agreed Letter of Credit."

"Seasonably". Section 1–204.

"Seller". Section 2–103.

"Term". Section 1–201.

§ 2–326. Sale on Approval and Sale or Return; Rights of Creditors°

(1) Unless otherwise agreed, if delivered goods may be returned by the buyer even though they conform to the contract, the transaction is

    (a) a "sale on approval" if the goods are delivered primarily for use, and

    (b) a "sale or return" if the goods are delivered primarily for resale.

(2) Goods held on approval are not subject to the claims of the buyer's creditors until acceptance; goods held on sale or return are subject to such claims while in the buyer's possession.

(3) Any "or return" term of a contract for sale is to be treated as a separate contract for sale within the statute of frauds section of this Article (Section 2–201) and as contradicting the sale aspect of the contract within the provisions of this Article on parol or extrinsic evidence (Section 2–202).

Definitional Cross References:

"Between merchants". Section 2–104.

"Buyer". Section 2–103.

"Conform". Section 2–106.

"Contract for sale". Section 2–106.

"Creditor". Section 1 201.

"Goods". Section 2–105.

"Sale". Section 2–106.

"Seller". Section 2–103.

§ 2–327. Special Incidents of Sale on Approval and Sale or Return

(1) Under a sale on approval unless otherwise agreed

    (a) although the goods are identified to the contract the risk of loss and the title do not pass to the buyer until acceptance; and

    (b) use of the goods consistent with the purpose of trial is not acceptance but failure seasonably to notify the seller of election to return the goods is acceptance, and if the goods conform to the contract acceptance of any part is acceptance of the whole; and

    (c) after due notification of election to return, the return is at the seller's risk and expense but a merchant buyer must follow any reasonable instructions.

o. Provisions about consignment transactions, once included in this section, have been replaced by provisions in Article 9.

(2) Under a sale or return unless otherwise agreed

    (a) the option to return extends to the whole or any commercial unit of the goods while in substantially their original condition, but must be exercised seasonably; and

    (b) the return is at the buyer's risk and expense.

Definitional Cross References:

"Agreed". Section 1–201.

"Buyer". Section 2–103.

"Commercial unit". Section 2–105.

"Conform". Section 2–106.

"Contract". Section 1–201.

"Goods". Section 2–105.

"Merchant". Section 2–104.

"Notifies". Section 1–201.

"Notification". Section 1–201.

"Sale on approval". Section 2–326.

"Sale or return". Section 2–326.

"Seasonably". Section 1–204.

"Seller". Section 2–103.

§ 2–328. Sale by Auction[p]

(1) In a sale by auction if goods are put up in lots each lot is the subject of a separate sale.

(2) A sale by auction is complete when the auctioneer so announces by the fall of the hammer or in other customary manner. Where a bid is made while the hammer is falling in acceptance of a prior bid the auctioneer may in his discretion reopen the bidding or declare the goods sold under the bid on which the hammer was falling.

(3) Such a sale is with reserve unless the goods are in explicit terms put up without reserve. In an auction with reserve the auctioneer may withdraw the goods at any time until he announces completion of the sale. In an auction without reserve, after the auctioneer calls for bids on an article or lot, that article or lot cannot be withdrawn unless no bid is made within a reasonable time. In either case a bidder may retract his bid until the auctioneer's announcement of completion of the sale, but a bidder's retraction does not revive any previous bid.

(4) If the auctioneer knowingly receives a bid on the seller's behalf or the seller makes or procures such a bid, and notice has not been given that liberty for such bidding is reserved, the buyer may at his option avoid the sale or take the goods at the price of the last good faith bid prior to the completion of the sale. This subsection shall not apply to any bid at a forced sale.

Definitional Cross References:

"Buyer". Section 2–103.

"Good faith". Section 1–201.

"Goods". Section 2–105.

"Lot". Section 2–105.

"Notice". Section 1–201.

p. R 2–328 makes alterations, largely stylistic, eliminating the terms "with re- serve" and "without reserve".

"Sale". Section 2–106.

"Seller". Section 2–103.

PART 4

TITLE, CREDITORS AND GOOD FAITH PURCHASERS

§ 2–401. Passing of Title; Reservation for Security; Limited Application of This Section

Each provision of this Article with regard to the rights, obligations and remedies of the seller, the buyer, purchasers or other third parties applies irrespective of title to the goods except where the provision refers to such title. Insofar as situations are not covered by the other provisions of this Article and matters concerning title become material the following rules apply:

(1) Title to goods cannot pass under a contract for sale prior to their identification to the contract (Section 2–501), and unless otherwise explicitly agreed the buyer acquires by their identification a special property as limited by this Act. Any retention or reservation by the seller of the title (property) in goods shipped or delivered to the buyer is limited in effect to a reservation of a security interest. Subject to these provisions and to the provisions of the Article on Secured Transactions (Article 9), title to goods passes from the seller to the buyer in any manner and on any conditions explicitly agreed on by the parties.

(2) Unless otherwise explicitly agreed title passes to the buyer at the time and place at which the seller completes his performance with reference to the physical delivery of the goods, despite any reservation of a security interest and even though a document of title is to be delivered at a different time or place; and in particular and despite any reservation of a security interest by the bill of lading

(a) if the contract requires or authorizes the seller to send the goods to the buyer but does not require him to deliver them at destination, title passes to the buyer at the time and place of shipment; but

(b) if the contract requires delivery at destination, title passes on tender there.

(3) Unless otherwise explicitly agreed where delivery is to be made without moving the goods,

(a) if the seller is to deliver a document of title, title passes at the time when and the place where he delivers such documents; or

(b) if the goods are at the time of contracting already identified and no documents are to be delivered, title passes at the time and place of contracting.

(4) A rejection or other refusal by the buyer to receive or retain the goods, whether or not justified, or a justified revocation of acceptance revests title to the goods in the seller. Such revesting occurs by operation of law and is not a "sale".

Definitional Cross References:

"Agreement". Section 1–201.

"Bill of lading". Section 1–201.

"Buyer". Section 2–103.

"Contract". Section 1–201.

"Contract for sale". Section 2–106.

"Delivery". Section 1–201.

"Document of title". Section 1–201.

"Good faith". Section 2–103.

"Goods". Section 2–105.

"Party". Section 1–201.

"Purchaser". Section 1–201.

"Receipt" of goods. Section 2–103.

"Remedy". Section 1–201.

"Rights". Section 1–201.

"Sale". Section 2–106.

"Security interest". Section 1–201.

"Seller". Section 2–103.

"Send". Section 1–201.

§ 2–402. Rights of Seller's Creditors Against Sold Goods

(1) Except as provided in subsections (2) and (3), rights of unsecured creditors of the seller with respect to goods which have been identified to a contract for sale are subject to the buyer's rights to recover the goods under this Article (Sections 2–502 and 2–716).

(2) A creditor of the seller may treat a sale or an identification of goods to a contract for sale as void if as against him a retention of possession by the seller is fraudulent under any rule of law of the state where the goods are situated, except that retention of possession in good faith and current course of trade by a merchant-seller for a commercially reasonable time after a sale or identification is not fraudulent.

(3) Nothing in this Article shall be deemed to impair the rights of creditors of the seller

> (a) under the provisions of the Article on Secured Transactions (Article 9); or

> (b) where identification to the contract or delivery is made not in current course of trade but in satisfaction of or as security for a pre-existing claim for money, security or the like and is made under circumstances which under any rule of law of the state where the goods are situated would apart from this Article constitute the transaction a fraudulent transfer or voidable preference.

Definitional Cross References:

"Contract for sale". Section 2–106.

"Creditor". Section 1–201.

"Good faith". Section 2–103.

"Goods". Section 2–105.

"Merchant". Section 2–104.

"Money". Section 1–201.

"Reasonable time". Section 1–204.

"Rights". Section 1–201.

"Sale". Section 2–106.

"Seller". Section 2–103.

§ **2–403.** Power to Transfer; Good Faith Purchase of Goods; "Entrusting"

(1) A purchaser of goods acquires all title which his transferor had or had power to transfer except that a purchaser of a limited interest acquires rights only to the extent of the interest purchased. A person with voidable title has power to transfer a good title to a good faith purchaser for value. When goods have been delivered under a transaction of purchase the purchaser has such power even though

(a) the transferor was deceived as to the identity of the purchaser, or

(b) the delivery was in exchange for a check which is later dishonored, or

(c) it was agreed that the transaction was to be a "cash sale", or

(d) the delivery was procured through fraud punishable as larcenous under the criminal law.

(2) Any entrusting of possession of goods to a merchant who deals in goods of that kind gives him power to transfer all rights of the entruster to a buyer in ordinary course of business.

(3) "Entrusting" includes any delivery and any acquiescence in retention of possession regardless of any condition expressed between the parties to the delivery or acquiescence and regardless of whether the procurement of the entrusting or the possessor's disposition of the goods have been such as to be larcenous under the criminal law.

(4) The rights of other purchasers of goods and of lien creditors are governed by the Articles on Secured Transactions (Article 9), Bulk Transfers (Article 6) and Documents of Title (Article 7).

Definitional Cross References:

"Buyer in ordinary course of business". Section 1–201.

"Good faith". Sections 1–201 and 2–103.

"Goods". Section 2–105.

"Person". Section 1–201.

"Purchaser". Section 1–201.

"Signed". Section 1–201.

"Term". Section 1–201.

"Value". Section 1–201.

PART 5

PERFORMANCE

§ 2–501. Insurable Interest in Goods; Manner of Identification of Goods

(1) The buyer obtains a special property and an insurable interest in goods by identification of existing goods as goods to which the contract refers even though the goods so identified are non-conforming and he has an option to return or reject them. Such identification can be made at any time and in any manner explicitly agreed to by the parties. In the absence of explicit agreement identification occurs

> (a) when the contract is made if it is for the sale of goods already existing and identified;

> (b) if the contract is for the sale of future goods other than those described in paragraph (c), when goods are shipped, marked or otherwise designated by the seller as goods to which the contract refers;

> (c) when the crops are planted or otherwise become growing crops or the young are conceived if the contract is for the sale of unborn young to be born within twelve months after contracting or for the sale of crops to be harvested within twelve months or the next normal harvest season after contracting whichever is longer.

(2) The seller retains an insurable interest in goods so long as title to or any security interest in the goods remains in him and where the identification is by the seller alone he may until default or insolvency or notification to the buyer that the identification is final substitute other goods for those identified.

(3) Nothing in this section impairs any insurable interest recognized under any other statute or rule of law.

Definitional Cross References:

"Agreement". Section 1–201.

"Contract". Section 1–201.

"Contract for sale". Section 2–106.

"Future goods". Section 2–105.

"Goods". Section 2–105.

"Notification". Section 1–201.

"Party". Section 1–201.

"Sale". Section 2–106.

"Security interest". Section 1–201.

"Seller". Section 2–103.

§ 2–502. Buyer's Right to Goods on Seller's Repudiation, Failure to Deliver, or Insolvency

(1) Subject to subsections (2) and (3) and even though the goods have not been shipped a buyer who has paid a part or all of the price of goods in which he has a special property under the provisions of the immediately preceding section may on making and keeping good a tender of any unpaid portion of their price recover them from the seller if:

(a) in the case of goods bought for personal, family, or household purposes,[q] the seller repudiates or fails to deliver as required by the contract; or

(b) in all cases, the seller becomes insolvent within ten days after receipt of the first installment on their price.

(2) The buyer's right to recover the goods under subsection (1) vests upon acquisition of a special property, even if the seller had not then repudiated or failed to deliver.

(3) If the identification creating his special property has been made by the buyer he acquires the right to recover the goods only if they conform to the contract for sale.

Definitional Cross References:

"Buyer". Section 2–103.

"Conform". Section 2–106.

"Contract for sale". Section 2–106.

"Goods". Section 2–105.

"Insolvent". Section 1–201.

"Right". Section 1–201.

"Seller". Section 2–103.

§ 2–503. Manner of Seller's Tender of Delivery

(1) Tender of delivery requires that the seller put and hold conforming goods at the buyer's disposition and give the buyer any notification reasonably necessary to enable him to take delivery. The manner, time and place for tender are determined by the agreement and this Article, and in particular

(a) tender must be at a reasonable hour, and if it is of goods they must be kept available for the period reasonably necessary to enable the buyer to take possession; but

(b) unless otherwise agreed the buyer must furnish facilities reasonably suited to the receipt of the goods.

(2) Where the case is within the next section respecting shipment tender requires that the seller comply with its provisions.

(3) Where the seller is required to deliver at a particular destination tender requires that he comply with subsection (1) and also in any appropriate case tender documents as described in subsections (4) and (5) of this section.

(4) Where goods are in the possession of a bailee and are to be delivered without being moved

(a) tender requires that the seller either tender a negotiable document of title covering such goods or procure acknowledgment by the bailee of the buyer's right to possession of the goods; but

---

q. In R 2–502 the reference is to goods "bought by a consumer".

(b) tender to the buyer of a non-negotiable document of title or of a written direction to the bailee to deliver is sufficient tender unless the buyer seasonably objects, and receipt by the bailee of notification of the buyer's rights fixes those rights as against the bailee and all third persons; but risk of loss of the goods and of any failure by the bailee to honor the non-negotiable document of title or to obey the direction remains on the seller until the buyer has had a reasonable time to present the document or direction, and a refusal by the bailee to honor the document or to obey the direction defeats the tender.

(5) Where the contract requires the seller to deliver documents

(a) he must tender all such documents in correct form, except as provided in this Article with respect to bills of lading in a set (subsection (2) of Section 2–323); and

(b) tender through customary banking channels is sufficient and dishonor of a draft accompanying the documents constitutes non-acceptance or rejection.

Definitional Cross References:

"Agreement". Section 1–201.	"Draft". Section 3–104.
"Bill of lading". Section 1–201.	"Goods". Section 2–105.
"Buyer". Section 2–103.	"Notification". Section 1–201.
"Conforming". Section 2–106.	"Reasonable time". Section 1–204.
"Contract". Section 1–201.	"Receipt of goods". Section 2–103.
"Delivery". Section 1–201.	"Rights". Section 1–201.
"Dishonor". Section 3–508.	"Seasonably". Section 1–204.
"Document of title". Section 1–201.	"Seller". Section 2–103.
	"Written". Section 1–201.

§ 2–504. Shipment by Seller

Where the seller is required or authorized to send the goods to the buyer and the contract does not require him to deliver them at a particular destination, then unless otherwise agreed he must

(a) put the goods in the possession of such a carrier and make such a contract for their transportation as may be reasonable having regard to the nature of the goods and other circumstances of the case; and

(b) obtain and promptly deliver or tender in due form any document necessary to enable the buyer to obtain possession of the goods or otherwise required by the agreement or by usage of trade; and

(c) promptly notify the buyer of the shipment.

Failure to notify the buyer under paragraph (c) or to make a proper contract under paragraph (a) is a ground for rejection only if material delay or loss ensues.

Definitional Cross References:

"Agreement". Section 1–201.

"Buyer" Section 2–103.

"Contract". Section 1–201.

"Delivery". Section 1–201.

"Goods". Section 2–105.

"Notifies". Section 1–201.

"Seller". Section 2–103.

"Send". Section 1–201.

"Usage of trade". Section 1–205.

§ 2–505. Seller's Shipment Under Reservation

(1) Where the seller has identified goods to the contract by or before shipment:

> (a) his procurement of a negotiable bill of lading to his own order or otherwise reserves in him a security interest in the goods. His procurement of the bill to the order of a financing agency or of the buyer indicates in addition only the seller's expectation of transferring that interest to the person named.

> (b) a non-negotiable bill of lading to himself or his nominee reserves possession of the goods as security but except in a case of conditional delivery (subsection (2) of Section 2–507) a non-negotiable bill of lading naming the buyer as consignee reserves no security interest even though the seller retains possession of the bill of lading.

(2) When shipment by the seller with reservation of a security interest is in violation of the contract for sale it constitutes an improper contract for transportation within the preceding section but impairs neither the rights given to the buyer by shipment and identification of the goods to the contract nor the seller's powers as a holder of a negotiable document.

Definitional Cross References:

"Bill of lading". Section 1–201.

"Buyer". Section 2–103.

"Consignee". Section 7–102.

"Contract". Section 1–201.

"Contract for sale". Section 2–106.

"Delivery". Section 1–201.

"Financing agency". Section 2–104.

"Goods". Section 2–105.

"Holder". Section 1–201.

"Person". Section 1–201.

"Security interest". Section 1–201.

"Seller". Section 2–103.

§ 2–506. Rights of Financing Agency

(1) A financing agency by paying or purchasing for value a draft which relates to a shipment of goods acquires to the extent of the payment or purchase and in addition to its own rights under the draft

and any document of title securing it any rights of the shipper in the goods including the right to stop delivery and the shipper's right to have the draft honored by the buyer.

(2) The right to reimbursement of a financing agency which has in good faith honored or purchased the draft under commitment to or authority from the buyer is not impaired by subsequent discovery of defects with reference to any relevant document which was apparently regular on its face.

Definitional Cross References:

"Buyer". Section 2–103.

"Document of title". Section 1–201.

"Draft". Section 3–104.

"Financing agency". Section 2–104.

"Good faith". Section 2–103.

"Goods". Section 2–105.

"Honor". Section 1–201.

"Purchase". Section 1–201.

"Rights". Section 1–201.

"Value". Section 1–201.

§ 2–507. Effect of Seller's Tender; Delivery on Condition

(1) Tender of delivery is a condition to the buyer's duty to accept the goods and, unless otherwise agreed, to his duty to pay for them. Tender entitles the seller to acceptance of the goods and to payment according to the contract.

(2) Where payment is due and demanded on the delivery to the buyer of goods or documents of title, his right as against the seller to retain or dispose of them is conditional upon his making the payment due.

Definitional Cross References:

"Buyer". Section 2–103.

"Contract". Section 1–201.

"Delivery". Section 1–201.

"Document of title". Section 1–201.

"Goods". Section 2–105.

"Rights". Section 1–201.

"Seller". Section 2–103.

§ 2–508. Cure by Seller of Improper Tender or Delivery; Replacement[r]

(1) Where any tender or delivery by the seller is rejected because non-conforming and the time for performance has not yet expired, the seller may seasonably notify the buyer of his intention to cure and may then within the contract time make a conforming delivery.

(2) Where the buyer rejects a non-conforming tender which the seller had reasonable grounds to believe would be acceptable with or without money allowance the seller may if he seasonably notifies the buyer have a further reasonable time to substitute a conforming tender.

r. R 2–508 expands and refines the seller's right to cure, and imposes limitations with respect to consumer contracts.

Definitional Cross References:

"Buyer". Section 2–103.

"Conforming". Section 2–106.

"Contract". Section 1–201.

"Money". Section 1–201.

"Notifies". Section 1–201.

"Reasonable time". Section 1–204.

"Seasonably". Section 1–204.

"Seller". Section 2–103.

§ 2–509. Risk of Loss in the Absence of Breach

(1) Where the contract requires or authorizes the seller to ship the goods by carrier

    (a) if it does not require him to deliver them at a particular destination, the risk of loss passes to the buyer when the goods are duly delivered to the carrier even though the shipment is under reservation (Section 2–505); but

    (b) if it does require him to deliver them at a particular destination and the goods are there duly tendered while in the possession of the carrier, the risk of loss passes to the buyer when the goods are there duly so tendered as to enable the buyer to take delivery.

(2) Where the goods are held by a bailee to be delivered without being moved, the risk of loss passes to the buyer

    (a) on his receipt of a negotiable document of title covering the goods, or

    (b) on acknowledgment by the bailee of the buyer's right to possession of the goods; or

    (c) after his receipt of a non-negotiable document of title or other written direction to deliver, as provided in subsection (4)(b) of Section 2–503.

(3) In any case not within subsection (1) or (2), the risk of loss passes to the buyer on his receipt of the goods if the seller is a merchant; otherwise the risk passes to the buyer on tender of delivery.[s]

(4) The provisions of this section are subject to contrary agreement of the parties and to the provisions of this Article on sale on approval (Section 2–327) and on effect of breach on risk of loss (Section 2–510).

Definitional Cross References:

"Agreement". Section 1–201.

"Buyer". Section 2–103.

"Contract". Section 1–201.

"Delivery". Section 1–201.

"Document of title". Section 1–201.

"Goods". Section 2–105.

"Merchant". Section 2–104.

"Party". Section 1–201.

"Receipt" of goods. Section 2–103.

"Sale on approval". Section 2–326.

"Seller". Section 2–103.

s. R 2–509(3) omits the qualification as to merchant-sellers.

§ 2–510. Effect of Breach on Risk of Loss

(1) Where a tender or delivery of goods so fails to conform to the contract as to give a right of rejection the risk of their loss remains on the seller until cure or acceptance.

(2) Where the buyer rightfully revokes acceptance he may to the extent of any deficiency in his effective insurance coverage treat the risk of loss as having rested on the seller from the beginning.

(3) Where the buyer as to conforming goods already identified to the contract for sale repudiates or is otherwise in breach before risk of their loss has passed to him, the seller may to the extent of any deficiency in his effective insurance coverage treat the risk of loss as resting on the buyer for a commercially reasonable time.

Definitional Cross References:

"Buyer". Section 2–103.

"Conform". Section 2–106.

"Contract for sale". Section 2–106.

"Goods". Section 2–105.

"Seller". Section 2–103.

§ 2–511. Tender of Payment by Buyer; Payment by Check

(1) Unless otherwise agreed tender of payment is a condition to the seller's duty to tender and complete any delivery.

(2) Tender of payment is sufficient when made by any means or in any manner current in the ordinary course of business unless the seller demands payment in legal tender and gives any extension of time reasonably necessary to procure it.

(3) Subject to the provisions of this Act on the effect of an instrument on an obligation (Section 3–802), payment by check is conditional and is defeated as between the parties by dishonor of the check on due presentment.

Definitional Cross References:

"Buyer". Section 2–103.

"Check". Section 3–104.

"Dishonor". Section 3–508.

"Party". Section 1–201.

"Reasonable time". Section 1–204.

"Seller". Section 2–103.

§ 2–512. Payment by Buyer Before Inspection

(1) Where the contract requires payment before inspection non-conformity of the goods does not excuse the buyer from so making payment unless

    (a) the non-conformity appears without inspection; or

    (b) despite tender of the required documents the circumstances would justify injunction against honor under the provisions of this Act (Section 5–114).

(2) Payment pursuant to subsection (1) does not constitute an acceptance of goods or impair the buyer's right to inspect or any of his remedies.

§ 2–513. Buyer's Right to Inspection of Goods

(1) Unless otherwise agreed and subject to subsection (3), where goods are tendered or delivered or identified to the contract for sale, the buyer has a right before payment or acceptance to inspect them at any reasonable place and time and in any reasonable manner. When the seller is required or authorized to send the goods to the buyer, the inspection may be after their arrival.

(2) Expenses of inspection must be borne by the buyer but may be recovered from the seller if the goods do not conform and are rejected.

(3) Unless otherwise agreed and subject to the provisions of this Article on C.I.F. contracts (subsection (3) of Section 2–321), the buyer is not entitled to inspect the goods before payment of the price when the contract provides

> (a) for delivery "C.O.D." or on other like terms; or
>
> (b) for payment against documents of title, except where such payment is due only after the goods are to become available for inspection.

(4) A place or method of inspection fixed by the parties is presumed to be exclusive but unless otherwise expressly agreed it does not postpone identification or shift the place for delivery or for passing the risk of loss. If compliance becomes impossible, inspection shall be as provided in this section unless the place or method fixed was clearly intended as an indispensable condition failure of which avoids the contract.

§ 2–514. When Documents Deliverable on Acceptance; When on Payment

Unless otherwise agreed documents against which a draft is drawn are to be delivered to the drawee on acceptance of the draft if it is payable more than three days after presentment; otherwise, only on payment.

Definitional Cross References:

"Delivery". Section 1–201.

"Draft". Section 3–104.

§ 2–515. Preserving Evidence of Goods in Dispute

In furtherance of the adjustment of any claim or dispute

    (a) either party on reasonable notification to the other and for the purpose of ascertaining the facts and preserving evidence has the right to inspect, test and sample the goods including such of them as may be in the possession or control of the other; and

    (b) the parties may agree to a third party inspection or survey to determine the conformity or condition of the goods and may agree that the findings shall be binding upon them in any subsequent litigation or adjustment.

Definitional Cross References:

"Conform". Section 2–106.

"Goods". Section 2–105.

"Notification". Section 1–201.

"Party". Section 1–201.

PART 6

BREACH, REPUDIATION AND EXCUSE

§ 2–601. Buyer's Rights on Improper Delivery

Subject to the provisions of this Article on breach in installment contracts (Section 2–612)[t] and unless otherwise agreed under the sections on contractual limitations of remedy (Sections 2–718 and 2–719), if the goods or the tender of delivery fail in any respect to conform to the contract, the buyer may

    (a) reject the whole; or

    (b) accept the whole; or

    (c) accept any commercial unit or units and reject the rest.

Definitional Cross References:

"Buyer". Section 2–103.

"Commercial unit". Section 2–105.

"Conform". Section 2–106.

"Contract". Section 1–201.

"Goods". Section 2–105.

"Installment contract". Section 2–612.

"Rights". Section 1–201.

§ 2–602. Manner and Effect of Rightful Rejection

(1) Rejection of goods must be within a reasonable time after their delivery or tender. It is ineffective unless the buyer seasonably notifies the seller.

t. R 2–601 makes the rule subject also to R 2–504, on shipment by seller.

(2) Subject to the provisions of the two following sections on rejected goods (Sections 2–603 and 2–604),

    (a) after rejection any exercise of ownership by the buyer with respect to any commercial unit is wrongful as against the seller; and

    (b) if the buyer has before rejection taken physical possession of goods in which he does not have a security interest under the provisions of this Article (subsection (3) of Section 2–711), he is under a duty after rejection to hold them with reasonable care at the seller's disposition for a time sufficient to permit the seller to remove them; but

    (c) the buyer has no further obligations with regard to goods rightfully rejected.

(3) The seller's rights with respect to goods wrongfully rejected are governed by the provisions of this Article on Seller's remedies in general (Section 2–703).

Definitional Cross References:

"Buyer". Section 2–103.
"Commercial unit". Section 2–105.
"Goods". Section 2–105.
"Merchant". Section 2–104.
"Notifies". Section 1–201.
"Reasonable time". Section 1–204.
"Remedy". Section 1–201.
"Rights". Section 1–201.
"Seasonably". Section 1–204.
"Security interest". Section 1–201.
"Seller". Section 2–103.

§ 2–603. Merchant Buyer's Duties as to Rightfully Rejected Goods

(1) Subject to any security interest in the buyer (subsection (3) of Section 2–711), when the seller has no agent or place of business at the market of rejection a merchant buyer is under a duty after rejection of goods in his possession or control to follow any reasonable instructions received from the seller with respect to the goods and in the absence of such instructions to make reasonable efforts to sell them for the seller's account if they are perishable or threaten to decline in value speedily. Instructions are not reasonable if on demand indemnity for expenses is not forthcoming.

(2) When the buyer sells goods under subsection (1), he is entitled to reimbursement from the seller or out of the proceeds for reasonable expenses of caring for and selling them, and if the expenses include no selling commission then to such commission as is usual in the trade or if there is none to a reasonable sum not exceeding ten per cent on the gross proceeds.

(3) In complying with this section the buyer is held only to good faith and good faith conduct hereunder is neither acceptance nor conversion nor the basis of an action for damages.

Definitional Cross References:

"Buyer".　Section 2–103.

"Good faith".　Section 1–201.

"Goods".　Section 2–105.

"Merchant".　Section 2–104.

"Security interest".　Section 1–201.

"Seller".　Section 2–102.

§ 2–604.　Buyer's Options as to Salvage of Rightfully Rejected Goods

Subject to the provisions of the immediately preceding section on perishables if the seller gives no instructions within a reasonable time after notification of rejection the buyer may store the rejected goods for the seller's account or reship them to him or resell them for the seller's account with reimbursement as provided in the preceding section. Such action is not acceptance or conversion.

Definitional Cross References:

"Buyer".　Section 2–103.

"Notification".　Section 1–201.

"Reasonable time".　Section 1–204.

"Seller".　Section 2–103.

§ 2–605.　Waiver of Buyer's Objections by Failure to Particularize

(1) The buyer's failure to state in connection with rejection a particular defect which is ascertainable by reasonable inspection precludes him from relying on the unstated defect to justify rejection or to establish breach

> (a) where the seller could have cured it if stated seasonably; or

> (b) between merchants when the seller has after rejection made a request in writing for a full and final written statement of all defects on which the buyer proposes to rely.[u]

(2) Payment against documents made without reservation of rights precludes recovery of the payment for defects apparent on the face of the documents.

Definitional Cross References:

"Between merchants".　Section 2–104.

"Buyer".　Section 2–103.

"Seasonably".　Section 1–204.

"Seller".　Section 2–103.

"Writing" and "written".　Section 1–201.

§ 2–606.　What Constitutes Acceptance of Goods

(1) Acceptance of goods occurs when the buyer

> (a) after a reasonable opportunity to inspect the goods signifies to the seller that the goods are conforming or that he will take or retain them in spite of their nonconformity; or

u.　R 2–605(1) narrows the range of the phrase here "to establish breach".

(b) fails to make an effective rejection (subsection (1) of Section 2–602), but such acceptance does not occur until the buyer has had a reasonable opportunity to inspect them; or

(c) does any act inconsistent with the seller's ownership; but if such act is wrongful as against the seller it is an acceptance only if ratified by him.

(2) Acceptance of a part of any commercial unit is acceptance of that entire unit.

Definitional Cross References:

"Buyer". Section 2–103.

"Commercial unit". Section 2–105.

"Goods". Section 2–105.

"Seller". Section 2–103.

§ 2–607. Effect of Acceptance; Notice of Breach; Burden of Establishing Breach After Acceptance; Notice of Claim or Litigation to Person Answerable Over

(1) The buyer must pay at the contract rate for any goods accepted.

(2) Acceptance of goods by the buyer precludes rejection of the goods accepted and if made with knowledge of a non-conformity cannot be revoked because of it unless the acceptance was on the reasonable assumption that the non-conformity would be seasonably cured but acceptance does not of itself impair any other remedy provided by this Article for non-conformity.

(3) Where a tender has been accepted.

(a) the buyer must within a reasonable time after he discovers or should have discovered any breach notify the seller of breach or be barred from any remedy;[v] and

(b) if the claim is one for infringement or the like (subsection (3) of Section 2–312) and the buyer is sued as a result of such a breach he must so notify the seller within a reasonable time after he receives notice of the litigation or be barred from any remedy over for liability established by the litigation.

(4) The burden is on the buyer to establish any breach with respect to the goods accepted.

(5) Where the buyer is sued for breach of a warranty or other obligation for which his seller is answerable over

(a) he may give his seller written notice of the litigation. If the notice states that the seller may come in and defend and that if the seller does not do so he will be bound in any

v. R 2–607(3)(2) limits the effect of non-notification to situations where the seller would suffer prejudice.

action against him by his buyer by any determination of fact common to the two litigations, then unless the seller after seasonable receipt of the notice does come in and defend he is so bound.

(b) if the claim is one for infringement or the like (subsection (3) of Section 2–312) the original seller may demand in writing that his buyer turn over to him control of the litigation including settlement or else be barred from any remedy over and if he also agrees to bear all expense and to satisfy any adverse judgment, then unless the buyer after seasonable receipt of the demand does turn over control the buyer is so barred.

(6) The provisions of subsection (3), (4) and (5) apply to any obligation of a buyer to hold the seller harmless against infringement or the like (subsection (3) of Section 2–312).

Definitional Cross References:

"Burden of establishing". Section 1–201.

"Buyer". Section 2–103.

"Conform". Section 2–106.

"Contract". Section 1–201.

"Goods". Section 2–105.

"Notifies". Section 1–201.

"Reasonable time". Section 1–204.

"Remedy". Section 1–201.

"Seasonably". Section 1–204.

§ 2–608. Revocation of Acceptance in Whole or in Part

(1) The buyer may revoke his acceptance of a lot or commercial unit whose non-conformity substantially impairs its value to him if he has accepted it

(a) on the reasonable assumption that its non-conformity would be cured and it has not been seasonably cured; or

(b) without discovery of such non-conformity if his acceptance was reasonably induced either by the difficulty of discovery before acceptance or by the seller's assurances.

(2) Revocation of acceptance must occur within a reasonable time after the buyer discovers or should have discovered the ground for it and before any substantial change in condition of the goods which is not caused by their own defects. It is not effective until the buyer notifies the seller of it.

(3) A buyer who so revokes has the same rights and duties with regard to the goods involved as if he had rejected them.

Definitional Cross References:

"Buyer". Section 2–103.

"Commercial unit". Section 2–105.

"Conform". Section 2–106.

"Goods". Section 2–105.

"Lot". Section 2–105.

"Notifies". Section 1–201.

"Reasonable time". Section 1–204.

"Rights". Section 1–201.

"Seasonably". Section 1–204.

"Seller". Section 2–103.

§ **2–609.** Right to Adequate Assurance of Performance

(1) A contract for sale imposes an obligation on each party that the other's expectation of receiving due performance will not be impaired. When reasonable grounds for insecurity arise with respect to the performance of either party the other may in writing demand adequate assurance of due performance and until he receives such assurance may if commercially reasonable suspend any performance for which he has not already received the agreed return.

(2) Between merchants the reasonableness of grounds for insecurity and the adequacy of any assurance offered shall be determined according to commercial standards.

(3) Acceptance of any improper delivery or payment does not prejudice the aggrieved party's right to demand adequate assurance of future performance.

(4) After receipt of a justified demand failure to provide within a reasonable time not exceeding thirty days such assurance of due performance as is adequate under the circumstances of the particular case is a repudiation of the contract.

Official Comment

Prior Uniform Statutory Provision: See Sections 53, 54(1)(b), 55 and 63(2), Uniform Sales Act.

Purposes:

1. The section rests on the recognition of the fact that the essential purpose of a contract between commercial men is actual performance and they do not bargain merely for a promise, or for a promise plus the right to win a lawsuit and that a continuing sense of reliance and security that the promised performance will be forthcoming when due, is an important feature of the bargain. If either the willingness or the ability of a party to perform declines materially between the time of contracting and the time for performance, the other party is threatened with the loss of a substantial part of what he has bargained for. A seller needs protection not merely against having to deliver on credit to a shaky buyer, but also against having to procure and manufacture the goods, perhaps turning down other customers. Once he has been given reason to believe that the buyer's performance has become uncertain, it is an undue hardship to force him to continue his own performance. Similarly, a buyer who believes that the seller's deliveries have become uncertain cannot safely wait for the due date of performance when he has been buying to assure himself of materials for his current manufacturing or to replenish his stock of merchandise.

2. Three measures have been adopted to meet the needs of commercial men in such situations. First, the aggrieved party is permitted to suspend his own performance and any preparation therefor, with excuse for any resulting necessary delay, until the situation has been clarified. "Suspend performance" under this section

means to hold up performance pending the outcome of the demand, and includes also the holding up of any preparatory action. This is the same principle which governs the ancient law of stoppage and seller's lien, and also of excuse of a buyer from prepayment if the seller's actions manifest that he cannot or will not perform. (Original Act, Section 63(2).)

Secondly, the aggrieved party is given the right to require adequate assurance that the other party's performance will be duly forthcoming. This principle is reflected in the familiar clauses permitting the seller to curtail deliveries if the buyer's credit becomes impaired, which when held within the limits of reasonableness and good faith actually express no more than the fair business meaning of any commercial contract.

Third, and finally, this section provides the means by which the aggrieved party may treat the contract as broken if his reasonable grounds for insecurity are not cleared up within a reasonable time. This is the principle underlying the law of anticipatory breach, whether by way of defective part performance or by repudiation. The present section merges these three principles of law and commercial practice into a single theory of general application to all sales agreements looking to future performance.

3. Subsection (2) of the present section requires that "reasonable" grounds and "adequate" assurance as used in subsection (1) be defined by commercial rather than legal standards. The express reference to commercial standards carries no connotation that the obligation of good faith is not equally applicable here.

Under commercial standards and in accord with commercial practice, a ground for insecurity need not arise from or be directly related to the contract in question. The law as to "de-pendence" or "independence" of promises within a single contract does not control the application of the present section.

Thus a buyer who falls behind in "his account" with the seller, even though the items involved have to do with separate and legally distinct contracts, impairs the seller's expectation of due performance. Again, under the same test, a buyer who requires precision parts which he intends to use immediately upon delivery, may have reasonable grounds for insecurity if he discovers that his seller is making defective deliveries of such parts to other buyers with similar needs. Thus, too, in a situation such as arose in Jay Dreher Corporation v. Delco Appliance Corporation, 93 F.2d 275 (C.C.A. 2, 1937), where a manufacturer gave a dealer an exclusive franchise for the sale of his product but on two or three occasions breached the exclusive dealing clause, although there was no default in orders, deliveries or payments under the separate sales contract between the parties, the aggrieved dealer would be entitled to suspend his performance of the contract for sale under the present section and to demand assurance that the exclusive dealing contract would be lived up to. There is no need for an explicit clause tying the exclusive franchise into the contract for the sale of goods since the situation itself ties the agreements together.

The nature of the sales contract enters also into the question of reasonableness. For example, a report from an apparently trustworthy source that the seller had shipped defective goods or was planning to ship them would normally give the buyer reasonable grounds for insecurity. But when the buyer has assumed the risk of payment before inspection of the goods, as in a sales contract on C.I.F. or similar cash against documents terms, that risk is not to be evaded by a demand for assurance. Therefore no ground for insecurity would exist under this section unless the report went to a ground which would excuse payment by the buyer.

4. What constitutes "adequate" assurance of due performance is subject to the same test of factual conditions. For example, where the buyer can make use of a defective delivery, a mere promise by a seller of good repute that he is giving the matter his attention and that the defect will not be repeated, is normally sufficient. Under the same circumstances, however, a similar statement by a known corner-cutter might well be considered insufficient without the posting of a guaranty or, if so demanded by the buyer, a speedy replacement of the delivery involved. By the same token where a delivery has defects, even though easily curable, which interfere with easy use by the buyer, no verbal assurance can be deemed adequate which is not accompanied by replacement, repair, money-allowance, or other commercially reasonable cure.

A fact situation such as arose in Corn Products Refining Co. v. Fasola, 94 N.J.L. 181, 109 A. 505 (1920) offers illustration both of reasonable grounds for insecurity and "adequate" assurance. In that case a contract for the sale of oils on 30 days' credit, 2% off for payment within–10 days, provided that credit was to be extended to the buyer only if his financial responsibility was satisfactory to the seller. The buyer had been in the habit of taking advantage of the discount but at the same time that he failed to make his customary 10 day payment, the seller heard rumors, in fact false, that the buyer's financial condition was shaky. Thereupon, the seller demanded cash before shipment or security satisfactory to him. The buyer sent a good credit report from his banker, expressed will-

ingness to make payments when due on the 30 day terms and insisted on further deliveries under the contract. Under this Article the rumors, although false, were enough to make the buyer's financial condition "unsatisfactory" to the seller under the contract clause. Moreover, the buyer's practice of taking the cash discounts is enough, apart from the contract clause, to lay a commercial foundation for suspicion when the practice is suddenly stopped. These matters, however, go only to the justification of the seller's demand for security, or his "reasonable grounds for insecurity".

The adequacy of the assurance given is not measured as in the type of "satisfaction" situation affected with intangibles, such as in personal service cases, cases involving a third party's judgment as final, or cases in which the whole contract is dependent on one party's satisfaction, as in a sale on approval. Here, the seller must exercise good faith and observe commercial standards. This Article thus approves the statement of the court in James B. Berry's Sons Co. of Illinois v. Monark Gasoline & Oil Co., Inc., 32 F.2d 74 (C.C.A.8, 1929), that the seller's satisfaction under such a clause must be based upon reason and must not be arbitrary or capricious; and rejects the purely personal "good faith" test of the Corn Products Refining Co. case, which held that in the seller's sole judgment, if for any reason he was dissatisfied, he was entitled to revoke the credit. In the absence of the buyer's failure to take the 2% discount as was his custom, the banker's report given in that case would have been "adequate" assurance under this Act, regardless of the language of the "satisfaction" clause. However, the seller is reasonably entitled to feel insecure at a sudden expansion of the buyer's use of a credit term, and should be entitled either to security or to a satisfactory explanation.

The entire foregoing discussion as to adequacy of assurance by way of explanation is subject to qualification when repeated occasions for the application of this section arise. This Act recognizes that repeated delinquencies must be viewed as cumulative. On the other hand, commercial sense also requires that if repeated claims for assurance are made under this section, the basis for these claims must be increasingly obvious.

5. A failure to provide adequate assurance of performance and thereby to re-establish the security of expectation, results in a breach only "by repudiation" under subsection (4). Therefore, the possibility is continued of retraction of the repudiation under the section dealing with that problem, unless the aggrieved party has acted on the breach in some manner.

The thirty day limit on the time to provide assurance is laid down to free the question of reasonable time from uncertainty in later litigation.

6. Clauses seeking to give the protected party exceedingly wide powers to cancel or readjust the contract when ground for insecurity arises must be read against the fact that good faith is a part of the obligation of the contract and not subject to modification by agreement and includes, in the case of a merchant, the reasonable observance of commercial standards of fair dealing in the trade. Such clauses can thus be effective to enlarge the protection given by the present section to a certain extent, to fix the reasonable time within which requested assurance must be given, or to define adequacy of the assurance in any commercially reasonable fashion. But any clause seeking to set up arbitrary standards for action is ineffective under this Article. Acceleration clauses are treated similarly in the Articles on Commercial Paper and Secured Transactions.

Cross References:

Point 3: Section 1–203.

Point 5: Section 2–611.

Point 6: Sections 1–203 and 1–208 and Articles 3 and 9.

Definitional Cross References:

"Aggrieved party". Section 1–201.

"Between merchants". Section 2–104.

"Contract". Section 1–201.

"Contract for sale". Section 2–106.

"Party". Section 1–201.

"Reasonable time". Section 1–204.

"Rights". Section 1–201.

"Writing". Section 1–201.

§ 2–610. Anticipatory Repudiation

When either party repudiates the contract with respect to a performance not yet due the loss of which will substantially impair the value of the contract to the other, the aggrieved party may

    (a) for a commercially reasonable time await performance by the repudiating party; or

    (b) resort to any remedy for breach (Section 2–703 or Section 2–711), even though he has notified the repudiating party that he would await the latter's performance and has urged retraction; and

    (c) in either case suspend his own performance or proceed in accordance with the provisions of this Article on the seller's right to identify goods to the contract notwithstanding breach or to salvage unfinished goods (Section 2–704).[w]

Definitional Cross References:

"Aggrieved party". Section 1–201.

"Contract". Section 1–201.

"Party". Section 1–201.

"Remedy". Section 1–201.

§ 2–611. Retraction of Anticipatory Repudiation

(1) Until the repudiating party's next performance is due he can retract his repudiation unless the aggrieved party has since the repudiation cancelled or materially changed his position or otherwise indicated that he considers the repudiation final.

(2) Retraction may be by any method which clearly indicates to the aggrieved party that the repudiating party intends to perform, but must include any assurance justifiably demanded under the provisions of this Article (Section 2–609).

(3) Retraction reinstates the repudiating party's rights under the contract with due excuse and allowance to the aggrieved party for any delay occasioned by the repudiation.

Definitional Cross References:

"Aggrieved party". Section 1–201.

"Cancellation". Section 2–106.

"Contract". Section 1–201.

"Party". Section 1–201.

"Rights". Section 1–201.

§ 2–612. "Installment Contract"; Breach

(1) An "installment contract" is one which requires or authorizes the delivery of goods in separate lots to be separately accepted, even though the contract contains a clause "each delivery is a separate contract" or its equivalent.

(2) The buyer may reject any installment which is non-conforming if the non-conformity substantially impairs the value of that installment and cannot be cured or if the non-conformity is a defect in the required documents; but if the non-conformity does not fall within subsection (3) and the seller gives adequate assurance of its cure the buyer must accept that installment.[x]

(3) Whenever non-conformity or default with respect to one or more installments substantially impairs the value of the whole contract there is a breach of the whole. But the aggrieved party reinstates the contract if he accepts a non-conforming installment without seasonably notifying of cancellation or if he brings an action with respect only to past installments or demands performance as to future installments.

w. R 2–610 introduces a new subsection (2) which describes language and conduct amounting to a repudiation.

x. R 2–612(2) omits the reference to incurable non-conformity.

Definitional Cross References:

"Action". Section 1–201.

"Aggrieved party". Section 1–201.

"Buyer". Section 2–103.

"Cancellation". Section 2–106.

"Conform". Section 2–106.

"Contract". Section 1–201.

"Lot". Section 2–105.

"Notifies". Section 1–201.

"Seasonably". Section 1–204.

"Seller". Section 2–103.

§ 2–613. Casualty to Identified Goods

Where the contract requires for its performance goods identified when the contract is made, and the goods suffer casualty without fault of either party before the risk of loss passes to the buyer, or in a proper case under a "no arrival, no sale" term (Section 2–324) then

(a) if the loss is total the contract is avoided; and

(b) if the loss is partial or the goods have so deteriorated as no longer to conform to the contract the buyer may nevertheless demand inspection and at his option either treat the contract as avoided or accept the goods with due allowance from the contract price for the deterioration or the deficiency in quantity but without further right against the seller.

Definitional Cross References:

"Buyer". Section 2–103.

"Conform". Section 2–106.

"Contract". Section 1–201.

"Fault". Section 1–201.

"Goods". Section 2–105.

"Party". Section 1–201.

"Rights". Section 1–201.

"Seller". Section 2–103.

§ 2–614. Substituted Performance

(1) Where without fault of either party the agreed berthing, loading, or unloading facilities fail or an agreed type of carrier becomes unavailable or the agreed manner of delivery otherwise becomes commercially impracticable but a commercially reasonable substitute is available, such substitute performance must be tendered and accepted.

(2) If the agreed means or manner of payment fails because of domestic or foreign governmental regulation, the seller may withhold or stop delivery unless the buyer provides a means or manner of payment which is commercially a substantial equivalent. If delivery has already been taken, payment by the means or in the manner provided by the regulation discharges the buyer's obligation unless the regulation is discriminatory, oppressive or predatory.

Definitional Cross References:

"Buyer". Section 2–103.

"Fault". Section 1–201.

"Party". Section 1–201.

"Seller". Section 2–103.

§ 2–615. Excuse by Failure of Presupposed Conditions

Except so far as a seller may have assumed a greater obligation and subject to the preceding section on substituted performance:

(a) Delay in delivery or non-delivery in whole or in part by a seller who complies with paragraphs (b) and (c) is not a breach of his duty under a contract for sale if performance as agreed has been made impracticable by the occurrence of a contingency the non-occurrence of which was a basic assumption on which the contract was made or by compliance in good faith with any applicable foreign or domestic governmental regulation or order whether or not it later proves to be invalid.

(b) Where the causes mentioned in paragraph (a) affect only a part of the seller's capacity to perform, he must allocate production and deliveries among his customers but may at his option include regular customers not then under contract as well as his own requirements for further manufacture. He may so allocate in any manner which is fair and reasonable.

(c) The seller must notify the buyer seasonably that there will be delay or non-delivery and, when allocation is required under paragraph (b), of the estimated quota thus made available for the buyer.

Official Comment

Prior Uniform Statutory Provision: None.

Purposes:

1. This section excuses a seller from timely delivery of goods contracted for, where his performance has become commercially impracticable because of unforeseen supervening circumstances not within the contemplation of the parties at the time of contracting. The destruction of specific goods and the problem of the use of substituted performance on points other than delay or quantity, treated elsewhere in this Article, must be distinguished from the matter covered by this section.

2. The present section deliberately refrains from any effort at an exhaustive expression of contingencies and is to be interpreted in all cases sought to be brought within its scope in terms of its underlying reason and purpose.

3. The first test for excuse under this Article in terms of basic assumption is a familiar one. The additional test of commercial impracticability (as contrasted with "impossibility," "frustration of performance" or "frustration of the venture") has been adopted in order to call attention to the commercial character of the criterion chosen by this Article.

4. Increased cost alone does not excuse performance unless the rise in cost is due to some unforeseen contingency which alters the essential nature of the performance. Neither is a rise or a collapse in the market in itself a justification, for that is exactly the type of business risk which business contracts made at fixed prices are intended to cover. But a severe shortage

of raw materials or of supplies due to a contingency such as war, embargo, local crop failure unforeseen shutdown of major sources of supply or the like, which either causes a marked increase in cost or altogether prevents the seller from securing supplies necessary to his performance, is within the contemplation of this section. (See Ford & Sons, Ltd., v. Henry Leetham & Sons, Ltd., 21 Com.Cas. 55 (1915, K.B.D.).)

5. Where a particular source of supply is exclusive under the agreement and fails through casualty, the present section applies rather than the provision on destruction or deterioration of specific goods. The same holds true where a particular source of supply is shown by the circumstances to have been contemplated or assumed by the parties at the time of contracting. (See Davis Co. v. Hoffmann–LaRoche Chemical Works, 178 App.Div. 855, 166 N.Y.S. 179 (1917) and International Paper Co. v. Rockefeller, 161 App. Div. 180, 146 N.Y.S. 371 (1914).) There is no excuse under this section, however, unless the seller has employed all due measures to assure himself that his source will not fail. (See Canadian Industrial Alcohol Co., Ltd., v. Dunbar Molasses Co., 258 N.Y. 194, 179 N.E. 383, 80 A.L.R. 1173 (1932) and Washington Mfg. Co. v. Midland Lumber Co., 113 Wash. 593, 194 P. 777 (1921).)

In the case of failure of production by an agreed source for causes beyond the seller's control, the seller should, if possible, be excused since production by an agreed source is without more a basic assumption of the contract. Such excuse should not result in relieving the defaulting supplier from liability nor in dropping into the seller's lap an unearned bonus of damages over. The flexible adjustment machinery of this Article provides the solution under the provision on the obligation of good faith. A condition to his making good the claim of excuse is the turning over

to the buyer of his rights against the defaulting source of supply to the extent of the buyer's contract in relation to which excuse is being claimed.

6. In situations in which neither sense nor justice is served by either answer when the issue is posed in flat terms of "excuse" or "no excuse," adjustment under the various provisions of this Article is necessary, especially the sections on good faith, on insecurity and assurance and on the reading of all provisions in the light of their purposes, and the general policy of this Act to use equitable principles in furtherance of commercial standards and good faith.

7. The failure of conditions which go to convenience or collateral values rather than to the commercial practicability of the main performance does not amount to a complete excuse. However, good faith and the reason of the present section and of the preceding one may properly be held to justify and even to require any needed delay involved in a good faith inquiry seeking a readjustment of the contract terms to meet the new conditions.

8. The provisions of this section are made subject to assumption of greater liability by agreement and such agreement is to be found not only in the expressed terms of the contract but in the circumstances surrounding the contracting, in trade usage and the like. Thus the exemptions of this section do not apply when the contingency in question is sufficiently foreshadowed at the time of contracting to be included among the business risks which are fairly to be regarded as part of the dickered terms, either consciously or as a matter of reasonable, commercial interpretation from the circumstances. (See Madeirense Do Brasil, S.A. v. Stulman–Emrick Lumber Co., 147 F.2d 399 (C.C.A., 2 Cir., 1945).) The exemption otherwise present through usage of trade under the

present section may also be expressly negated by the language of the agreement. Generally, express agreements as to exemptions designed to enlarge upon or supplant the provisions of this section are to be read in the light of mercantile sense and reason, for this section itself sets up the commercial standard for normal and reasonable interpretation and provides a minimum beyond which agreement may not go.

Agreement can also be made in regard to the consequences of exemption as laid down in paragraphs (b) and (c) and the next section on procedure on notice claiming excuse.

9. The case of a farmer who has contracted to sell crops to be grown on designated land may be regarded as falling either within the section on casualty to identified goods or this section, and he may be excused, when there is a failure of the specific crop, either on the basis of the destruction of identified goods or because of the failure of a basic assumption of the contract.

Exemption of the buyer in the case of a "requirements" contract is covered by the "Output and Requirements" section both as to assumption and allocation of the relevant risks. But when a contract by a manufacturer to buy fuel or raw material makes no specific reference to a particular venture and no such reference may be drawn from the circumstances, commercial understanding views it as a general deal in the general market and not conditioned on any assumption of the continuing operation of the buyer's plant. Even when notice is given by the buyer that the supplies are needed to fill a specific contract of a normal commercial kind, commercial understanding does not see such a supply contract as conditioned on the continuance of the buyer's further contract for outlet. On the other hand, where the buyer's contract is in reasonable commercial understanding conditioned on a definite and specific venture or assumption as, for instance, a war procurement subcontract known to be based on a prime contract which is subject to termination, or a supply contract for a particular construction venture, the reason of the present section may well apply and entitle the buyer to the exemption.

10. Following its basic policy of using commercial practicability as a test for excuse, this section recognizes as of equal significance either a foreign or domestic regulation and disregards any technical distinctions between "law," "regulation," "order" and the like. Nor does it make the present action of the seller depend upon the eventual judicial determination of the legality of the particular governmental action. The seller's good faith belief in the validity of the regulation is the test under this Article and the best evidence of his good faith is the general commercial acceptance of the regulation. However, governmental interference cannot excuse unless it truly "supervenes" in such a manner as to be beyond the seller's assumption of risk. And any action by the party claiming excuse which causes or colludes in inducing the governmental action preventing his performance would be in breach of good faith and would destroy his exemption.

11. An excused seller must fulfill his contract to the extent which the supervening contingency permits, and if the situation is such that his customers are generally affected he must take account of all in supplying one. Subsections (a) and (b), therefore, explicitly permit in any proration a fair and reasonable attention to the needs of regular customers who are probably relying on spot orders for supplies. Customers at different stages of the manufacturing process may be fairly treated by including the seller's manufacturing

requirements. A fortiori, the seller may also take account of contracts later in date than the one in question. The fact that such spot orders may be closed at an advanced price causes no difficulty, since any allocation which exceeds normal past requirements will not be reasonable. However, good faith requires, when prices have advanced, that the seller exercise real care in making his allocations, and in case of doubt his contract customers should be favored and supplies prorated evenly among them regardless of price. Save for the extra care thus required by changes in the market, this section seeks to leave every reasonable business leeway to the seller.

Cross References:

Point 1: Sections 2-613 and 2-614.

Point 2: Section 1-102.

Point 5: Sections 1-203 and 2-613.

Point 6: Sections 1-102, 1-203 and 2-609.

Point 7: Section 2-614.

Point 8: Sections 1-201, 2-302 and 2-616.

Point 9: Sections 1-102, 2-306 and 2-613.

Definitional Cross References:

"Between merchants". Section 2-104.

"Buyer". Section 2-103.

"Contract". Section 1-201.

"Contract for sale". Section 2-106.

"Good faith". Section 1-201.

"Merchant". Section 2-104.

"Notifies". Section 1-201.

"Seasonably". Section 1-204.

"Seller". Section 2-103.

§ 2-616. Procedure on Notice Claiming Excuse

(1) Where the buyer receives notification of a material or indefinite delay or an allocation justified under the preceding section he may by written notification to the seller as to any delivery concerned, and where the prospective deficiency substantially impairs the value of the whole contract under the provisions of this Article relating to breach of installment contracts (Section 2-612), then also as to the whole,

> (a) terminate and thereby discharge any unexecuted portion of the contract; or
>
> (b) modify the contract by agreeing to take his available quota in substitution.

(2) If after receipt of such notification from the seller the buyer fails so to modify the contract within a reasonable time not exceeding thirty days the contract lapses with respect to any deliveries affected.

(3) The provisions of this section may not be negated by agreement except in so far as the seller has assumed a greater obligation under the preceding section.

Definitional Cross References:

"Buyer". Section 2-103.

"Contract". Section 1-201.

"Installment contract". Section 2-612.

"Notification". Section 1-201.

"Reasonable time". Section 1-204.

"Seller". Section 2–103.

"Termination". Section 2–106.

"Written". Section 1–201.

PART 7

REMEDIES

§ 2–701. Remedies for Breach of Collateral Contracts Not Impaired

Remedies for breach of any obligation or promise collateral or ancillary to a contract for sale are not impaired by the provisions of this Article.

Definitional Cross References:

"Contract for sale". Section 2–106.

"Remedy". Section 1–201.

§ 2–702. Seller's Remedies on Discovery of Buyer's Insolvency

(1) Where the seller discovers the buyer to be insolvent he may refuse delivery except for cash including payment for all goods theretofore delivered under the contract, and stop delivery under this Article (Section 2–705).

(2) Where the seller discovers that the buyer has received goods on credit while insolvent he may reclaim the goods upon demand made within ten days after the receipt, but if misrepresentation of solvency has been made to the particular seller in writing within three months before delivery the ten day limitation does not apply.[y] Except as provided in this subsection the seller may not base a right to reclaim goods on the buyer's fraudulent or innocent misrepresentation of solvency or of intent to pay.

(3) The seller's right to reclaim under subsection (2) is subject to the rights of a buyer in ordinary course or other good faith purchaser under this Article (Section 2–403). Successful reclamation of goods excludes all other remedies with respect to them.

Definitional Cross References:

"Buyer". Section 2–103.

"Buyer in ordinary course of business". Section 1–201.

"Contract". Section 1–201.

"Good faith". Section 1–201.

"Goods". Section 2–105.

"Insolvent". Section 1–201.

"Person". Section 1–201.

"Purchaser". Section 1–201.

y. R 2–702(2) substitutes "a reasonable time" for "ten days" and eliminates the exception for a written misrepresentation of solvency.

77

"Receipt" of goods. Section 2–103.   "Seller". Section 2–103.

"Remedy". Section 1–201.   "Writing". Section 1–201.

"Rights". Section 1–201.

§ 2–703. Seller's Remedies in General[z]

Where the buyer wrongfully rejects or revokes acceptance of goods or fails to make a payment due on or before delivery or repudiates with respect to a part or the whole, then with respect to any goods directly affected and, if the breach is of the whole contract (Section 2–612), then also with respect to the whole undelivered balance, the aggrieved seller may

(a) withhold delivery of such goods;

(b) stop delivery by any bailee as hereafter provided (Section 2–705);

(c) proceed under the next section respecting goods still unidentified to the contract;

(d) resell and recover damages as hereafter provided (Section 2–706);

(e) recover damages for non-acceptance (Section 2–708) or in a proper case the price (Section 2–709);

(f) cancel.

Definitional Cross References: "Contract". Section 1–201.

"Aggrieved party". Section 1–201.   "Goods". Section 2–105.

"Buyer". Section 2–103.   "Remedy". Section 1–201.

"Cancellation". Section 2–106.   "Seller". Section 2–103.

§ 2–704. Seller's Right to Identify Goods to the Contract Notwithstanding Breach or to Salvage Unfinished Goods

(1) An aggrieved seller under the preceding section may

(a) identify to the contract conforming goods not already identified if at the time he learned of the breach they are in his possession or control;

(b) treat as the subject of resale goods which have demonstrably been intended for the particular contract even though those goods are unfinished.

(2) Where the goods are unfinished an aggrieved seller may in the exercise of reasonable commercial judgment for the purposes of avoiding loss and of effective realization either complete the manufacture and

z. R 2–703 introduces a nonexclusive definition of "breach of contract by the buyer" and contains an expanded list of seller's remedies.

wholly identify the goods to the contract or cease manufacture and resell for scrap or salvage value or proceed in any other reasonable manner.

Definitional Cross References:

"Aggrieved party". Section 1–201.

"Conforming". Section 2–106.

"Contract". Section 1–201.

"Goods". Section 2–105.

"Rights". Section 1–201.

"Seller". Section 2–103.

§ 2–705. Seller's Stoppage of Delivery in Transit or Otherwise

(1) The seller may stop delivery of goods in the possession of a carrier or other bailee when he discovers the buyer to be insolvent (Section 2–702) and may stop delivery of carload, truckload, planeload or larger shipments of express or freight when the buyer repudiates or fails to make a payment due before delivery or if for any other reason the seller has a right to withhold or reclaim the goods.

(2) As against such buyer the seller may stop delivery until

    (a) receipt of the goods by the buyer; or

    (b) acknowledgment to the buyer by any bailee of the goods except a carrier that the bailee holds the goods for the buyer; or

    (c) such acknowledgment to the buyer by a carrier by reshipment or as warehouseman; or

    (d) negotiation to the buyer of any negotiable document of title covering the goods.

(3)

    (a) To stop delivery the seller must so notify as to enable the bailee by reasonable diligence to prevent delivery of the goods.

    (b) After such notification the bailee must hold and deliver the goods according to the directions of the seller but the seller is liable to the bailee for any ensuing charges or damages.

    (c) If a negotiable document of title has been issued for goods the bailee is not obliged to obey a notification to stop until surrender of the document.

    (d) A carrier who has issued a non-negotiable bill of lading is not obliged to obey a notification to stop received from a person other than the consignor.

Definitional Cross References:

"Buyer". Section 2–103.

"Contract for sale". Section 2–106.

"Document of title". Section 1–201.

"Goods". Section 2–105.

"Insolvent". Section 1–201.

"Notification". Section 1–201.

"Receipt" of goods. Section 2–103.

"Rights". Section 1–201.

"Seller". Section 2–103.

§ 2–706.   Seller's Resale Including Contract for Resale[aa]

(1) Under the conditions stated in Section 2–703 on seller's remedies, the seller may resell the goods concerned or the undelivered balance thereof. Where the resale is made in good faith and in a commercially reasonable manner the seller may recover the difference between the resale price and the contract price together with any incidental damages allowed under the provisions of this Article (Section 2–710), but less expenses saved in consequence of the buyer's breach.

(2) Except as otherwise provided in subsection (3) or unless otherwise agreed resale may be at public or private sale including sale by way of one or more contracts to sell or of identification to an existing contract of the seller. Sale may be as a unit or in parcels and at any time and place and on any terms but every aspect of the sale including the method, manner, time, place and terms must be commercially reasonable. The resale must be reasonably identified as referring to the broken contract, but it is not necessary that the goods be in existence or that any or all of them have been identified to the contract before the breach.

(3) Where the resale is at private sale the seller must give the buyer reasonable notification of his intention to resell.

(4) Where the resale is at public sale

    (a) only identified goods can be sold except where there is a recognized market for a public sale of futures in goods of the kind; and

    (b) it must be made at a usual place or market for public sale if one is reasonably available and except in the case of goods which are perishable or threaten to decline in value speedily the seller must give the buyer reasonable notice of the time and place of the resale; and

    (c) if the goods are not to be within the view of those attending the sale the notification of sale must state the place where the goods are located and provide for their reasonable inspection by prospective bidders; and

    (d) the seller may buy.

(5) A purchaser who buys in good faith at a resale takes the goods free of any rights of the original buyer even though the seller fails to comply with one or more of the requirements of this section.

aa. R 2–706 includes a new subsection (7) providing that a seller's failure to resell does not bar the seller from any other remedy. As to consequential damages, see footnote ee below.

(6) The seller is not accountable to the buyer for any profit made on any resale. A person in the position of a seller (Section 2–707) or a buyer who has rightfully rejected or justifiably revoked acceptance must account for any excess over the amount of his security interest, as hereinafter defined (subsection (3) of Section 2–711).

Definitional Cross References:

"Buyer". Section 2–103.

"Contract". Section 1–201.

"Contract for sale". Section 2–106.

"Good faith". Section 2–103.

"Goods". Section 2–105.

"Merchant". Section 2–104.

"Notification". Section 1–201.

"Person in position of seller". Section 2–707.

"Purchase". Section 1–201.

"Rights". Section 1–201.

"Sale". Section 2–106.

"Security interest". Section 1–201.

"Seller". Section 2–103.

§ 2–707. "Person in the Position of a Seller"

(1) A "person in the position of a seller" includes as against a principal an agent who has paid or become responsible for the price of goods on behalf of his principal or anyone who otherwise holds a security interest or other right in goods similar to that of a seller.

(2) A person in the position of a seller may as provided in this Article withhold or stop delivery (Section 2–705) and resell (Section 2–706) and recover incidental damages (Section 2–710).

Definitional Cross References:

"Consignee". Section 7–102.

"Consignor". Section 7–102.

"Goods" Section 2–105.

"Security interest". Section 1–201.

"Seller". Section 2–103.

§ 2–708. Seller's Damages for Non-acceptance or Repudiation

(1) Subject to subsection (2) and to the provisions of this Article with respect to proof of market price (Section 2–723), the measure of damages for non-acceptance or repudiation by the buyer is the difference between the market price at the time and place for tender and the unpaid contract price together with any incidental damages provided in this Article (Section 2–710), but less expenses saved in consequence of the buyer's breach.[bb]

(2) If the measure of damages provided in subsection (1) is inadequate to put the seller in as good a position as performance would have done then the measure of damages is the profit (including reasonable overhead) which the seller would have made from full performance by the buyer, together with any incidental damages provided in this Article

bb. R 2–708(1)(b), on damages for buyer's repudiation, calls for consulting the market price at a time keyed to a commercially reasonable time after the seller

(Section 2–710), due allowance for costs reasonably incurred and due credit for payments or proceeds of resale.[cc]

Definitional Cross References:
  "Buyer". Section 2–103.
  "Contract". Section 1–201.

"Seller". Section 2–103.

§ 2–709. Action for the Price

(1) When the buyer fails to pay the price as it becomes due the seller may recover, together with any incidental damages under the next section, the price

    (a) of goods accepted or of conforming goods lost or damaged within a commercially reasonable time after risk of their loss has passed to the buyer; and

    (b) of goods identified to the contract if the seller is unable after reasonable effort to resell them at a reasonable price or the circumstances reasonably indicate that such effort will be unavailing.[dd]

(2) Where the seller sues for the price he must hold for the buyer any goods which have been identified to the contract and are still in his control except that if resale becomes possible he may resell them at any time prior to the collection of the judgment. The net proceeds of any such resale must be credited to the buyer and payment of the judgment entitles him to any goods not resold.

(3) After the buyer has wrongfully rejected or revoked acceptance of the goods or has failed to make a payment due or has repudiated (Section 2–610), a seller who is held not entitled to the price under this section shall nevertheless be awarded damages for non-acceptance under the preceding section.

Definitional Cross References:
  "Action". Section 1–201.
  "Buyer". Section 2–103.
  "Conforming". Section 2–106.

"Contract". Section 1–201.

"Goods". Section 2–105.

"Seller". Section 2–103.

§ 2–710. Seller's Incidental Damages[ee]

Incidental damages to an aggrieved seller include any commercially reasonable charges, expenses or commissions incurred in stopping delivery, in the transportation, care and custody of goods after the buyer's

learned of the repudiation. As to consequential damages, see footnote ee below.

  cc. R 2–708(2) refers not only to subsection (1) but also to R 2–706. The final phrase, beginning with "due allowance," is deleted.

  dd. As to consequential damages, see footnote ee below.

  ee. R 2–710(2) contains a nonexclusive definition of "consequential damages re-

sulting from the buyer's breach". A seller's recovery of consequential damages is provided for in R 2–706(1), R 2–708(1), and R 2–709. The drafters have acknowledged that sellers rarely suffer consequential damages. See also R 2–710(3), as to protecting consumers against liability for consequential damages.

breach, in connection with return or resale of the goods or otherwise resulting from the breach.

Definitional Cross References:

"Aggrieved party". Section 1–201.
"Buyer". Section 2–103.
"Goods". Section 2–105.
"Seller". Section 2–103.

§ 2–711. Buyer's Remedies in General; Buyer's Security Interest in Rejected Goods[ff]

(1) Where the seller fails to make delivery or repudiates or the buyer rightfully rejects or justifiably revokes acceptance then with respect to any goods involved, and with respect to the whole if the breach goes to the whole contract (Section 2–612), the buyer may cancel and whether or not he has done so may in addition to recovering so much of the price as has been paid

    (a) "cover" and have damages under the next section as to all the goods affected whether or not they have been identified to the contract; or

    (b) recover damages for non-delivery as provided in this Article (Section 2–713).

(2) Where the seller fails to deliver or repudiates the buyer may also

    (a) if the goods have been identified recover them as provided in this Article (Section 2–502); or

    (b) in a proper case obtain specific performance or replevy the goods as provided in this Article (Section 2–716).

(3) On rightful rejection or justifiable revocation of acceptance a buyer has a security interest in goods in his possession or control for any payments made on their price and any expenses reasonably incurred in their inspection, receipt, transportation, care and custody and may hold such goods and resell them in like manner as an aggrieved seller (Section 2–706).

Definitional Cross References:

"Aggrieved party". Section 1–201.
"Buyer". Section 2–103.
"Cancellation". Section 2–106.
"Contract". Section 1–201.
"Cover". Section 2–712.
"Goods". Section 2–105.
"Notifies". Section 1–201.
"Receipt" of goods. Section 2–103.
"Remedy". Section 1–201.
"Security interest". Section 1–201.
"Seller". Section 2–103.

§ 2–712. "Cover"; Buyer's Procurement of Substitute Goods

(1) After a breach within the preceding section the buyer may "cover" by making in good faith and without unreasonable delay any

ff. R 2–711(1) introduces a nonexclusive definition of "breach of contract by the seller". The buyers' remedies are revised and the list is expanded.

reasonable purchase of or contract to purchase goods in substitution for those due from the seller.[gg]

(2) The buyer may recover from the seller as damages the difference between the cost of cover and the contract price together with any incidental or consequential damages as hereinafter defined (Section 2–715), but less expenses saved in consequence of the seller's breach.

(3) Failure of the buyer to effect cover within this section does not bar him from any other remedy.

Definitional Cross References:

"Buyer". Section 2–103.

"Contract". Section 1–201.

"Good faith". Section 2–103.

"Goods". Section 2–105.

"Purchase". Section 1–201.

"Remedy". Section 1–201.

"Seller". Section 2–103.

§ 2–713. Buyer's Damages for Non-delivery or Repudiation[hh]

(1) Subject to the provisions of this Article with respect to proof of market price (Section 2–723), the measure of damages for non-delivery or repudiation by the seller is the difference between the market price at the time when the buyer learned of the breach and the contract price together with any incidental and consequential damages provided in this Article (Section 2–715), but less expenses saved in consequence of the seller's breach.

(2) Market price is to be determined as of the place for tender or, in cases of rejection after arrival or revocation of acceptance, as of the place of arrival.

Definitional Cross References:

"Buyer". Section 2–103.

"Contract". Section 1–201.

"Seller". Section 2–103.

§ 2–714. Buyer's Damages for Breach in Regard to Accepted Goods

(1) Where the buyer has accepted goods and given notification (subsection (3) of Section 2–607) he may recover as damages for any non-conformity of tender the loss resulting in the ordinary course of events from the seller's breach as determined in any manner which is reasonable.

(2) The measure of damages for breach of warranty is the difference at the time and place of acceptance between the value of the goods accepted and the value they would have had if they had been as

gg. In lieu of the first seven words, R 2–712(1) mentions specific kinds of conduct by the seller and the buyer.

hh. R 2–713(1)(a), on damages for seller's failure to deliver, omits reference to the time "when the buyer learned of the breach". But subsection (1)(b), on damages for seller's repudiation, calls for consulting the market price at a time keyed to a commercially reasonable time after the buyer learned of the repudiation. Subsection

warranted, unless special circumstances show proximate damages of a different amount.

(3) In a proper case any incidental and consequential damages under the next section may also be recovered.

§ 2–715. Buyer's Incidental and Consequential Damages

(1) Incidental damages resulting from the seller's breach include expenses reasonably incurred in inspection, receipt, transportation and care and custody of goods rightfully rejected, any commercially reasonable charges, expenses or commissions in connection with effecting cover and any other reasonable expense incident to the delay or other breach.

(2) Consequential damages resulting from the seller's breach include

(a) any loss resulting from general or particular requirements and needs of which the seller at the time of contracting had reason to know and which could not reasonably be prevented by cover or otherwise; and

(b) injury to person or property proximately resulting from any breach of warranty.

§ 2–716. Buyer's Right to Specific Performance or Replevin

(1) Specific performance may be decreed where the goods are unique or in other proper circumstances.[ii]

(2) The decree for specific performance may include such terms and conditions as to payment of the price, damages, or other relief as the court may deem just.

(3) The buyer has a right of replevin for goods identified to the contract if after reasonable effort he is unable to effect cover for such goods or the circumstances reasonably indicate that such effort will be unavailing or if the goods have been shipped under reservation and satisfaction of the security interest in them has been made or tendered. In the case of goods bought for personal, family, or household purposes,

(1)(a), on damages in other situations, calls for consulting the market at the time for tender.

ii. R 2–716(1) provides that, except in a consumer contract, the parties can agree to specific performance.

the buyer's right of replevin vests upon acquisition of a special property, even if the seller had not then repudiated or failed to deliver.

Definitional Cross References:

"Buyer". Section 2–103.

"Goods". Section 1–201.

"Rights". Section 1–201.

§ 2–717. Deduction of Damages From the Price

The buyer on notifying the seller of his intention to do so may deduct all or any part of the damages resulting from any breach of the contract from any part of the price still due under the same contract.

Definitional Cross References:

"Buyer". Section 2–103.

"Notifies". Section 1–201.

§ 2–718. Liquidation or Limitation of Damages; Deposits[jj]

(1) Damages for breach by either party may be liquidated in the agreement but only at an amount which is reasonable in the light of the anticipated or actual harm caused by the breach, the difficulties of proof of loss, and the inconvenience or non-feasibility of otherwise obtaining an adequate remedy. A term fixing unreasonably large liquidated damages is void as a penalty.

(2) Where the seller justifiably withholds delivery of goods because of the buyer's breach, the buyer is entitled to restitution of any amount by which the sum of his payments exceeds

>   (a) the amount to which the seller is entitled by virtue of terms liquidating the seller's damages in accordance with subsection (1), or

>   (b) in the absence of such terms, twenty per cent of the value of the total performance for which the buyer is obligated under the contract or $500, whichever is smaller.

(3) The buyer's right to restitution under subsection (2) is subject to offset to the extent that the seller establishes

>   (a) a right to recover damages under the provisions of this Article other than subsection (1), and

---

jj. R 2–718(1) draws a distinction between consumer contracts and others, confining the test for the latter to what is reasonable in the light of anticipated or actual harm. It omits the second sentence, and refers to R 2–719 on the enforceability of a term that "limits but does not liquidate" damages.

R 2–718(2) adds to the situations in which restitution is owed. It omits original clause (b).

(b) the amount or value of any benefits received by the buyer directly or indirectly by reason of the contract.

(4) Where a seller has received payment in goods their reasonable value or the proceeds of their resale shall be treated as payments for the purposes of subsection (2); but if the seller has notice of the buyer's breach before reselling goods received in part performance, his resale is subject to the conditions laid down in this Article on resale by an aggrieved seller (Section 2–706).

Definitional Cross References:

"Aggrieved party". Section 1–201.   "Goods". Section 2–105.

"Agreement". Section 1–201.   "Action". 1–201.

"Buyer". Section 2–103.   "Seller". Section 2–103.

"Term". Section 1–201.

§ 2–719. Contractual Modification or Limitation of Remedy

(1) Subject to the provisions of subsections (2) and (3) of this section and of the preceding section on liquidation and limitation of damages,

    (a) the agreement may provide for remedies in addition to or in substitution for those provided in this Article and may limit or alter the measure of damages recoverable under this Article, as by limiting the buyer's remedies to return of the goods and repayment of the price or to repair and replacement of non-conforming goods or parts; and

    (b) resort to a remedy as provided is optional unless the remedy is expressly agreed to be exclusive, in which case it is the sole remedy.

(2) Where circumstances cause an exclusive or limited remedy to fail of its essential purpose, remedy may be had as provided in this Act.

(3) Consequential damages may be limited or excluded unless the limitation or exclusion is unconscionable. Limitation of consequential damages for injury to the person in the case of consumer goods is prima facie unconscionable but limitation of damages where the loss is commercial is not.

Definitional Cross References:

"Agreement". Section 1–201.   "Contract". Section 1–201.

"Buyer". Section 2–103.   "Goods". Section 2–105.

"Conforming". Section 2–106.   "Remedy". Section 1–201.

"Seller". Section 2–103.

§ 2–720. Effect of "Cancellation" or "Rescission" on Claims for Antecedent Breach

Unless the contrary intention clearly appears, expressions of "cancellation" or "rescission" of the contract or the like shall not be construed as a renunciation or discharge of any claim in damages for an antecedent breach.

Definitional Cross References:

"Cancellation". Section 2–106.

"Contract". Section 1–201.

§ 2–721. Remedies for Fraud

Remedies for material misrepresentation or fraud include all remedies available under this Article for non-fraudulent breach. Neither rescission or a claim for rescission of the contract for sale nor rejection or return of the goods shall bar or be deemed inconsistent with a claim for damages or other remedy.

Definitional Cross References: "Goods". Section 1–201.

"Contract for sale". Section 2–106.   "Remedy". Section 1–201.

§ 2–722. Who Can Sue Third Parties for Injury to Goods

Where a third party so deals with goods which have been identified to a contract for sale as to cause actionable injury to a party to that contract

(a) a right of action against the third party is in either party to the contract for sale who has title to or a security interest or a special property or an insurable interest in the goods; and if the goods have been destroyed or converted a right of action is also in the party who either bore the risk of loss under the contract for sale or has since the injury assumed that risk as against the other;

(b) if at the time of the injury the party plaintiff did not bear the risk of loss as against the other party to the contract for sale and there is no arrangement between them for disposition of the recovery, his suit or settlement is, subject to his own interest, as a fiduciary for the other party to the contract;

(c) either party may with the consent of the other sue for the benefit of whom it may concern.

Definitional Cross References: "Goods". Section 2–105.

"Action". Section 1–201.   "Party". Section 1–201.

"Buyer". Section 2–103.   "Rights". Section 1–201.

"Contract for sale". Section 2–106.   "Security interest". Section 1–201.

§ 2–723. Proof of Market Price: Time and Place[kk]

(1) If an action based on anticipatory repudiation comes to trial before the time for performance with respect to some or all of the goods, any damages based on market price (Section 2–708 or Section 2–713)

kk. R 2–723 omits original subsection (1).

shall be determined according to the price of such goods prevailing at the time when the aggrieved party learned of the repudiation.

(2) If evidence of a price prevailing at the times or places described in this Article is not readily available the price prevailing within any reasonable time before or after the time described or at any other place which in commercial judgment or under usage of trade would serve as a reasonable substitute for the one described may be used, making any proper allowance for the cost of transporting the goods to or from such other place.

(3) Evidence of a relevant price prevailing at a time or place other than the one described in this Article offered by one party is not admissible unless and until he has given the other party such notice as the court finds sufficient to prevent unfair surprise.

Definitional Cross References:

"Action". Section 1–201.

"Aggrieved party". Section 1–201.

"Goods". Section 2–105.

"Notifies". Section 1–201.

"Party". Section 1–201.

"Reasonable time". Section 1–204.

"Usage of trade". Section 1–205.

§ 2–724. **Admissibility of Market Quotations**

Whenever the prevailing price or value of any goods regularly bought and sold in any established commodity market is in issue, reports in official publications or trade journals or in newspapers or periodicals of general circulation published as the reports of such market shall be admissible in evidence. The circumstances of the preparation of such a report may be shown to affect its weight but not its admissibility.

Definitional Cross Reference:

"Goods". Section 2–105.

§ 2–725. **Statute of Limitations in Contracts for Sale**[ll]

(1) An action for breach of any contract for sale must be commenced within four years after the cause of action has accrued. By the original agreement the parties may reduce the period of limitation to not less than one year but may not extend it.

(2) A cause of action accrues when the breach occurs, regardless of the aggrieved party's lack of knowledge of the breach. A breach of warranty occurs when tender of delivery is made, except that where a warranty explicitly extends to future performance of the goods and discovery of the breach must await the time of such performance the cause of action accrues when the breach is or should have been discovered.

ll. R 2–725 replaces original subsections (1) and (2) with a much more elaborate set of rules in subsections (1)–(3).

(3) Where an action commenced within the time limited by subsection (1) is so terminated as to leave available a remedy by another action for the same breach such other action may be commenced after the expiration of the time limited and within six months after the termination of the first action unless the termination resulted from voluntary discontinuance or from dismissal for failure or neglect to prosecute.

(4) This section does not alter the law on tolling of the statute of limitations nor does it apply to causes of action which have accrued before this Act becomes effective.

Definitional Cross References:

"Action". Section 1–201.

"Aggrieved party". Section 1–201.

"Agreement". Section 1–201.

"Contract for sale". Section 2–106.

"Goods". Section 2–105.

"Party". Section 1–201.

"Remedy". Section 1–201.

"Term". Section 1–201.

"Termination". Section 2–106.

ARTICLE 3. NEGOTIABLE INSTRUMENTS

§ 3–311. Accord and Satisfaction by Use of Instrument

(a) If a person against whom a claim is asserted proves that (i) that person in good faith tendered an instrument to the claimant as full satisfaction of the claim, (ii) the amount of the claim was unliquidated or subject to a bona fide dispute, and (iii) the claimant obtained payment of the instrument, the following subsections apply.

(b) Unless subsection (c) applies, the claim is discharged if the person against whom the claim is asserted proves that the instrument or an accompanying written communication contained a conspicuous statement to the effect that the instrument was tendered as full satisfaction of the claim.

(c) Subject to subsection (d), a claim is not discharged under subsection (b) if either of the following applies:

(1) The claimant, if an organization, proves that (i) within a reasonable time before the tender, the claimant sent a conspicuous statement to the person against whom the claim is asserted that communications concerning disputed debts, including an instrument tendered as full satisfaction of a debt, are to be sent to a designated person, office, or place, and (ii) the instrument or accompanying communication was not received by that designated person, office, or place.

(2) The claimant, whether or not an organization, proves that within 90 days after payment of the instrument, the claimant tendered repayment of the amount of the instrument to the person against whom the claim is asserted. This paragraph does not apply if the claimant is an organization that sent a statement complying with paragraph (1)(i).

(d) A claim is discharged if the person against whom the claim is asserted proves that within a reasonable time before collection of the instrument was initiated, the claimant, or an agent of the claimant having direct responsibility with respect to the disputed obligation, knew that the instrument was tendered in full satisfaction of the claim.

*

UNIFORM COMMERCIAL CODE

2003 OFFICIAL TEXT

ARTICLE 1. GENERAL PROVISIONS

PART 1.   GENERAL PROVISIONS

ARTICLE 1. GENERAL PROVISIONS

PART 1

GENERAL PROVISIONS

§ 1–101. Short Titles.

(a) This [Act] may be cited as the Uniform Commercial Code.

(b) This article may be cited as Uniform Commercial Code C General Provisions.

§ 1–102. Scope of Article.

This article applies to a transaction to the extent that it is governed by another article of [the Uniform Commercial Code].

§ 1–103. Construction of Act to Promote its Purposes and Policies; Applicability of Supplemental Principles of Law.

(a) [The Uniform Commercial Code] must be liberally construed and applied to promote its underlying purposes and policies, which are:

(1) to simplify, clarify, and modernize the law governing commercial transactions;

(2) to permit the continued expansion of commercial practices through custom, usage, and agreement of the parties; and

(3) to make uniform the law among the various jurisdictions.

(b) Unless displaced by the particular provisions of [the Uniform Commercial Code], the principles of law and equity, including the law merchant and the law relative to capacity to contract, principal and agent, estoppel, fraud, misrepresentation, duress, coercion, mistake, bankruptcy, and other validating or invalidating cause supplement its provisions.

§ 1–104. Construction Against Implied Repeal.

[The Uniform Commercial Code] being a general act intended as a unified coverage of its subject matter, no part of it shall be deemed to be impliedly repealed by subsequent legislation if such construction can reasonably be avoided.

§ 1–105. Severability

If any provision or clause of [the Uniform Commercial Code] or its application to any person or circumstance is held invalid, the invalidity does not affect other provisions or applications of [the Uniform Commercial Code] which can be given effect without the invalid provision or application, and to this end the provisions of [the Uniform Commercial Code] are severable.

§ 1–106. Use of Singular and Plural; Gender

In [the Uniform Commercial Code], unless the statutory context otherwise requires:

(1) words in the singular number include the plural, and those in the plural include the singular; and

(2) words of any gender also refer to any other gender.

§ 1–107. Section Captions.

Section captions are part of [the Uniform Commercial Code].

§ 1–108. Relation to Electronic Signatures in Global and National Commerce Act.

This [Act] modifies, limits, and supersedes the federal Electronic Signature in Global and National Commerce Act, (15 U.S.C. Section 7001, et seq.) but does not modify, limit, or supersede Section 101(c) of that act (15 U.S.C. Section 7001(c)) or authorize electronic delivery of any of the notices described in Section 103(h) of that act (15 U.S.C. Section 103(b)).

PART 2

GENERAL DEFINITIONS AND PRINCIPLES OF INTERPRETATION

§ 1–201. General Definitions.

(a) Unless the context otherwise requires, words or phrases defined in this section, or in the additional definitions contained in other articles of [the Uniform Commercial Code] that apply to particular articles or parts thereof, have the meanings stated.

(b) Subject to definitions contained in other articles of [the Uniform Commercial Code] that apply to particular articles or parts thereof:

(1) "Action", in the sense of a judicial proceeding, includes recoupment, counterclaim, set-off, suit in equity, and any other proceeding in which rights are determined.

(2) "Aggrieved party" means a party entitled to pursue a remedy.

(3) "Agreement", as distinguished from "contract", means the bargain of the parties in fact, as found in their language or inferred from other circumstances, including course of performance, course of dealing, or usage of trade as provided in Section 1–303.

(4) "Bank" means a person engaged in the business of banking and includes a savings bank, savings and loan association, credit union, and trust company.

(5) "Bearer" means a person in possession of a negotiable instrument, document of title, or certificated security that is payable to bearer or indorsed in blank.

(6) "Bill of lading" means a document evidencing the receipt of goods for shipment issued by a person engaged in the business of transporting or forwarding goods.

(7) "Branch" includes a separately incorporated foreign branch of a bank.

(8) "Burden of establishing" a fact means the burden of persuading the trier of fact that the existence of the fact is more probable than its nonexistence.

(9) "Buyer in ordinary course of business" means a person that buys goods in good faith, without knowledge that the sale violates the rights of another person in the goods, and in the ordinary course from a person, other than a pawnbroker, in the business of selling goods of that kind. A person buys goods in the ordinary course if the sale to the person comports with the usual or customary practices in the kind of business in which the seller is engaged or with the seller's own usual or customary practices. A person that sells oil, gas, or other minerals at the wellhead or minehead is a person in the business of selling goods of that kind. A buyer in ordinary course of business may buy for cash, by exchange of other property, or on secured or unsecured credit, and may acquire goods or documents of title under a preexisting contract for sale. Only a buyer that takes possession of the goods or has a right to recover the goods from the seller under Article 2 may be a buyer in ordinary course of business. "Buyer in ordinary course of business" does not include a person that acquires goods in a transfer in bulk or as security for or in total or partial satisfaction of a money debt.

(10) "Conspicuous", with reference to a term, means so written, displayed, or presented that a reasonable person against which it is to operate ought to have noticed it. Whether a term is "conspicuous" or not is a decision for the court. Conspicuous terms include the following:

   (A) a heading in capitals equal to or greater in size than the surrounding text, or in contrasting type, font, or color to the surrounding text of the same or lesser size; and

   (B) language in the body of a record or display in larger type than the surrounding text, or in contrasting type, font, or color to the surrounding text of the same size, or set off from surrounding text of the same size by symbols or other marks that call attention to the language.

(11) "Consumer" means an individual who enters into a transaction primarily for personal, family, or household purposes.

(12) "Contract", as distinguished from "agreement", means the total legal obligation that results from the parties' agreement as determined by [the Uniform Commercial Code] as supplemented by any other applicable laws.

(13) "Creditor" includes a general creditor, a secured creditor, a lien creditor, and any representative of creditors, including an assignee for the benefit of creditors, a trustee in bankruptcy, a receiver in equity, and an executor or administrator of an insolvent debtor's or assignor's estate.

(14) "Defendant" includes a person in the position of defendant in a counterclaim, cross-claim, or third-party claim.

(15) "Delivery", with respect to an instrument, document of title, or chattel paper, means voluntary transfer of possession.

(16) "Document of title" includes bill of lading, dock warrant, dock receipt, warehouse receipt or order for the delivery of goods, and also any other document which in the regular course of business or financing is treated as adequately evidencing that the person in possession of it is entitled to receive, hold, and dispose of the document and the goods it covers. To be a document of title, a document must purport to be issued by or addressed to a bailee and purport to cover goods in the bailee's possession which are either identified or are fungible portions of an identified mass.

(17) "Fault" means a default, breach, or wrongful act or omission.

(18) "Fungible goods" means:

(A) goods of which any unit, by nature or usage of trade, is the equivalent of any other like unit; or

(B) goods that by agreement are treated as equivalent.

(19) "Genuine" means free of forgery or counterfeiting.

(20) "Good faith," except as otherwise provided in Article 5, means honesty in fact and the observance of reasonable commercial standards of fair dealing.

(21) "Holder" means:

(A) the person in possession of a negotiable instrument that is payable either to bearer or to an identified person that is the person in possession; or

(B) the person in possession of a document of title if the goods are deliverable either to bearer or to the order of the person in possession.

(22) "Insolvency proceeding" includes an assignment for the benefit of creditors or other proceeding intended to liquidate or rehabilitate the estate of the person involved.

(23) "Insolvent" means:

(A) having generally ceased to pay debts in the ordinary course of business other than as a result of bona fide dispute;

    (B) being unable to pay debts as they become due; or

    (C) being insolvent within the meaning of federal bankruptcy law.

(24) "Money" means a medium of exchange currently authorized or adopted by a domestic or foreign government. The term includes a monetary unit of account established by an intergovernmental organization or by agreement between two or more countries.

(25) "Organization" means a person other than an individual.

(26) "Party", as distinguished from "third party", means a person that has engaged in a transaction or made an agreement subject to [the Uniform Commercial Code].

(27) "Person" means an individual, corporation, business trust, estate, trust, partnership, limited liability company, association, joint venture, government, government subdivision, agency, or instrumentality, public corporation, or any other legal or commercial entity.

(28) "Present value" means the amount as of a date certain of one or more sums payable in the future, discounted to the date certain by use of either an interest rate specified by the parties if that rate is not manifestly unreasonable at the time the transaction is entered into or, if an interest rate is not so specified, a commercially reasonable rate that takes into account the facts and circumstances at the time the transaction is entered into.

(29) "Purchase" means taking by sale, lease, discount, negotiation, mortgage, pledge, lien, security interest, issue or reissue, gift, or any other voluntary transaction creating an interest in property.

(30) "Purchaser" means a person that takes by purchase.

(31) "Record" means information that is inscribed on a tangible medium or that is stored in an electronic or other medium and is retrievable in perceivable form.

(32) "Remedy" means any remedial right to which an aggrieved party is entitled with or without resort to a tribunal.

(33) "Representative" means a person empowered to act for another, including an agent, an officer of a corporation or association, and a trustee, executor, or administrator of an estate.

(34) "Right" includes remedy.

(35) "Security interest" means an interest in personal property or fixtures which secures payment or performance of an obligation. "Security interest" includes any interest of a consignor

and a buyer of accounts, chattel paper, a payment intangible, or a promissory note in a transaction that is subject to Article 9. . . .[a] Whether a transaction in the form of a lease creates a "security interest" is determined pursuant to Section 1–203.

(36) "Send" in connection with a writing, record, or notice means:

　(A) to deposit in the mail or deliver for transmission by any other usual means of communication with postage or cost of transmission provided for and properly addressed and, in the case of an instrument, to an address specified thereon or otherwise agreed, or if there be none to any address reasonable under the circumstances; or

　(B) in any other way to cause to be received any record or notice within the time it would have arrived if properly sent.

(37) "Signed" includes using any symbol executed or adopted with present intention to adopt or accept a writing.

(38) "State" means a State of the United States, the District of Columbia, Puerto Rico, the United States Virgin Islands, or any territory or insular possession subject to the jurisdiction of the United States.

(39) "Surety" includes a guarantor or other secondary obligor.

(40) "Term" means a portion of an agreement that relates to a particular matter.

(41) "Unauthorized signature" means a signature made without actual, implied, or apparent authority. The term includes a forgery.

(42) "Warehouse receipt" means a receipt issued by a person engaged in the business of storing goods for hire.

(43) "Writing" includes printing, typewriting, or any other intentional reduction to tangible form. "Written" has a corresponding meaning.

§ 1–202. Notice; Knowledge

(a) Subject to subsection (f), a person has "notice" of a fact if the person:

(1) has actual knowledge of it;

(2) has received a notice or notification of it; or

(3) from all the facts and circumstances known to the person at the time in question, has reason to know that it exists.

---

a. Three sentences refining the definition further are omitted here.

(b) "Knowledge" means actual knowledge. "Knows" has a corresponding meaning.

(c) "Discover", "learn", or words of similar import refer to knowledge rather than to reason to know.

(d) A person "notifies" or "gives" a notice or notification to another person by taking such steps as may be reasonably required to inform the other person in ordinary course, whether or not the other person actually comes to know of it.

(e) Subject to subsection (f), a person "receives" a notice or notification when:

(1) it comes to that person's attention; or

(2) it is duly delivered in a form reasonable under the circumstances at the place of business through which the contract was made or at another location held out by that person as the place for receipt of such communications.

(f) Notice, knowledge, or a notice or notification received by an organization is effective for a particular transaction from the time it is brought to the attention of the individual conducting that transaction and, in any event, from the time it would have been brought to the individual's attention if the organization had exercised due diligence. An organization exercises due diligence if it maintains reasonable routines for communicating significant information to the person conducting the transaction and there is reasonable compliance with the routines. Due diligence does not require an individual acting for the organization to communicate information unless the communication is part of the individual's regular duties or the individual has reason to know of the transaction and that the transaction would be materially affected by the information.

§ 1–203. Lease Distinguished from Security Interest.

[*The text of this section is not reproduced here.*]

§ 1–204. Value.

Except as otherwise provided in articles 3, 4, [and] 5, [and 6], a person gives value for rights if the person acquires them:

(1) in return for a binding commitment to extend credit or for the extension of immediately available credit, whether or not drawn upon and whether or not a charge-back is provided for in the event of difficulties in collection;

(2) as security for, or in total or partial satisfaction of, a preexisting claim;

(3) by accepting delivery under a pre-existing contract for purchase; or

(4) in return for any consideration sufficient to support a simple contract.

§ 1–205. Reasonable Time; Seasonableness.

(1) Whether a time for taking an action required by [the Uniform Commercial Code] is reasonable depends on the nature, purpose, and circumstances of the action.

(3) An action is taken seasonably if it is taken at or within the time agreed or, if no time is agreed, at or within a reasonable time.

§ 1–206. Presumptions.

Whenever [the Uniform Commercial Code] creates a "presumption" with respect to a fact, or provides that a fact is "presumed," the trier of fact must find the existence of the fact unless and until evidence is introduced that supports a finding of its nonexistence.

Legislative Note: Former Section 1–206, a Statute of Frauds for sales of "kinds of personal property not otherwise covered," has been deleted. The other articles of the Uniform Commercial Code make individual determinations as to requirements for memorializing transactions within their scope, so that the primary effect of former Section 1–206 was to impose a writing requirement on sales transactions not otherwise governed by the UCC. Deletion of former Section 1–206 does not constitute a recommendation to legislatures as to whether such sales transactions should be covered by a Statute of Frauds; rather, it reflects a determination that there is no need for uniform commercial law to resolve that issue.

PART 3

TERRITORIAL APPLICABILITY AND GENERAL RULES

§ 1–301. Territorial Applicability; Parties' Power to Choose Applicable Law.

(a) In this section:

(1) "Domestic transaction" means a transaction other than an international transaction.

(2) "International transaction" means a transaction that bears a reasonable relation to a country other than the United States.

(b) This section applies to a transaction to the extent that it is governed by another article of the [Uniform Commercial Code].

(c) Except as otherwise provided in this section:

(1) an agreement by parties to a domestic transaction that any or all of their rights and obligations are to be determined by the law of

this State or of another State is effective, whether or not the transaction bears a relation to the State designated; and

(2) an agreement by parties to an international transaction that any or all of their rights and obligations are to be determined by the law of this State or of another State or country is effective, whether or not the transaction bears a relation to the State or country designated.

(d) In the absence of an agreement effective under subsection (c), and except as provided in subsections (e) and (g), the rights and obligations of the parties are determined by the law that would be selected by application of this State's conflict of laws principles.

(e) If one of the parties to a transaction is a consumer, the following rules apply:

(1) An agreement referred to in subsection (c) is not effective unless the transaction bears a reasonable relation to the State or country designated.

(2) Application of the law of the State or country determined pursuant to subsection (c) or (d) may not deprive the consumer of the protection of any rule of law governing a matter within the scope of this section, which both is protective of consumers and may not be varied by agreement:

(A) of the State or country in which the consumer principally resides, unless subparagraph (B) applies; or

(B) if the transaction is a sale of goods, of the State or country in which the consumer both makes the contract and takes delivery of those goods, if such State or country is not the State or country in which the consumer principally resides.

(f) An agreement otherwise effective under subsection (c) is not effective to the extent that application of the law of the State or country designated would be contrary to a fundamental policy of the State or country whose law would govern in the absence of agreement under subsection (d).

(g) To the extent that [the Uniform Commercial Code] governs a transaction, if one of the following provisions of [the Uniform Commercial Code] specifies the applicable law, that provision governs and a contrary agreement is effective only to the extent permitted by the law so specified:

(1) Section 2–402;

(2) Sections 2A–105 and 2A–106;

(3) Section 4–102;

(4) Section 4A–507;

(5) Section 5–116;

[(6) Section 6–103;]

(7) Section 8–110;

(8) Sections 9–301 through 9–307.

§ 1–302. Variation By Agreement.

(a) Except as otherwise provided in subsection (b) or elsewhere in [the Uniform Commercial Code], the effect of provisions of [the Uniform Commercial Code] may be varied by agreement.

(b) The obligations of good faith, diligence, reasonableness, and care prescribed by [the Uniform Commercial Code] may not be disclaimed by agreement. The parties, by agreement, may determine the standards by which the performance of those obligations is to be measured if those standards are not manifestly unreasonable. Whenever [the Uniform Commercial Code] requires an action to be taken within a reasonable time, a time that is not manifestly unreasonable may be fixed by agreement.

(c) The presence in certain provisions of [the Uniform Commercial Code] of the phrase "unless otherwise agreed", or words of similar import, does not imply that the effect of other provisions may not be varied by agreement under this section.

§ 1–303. Course of Performance, Course of Dealing, and Usage of Trade.

(a) A "course of performance" is a sequence of conduct between the parties to a particular transaction that exists if:

(1) the agreement of the parties with respect to the transaction involves repeated occasions for performance by a party; and

(2) the other party, with knowledge of the nature of the performance and opportunity for objection to it, accepts the performance or acquiesces in it without objection.

(b) A "course of dealing" is a sequence of conduct concerning previous transactions between the parties to a particular transaction that is fairly to be regarded as establishing a common basis of understanding for interpreting their expressions and other conduct.

(c) A "usage of trade" is any practice or method of dealing having such regularity of observance in a place, vocation, or trade as to justify an expectation that it will be observed with respect to the transaction in question. The existence and scope of such a usage must be proved as facts. If it is established that such a usage is embodied in a trade code or similar record, the interpretation of the record is a question of law.

(d) A course of performance or course of dealing between the parties or usage of trade in the vocation or trade in which they are engaged or of which they are or should be aware is relevant in ascertaining the meaning of the parties' agreement, may give particular meaning to specific terms of the agreement, and may supplement or qualify the terms of the agreement. A usage of trade applicable in the place in which part of the performance under the agreement is to occur may be so utilized as to that part of the performance.

(e) Except as otherwise provided in subsection (f), the express terms of an agreement and any applicable course of performance, course of dealing, or usage of trade must be construed whenever reasonable as consistent with each other. If such a construction is unreasonable:

(1) express terms prevail over course of performance, course of dealing, and usage of trade;

(2) course of performance prevails over course of dealing and usage of trade; and

(3) course of dealing prevails over usage of trade.

(f) Subject to Section 2–209, a course of performance is relevant to show a waiver or modification of any term inconsistent with the course of performance.

(g) Evidence of a relevant usage of trade offered by one party is not admissible unless that party has given the other party notice that the court finds sufficient to prevent unfair surprise to the other party.

§ 1–304. Obligation of Good Faith.

Every contract or duty within [the Uniform Commercial Code] imposes an obligation of good faith in its performance and enforcement.

§ 1–305. Remedies to be Liberally Administered.

(a) The remedies provided by [the Uniform Commercial Code] must be liberally administered to the end that the aggrieved party may be put in as good a position as if the other party had fully performed but neither consequential or special damages nor penal damages may be had except as specifically provided in [the Uniform Commercial Code] or by other rule of law.

(b) Any right or obligation declared by [the Uniform Commercial Code] is enforceable by action unless the provision declaring it specifies a different and limited effect.

§ 1–306. Waiver or Renunciation of Claim or Right After Breach.

A claim or right arising out of an alleged breach may be discharged in whole or in part without consideration by agreement of the aggrieved party in an authenticated record.

§ 1–307. Prima Facie Evidence by Third Party Documents

A document in due form purporting to be a bill of lading, policy or certificate of insurance, official weigher's or inspector's certificate, consular invoice, or any other document authorized or required by the contract to be issued by a third party is prima facie evidence of its own authenticity and genuineness and of the facts stated in the document by the third party.

§ 1–308. Performance or Acceptance Under Reservation of Rights.

(a) A party that with explicit reservation of rights performs or promises performance or assents to performance in a manner demanded or offered by the other party does not thereby prejudice the rights reserved. Such words as "without prejudice", "under protest", or the like are sufficient.

(b) Subsection (a) does not apply to an accord and satisfaction.

§ 1–309. Option to Accelerate at Will.

A term providing that one party or that party's successor in interest may accelerate payment or performance or require collateral or additional collateral "at will" or "when the party deems itself insecure," or words of similar import, means that the party has power to do so only if that party in good faith believes that the prospect of payment or performance is impaired. The burden of establishing lack of good faith is on the party against which the power has been exercised.

§ 1–310. Subordinated Obligations.

An obligation may be issued as subordinated to performance of another obligation of the person obligated, or a creditor may subordinate its right to performance of an obligation by agreement with either the person obligated or another creditor of the person obligated. Subordination does not create a security interest as against either the common debtor or a subordinated creditor.

ARTICLE 2. SALES[1]

PART 1

SHORT TITLE, GENERAL CONSTRUCTION AND SUBJECT MATTER

§ 2–101. Short Title.

This Article shall be known and may be cited as Uniform Commercial Code Sales.

§ 2–102. Scope; Certain Security and Other Transactions Excluded From This Article.

Unless the context otherwise requires, this Article applies to transactions in goods; it does not apply to any transaction which although in the form of an unconditional contract to sell or present sale is intended to operate only as a security transaction nor does this Article impair or repeal any statute regulating sales to consumers, farmers or other specified classes of buyers.

Definitional Cross References:

"Contract". Section 1–201.

"Contract for sale". Section 2–106.

"Present sale". Section 2–106.

"Sale". Section 2–106.

§ 2–103. Definitions and Index of Definitions.

(1) In this article unless the context otherwise requires

(a) "Buyer" means a person that buys or contracts to buy goods.

(b) "Conspicuous", with reference to a term, means so written, displayed, or presented that a reasonable person against which it is to operate ought to have noticed it. A term in an electronic record intended to evoke a response by an electronic agent is conspicuous if it is presented in a form that would enable a reasonably configured electronic agent to take it into account or react to it without review of the record by an individual. Whether a term is "conspicuous" or not is a decision for the court. Conspicuous terms include the following:

(i) for a person:

(A) a heading in capitals equal to or greater in size than the surrounding text, or in contrasting type, font, or color to the surrounding text of the same or lesser size and;

(B) language in the body of a record or display in larger type than the surrounding text, or in contrasting type, font, or color to the surrounding text of the same size, or set off from surrounding text of the same size by

1. As submiited to the American Law Institute in May, 2003.

symbols or other marks that call attention to the language; and

    (ii) for a person or an electronic agent, a term that is so placed in a record or display that the person or electronic agent cannot proceed without taking action with respect to the particular term.

(c) "Consumer" means an individual who buys or contracts to buy goods that, at the time of contracting, are intended by the individual to be used primarily for personal, family, or household purposes.

(d) "Consumer contract" means a contract between a merchant seller and a consumer.

(e) "Delivery" means the voluntary transfer of physical possession or control of goods.

(f) "Electronic" means relating to technology having electrical, digital, magnetic, wireless, optical, electromagnetic, or similar capabilities.

(g) "Electronic agent" means a computer program or an electronic or other automated means used independently to initiate an action or respond to electronic records or performances in whole or in part, without review or action by an individual.

(h) "Electronic record" means a record created, generated, sent, communicated, received, or stored by electronic means.

(i) "Foreign exchange transaction" means a transaction in which one party agrees to deliver a quantity of a specified money or unit of account in consideration of the other party's agreement to deliver another quantity of a different money or unit of account either currently or at a future date, and in which delivery is to be through funds transfer, book entry accounting, or other form of payment order, or other agreed means to transfer a credit balance. The term includes a transaction of this type involving two or more moneys and spot, forward, option, or other products derived from underlying moneys and any combination of these transactions. The term does not include a transaction involving two or more moneys in which one or both of the parties is obligated to make physical delivery, at the time of contracting or in the future, of banknotes, coins, or other form of legal tender or specie.

(j) "Good faith" means honesty in fact and the observance of reasonable commercial standards of fair dealing.

Legislative Note: This definition should not be adopted if the jurisdiction has enacted revised Article 1.

(k) "Goods" means all things that are movable at the time of identification to a contract for sale. The term includes future goods, specially manufactured goods, the unborn young of animals, growing crops, and other identified things attached to realty as described in Section 2–107. The term does not include information, the money in which the price is to be paid, investment securities under Article 8, the subject matter of foreign exchange transactions, or choses in action.

(*l*) "Receipt of goods" means taking physical possession of them.

(m) "Record" means information that is inscribed on a tangible medium or that is stored in an electronic or other medium and is retrievable in perceivable form.

Legislative Note: This definition should not be adopted if the jurisdiction has enacted revised Article 1.

(n) "Remedial promise" means a promise by the seller to repair or replace the goods or to refund all or part of the price of goods upon the happening of a specified event.

(*o*) "Seller" means a person that sells or contracts to sell goods.

(p) "Sign" means, with present intent to authenticate or adopt a record:

(i) to execute or adopt a tangible symbol; or

(ii) to attach to or logically associate with the record an electronic sound, symbol, or process.

(2) Other definitions applying to this Article or to specified Parts thereof, and the sections in which they appear are.

"Acceptance". Section 2–206.

"Between merchants". Section 2–104.

"Cancellation". Section 2–106.

"Commercial unit". Section 2–105.

"Conforming to contract". Section 2–106.

"Contract for sale". Section 2–106.

"Cover". Section 2–712.

"Entrusting". Section 2–403.

"Financing agency". Section 2–104.

"Future goods". Section 2–105.

"Goods". Section 2–103.

"Identification". Section 2–501.

"Installment contract". Section 2–612.

"Lot". Section 2–105.

"Merchant". Section 2–104.

"Person in position of seller". Section 2–707.

"Present sale". Section 2–106.

"Sale". Section 2–106.

"Sale on approval". Section 2–326.

"Sale or return". Section 2–326.

"Termination". Section 2–106.

(3) The following definitions in other Articles apply to this Article:

"Check". Section 3–104(f).

"Consumer goods". Section 9–102(a)(23).

"Dishonor". Section 3–502.

"Draft". Section 3–104(e).

"Injunction against honor". Section 5–109(b).

"Letter of credit". Section 5–102(a)(10).

(4) In addition Article 1 contains general definitions and principles of construction and interpretation applicable throughout this Article.

§ 2–104. Definitions: "Merchant"; "Between Merchants"; "Financing Agency"

(1) "Merchant" means a person that deals in goods of the kind or otherwise holds itself out by occupation as having knowledge or skill peculiar to the practices or goods involved in the transaction or to which the knowledge or skill may be attributed by the person's employment of an agent or broker or other intermediary that holds itself out by occupation as having the knowledge or skill.

(2) "Financing agency" means a bank, finance company or other person that in the ordinary course of business makes advances against goods or documents of title or that by arrangement with either the seller or the buyer intervenes in ordinary course to make or collect payment due or claimed under the contract for sale, as by purchasing or paying the seller's draft or making advances against it or by merely taking it for collection whether or not documents of title accompany the draft. "Financing agency" includes also a bank or other person that similarly intervenes between persons that are in the position of seller and buyer in respect to the goods (Section 2–707).

(3) "Between merchants" means in any transaction with respect to which both parties are chargeable with the knowledge or skill of merchants.

Definitional Cross References:

"Bank". Section 1–201.

"Buyer". Section 2–103.

"Contract for sale". Section 2–106.

"Document of title". Section 1–201.   "Person". Section 1–201.

"Draft". Section 3–104(e).   "Purchase". Section 1–201.

"Goods". Section 2–103.   "Seller". Section 2–103.

§ 2–105. Definitions: Transferability; "Future" Goods; "Lot"; "Commercial Unit".

(1) Goods must be both existing and identified before any interest in them can pass. Goods which are not both existing and identified are "future" goods. A purported present sale of future goods or of any interest therein operates as a contract to sell.

(2) There may be a sale of a part interest in existing identified goods.

(3) An undivided share in an identified bulk of fungible goods is sufficiently identified to be sold although the quantity of the bulk is not determined. Any agreed proportion of such a bulk or any quantity thereof agreed upon by number, weight or other measure may to the extent of the seller's interest in the bulk be sold to the buyer that then becomes an owner in common.

(4) "Lot" means a parcel or a single article which is the subject matter of a separate sale or delivery, whether or not it is sufficient to perform the contract.

(5) "Commercial unit" means such a unit of goods as by commercial usage is a single whole for purposes of sale and division of which materially impairs its character or value on the market or in use. A commercial unit may be a single article (as a machine) or a set of articles (as a suite of furniture or an assortment of sizes) or a quantity (as a bale, gross, or carload) or any other unit treated in use or in the relevant market as a single whole.

Definitional Cross References: "Money". Section 1–201.

"Buyer". Section 2–103.   "Present sale". Section 2–106.

"Contract". Section 1–201.

"Contract for sale". Section 2–106.   "Sale". Section 2–106.

"Fungible". Section 1–201.   "Seller". Section 2–103.

§ 2–106. Definitions: "Contract"; "Agreement"; "Contract for Sale"; "Sale"; "Present Sale"; "Conforming" to Contract; "Termination"; "Cancellation".

(1) In this Article unless the context otherwise requires "contract" and "agreement" are limited to those relating to the present or future sale of goods. "Contract for sale" includes both a present sale of goods and a contract to sell goods at a future time. A "sale" consists in the passing of title from the seller to the buyer for a price (Section 2–401). A

"present sale" means a sale which is accomplished by the making of the contract.

(2) Goods or conduct including any part of a performance are "conforming" or conform to the contract when they are in accordance with the obligations under the contract.

(3) "Termination" occurs when either party pursuant to a power created by agreement or law puts an end to the contract otherwise than for its breach. On "termination" all obligations which are still executory on both sides are discharged but any right based on prior breach or performance survives.

(4) "Cancellation" occurs when either party puts an end to the contract for breach by the other and its effect is the same as that of "termination" except that the cancelling party also retains any remedy for breach of the whole contract or any unperformed balance.

Definitional Cross References:

"Agreement". Section 1–201.

"Buyer". Section 2–103.

"Contract". Section 1–201.

"Goods". Section 2–103.

"Party". Section 1–201.

"Remedy". Section 1–201.

"Rights". Section 1–201.

"Seller". Section 2–103.

§ 2–107. Goods to Be Severed From Realty: Recording.

(1) A contract for the sale of minerals or the like (including oil and gas) or a structure or its materials to be removed from realty is a contract for the sale of goods within this Article if they are to be severed by the seller but until severance a purported present sale thereof which is not effective as a transfer of an interest in land is effective only as a contract to sell.

(2) A contract for the sale apart from the land of growing crops or other things attached to realty and capable of severance without material harm thereto but not described in subsection (1) or of timber to be cut is a contract for the sale of goods within this Article whether the subject matter is to be severed by the buyer or by the seller even though it forms part of the realty at the time of contracting, and the parties can by identification effect a present sale before severance.

(3) The provisions of this section are subject to any third party rights provided by the law relating to realty records, and the contract for sale may be executed and recorded as a document transferring an interest in land and shall then constitute notice to third parties of the buyer's rights under the contract for sale.

Definitional Cross References:

"Buyer". Section 2–103.

"Contract". Section 1–201.

"Contract for sale". Section 2–106.

"Goods". Section 2–103.

"Party". Section 1–201.

"Present sale". Section 2–106.

"Rights". Section 1–201.

"Seller". Section 2–103.

§ 2–108. Transactions Subject to Other Law.

(1) A transaction subject to this article is also subject to any applicable:

  (a) [list any certificate of title statutes of this State covering automobiles, trailers, mobile homes, boats, farm tractors, or the like], except with respect to the rights of a buyer in ordinary course of business under Section 2–403(2) which arise before a certificate of title covering the goods is effective in the name of any other buyer;

  (b) rule of law that establishes a different rule for consumers; or

  (c) statute of this state applicable to the transaction is subject, such as a statute dealing with:

    (i) the sale or lease of agricultural products;

    (ii) the transfer of human blood, blood products, human tissues, or parts;

    (iii) the consignment or transfer by artists of works of art or fine prints;

    (iv) distribution agreements, franchises, and other relationships through which goods are sold;

    (v) the misbranding or adulteration of food products or drugs; and

    (vi) dealers in particular products, such as automobiles, motorized wheelchairs, agricultural equipment, and hearing aids.

(2) Except for the rights of a buyer in ordinary course of business under subsection (1)(a), in the event of a conflict between this article and a law referred to in subsection (1), that law governs.

(3) For purposes of this article, failure to comply with a law referred to in subsection (1) has only the effect specified in that law.

(4) This article modifies, limits, and supersedes the federal Electronic Signatures in Global and National Commerce Act, 15 U.S.C. Section 7001 et seq., except that nothing in this article modifies, limits, or supersedes Section 7001(c) of that Act or authorizes electronic delivery of any of the notices described in Section 7003(b) of that Act.

Definitional Cross Reference:

"Lease". Section 1–203.

PART 2

FORM, FORMATION, TERMS AND READJUSTMENT OF CONTRACT; ELECTRONIC CONTRACTING

§ 2–201. Formal Requirement; Statute of Frauds.

(1) A contract for the sale of goods for the price of $5,000 or more is not enforceable by way of action or defense unless there is some record sufficient to indicate that a contract for sale has been made between the parties and signed by the party against which enforcement is sought or by the party's authorized agent or broker. A record is not insufficient because it omits or incorrectly states a term agreed upon but the contract is not enforceable under this subsection beyond the quantity of goods shown in the record.

(2) Between merchants if within a reasonable time a record in confirmation of the contract and sufficient against the sender is received and the party receiving it has reason to know its contents, it satisfies the requirements of subsection (1) against the recipient unless notice of objection to its contents is given in a record within 10 days after it is received.

(3) A contract which does not satisfy the requirements of subsection (1) but which is valid in other respects is enforceable

   (a) if the goods are to be specially manufactured for the buyer and are not suitable for sale to others in the ordinary course of the seller's business and the seller, before notice of repudiation is received and under circumstances which reasonably indicate that the goods are for the buyer, has made either a substantial beginning of their manufacture or commitments for their procurement; or

   (b) if the party against which enforcement is sought admits in the party's pleading, or in the party's testimony or otherwise under oath that a contract for sale was made, but the contract is not enforceable under this paragraph beyond the quantity of goods admitted; or

   (c) with respect to goods for which payment has been made and accepted or which have been received and accepted (Sec. 2–606).

(4) A contract that is enforceable under this section is not unenforceable merely because it is not capable of being performed within one year or any other period after its making.

Definitional Cross References:

"Action". Section 1–201.

"Between merchants". Section 2–104.

"Buyer". Section 2–103.

"Contract". Section 1–201.

"Contract for sale". Section 2–106.

"Goods". Section 2–103.

"Notice". Section 1–202.

"Party". Section 1–201.

"Reasonable time". Section 1–205.

"Record". Section 2–103.

"Sale". Section 2–106.

"Seller". Section 2–103.

§ 2–202. Final Expression in a Record: Parol or Extrinsic Evidence.

(1) Terms with respect to which the confirmatory records of the parties agree or which are otherwise set forth in a record intended by the parties as a final expression of their agreement with respect to such terms as are included therein may not be contradicted by evidence of any prior agreement or of a contemporaneous oral agreement but may be supplemented by evidence of:

(a) course of performance, course of dealing or usage of trade (Section 1–303); and

(b) consistent additional terms unless the court finds the record to have been intended also as a complete and exclusive statement of the terms of the agreement.

(2) Terms in a record may be explained by evidence of course of performance, course of dealing, or usage of trade without a preliminary determination by the court that the language used is ambiguous.

Legislative Note: The cross-references in subsection (1)(a) should not be changed if the jurisdiction has not adopted revised Article 1.

Definitional Cross References:

"Agreement". Section 1–201.

"Course of dealing". Section 1–303.

"Course of performance". Section 1–303.

"Parties". Section 1–201.

"Record". Section 2–103.

"Term". Section 1–201.

"Usage of trade". Section 1–303.

"Written" and "writing". Section 1–201.

§ 2–203. Seals Inoperative.

The affixing of a seal to a record evidencing a contract for sale or an offer to buy or sell goods does not constitute the record a sealed instrument and the law with respect to sealed instruments does not apply to such a contract or offer.

Definitional Cross References:

"Contract for sale". Section 2–106.

"Goods". Section 2–103.

"Record". Section 2–103.

§ 2–204. Formation in General.

(1) A contract for sale of goods may be made in any manner sufficient to show agreement, including offer and acceptance, conduct by both parties which recognizes the existence of such a contract, the interaction of electronic agents, and the interaction of an electronic agent and an individual.

(2) An agreement sufficient to constitute a contract for sale may be found even though the moment of its making is undetermined.

(3) Even though one or more terms are left open a contract for sale does not fail for indefiniteness if the parties have intended to make a contract and there is a reasonably certain basis for giving an appropriate remedy.

(4) Except as otherwise provided in Sections 2–211 through 2–213, the following rules apply:

(a) A contract may be formed by the interaction of electronic agents of the parties, even if no individual was aware of or reviewed the electronic agents' actions or the resulting terms and agreements.

(b) A contract may be formed by the interaction of an electronic agent and an individual acting on the individual's own behalf or for another person. A contract is formed if the individual takes actions that the individual is free to refuse to take or makes a statement, and the individual has reason to know that the actions or statement will:

(i) cause the electronic agent to complete the transaction or performance; or

(ii) indicate acceptance of an offer, regardless of other expressions or actions by the individual to which the electronic agent cannot react.

Definitional Cross References:

"Agreement". Section 1–201.

"Contract". Section 1–201.

"Contract for sale". Section 2–106.

"Electronic". Section 2–103.

"Electronic agents". Section 2–103.

"Goods". Section 2–103.

"Party". Section 1–201.

"Remedy". Section 1–201.

"Term". Section 1–201.

§ 2–205. Firm Offers.

An offer by a merchant to buy or sell goods in a signed record which by its terms gives assurance that it will be held open is not revocable, for lack of consideration, during the time stated or if no time is stated for a reasonable time, but in no event may such period of irrevocability exceed three months, but any such term of assurance in a form supplied by the offeree must be separately signed by the offeror.

Definitional Cross References:

"Goods". Section 2–103.

"Merchant". Section 2–104.

"Record". Section 2–103.

"Signed". Section 1–201.

§ 2–206. Offer and Acceptance in Formation of Contract.

(1) Unless otherwise unambiguously indicated by the language or circumstances

(a) an offer to make a contract shall be construed as inviting acceptance in any manner and by any medium reasonable in the circumstances;

(b) an order or other offer to buy goods for prompt or current shipment shall be construed as inviting acceptance either by a prompt promise to ship or by the prompt or current shipment of conforming or nonconforming goods, but the shipment of non-conforming goods is not an acceptance if the seller seasonably notifies the buyer that the shipment is offered only as an accommodation to the buyer.

(2) Where the beginning of a requested performance is a reasonable mode of acceptance an offeror that is not notified of acceptance within a reasonable time may treat the offer as having lapsed before acceptance.

(3) A definite and seasonable expression of acceptance in a record operates as an acceptance even if it contains terms additional to or different from the offer.

Definitional Cross References:

"Buyer". Section 2–103.

"Conforming". Section 2–106.

"Contract". Section 1–201.

"Goods". Section 2–103.

"Notifies". Section 1–202.

"Reasonable time". Section 1–205.

§ 2–207. Terms of Contract; Effect of Confirmation.

Subject to Section 2–202, if (i) conduct by both parties recognizes the existence of a contract although their records do not otherwise establish a contract, (ii) a contract is formed by an offer and acceptance, or (iii) a contract formed in any manner is confirmed by a record that contains terms additional to or different from those in the contract being confirmed, the terms of the contract, are:

(a) terms that appear in the records of both parties;

(b) terms, whether in a record or not, to which both parties agree; and

(c) terms supplied or incorporated under any provision of this Act.

Definitional Cross References:

"Agree". Section 1–201.

"Acceptance". Section 2–206.

"Contract". Section 1–201.

"Offer". Section 2–204.

"Parties". Section 1–201.

"Records". Section 2–103.

"Terms". Section 1–201.

§ 2–208. Reserved.

Legislative Note: This section should not be repealed if the jurisdiction has not adopted revised Article 1.

§ 2–209. Modification; Rescission and Waiver.

(1) An agreement modifying a contract within this Article needs no consideration to be binding.

(2) An agreement in a signed record which excludes modification or rescission except by a signed record cannot be otherwise modified or rescinded, but except as between merchants such a requirement in a form supplied by the merchant must be separately signed by the other party.

(3) The requirements of the statute of frauds section of this Article (Section 2–201) must be satisfied if the contract as modified is within its provisions.

(4) Although an attempt at modification or rescission does not satisfy the requirements of subsection (2) or (3) it can operate as a waiver.

(5) A party that has made a waiver affecting an executory portion of the contract may retract the waiver by reasonable notification received by the other party that strict performance will be required of any term waived, unless the retraction would be unjust in view of a material change of position in reliance on the waiver.

Definitional Cross References:

"Agreement". Section 1–201.

"Between merchants". Section 2–104.

"Contract". Section 1–201.

"Merchant". Section 2–104.

"Notification". Section 1–202.

"Signed". Section 1–201.

"Statute of frauds". Section 2–201.

"Term". Section 1–201.

"Writing". Section 1–201.

§ 2–210. Delegation of Performance; Assignment of Rights.

(1) If the seller or buyer assigns rights under a contract, the following rules apply:

(a) Subject to paragraph (b) and except as otherwise provided in Section 9–406 or as otherwise agreed, all rights of the seller or the buyer may be assigned unless the assignment would materially change the duty of the other party, increase materially the burden or risk imposed on that party by the contract, or impair materially that party's chance of obtaining return performance. A right to damages for breach of the whole contract or a right arising out of the assignor's due performance of its entire obligation may be assigned despite an agreement otherwise.

(b) The creation, attachment, perfection, or enforcement of a security interest in the seller's interest under a contract is not an assignment that materially changes the duty of or materially increases the burden or risk imposed on the buyer or materially impairs the buyer's chance of obtaining return performance under paragraph (a) unless, and only to the extent that, enforcement of the security interest results in a delegation of a material performance of the seller. Even in that event, the creation, attachment, perfection, and enforcement of the security interest remain effective. However, the seller is liable to the buyer for damages caused by the delegation to the extent that the damages could not reasonably be prevented by the buyer, and a court may grant other appropriate relief, including cancellation of the contract or an injunction against enforcement of the security interest or consummation of the enforcement.

(2) If the seller or buyer delegates performance of its duties under a contract, the following rules apply:

(a) A party may perform its duties through a delegate unless otherwise agreed or unless the other party has a substantial interest in having the original promisor perform or control the acts required by the contract. Delegation of performance does not relieve the delegating party of any duty to perform or liability for breach.

(b) Acceptance of a delegation of duties by the assignee constitutes a promise to perform those duties. The promise is enforceable by either the assignor or the other party to the original contract.

(c) The other party may treat any delegation of duties as creating reasonable grounds for insecurity and may without prejudice to its rights against the assignor demand assurances from the assignee under Section 2–609.

(d) A contractual term prohibiting the delegation of duties otherwise delegable under paragraph (a) is enforceable, and an attempted delegation is not effective.

(3) An assignment of "the contract" or of "all my rights under the contract" or an assignment in similar general terms is an assignment of rights and unless the language or the circumstances, as in an assignment for security, indicate the contrary, it is also a delegation of performance of the duties of the assignor.

(4) Unless the circumstances indicate the contrary a prohibition of assignment of "the contract" is to be construed as barring only the delegation to the assignee of the assignor's performance.

Definitional Cross References:

"Agreement". Section 1–201.

"Buyer". Section 2–103.

"Contract". Section 1–201.

"Party". Section 1–201.

"Rights". Section 1–201.

"Seller". Section 2–103.

"Term". Section 1–201.

§ 2–211. Legal Recognition of Electronic Contracts, Records and Signatures.

(1) A record or signature may not be denied legal effect or enforceability solely because it is in electronic form.

(2) A contract may not be denied legal effect or enforceability solely because an electronic record was used in its formation.

(3) This article does not require a record or signature to be created, generated, sent, communicated, received, stored, or otherwise processed by electronic means or in electronic form.

(4) A contract formed by the interaction of an individual and an electronic agent under Section 2–204(4)(b) does not include terms provided by the individual if the individual had reason to know that the agent could not react to the terms as provided.

Definitional Cross References:

"Contract". Section 1–201.

"Electronic". Section 2–103.

"Electronic agent". Section 2–103.

"Electronic record". Section 2–103.

"Record". Section 2–103.

"Signature". Section 1–201.

§ 2–212. Attribution.

An electronic record or electronic signature is attributable to a person if it was the act of the person or the person's electronic agent or the person is otherwise legally bound by the act.

Definitional Cross References:

"Contract". Section 1–201.

"Electronic". Section 2–103.

"Electronic agent". Section 2–103.

"Electronic record". Section 2–103.

"Record". Section 2–103.

"Signature". Section 1–201.

§ 2–213. Electronic Communication.

(1) If the receipt of an electronic communication has a legal effect, it has that effect even if no individual is aware of its receipt.

(2) Receipt of an electronic acknowledgment of an electronic communication establishes that the communication was received but, in itself, does not establish that the content sent corresponds to the content received.

Definitional Cross References:

"Electronic". Section 2–103.

"Sent". Section 1–201.

PART 3

GENERAL OBLIGATION AND CONSTRUCTION OF CONTRACT

§ 2–301. General Obligations of Parties.

The obligation of the seller is to transfer and deliver and that of the buyer is to accept and pay in accordance with the contract.

Definitional Cross References:

"Buyer". Section 2–103.

"Contract". Section 1–201.

"Party". Section 1–201.

"Seller". Section 2–103.

§ 2–302. Unconscionable Contract or Term.

(1) If the court as a matter of law finds the contract or any term of the contract to have been unconscionable at the time it was made the court may refuse to enforce the contract, or it may enforce the remainder of the contract without the unconscionable term, or it may so limit the application of any unconscionable term as to avoid any unconscionable result.

(2) When it is claimed or appears to the court that the contract or any term thereof may be unconscionable the parties shall be afforded a reasonable opportunity to present evidence as to its commercial setting, purpose and effect to aid the court in making the determination.

Definitional Cross References:

"Contract". Section 1–201.

"Term". Section 1–201.

§2–303. Allocation or Division of Risks.

Where this Article allocates a risk or a burden as between the parties—unless otherwise agreed—the agreement may not only shift the allocation but may also divide the risk or burden.

Definitional Cross References:

"Party". Section 1–201.

"Agreement". Section 1–201.

§ 2–304. Price Payable in Money, Goods, Realty, or Otherwise.

(1) The price can be made payable in money or otherwise. If it is payable in whole or in part in goods each party is a seller of the goods which that party is to transfer.

(2) Even though all or part of the price is payable in an interest in realty the transfer of the goods and the seller's obligations with reference to them are subject to this Article, but not the transfer of the interest in realty or the transferor's obligations in connection therewith.

Definitional Cross References:

"Goods". Section 2–103.

"Money". Section 1–201.

"Party". Section 1–201.

"Seller". Section 2–103.

§ 2–305. Open Price Term.

(1) The parties if they so intend can conclude a contract for sale even though the price is not settled. In such a case the price is a reasonable price at the time for delivery if

(a) nothing is said as to price; or

(b) the price is left to be agreed by the parties and they fail to agree; or

(c) the price is to be fixed in terms of some agreed market or other standard as set or recorded by a third person or agency and it is not so set or recorded.

(2) A price to be fixed by the seller or by the buyer means a price to be fixed in good faith.

(3) When a price left to be fixed otherwise than by agreement of the parties fails to be fixed through fault of one party the other may at the party's option treat the contract as canceled or the party may fix a reasonable price.

(4) Where, however, the parties intend not to be bound unless the price be fixed or agreed and it is not fixed or agreed there is no contract. In such a case the buyer must return any goods already received or if unable so to do must pay their reasonable value at the time of delivery and the seller must return any portion of the price paid on account.

Definitional Cross References:

"Agreement". Section 1–201.

"Burden of establishing". Section 1–201.

"Buyer". Section 2–103.

"Cancellation". Section 2–106.

"Contract". Section 1–201.

"Contract for sale". Section 2–106.

"Goods". Section 2–103.

"Party". Section 1–201.

"Receipt of goods". Section 2–103.

"Seller". Section 2–103.

"Term". Section 1–201.

§ 2–306. Output, Requirements and Exclusive Dealings.

(1) A term which measures the quantity by the output of the seller or the requirements of the buyer means such actual output or requirements as may occur in good faith, except that no quantity unreasonably disproportionate to any stated estimate or in the absence of a stated estimate to any normal or otherwise comparable prior output or requirements may be tendered or demanded.

(2) A lawful agreement by either the seller or the buyer for exclusive dealing in the kind of goods concerned imposes unless otherwise agreed an obligation by the seller to use best efforts to supply the goods and by the buyer to use best efforts to promote their sale.

Definitional Cross References:

"Agreement". Section 1–201.

"Buyer". Section 2–103.

"Contract for sale". Section 2–106.

"Goods". Section 2–103.

"Good faith". Section 2–103.

"Party". Section 1–201.

"Seller". Section 2–103.

"Term". Section 1–201.

§ 2–307. Delivery in Single Lot or Several Lots.

Unless otherwise agreed all goods called for by a contract for sale must be tendered in a single delivery and payment is due only on such tender but where the circumstances give either party the right to make or demand delivery in lots the price if it can be apportioned may be demanded for each lot.

Definitional Cross References:

"Contract for sale". Section 2–106.

"Goods". Section 2–103.

"Lot". Section 2–105.

"Party". Section 1–201.

"Rights". Section 1–201.

§ 2–308. Absence of Specified Place for Delivery.

Unless otherwise agreed

(a) the place for delivery of goods is the seller's place of business or if it has none the seller's residence; but

(b) in a contract for sale of identified goods which to the knowledge of the parties at the time of contracting are in some other place, that place is the place for their delivery; and

(c) documents of title may be delivered through customary banking channels.

Definitional Cross References:

"Contract for sale". Section 2–106.

"Delivery". Section 2–103.

"Document of title". Section 1–201.

"Goods". Section 2–103.

"Party". Section 1–201.

"Seller". Section 2–103

§ 2–309. Absence of Specific Time Provisions; Notice of Termination.

(1) The time for shipment or delivery or any other action under a contract if not provided in this Article or agreed upon shall be a reasonable time.

(2) Where the contract provides for successive performances but is indefinite in duration it is valid for a reasonable time but unless otherwise agreed may be terminated at any time by either party.

(3) Termination of a contract by one party except on the happening of an agreed event requires that reasonable notification be received by the other party and an agreement dispensing with notification is invalid if its operation would be unconscionable. A term specifying standards for the nature and timing of notice is enforceable if the standards are not manifestly unreasonable.

Definitional Cross References:

"Agreement". Section 1–201.

"Contract". Section 1–201.

"Notification". Section 1–202.

"Party". Section 1–201.

"Reasonable time". Section 1–205.

"Termination". Section 2–106.

§ 2–310. Open Time for Payment or Running of Credit Authority to Ship Under Reservation.

Unless otherwise agreed

(a) payment is due at the time and place at which the buyer is to receive the goods even though the place of shipment is the place of delivery; and

(b) if the seller is required or authorized to send the goods the seller may ship them under reservation, and may tender the documents of title, but the buyer may inspect the goods after their arrival before payment is due unless such inspection is inconsistent with the terms of the contract (Section 2–513); and

(c) if tender of delivery is agreed to be made by way of documents of title otherwise than by subsection (b) then payment is due at the time and place at which the buyer is to receive the documents regardless of where the goods are to be received; and

(d) where the seller is required or authorized to ship the goods on credit the credit period runs from the time of shipment but postdating the invoice or delaying its dispatch will correspondingly delay the starting of the credit period.

Definitional Cross References:

"Agreement". Section 1–201.

"Buyer". Section 2–103.

"Delivery". Section 2–103.

"Document of title". Section 1–201.

"Goods". Section 2–103.

"Receipt of goods". Section 2–103.

"Seller". Section 2–103.

"Send". Section 1–201.

"Tender of delivery". Sections 2–503 and 2–507.

"Term". Section 1–201.

§ 2–311. Options and Cooperation Respecting Performance.

(1) An agreement for sale which is otherwise sufficiently definite (subsection (3) of Section 2–204) to be a contract is not made invalid by the fact that it leaves particulars of performance to be specified by one of the parties. Any such specification must be made in good faith and within limits set by commercial reasonableness.

(2) Unless otherwise agreed specifications relating to assortment of the goods are at the buyer's option and specifications or arrangements relating to shipment are at the seller's option.

(3) Where such specification would materially affect the other party's performance but is not seasonably made or where one party's cooperation is necessary to the agreed performance of the other but is not seasonably forthcoming, the other party in addition to all other remedies

(a) is excused for any resulting delay in that party's performance; and

(b) may also either proceed to perform in any reasonable manner or after the time for a material part of that party's performance treat the failure to specify or to cooperate as a breach by failure to deliver or accept the goods.

Definitional Cross References:

"Agreement". Section 1–201.

"Buyer". Section 2–103.

"Contract for sale". Section 2–106.

"Goods". Section 2–103.

"Party". Section 1–201.

"Remedy". Section 1–201.

"Seasonably". Section 1–205.

"Seller". Section 2–103.

§ 2–312. Warranty of Title and Against Infringement: Buyer's Obligation Against Infringement.

(1) Subject to subsection (3) there is in a contract for sale a warranty by the seller that

(a) the title conveyed shall be good and its transfer rightful and shall not unreasonably expose the buyer to litigation because of any colorable claim to or interest in the goods; and

(b) the goods shall be delivered free from any security interest or other lien or encumbrance of which the buyer at the time of contracting has no knowledge.

(2) Unless otherwise agreed a seller that is a merchant regularly dealing in goods of the kind warrants that the goods shall be delivered free of the rightful claim of any third person by way of infringement or the like but a buyer that furnishes specifications to the seller must hold the seller harmless against any such claim that arises out of compliance with the specifications.

(3) A warranty under this section may be disclaimed or modified only by specific language or by circumstances that give the buyer reason to know that the seller does not claim title, that the seller is purporting to sell only the right or title as the seller or a third person may have, or that the seller is selling subject to any claims of infringement or the like.

Definitional Cross References:

"Agreement". Section 1–201.

"Buyer". Section 2–103.

"Contract for sale". Section 2–106.

"Goods". Section 2–103.

"Merchant". Section 2–104.

"Person". Section 1–201.

"Right". Section 1–201.

"Seller". Section 2–103.

§ 2–313. Express Warranties By Affirmation, Promise, Description, Sample; Remedial Promise.

(1) In this section, "immediate buyer" means a buyer that enters into a contract with the seller.

127

(2) Express warranties by the seller to the immediate buyer are created as follows:

    (a) Any affirmation of fact or promise made by the seller which relates to the goods and becomes part of the basis of the bargain creates an express warranty that the goods shall conform to the affirmation or promise.

    (b) Any description of the goods which is made part of the basis of the bargain creates an express warranty that the goods shall conform to the description.

    (c) Any sample or model which is made part of the basis of the bargain creates an express warranty that the whole of the goods shall conform to the sample or model.

(3) It is not necessary to the creation of an express warranty that the seller use formal words such as "warrant" or "guarantee" or that the seller have a specific intention to make a warranty, but an affirmation merely of the value of the goods or a statement purporting to be merely the seller's opinion or commendation of the goods does not create a warranty.

(4) Any remedial promise made by the seller to the immediate buyer creates an obligation that the promise will be performed upon the happening of the specified event.

Definitional Cross References:

"Buyer". Section 2–103.

"Conforming". Section 2–106.

"Goods". Section 2–103.

"Remedial promise". Section 2–103.

"Seller". Section 2–103.

"Tender of delivery". Sections 2–503 and 2–507.

§ 2–313A. Obligation to Remote Purchaser Created By Record Packaged With or Accompanying Goods.

(1) In this section:

    (a) "Immediate buyer" means a buyer that enters into a contract with the seller.

    (b) "Remote purchaser" means a person that buys or leases goods from an immediate buyer or other person in the normal chain of distribution.

(2) This section applies only to new goods and goods sold or leased as new goods in a transaction of purchase in the normal chain of distribution.

(3) If in a record packaged with or accompanying the goods the seller makes an affirmation of fact or promise that relates to the goods, provides a description that relates to the goods, or makes a remedial promise, and the seller reasonably expects the record to be, and the record is, furnished to the remote purchaser, the seller has an obligation to the remote purchaser that:

(a) the goods will conform to the affirmation of fact, promise or description unless a reasonable person in the position of the remote purchaser would not believe that the affirmation of fact, promise or description created an obligation; and

(b) the seller will perform the remedial promise.

(4) It is not necessary to the creation of an obligation under this section that the seller use formal words such as "warrant" or "guarantee" or that the seller have a specific intention to undertake an obligation, but an affirmation merely of the value of the goods or a statement purporting to be merely the seller's opinion or commendation of the goods does not create an obligation.

(5) The following rules apply to the remedies for breach of an obligation created under this section:

(a) The seller may modify or limit the remedies available to the remote purchaser if the modification or limitation is furnished to the remote purchaser no later than the time of purchase or if the modification or limitation is contained in the record that contains the affirmation of fact, promise or description.

(b) Subject to a modification or limitation of remedy, a seller in breach is liable for incidental or consequential damages under Section 2–715, but not for lost profits.

(c) The remote purchaser may recover as damages for breach of a seller's obligation arising under subsection (2) the loss resulting in the ordinary course of events as determined in any reasonable manner.

(6) An obligation that is not a remedial promise is breached if the goods did not conform to the affirmation of fact, promise or description creating the obligation when the goods left the seller's control.

Legislative Note: To maintain their relative positions in this Act, Sections 2–313A and 2–313B may have to be renumbered according to the convention used by a particular state. For example, in some states they may be designated as 2–313.1 and 2–313.2.

Definitional Cross References:

"Buyer". Section 2–103.

"Conforming". Section 2–106.

"Goods". Section 2–103.

"Lease". Section 1–203.

"Purchase". Section 1–201.

"Record". Section 2–103.

"Remedial promise". Section 2–103.

"Remedy". Section 1–201.

"Sale". Section 2–106.

"Seller". Section 2–103.

§ 2–313B. Obligation to Remote Purchaser Created By Communication to the Public.

(1) In this section:

(a) "Immediate buyer" means a buyer that enters into a contract with the seller.

(b) "Remote purchaser" means a person that buys or leases goods from an immediate buyer or other person in the normal chain of distribution.

(2) This section applies only to new goods and goods sold or leased as new goods in a transaction of purchase in the normal chain of distribution.

(3) If in an advertisement or a similar communication to the public a seller makes an affirmation of fact or promise that relates to the goods, provides a description that relates to the goods, or makes a remedial promise, and the remote purchaser enters into a transaction of purchase with knowledge of and with the expectation that the goods will conform to the affirmation of fact, promise, or description, or that the seller will perform the remedial promise, the seller has an obligation to the remote purchaser that:

(a) the goods will conform to the affirmation of fact, promise or description unless a reasonable person in the position of the remote purchaser would not believe that the affirmation of fact, promise or description created an obligation; and

(b) the seller will perform the remedial promise.

(4) It is not necessary to the creation of an obligation under this section that the seller use formal words such as "warrant" or "guarantee" or that the seller have a specific intention to undertake an obligation, but an affirmation merely of the value of the goods or a statement purporting to be merely the seller's opinion or commendation of the goods does not create an obligation.

(5) The following rules apply to the remedies for breach of an obligation created under this section:

(a) The seller may modify or limit the remedies available to the remote purchaser if the modification or limitation is furnished to the remote purchaser no later than the time of purchase. The modification or limitation may be furnished as part of the communication that contains the affirmation of fact, promise or description.

(b) Subject to a modification or limitation of remedy, a seller in breach is liable for incidental or consequential damages under Section 2–715, but not for lost profits.

(c) The remote purchaser may recover as damages for breach of a seller's obligation arising under subsection (2) the loss resulting in the ordinary course of events as determined in any reasonable manner.

(6) An obligation that is not a remedial promise is breached if the goods did not conform to the affirmation of fact, promise or description creating the obligation when the goods left the seller's control.

Legislative Note: In order to maintain their relative positions in this Act, Sections 2–313A and 2–313B may have to be renumbered according to the convention used by a particular state. For example, in some states they may be designated as 2–313.1 and 2–313.2.

Definitional Cross References:

"Buyer". Section 2–103.

"Conforming". Section 2–106.

"Goods". Section 2–103.

"Lease". Section 1–203.

"Purchase". Section 1–201.

"Record". Section 2–103.

"Remedial promise". Section 2–103.

"Remedy". Section 1–201.

"Sale". Section 2–106.

"Seller". Section 2–103.

§ 2–314. Implied Warranty: Merchantability; Usage of Trade.

(1) Unless excluded or modified (Section 2–316), a warranty that the goods shall be merchantable is implied in a contract for their sale if the seller is a merchant with respect to goods of that kind. Under this section the serving for value of food or drink to be consumed either on the premises or elsewhere is a sale.

(2) Goods to be merchantable must be at least such as

(a) pass without objection in the trade under the contract description; and

(b) in the case of fungible goods, are of fair average quality within the description; and

(c) are fit for the ordinary purposes for which goods of that description are used; and

(d) run, within the variations permitted by the agreement, of even kind, quality and quantity within each unit and among all units involved; and

(e) are adequately contained, packaged, and labeled as the agreement may require; and

(f) conform to the promise or affirmations of fact made on the container or label if any.

(3) Unless excluded or modified (Section 2–316) other implied warranties may arise from course of dealing or usage of trade.

Definitional Cross References:

"Agreement". Section 1–201.

"Contract". Section 1–201.

"Contract for sale". Section 2–106.

"Goods". Section 2–103.

"Merchant". Section 2–104.

"Seller". Section 2–103.

§ 2–315. Implied Warranty: Fitness for Particular Purpose.

Where the seller at the time of contracting has reason to know any particular purpose for which the goods are required and that the buyer is relying on the seller's skill or judgment to select or furnish suitable goods, there is unless excluded or modified under the next section an implied warranty that the goods shall be fit for such purpose.

Definitional Cross References: "Seller". Section 2–103.

"Buyer". Section 2–103.

"Goods". Section 2–103.

§ 2–316. Exclusion or Modification of Warranties.

(1) Words or conduct relevant to the creation of an express warranty and words or conduct tending to negate or limit warranty shall be construed wherever reasonable as consistent with each other; but subject to the provisions of this Article on parol or extrinsic evidence (Section 2–202) negation or limitation is inoperative to the extent that such construction is unreasonable.

(2) Subject to subsection (3), to exclude or modify the implied warranty of merchantability or any part of it in a consumer contract the language must be in a record, be conspicuous, and state "The seller undertakes no responsibility for the quality of the goods except as otherwise provided in this contract," and in any other contract the language must mention merchantability and in case of a record must be conspicuous. Subject to subsection (3), to exclude or modify the implied warranty of fitness, the exclusion must be in a record and be conspicuous. Language to exclude all implied warranties of fitness in a consumer contract must state "The seller assumes no responsibility that the goods will be fit for any particular purpose for which you may be buying these goods, except as otherwise provided in the contract," and in any other contract the language is sufficient if it states, for example, that "There are no warranties that extend beyond the description on the face hereof." Language that satisfies the requirements of this subsection for the exclusion and modification of a warranty in a consumer contract also satisfies the requirements for any other contract.

(3) Notwithstanding subsection (2):

(a) unless the circumstances indicate otherwise, all implied warranties are excluded by expressions like "as is", "with all faults" or other language which in common understanding calls the buyer's attention to the exclusion of warranties, makes plain that there is no implied warranty, and, in a consumer contract evidenced by a record, is set forth conspicuously in the record; and

(b) when the buyer before entering into the contract has examined the goods or the sample or model as fully as desired or has refused to examine the goods after a demand by the seller there is no implied warranty with regard to defects which an examination ought in the circumstances to have revealed to the buyer; and

(c) an implied warranty can also be excluded or modified by course of dealing or course of performance or usage of trade.

(4) Remedies for breach of warranty can be limited in accordance with the provisions of this article on liquidation or limitation of damages and on contractual modification of remedy (Sections 2–718 and 2–719).

Definitional Cross References:

"Agreement". Section 1–201.

"Buyer". Section 2–103.

"Conspicuous". Section 2–103.

"Consumer contract". Section 2–103.

"Contract". Section 1–201.

"Course of dealing". Section 1–303.

"Goods". Section 2–103.

"Record". Section 2–103.

"Remedy". Section 1–201.

"Seller". Section 2–103.

"Usage of trade". Section 1–303.

§ 2–317. Cumulation and Conflict of Warranties Express or Implied.

Warranties whether express or implied shall be construed as consistent with each other and as cumulative, but if such construction is unreasonable the intention of the parties shall determine which warranty is dominant. In ascertaining that intention the following rules apply:

(a) Exact or technical specifications displace an inconsistent sample or model or general language of description.

(b) A sample from an existing bulk displaces inconsistent general language of description.

(c) Express warranties displace inconsistent implied warranties other than an implied warranty of fitness for a particular purpose.

Definitional Cross Reference:

"Party". Section 1–201.

§ 2–318. Third Party Beneficiaries of Warranties and Obligations.

(1) In this section:

(a) "Immediate buyer" means a buyer that enters into a contract with the seller.

(b) "Remote purchaser" means a person that buys or leases goods from an immediate buyer or other person in the normal chain of distribution.

Alternative A to subsection (2)

(2) A seller's warranty to an immediate buyer, whether express or implied, a seller's remedial promise to an immediate buyer, or a seller's obligation to a remote purchaser under Section 2–313A or 2–313B extends to any natural person who is in the family or household of the immediate buyer or the remote purchaser or who is a guest in the home

of either if it is reasonable to expect that the person may use, consume or be affected by the goods and who is injured in person by breach of the warranty, remedial promise or obligation. A seller may not exclude or limit the operation of this section.

Alternative B to subsection (2)

(2) A seller's warranty to an immediate buyer, whether express or implied, a seller's remedial promise to an immediate buyer, or a seller's obligation to a remote purchaser under Section 2–313A or 2–313B extends to any natural person who may reasonably be expected to use, consume or be affected by the goods and who is injured in person by breach of the warranty, remedial promise or obligation. A seller may not exclude or limit the operation of this section.

Alternative C to subsection (2)

(2) A seller's warranty to an immediate buyer, whether express or implied, a seller's remedial promise to an immediate buyer, or a seller's obligation to a remote purchaser under Section 2–313A or 2–313B extends to any person that may reasonably be expected to use, consume or be affected by the goods and that is injured by breach of the warranty, remedial promise or obligation. A seller may not exclude or limit the operation of this section with respect to injury to the person of an individual to whom the warranty, remedial promise or obligation extends.

Definitional Cross References:

"Buyer". Section 2–103.

"Contract". Section 1–201.

"Goods". Section 2–103.

"Lease". Section 1–203.

"Remedial promise". Section 2–103.

"Seller". Section 2–103.

§ 2–319. Reserved.

Legislative Note: Sections 2–319 through 2–324 have been eliminated because they are inconsistent with modern commercial practices.

§ 2–320. Reserved.

§ 2–321. Reserved.

§ 2–322. Reserved.

§ 2–323. Reserved.

§ 2–324. Reserved.

§ 2–325. Failure to Pay By Agreed Letter of Credit.

If the parties agree that the primary method of payment will be by letter of credit, the following rules apply:

  (a) The buyer's obligation to pay is suspended by seasonable delivery to the seller of a letter of credit issued or confirmed by a financing agency of good repute in which the issuer and any confirmer undertake to pay against presentation of documents that evidence delivery of the goods.

(b) Failure of a party seasonably to furnish a letter of credit as agreed is a breach of the contract for sale.

(c) If the letter of credit is dishonored or repudiated, the seller, on seasonable notification, may require payment directly from the buyer.

Definitional Cross References:

"Agree". Section 1–201.

"Buyer". Section 2–103.

"Delivery". Section 2–103.

"Dishonored". Section 3–502.

"Financing agency". Section 2–104.

"Letter of credit" Section 5–102(a)(10).

"Notification". Section 1–202.

"Party". Section 1–201.

"Seasonable". Section 1–205.

"Seller". Section 2–103.

§ 2–326. Sale on Approval and Sale or Return.

(1) Unless otherwise agreed, if delivered goods may be returned by the buyer even though they conform to the contract, the transaction is

(a) a "sale on approval" if the goods are delivered primarily for use, and

(b) a "sale or return" if the goods are delivered primarily for resale.

(2) Goods held on approval are not subject to the claims of the buyer's creditors until acceptance; goods held on sale or return are subject to such claims while in the buyer's possession.

(3) Any "or return" term of a contract for sale is to be treated as a separate contract for sale within the statute of frauds section of this Article (Section 2–201) and as contradicting the sale aspect of the contract within the provisions of this Article on parol or extrinsic evidence (Section 2–202).

Definitional Cross References:

"Buyer". Section 2–103.

"Conform to the contract". Section 2–106.

"Creditor". Section 1–201.

"Delivered". Section 2–103.

"Goods". Section 1–203.

"Sale". Section 2–106.

"Sale on approval". Section 2–326.

"Statute of frauds". Section 2–201.

§ 2–327. Special Incidents of Sale on Approval and Sale or Return.

(1) Under a sale on approval unless otherwise agreed

(a) although the goods are identified to the contract the risk of loss and the title do not pass to the buyer until acceptance; and

(b) use of the goods consistent with the purpose of trial is not acceptance but failure seasonably to notify the seller of election to return the goods is acceptance, and if the goods conform to the contract acceptance of any part is acceptance of the whole; and

(c) after due notification of election to return, the return is at the seller's risk and expense but a merchant buyer must follow any reasonable instructions.

(2) Under a sale or return unless otherwise agreed

(a) the option to return extends to the whole or any commercial unit of the goods while in substantially their original condition, but must be exercised seasonably; and

(b) the return is at the buyer's risk and expense.

Definitional Cross References:

"Agreed". Section 1–201.

"Buyer". Section 2–103.

"Commercial unit". Section 2–105.

"Conform". Section 2–106.

"Contract". Section 1–201.

"Goods". Section 2–103.

"Merchant". Section 2–104.

"Notification". Section 1–202.

"Notifies". Section 1–202.

"Sale on approval". Section 2–326.

"Sale or return". Section 2–326

"Seasonably". Section 1–206.

"Seller". Section 2–103.

§ 2–328. Sale By Auction.

(1) In a sale by auction if goods are put up in lots each lot is the subject of a separate sale.

(2) A sale by auction is complete when the auctioneer so announces by the fall of the hammer or in other customary manner. Where a bid is made during the process of completing the sale but before a prior bid is accepted the auctioneer has discretion to reopen the bidding or to declare the goods sold under the prior bid.

(3) A sale by auction is subject to the seller's right to withdraw the goods unless at the time the goods are put up or during the course of the auction it is announced in express terms that the right to withdraw the goods is not reserved. In an auction in which the right to withdraw the goods is reserved, the auctioneer may withdraw the goods at any time until completion of the sale is announced by the auctioneer. In an auction in which the right to withdraw the goods is not reserved, after the auctioneer calls for bids on an article or lot, the article or lot cannot be withdrawn unless no bid is made within a reasonable time. In either case a bidder may retract a bid until the auctioneer's announcement of completion of the sale, but a bidder's retraction does not revive any previous bid.

(4) If the auctioneer knowingly receives a bid on the seller's behalf or the seller makes or procures such a bid, and notice has not been given that liberty for such bidding is reserved, the buyer may at the buyer's

option avoid the sale or take the goods at the price of the last good faith bid prior to the completion of the sale. This subsection shall not apply to any bid at an auction required by law.

Definitional Cross References:

"Buyer". Section 2–103.

"Goods". Section 2–103.

"Lot". Section 2–105.

"Notice". Section 1–202.

"Reasonable time". Section 1–205.

"Sale". Section 2–106.

"Seller". Section 2–103.

"Terms". Section 1–201.

PART 4

TITLE, CREDITORS AND GOOD FAITH PURCHASERS

§ 2–401. Passing of Title; Reservation for Security; Limited Application of This Section.

Each provision of this Article with regard to the rights, obligations and remedies of the seller, the buyer, purchasers or other third parties applies irrespective of title to the goods except where the provision refers to such title. Insofar as situations are not covered by the other provisions of this Article and matters concerning title become material the following rules apply:

(1) Title to goods cannot pass under a contract for sale prior to their identification to the contract (Section 2–501), and unless otherwise explicitly agreed the buyer acquires by their identification a special property as limited by this Act. Any retention or reservation by the seller of the title (property) in goods shipped or delivered to the buyer is limited in effect to a reservation of a security interest. Subject to these provisions and to the provisions of the Article on Secured Transactions (Article 9), title to goods passes from the seller to the buyer in any manner and on any conditions explicitly agreed on by the parties.

(2) Unless otherwise explicitly agreed title passes to the buyer at the time and place at which the seller completes performance with reference to the delivery of the goods, despite any reservation of a security interest and even though a document of title is to be delivered at a different time or place; and in particular and despite any reservation of a security interest by the bill of lading

(a) if the contract requires or authorizes the seller to send the goods to the buyer but does not require the seller to deliver them at destination, title passes to the buyer at the time and place of shipment; but

(b) if the contract requires delivery at destination, title passes on tender there.

(3) Unless otherwise explicitly agreed where delivery is to be made without moving the goods,

(a) if the seller is to deliver a document of title, title passes at the time when and the place where the seller delivers such documents; or

(b) if the goods are at the time of contracting already identified and no documents are to be delivered, title passes at the time and place of contracting.

(4) A rejection or other refusal by the buyer to receive or retain the goods, whether or not justified, or a justified revocation of acceptance revests title to the goods in the seller. Such revesting occurs by operation of law and is not a "sale".

Definitional Cross References:

"Agreement". Section 1–201.

"Bill of lading". Section 1–201.

"Buyer". Section 2–103.

"Contract". Section 1–201.

"Contract for sale". Section 2–106.

"Delivery". Section 2–103.

"Document of title". Section 1–201.

"Goods". Section 2–103.

"Party". Section 1–201.

"Purchaser". Section 1–201.

"Receipt" of goods. Section 2–103.

"Remedy". Section 1–201.

"Rights". Section 1–201.

"Sale". Section 2–106.

"Security interest". Section 1–201.

"Seller". Section 2–103.

"Send". Section 1–201.

§ 2–402. Rights of Seller's Creditors Against Sold Goods.

(1) Except as provided in subsections (2) and (3), rights of unsecured creditors of the seller with respect to goods which have been identified to a contract for sale are subject to the buyer's rights to recover the goods under this Article (Sections 2–502 and 2–716).

(2) A creditor of the seller may treat a sale or an identification of goods to a contract for sale as void if as against the creditor a retention of possession by the seller is fraudulent under any rule of law of the state where the goods are situated, except that retention of possession in good faith and current course of trade by a merchant-seller for a commercially reasonable time after a sale or identification is not fraudulent.

(3) Except as otherwise provided in Section 2–403(2), nothing in this Article shall be deemed to impair the rights of creditors of the seller

(a) under the provisions of the Article on Secured Transactions (Article 9); or

(b) where identification to the contract or delivery is made not in current course of trade but in satisfaction of or as security for a pre-existing claim for money, security or the like and is made under circumstances which under any rule of law of the state where the goods are situated would apart from this Article constitute the transaction a fraudulent transfer or voidable preference.

Definitional Cross References:

"Contract for sale". Section 2–106.

"Creditor". Section 1–201.

"Goods". Section 2–103.

"Merchant". Section 2–104.

"Money". Section 1–201.

"Reasonable time". Section 2–205.

"Rights". Section 1–201.

"Sale". Section 2–106.

"Seller". Section 2–103.

§ 2–403. Power to Transfer; Good Faith Purchase of Goods; "Entrusting".

(1) A purchaser of goods acquires all title which the purchaser's transferor had or had power to transfer except that a purchaser of a limited interest acquires rights only to the extent of the interest purchased. A person with voidable title has power to transfer a good title to a good faith purchaser for value. When goods have been delivered under a transaction of purchase the purchaser has such power even though

(a) the transferor was deceived as to the identity of the purchaser, or

(b) the delivery was in exchange for a check which is later dishonored, or

(c) it was agreed that the transaction was to be a "cash sale", or

(d) the delivery was procured through criminal fraud.

(2) Any entrusting of goods to a merchant that deals in goods of that kind gives the merchant power to transfer all of the entruster's rights to the goods and to transfer the goods free of any interest of the entruster to a buyer in ordinary course of business.

(3) "Entrusting" includes any delivery and any acquiescence in retention of possession regardless of any condition expressed between the parties to the delivery or acquiescence and regardless of whether the procurement of the entrusting or the possessor's disposition of the goods have been such as to be punishable under the criminal law.

[*Legislative Note: If a state adopts the repealer of Article 6CBulk Transfers (Alternative A), subsection (4) should read as follows:*]

(4) The rights of other purchasers of goods and of lien creditors are governed by the Articles on Secured Transactions (Article 9) and Documents of Title (Article 7).

[*Legislative Note: If a state adopts revised Article 6CBulk Sales (Alternative B), subsection (4) should read as follows:*]

(4) The rights of other purchasers of goods and of lien creditors are governed by the Articles on Secured Transactions (Article 9), Bulk Sales (Article 6) and Documents of Title (Article 7).

Definitional Cross References:

"Buyer in ordinary course of business". Section 1–201.

"Delivery". Section 2–103.

"Dishonor". Section 3–502.

"Goods". Section 2–103.

"Person". Section 1–201.

"Purchaser". Section 1–201.

"Signed". Section 1–201.

"Term". Section 1–201.

"Value". Section 1–204.

PART 5

PERFORMANCE

§ 2–501. Insurable Interest in Goods; Manner of Identification of Goods.

(1) The buyer obtains a special property and an insurable interest in goods by identification of existing goods as goods to which the contract refers even though the goods so identified are non-conforming and the buyer has an option to return or reject them. Such identification can be made at any time and in any manner explicitly agreed to by the parties. In the absence of explicit agreement identification occurs

(a) when the contract is made if it is for the sale of goods already existing and identified;

(b) if the contract is for the sale of future goods other than those described in paragraph (c), when goods are shipped, marked or otherwise designated by the seller as goods to which the contract refers;

(c) when the crops are planted or otherwise become growing crops or the young are conceived if the contract is for the sale of unborn young to be born within twelve months after contracting or for the sale of crops to be harvested within twelve months or the next normal harvest season after contracting whichever is longer.

(2) The seller retains an insurable interest in goods so long as title to or any security interest in the goods remains in the seller and where the identification is by the seller alone the seller may until default or insolvency or notification to the buyer that the identification is final substitute other goods for those identified.

(3) Nothing in this section impairs any insurable interest recognized under any other statute or rule of law.

Definitional Cross References:

"Agreement". Section 1–201.

"Buyer". Section 2–103.

"Contract". Section 1–201.

"Contract for sale". Section 2–106.

"Future goods". Section 2–105.

"Goods". Section 2–109.

"Notification". Section 1–202.

"Party". Section 1–201.

"Sale". Section 2–106.

"Security interest". Section 1–201.

"Seller". Section 2–103.

§ 2–502. Buyer's Right to Goods on Seller's Insolvency.

(1) Subject to subsections (2) and (3) and even though the goods have not been shipped a buyer that has paid a part or all of the price of goods in which the buyer has a special property under the provisions of the immediately preceding section may on making and keeping good a tender of any unpaid portion of their price recover them from the seller if:

(a) in the case of goods bought by a consumer, the seller repudiates or fails to deliver as required by the contract; or

(b) in all cases, the seller becomes insolvent within ten days after receipt of the first installment on their price.

(2) The buyer's right to recover the goods under subsection (1) vests upon acquisition of a special property, even if the seller had not then repudiated or failed to deliver.

(3) If the identification creating the special property has been made by the buyer, the buyer acquires the right to recover the goods only if they conform to the contract for sale.

Definitional Cross References:

"Buyer". Section 2–103.	"Deliver". Section 1–201.
"Consumer". Section 2–103.	"Goods". Section 2–103.
"Conform". Section 2–106.	"Insolvent". Section 1–201.
"Contract for sale". Section 2–106.	"Rights". Section 1–201.
	"Seller". Section 2–103.

§ 2–503. Manner of Seller's Tender of Delivery.

(1) Tender of delivery requires that the seller put and hold conforming goods at the buyer's disposition and give the buyer any notification reasonably necessary to enable the buyer to take delivery. The manner, time and place for tender are determined by the agreement and this Article, and in particular

(a) tender must be at a reasonable hour, and if it is of goods they must be kept available for the period reasonably necessary to enable the buyer to take possession; but

(b) unless otherwise agreed the buyer must furnish facilities reasonably suited to the receipt of the goods.

(2) Where the case is within the next section respecting shipment tender requires that the seller comply with its provisions.

(3) Where the seller is required to deliver at a particular destination tender requires that the seller comply with subsection (1) and also in any

appropriate case tender documents as described in subsections (4) and (5) of this section.

(4) Where goods are in the possession of a bailee and are to be delivered without being moved

    (a) tender requires that the seller either tender a negotiable document of title covering such goods or procure acknowledgment by the bailee to the buyer of the buyer's right to possession of the goods; but

    (b) tender to the buyer of a non-negotiable document of title or of a record directing the bailee to deliver is sufficient tender unless the buyer seasonably objects, and except as otherwise provided in Article 9 receipt by the bailee of notification of the buyer's rights fixes those rights as against the bailee and all third persons; but risk of loss of the goods and of any failure by the bailee to honor the non-negotiable document of title or to obey the direction remains on the seller until the buyer has had a reasonable time to present the document or direction, and a refusal by the bailee to honor the document or to obey the direction defeats the tender.

(5) Where the contract requires the seller to deliver documents

    (a) the seller must tender all such documents in correct form; and

    (b) tender through customary banking channels is sufficient and dishonor of a draft accompanying the documents constitutes non-acceptance or rejection.

Definitional Cross References:

"Agreement". Section 1–201.

"Buyer". Section 2–103.

"Conforming". Section 2–106.

"Contract". Section 1–201.

"Delivery". Section 2–103.

"Dishonor". Section 3–502.

"Document of title". Section 1–201.

"Draft". Section 3–104(e).

"Goods". Section 2–103.

"Notification". Section 1–202.

"Reasonable time". Section 1–205.

"Receipt" of goods. Section 2–103.

"Record". Section 2–103.

"Rights". Section 1–201.

"Seasonably". Section 1–205.

"Seller". Section 2–103.

§ 2–504. Shipment By Seller.

Where the seller is required or authorized to send the goods to the buyer and the contract does not require the seller to deliver them at a particular destination, then unless otherwise agreed the seller must

    (a) put conforming goods in the possession of a carrier and make a proper contract for their transportation, having regard to the nature of the goods and other circumstances of the case; and

    (b) obtain and promptly deliver or tender in due form any document necessary to enable the buyer to obtain possession of the goods or otherwise required by the agreement or by usage of trade; and

(c) promptly notify the buyer of the shipment.

Failure to notify the buyer under paragraph (c) or to make a proper contract under paragraph (a) is a ground for rejection only if material delay or loss ensues.

Definitional Cross References:

"Agreement". Section 1–201.
"Buyer". Section 2–103.
"Conforming". Section 2–106.
"Contract". Section 1–201.
"Delivery". Section 2–103.

"Goods". Section 2–108.
"Notifies". Section 1–202.
"Seller". Section 2–103.
"Send". Section 1–201.
"Usage of trade". Section 1–303.

§ 2–505. Seller's Shipment Under Reservation.

(1) Where the seller has identified goods to the contract by or before shipment:

(a) the seller's procurement of a negotiable bill of lading to the seller's own order or otherwise reserves in the seller a security interest in the goods. The seller's procurement of the bill to the order of a financing agency or of the buyer indicates in addition only the seller's expectation of transferring that interest to the person named.

(b) a non-negotiable bill of lading to the seller or the seller's nominee reserves possession of the goods as security but except in a case when a seller has a right to reclaim the goods under subsection (2) of Section 2–507 a non-negotiable bill of lading naming the buyer as consignee reserves no security interest even though the seller retains possession of the bill of lading.

(2) When shipment by the seller with reservation of a security interest is in violation of the contract for sale, it constitutes an improper contract for transportation within the preceding section but impairs neither the rights given to the buyer by shipment and identification of the goods to the contract nor the seller's powers as a holder of a negotiable document.

Definitional Cross References:

"Bill of lading". Section 1–201.
"Buyer". Section 2–103.
"Contract". Section 1–201.
"Contract for sale". Section 2–106.
"Delivery". Section 2–103.

"Financing agency". Section 2–104.
"Goods". Section 2–103.
"Holder". Section 1–201.
"Person". Section 1–201.
"Security interest". Section 1–201.
"Seller". Section 2–103.

§ 2–506. Rights of Financing Agency.

(1) Except as otherwise provided in Article 5, a financing agency by paying or purchasing for value a draft which relates to a shipment of goods acquires to the extent of the payment or purchase and in addition to its own rights under the draft and any document of title securing it any rights of the shipper in the goods including the right to stop delivery and the shipper's right to have the draft honored by the buyer.

(2) The right to reimbursement of a financing agency which has in good faith honored or purchased the draft under commitment to or authority from the buyer is not impaired by subsequent discovery of defects with reference to any relevant document which was apparently regular on its face.

Definitional Cross References:

"Buyer". Section 2–103.

"Document of title". Section 1–201.

"Draft". Section 3–104(e).

"Financing agency". Section 2–104.

"Good faith". Section 2–103.

"Goods". Section 2–103.

"Purchase". Section 1–201.

"Rights". Section 1–201.

"Value". Section 1–204.

§ 2–507. Effect of Seller's Tender; Delivery on Condition.

(1) Tender of delivery is a condition to the buyer's duty to accept the goods and, unless otherwise agreed, to the buyer's duty to pay for them. Tender entitles the seller to acceptance of the goods and to payment according to the contract.

(2) Where payment is due and demanded on the delivery to the buyer of goods or documents of title, the seller may reclaim the goods delivered upon a demand made within a reasonable time after the seller discovers or should have discovered that payment was not made.

(3) The seller's right to reclaim under subsection (2) is subject to the rights of a buyer in ordinary course or other good-faith purchaser for value under this Article (Section 2–403).

Definitional Cross References:

"Buyer". Section 2–103.

"Contract". Section 1–201.

"Delivery". Section 2–103.

"Document of title". Section 1–201.

"Goods". Section 2–103.

"Good faith". Section 2–103.

"Reasonable time". Section 1–205.

"Rights". Section 1–201.

"Seller". Section 2–103.

"Value". Section 1–204.

§ 2–508. Cure By Seller of Improper Tender or Delivery; Replacement.

(1) Where the buyer rejects goods or a tender of delivery under Section 2–601 or 2–612 or, except in a consumer contract, justifiably revokes acceptance under Section 2–608(1)(b) and the agreed time for

performance has not expired, a seller that has performed in good faith, upon seasonable notice to the buyer and at the seller's own expense, may cure the breach of contract by making a conforming tender of delivery within the agreed time. The seller shall compensate the buyer for all of the buyer's reasonable expenses caused by the seller's breach of contract and subsequent cure.

(2) Where the buyer rejects goods or a tender of delivery under Section 2–601 or 2–612 or, except in a consumer contract, justifiably revokes acceptance under Section 2–608(1)(b) and the agreed time for performance has expired, a seller that has performed in good faith, upon seasonable notice to the buyer and at the seller's own expense, may cure the breach of contract, if the cure is appropriate and timely under the circumstances, by making a tender of conforming goods. The seller shall compensate the buyer for all of the buyer's reasonable expenses caused by the seller's breach of contract and subsequent cure.

Definitional Cross References:

"Agreement". Section 1–201.

"Buyer". Section 2–103.

"Conforming". Section 2–106.

"Consumer contract". Section 2–103.

"Contract". Section 1–201.

"Delivery". Section 2–103.

"Good faith". Section 2–103.

"Goods". Section 2–103.

"Notice". Section 1–202.

"Reasonable time". Section 1–205.

"Seasonable". Section 1–205.

"Seller". Section 2–103.

"Tender of delivery". Sections 2–503 and 2–507.

§ 2–509. Risk of Loss in the Absence of Breach.

(1) Where the contract requires or authorizes the seller to ship the goods by carrier

    (a) if it does not require the seller to deliver them at a particular destination, the risk of loss passes to the buyer when the goods are delivered to the carrier even though the shipment is under reservation (Section 2–505); but

    (b) if it does require the seller to deliver them at a particular destination and the goods are there tendered while in the possession of the carrier, the risk of loss passes to the buyer when the goods are there so tendered as to enable the buyer to take delivery.

(2) Where the goods are held by a bailee to be delivered without being moved, the risk of loss passes to the buyer

    (a) on the buyer's receipt of a negotiable document of title covering the goods; or

    (b) on acknowledgment by the bailee to the buyer of the buyer's right to possession of the goods; or

(c) after the buyer's receipt of a non-negotiable document of title or other direction to deliver in a record, as provided in subsection (4)(b) of Section 2–503.

(3) In any case not within subsection (1) or (2), the risk of loss passes to the buyer on the buyer's receipt of the goods.

(4) The provisions of this section are subject to contrary agreement of the parties and to the provisions of this Article on sale on approval (Section 2–327) and on effect of breach on risk of loss (Section 2–510).

Definitional Cross References:

"Agreement". Section 1–201.

"Buyer". Section 2–103.

"Contract". Section 1–201.

"Delivery". Section 2–103.

"Document of title". Section 1–201.

"Goods". Section 2–103.

"Party". Section 1–201.

"Receipt" of goods. Section 2–103.

"Sale on approval". Section 2–326.

"Seller". Section 2–103.

§ 2–510. Effect of Breach on Risk of Loss.

(1) Where a tender or delivery of goods so fails to conform to the contract as to give a right of rejection the risk of their loss remains on the seller until cure or acceptance.

(2) Where the buyer rightfully revokes acceptance the buyer may to the extent of any deficiency in the buyer's effective insurance coverage treat the risk of loss as having rested on the seller from the beginning.

(3) Where the buyer as to conforming goods already identified to the contract for sale repudiates or is otherwise in breach before risk of their loss has passed to the buyer, the seller may to the extent of any deficiency in the seller's effective insurance coverage treat the risk of loss as resting on the buyer for a commercially reasonable time.

Definitional Cross References:

"Buyer". Section 2–103.

"Conform". Section 2–106.

"Contract for sale". Section 2–106.

"Goods". Section 2–103.

"Seller". Section 2–103.

"Tender of delivery". Sections 2–503 and 2–507.

§ 2–511. Tender of Payment By Buyer; Payment By Check.

(1) Unless otherwise agreed tender of payment is a condition to the seller's duty to tender and complete any delivery.

(2) Tender of payment is sufficient when made by any means or in any manner current in the ordinary course of business unless the seller demands payment in legal tender and gives any extension of time reasonably necessary to procure it.

(3) Subject to the provisions of this Act on the effect of an instrument on an obligation (Section 3 310), payment by check is conditional and is defeated as between the parties by dishonor of the check on due presentment.

Definitional Cross References:

"Buyer". Section 2–103.

"Check". Section 3–104(f).

"Dishonor". Section 3–502.

"Party". Section 1–201.

"Reasonable time". Section 1–205.

"Seller". Section 2–103.

§ 2–512. Payment By Buyer Before Inspection.

(1) Where the contract requires payment before inspection non-conformity of the goods does not excuse the buyer from so making payment unless

(a) the non-conformity appears without inspection; or

(b) despite tender of the required documents the circumstances would justify injunction against honor under this Act (Section 5–109(b)).

(2) Payment pursuant to subsection (1) does not constitute an acceptance of goods or impair the buyer's right to inspect or any of the buyer's remedies.

Definitional Cross References:

"Buyer". Section 2–103.

"Conform". Section 2–106.

"Contract." Section 1–201.

"Financing agency". Section 2–104.

"Goods". Section 2–103.

"Remedy". Section 1–201.

"Rights". Section 1–201.

§ 2–513. Buyer's Right to Inspection of Goods.

(1) Unless otherwise agreed and subject to subsection (3), where goods are tendered or delivered or identified to the contract for sale, the buyer has a right before payment or acceptance to inspect them at any reasonable place and time and in any reasonable manner. When the seller is required or authorized to send the goods to the buyer, the inspection may be after their arrival.

(2) Expenses of inspection must be borne by the buyer but may be recovered from the seller if the goods do not conform and are rejected.

(3) Unless otherwise agreed the buyer is not entitled to inspect the goods before payment of the price when the contract provides

(a) for delivery on terms that under applicable course of performance, course of dealing, or usage of trade are interpreted to preclude inspection before payment; or

(b) for payment against documents of title, except where such payment is due only after the goods are to become available for inspection.

(4) A place, method or standard of inspection fixed by the parties is presumed to be exclusive but unless otherwise expressly agreed it does not postpone identification or shift the place for delivery or for passing

the risk of loss. If compliance becomes impossible, inspection shall be as provided in this section unless the place, method or standard fixed was clearly intended as an indispensable condition failure of which avoids the contract.

Definitional Cross References:

"Buyer". Section 2–103.

"Conform". Section 2–106.

"Contract". Section 1–201.

"Contract for sale". Section 2–106.

"Course of performance". Section 1–303.

"Document of title". Section 1–201.

"Goods". Section 2–103.

"Party". Section 1–201.

"Presumed". Section 1–201.

"Reasonable time". Section 1–205.

"Rights". Section 1–201.

"Seller". Section 2–103.

"Send". Section 1–201.

"Term". Section 1–201.

"Usage of trade". Section 1–303.

§ 2–514. When Documents Deliverable on Acceptance; When on Payment.

Unless otherwise agreed and except as otherwise provided in Article 5, documents against which a draft is drawn are to be delivered to the drawee on acceptance of the draft if it is payable more than three days after presentment; otherwise, only on payment.

Definitional Cross References:

"Delivery". Section 2–103.

"Draft". Section 3–104(e).

§ 2–515. Preserving Evidence of Goods in Dispute.

In furtherance of the adjustment of any claim or dispute

    (a) either party on reasonable notification to the other and for the purpose of ascertaining the facts and preserving evidence has the right to inspect, test and sample the goods including such of them as may be in the possession or control of the other; and

    (b) the parties may agree to a third party inspection or survey to determine the conformity or condition of the goods and may agree that the findings shall be binding upon them in any subsequent litigation or adjustment.

Definitional Cross References:

"Conform". Section 2–106.

"Goods". Section 2–103.

"Notification". Section 1–202.

"Party". Section 1–201.

PART 6

BREACH, REPUDIATION AND EXCUSE

§ 2–601. Buyer's Rights on Improper Delivery.

Subject to the provisions of this Article on breach in installment contracts (Section 2–612) and on shipment by seller (Section 2–504), and unless otherwise agreed under the sections on contractual limitations of remedy (Sections 2–718 and 2–719), if the goods or the tender of delivery fail in any respect to conform to the contract, the buyer may

(a) reject the whole; or

(b) accept the whole; or

(c) accept any commercial unit or units and reject the rest.

Definitional Cross References:
"Buyer". Section 2–103.
"Commercial unit". Section 2–103.
"Conform". Section 2–105.
"Contract". Section 1–201.
"Goods". Section 2–103.

"Installment contract". Section 2–612.
"Rights". Section 1–201.
"Seller". Section 2–103.
"Tender of delivery". Sections 2–503 and 2–507.

§ 2–602. Manner and Effect of Rejection.

(1) Rejection of goods must be within a reasonable time after their delivery or tender. It is ineffective unless the buyer seasonably notifies the seller.

(2) Subject to Sections 2–603, 2–604 and Section 2–608(4),

(a) after rejection any exercise of ownership by the buyer with respect to any commercial unit is wrongful as against the seller; and

(b) if the buyer has before rejection taken physical possession of goods in which the buyer does not have a security interest under the provisions of this Article (subsection (3) of Section 2–711), the buyer is under a duty after rejection to hold them with reasonable care at the seller's disposition for a time sufficient to permit the seller to remove them; but

(c) the buyer has no further obligations with regard to goods rightfully rejected.

(3) The seller's rights with respect to goods wrongfully rejected are governed by the provisions of this Article on Seller's remedies in general (Section 2–703).

Definitional Cross References:
"Buyer". Section 2–103.

"Commercial unit". Section 2–105.
"Goods". Section 2–103.

"Notifies". Section 1–202.

"Reasonable time". Section 1–205.

"Remedy". Section 1–201.

"Rights". Section 1–201.

"Seasonable". Section 1–205.

"Security interest". Section 1–201.

"Seller". Section 2–103.

§ 2–603. Merchant Buyer's Duties as to Rejected Goods.

(1) Subject to any security interest in the buyer (subsection (3) of Section 2–711), when the seller has no agent or place of business at the market of rejection a merchant buyer is under a duty after rejection of goods in the buyer's possession or control to follow any reasonable instructions received from the seller with respect to the goods and in the absence of such instructions to make reasonable efforts to sell them for the seller's account if they are perishable or threaten to decline in value speedily. In the case of a rightful rejection instructions are not reasonable if on demand indemnity for expenses is not forthcoming.

(2) When the buyer sells goods under subsection (1) following a rightful rejection, the buyer is entitled to reimbursement from the seller or out of the proceeds for reasonable expenses of caring for and selling them, and if the expenses include no selling commission then to such commission as is usual in the trade or if there is none to a reasonable sum not exceeding ten per cent on the gross proceeds.

(3) In complying with this section the buyer is held only to good faith and good faith conduct hereunder is neither acceptance nor conversion nor the basis of an action for damages.

Definitional Cross References:

"Buyer". Section 2–103.

"Good faith". Section 2–103.

"Goods". Section 2–103.

"Merchant". Section 2–104.

"Security interest". Section 1–201.

"Seller". Section 2–103.

§ 2–604. Buyer's Options as to Salvage of Rejected Goods.

Subject to the provisions of the immediately preceding section on perishables if the seller gives no instructions within a reasonable time after notification of rejection, the buyer may store the rejected goods for the seller's account or reship them to the seller or resell them for the seller's account with reimbursement as provided in the preceding section. Such action is not acceptance or conversion.

Definitional Cross References:

"Buyer". Section 2–103.

"Goods". Section 2–103.

"Seller". Section 2–103.

§ 2–605. Waiver of Buyer's Objections By Failure to Particularize.

(1) The buyer's failure to state in connection with rejection a particular defect or in connection with revocation of acceptance a defect

that justifies revocation precludes the buyer from relying on the unstated defect to justify rejection or revocation of acceptance if the defect is ascertainable by reasonable inspection

  (a) where the seller had a right to cure the defect and could have cured it if stated seasonably; or

  (b) between merchants when the seller has after rejection made a request in a record for a full and final statement in record form of all defects on which the buyer proposes to rely.

  (2) A buyer's payment against documents tendered to the buyer made without reservation of rights precludes recovery of the payment for defects apparent on the face of the documents.

Definitional Cross References:

"Between merchants". Section 2–104.

"Buyer". Section 2–103.

"Record". Section 2–103.

"Seasonably". Section 1–205.

"Seller". Section 2–103.

§ 2–606. What Constitutes Acceptance of Goods.

  (1) Acceptance of goods occurs when the buyer

  (a) after a reasonable opportunity to inspect the goods signifies to the seller that the goods are conforming or that the buyer will take or retain them in spite of their non-conformity; or

  (b) fails to make an effective rejection (subsection (1) of Section 2–602), but such acceptance does not occur until the buyer has had a reasonable opportunity to inspect them; or

  (c) except as otherwise provided in Section 2–608(4), does any act inconsistent with the seller's ownership if the act is ratified by the seller.

  (2) Acceptance of a part of any commercial unit is acceptance of that entire unit.

Definitional Cross References

"Buyer". Section 2–103.

"Commercial unit". Section 2–105.

"Goods". Section 2–103.

"Seller". Section 2–103.

§ 2–607. Effect of Acceptance; Notice of Breach; Burden of Establishing Breach After Acceptance; Notice of Claim or Litigation to Person Answerable Over.

  (1) The buyer must pay at the contract rate for any goods accepted.

  (2) Acceptance of goods by the buyer precludes rejection of the goods accepted and if made with knowledge of a non-conformity cannot be revoked because of it unless the acceptance was on the reasonable assumption that the non-conformity would be seasonably cured but

acceptance does not of itself impair any other remedy provided by this Article for non-conformity.

(3) Where a tender has been accepted

(a) the buyer must within a reasonable time after the buyer discovers or should have discovered any breach notify the seller. However, failure to give timely notice bars the buyer from a remedy only to the extent that the seller is prejudiced by the failure and

(b) if the claim is one for infringement or the like (subsection (3) of Section 2–312) and the buyer is sued as a result of such a breach the buyer must so notify the seller within a reasonable time after the buyer receives notice of the litigation or be barred from any remedy over for liability established by the litigation.

(4) The burden is on the buyer to establish any breach with respect to the goods accepted.

(5) Where the buyer is sued for indemnity, breach of a warranty or other obligation for which another party is answerable over

(a) the buyer may give the other party notice of the litigation in a record. If the notice states that the other party may come in and defend and that if the other party does not do so the other party will be bound in any action against the other party by the buyer by any determination of fact common to the two litigations, then unless the other party after seasonable receipt of the notice does come in and defend the other party is so bound.

(b) if the claim is one for infringement or the like (subsection (3) of Section 2–312) the original seller may demand in a record that its buyer turn over to it control of the litigation including settlement or else be barred from any remedy over and if it also agrees to bear all expense and to satisfy any adverse judgment, then unless the buyer after seasonable receipt of the demand does turn over control the buyer is so barred.

(6) The provisions of subsections (3), (4) and (5) apply to any obligation of a buyer to hold the seller harmless against infringement or the like (subsection (3) of Section 2–312).

Definitional Cross References:

"Burden of establishing". Section 1–205.

"Buyer". Section 2–103.

"Conform". Section 1–206.

"Contract". Section 1–201.

"Goods". Section 2–103.

"Notice". Section 1–202.

"Reasonable time". Section 1–201.

"Remedy". Section 1–201.

"Seasonably". Section 1–205.

§ 2–608. Revocation of Acceptance in Whole or in Part.

(1) The buyer may revoke acceptance of a lot or commercial unit whose non-conformity substantially impairs its value to the buyer if the buyer has accepted it

(a) on the reasonable assumption that its non-conformity would be cured and it has not been seasonably cured; or

(b) without discovery of such non-conformity if the buyer's acceptance was reasonably induced either by the difficulty of discovery before acceptance or by the seller's assurances.

(2) Revocation of acceptance must occur within a reasonable time after the buyer discovers or should have discovered the ground for it and before any substantial change in condition of the goods which is not caused by their own defects. The revocation is not effective until the buyer notifies the seller of it.

(3) A buyer that so revokes has the same rights and duties with regard to the goods involved as if the buyer had rejected them.

(4) If a buyer uses the goods after a rightful rejection or justifiable revocation of acceptance, the following rules apply:

(a) Any use by the buyer which is unreasonable under the circumstances is wrongful as against the seller and is an acceptance only if ratified by the seller.

(b) Any use of the goods which is reasonable under the circumstances is not wrongful as against the seller and is not an acceptance, but in an appropriate case the buyer is obligated to the seller for the value of the use to the buyer.

Definitional Cross References:

"Buyer". Section 2–103.

"Commercial unit". Section 2–105.

"Conform". Section 2–106.

"Goods". Section 2–103.

"Notifies". Section 1–202.

"Reasonable time". Section 1–205.

"Rights". Section 1–201.

"Seasonably". Section 1–205.

"Seller". Section 2–103.

"Value". Section 1–204.

§ 2–609. Right to Adequate Assurance of Performance.

(1) A contract for sale imposes an obligation on each party that the other's expectation of receiving due performance will not be impaired. When reasonable grounds for insecurity arise with respect to the performance of either party the other may demand in a record adequate assurance of due performance and until the party receives the assurance may if commercially reasonable suspend any performance for which it has not already received the agreed return.

(2) Between merchants the reasonableness of grounds for insecurity and the adequacy of any assurance offered shall be determined according to commercial standards.

(3) Acceptance of any improper delivery or payment does not prejudice the aggrieved party's right to demand adequate assurance of future performance.

(4) After receipt of a justified demand failure to provide within a reasonable time not exceeding thirty days such assurance of due performance as is adequate under the circumstances of the particular case is a repudiation of the contract.

Definitional Cross References:

"Aggrieved party". Section 1–201.

"Between Merchants". Section 2–104.

"Contract". Section 1–201.

"Contract for sale". Section 2–106.

"Party". Section 1–201.

"Reasonable time". Section 1–205.

"Record". Section 2–103.

"Rights". Section 1–201.

§ 2–610. Anticipatory Repudiation.

(1) When either party repudiates the contract with respect to a performance not yet due the loss of which will substantially impair the value of the contract to the other, the aggrieved party may

    (a) for a commercially reasonable time await performance by the repudiating party; or

    (b) resort to any remedy for breach (Section 2–703 or Section 2–711), even though the aggrieved party has notified the repudiating party that it would await the latter's performance and has urged retraction; and

    (c) in either case suspend performance or proceed in accordance with the provisions of this Article on the seller's right to identify goods to the contract notwithstanding breach or to salvage unfinished goods (Section 2–704).

(2) Repudiation includes language that a reasonable person would interpret to mean that the other party will not or cannot make a performance still due under the contract or voluntary, affirmative conduct that would appear to a reasonable person to make a future performance by the other party impossible.

Definitional Cross References

"Aggrieved party". Section 1–201.

"Contract". Section 1–201.

"Party". Section 1–201.

"Remedy". Section 1–201.

§ 2–611. Retraction of Anticipatory Repudiation.

(1) Until the repudiating party's next performance is due that party can retract the repudiation unless the aggrieved party has since the repudiation canceled or materially changed position or otherwise indicated that the repudiation is final.

(2) Retraction may be by any method which clearly indicates to the aggrieved party that the repudiating party intends to perform, but must

include any assurance justifiably demanded under the provisions of this Article (Section 2–609).

(3) Retraction reinstates the repudiating party's rights under the contract with due excuse and allowance to the aggrieved party for any delay occasioned by the repudiation.

Definitional Cross References:

"Aggrieved party". Section 1–201.

"Cancellation". Section 2–106.

"Contract". Section 1–201.

"Party". Section 1–201.

"Rights". Section 1–201.

§ 2–612. "Installment Contract"; Breach.

(1) An "installment contract" is one which requires or authorizes the delivery of goods in separate lots to be separately accepted, even though the contract contains a clause "each delivery is a separate contract" or its equivalent.

(2) The buyer may reject any installment which is non-conforming if the non-conformity substantially impairs the value of that installment to the buyer or if the non-conformity is a defect in the required documents; but if the non-conformity does not fall within subsection (3) and the seller gives adequate assurance of its cure the buyer must accept that installment.

(3) Whenever non-conformity or default with respect to one or more installments substantially impairs the value of the whole contract there is a breach of the whole. But the aggrieved party reinstates the contract if the party accepts a non-conforming installment without seasonably notifying of cancellation or if the party brings an action with respect only to past installments or demands performance as to future installments.

Definitional Cross References:

"Action". Section 1–201.

"Aggrieved party". Section 1–201.

"Buyer". Section 2–103.

"Cancellation". Section 2–106.

"Conform". Section 2–106.

"Contract". Section 1–201.

"Lot". Section 2–105.

"Notifies". Section 1–202.

"Party". Section 1–201.

"Seasonably". Section 1–205.

"Seller". Section 2–103.

§ 2–613. Casualty to Identified Goods.

Where the contract requires for its performance goods identified when the contract is made, and the goods suffer casualty without fault of either party before the risk of loss passes to the buyer then

(a) if the loss is total the contract is terminated; and

(b) if the loss is partial or the goods have so deteriorated as no longer to conform to the contract the buyer may nevertheless demand inspection and at its option either treat the contract as terminated or accept the goods with due allowance from the contract price for the deterioration or the deficiency in quantity but without further right against the seller.

Definitional Cross References:

"Buyer". Section 2–103.

"Conform". Section 2–106.

"Contract". Section 1–201.

"Fault". Section 1–201.

"Goods". Section 2–103.

"Party". Section 1–201.

"Rights". Section 1–201.

"Seller". Section 2–103.

"Terminated". Section 2–106.

§ 2–614. Substituted Performance.

(1) Where without fault of either party the agreed berthing, loading, or unloading facilities fail or an agreed type of carrier becomes unavailable or the agreed manner of delivery otherwise becomes commercially impracticable but a commercially reasonable substitute is available, such substitute performance must be tendered and accepted.

(2) If the agreed means or manner of payment fails because of domestic or foreign governmental regulation, the seller may withhold or stop delivery unless the buyer provides a means or manner of payment which is commercially a substantial equivalent. If delivery has already been taken, payment by the means or in the manner provided by the regulation discharges the buyer's obligation unless the regulation is discriminatory, oppressive or predatory.

Definitional Cross References:

"Buyer". Section 2–103.

"Delivery". Section 2–103.

"Fault". Section 1–201.

"Party". Section 1–201.

"Seller". Section 2–103.

§ 2–615. Excuse By Failure of Presupposed Conditions.

Except so far as a seller may have assumed a greater obligation and subject to the preceding section on substituted performance:

(a) Delay in performance or non-performance in whole or in part by a seller that complies with paragraphs (b) and (c) is not a breach of the seller's duty under a contract for sale if performance as agreed has been made impracticable by the occurrence of a contingency the non-occurrence of which was a basic assumption on which the contract was made or by compliance in good faith with any applicable foreign or domestic governmental regulation or order whether or not it later proves to be invalid.

(b) Where the causes mentioned in paragraph (a) affect only a part of the seller's capacity to perform, the seller must allocate production and deliveries among its customers but may at its option include regular customers not then under contract as well as its own requirements for further manufacture. The seller may so allocate in any manner which is fair and reasonable.

(c) The seller must notify the buyer seasonably that there will be delay or non-delivery and, when allocation is required under paragraph (b), of the estimated quota thus made available for the buyer.

Definitional Cross References:

"Buyer". Section 2–103.

"Contract". Section 1–201.

"Contract for sale". Section 2–106.

"Good faith". Section 2–103.

"Notifies". Section 1–202.

"Seasonably". Section 1–205.

"Seller". Section 2–103.

§ 2–616. Procedure on Notice Claiming Excuse.

(1) Where the buyer receives notification of a material or indefinite delay or an allocation justified under the preceding section it may by notification in a record to the seller as to any delivery concerned, and where the prospective deficiency substantially impairs the value of the whole contract under the provisions of this Article relating to breach of installment contracts (Section 2–612), then also as to the whole,

(a) terminate and thereby discharge any unexecuted portion of the contract; or

(b) modify the contract by agreeing to take its available quota in substitution.

(2) If after receipt of notification from the seller the buyer fails to modify the contract within a reasonable time not exceeding thirty days the contract is terminated with respect to any performance affected.

(3) The provisions of this section may not be negated by agreement except in so far as the seller has assumed a greater obligation under the preceding section.

Definitional Cross References:

"Buyer". Section 2–103.

"Contract". Section 1–201.

"Installment contract". Section 2–612.

"Notification". Section 1–202.

"Reasonable time". Section 1–205.

"Record". Section 2–103.

"Seller". Section 2–103.

"Termination". Section 2–106.

PART 7

REMEDIES

§ 2–701. Remedies for Breach of Collateral Contracts Not Impaired.

Remedies for breach of any obligation or promise collateral or ancillary to a contract for sale are not impaired by the provisions of this Article.

Definitional Cross References:

"Contract for sale". Section 2–106.

"Remedy". Section 1–201.

§ 2–702. Seller's Remedies on Discovery of Buyer's Insolvency.

(1) Where the seller discovers the buyer to be insolvent the seller may refuse delivery except for cash including payment for all goods theretofore delivered under the contract, and stop delivery under this Article (Section 2–705).

(2) Where the seller discovers that the buyer has received goods on credit while insolvent the seller may reclaim the goods upon demand made within a reasonable time after the buyer's receipt of the goods. Except as provided in this subsection the seller may not base a right to reclaim goods on the buyer's fraudulent or innocent misrepresentation of solvency or of intent to pay.

(3) The seller's right to reclaim under subsection (2) is subject to the rights of a buyer in ordinary course or other good-faith purchaser for value under this Article (Section 2–403). Successful reclamation of goods excludes all other remedies with respect to them.

Definitional Cross References:

"Buyer". Section 2–103.

"Buyer in ordinary course of business". Section 1–201.

"Contract". Section 1–201.

"Good faith". Section 2–103.

"Goods". Section 1–203.

"Insolvent". Section 1–201.

"Person". Section 1–201.

"Purchaser". Section 1–201.

"Reasonable time". Section 2–103.

"Remedy". Section 1–201.

"Receipt of goods". Section 2–103.

"Rights". Section 1–201.

"Seller". Section 2–103.

"Tender of delivery". Sections 2–503 and 2–507.

"Value". Section 1–204.

§ 2–703. Seller's Remedies in General.

(1) A breach of contract by the buyer includes the buyer's wrongful rejection or wrongful attempt to revoke acceptance of goods, wrongful failure to perform a contractual obligation, failure to make a payment when due, and repudiation.

(2) If the buyer is in breach of contract the seller, to the extent provided for by this Act or other law, may:

(a) withhold delivery of the goods;

(b) stop delivery of the goods under Section 2–705;

(c) proceed under Section 2–704 with respect to goods unidentified to the contract or unfinished;

(d) reclaim the goods under Section 2-507(2) or 2-702(2);

(e) require payment directly from the buyer under Section 2-325(c);

(f) cancel;

(g) resell and recover damages under Section 2-706;

(h) recover damages for nonacceptance or repudiation under Section 2-708(1);

(i) recover lost profits under Section 2-708(2);

(j) recover the price under Section 2-709;

(k) obtain specific performance under Section 2-716;

(*l*) recover liquidated damages under Section 2-718;

(m) in other cases, recover damages in any manner that is reasonable under the circumstances.

(3) If a buyer becomes insolvent, the seller may:

(a) withhold delivery under Section 2-702(1);

(b) stop delivery of the goods under Section 2-705;

(c) reclaim the goods under Section 2-702(2).

Definitional Cross References:

"Buyer". Section 2-103.

"Cancel". Section 2-106.

"Contract". Section 1-201.

"Delivery". Section 2-103.

"Goods". Section 2-103.

"Insolvent". Section 1-201.

"Remedy". Section 1-201.

"Seller". Section 2-103.

§ 2-704. Seller's Right to Identify Goods to the Contract Notwithstanding Breach or to Salvage Unfinished Goods.

(1) An aggrieved seller under the preceding section may

(a) identify to the contract conforming goods not already identified if at the time the seller learned of the breach the goods are in the seller's possession or control;

(b) treat as the subject of resale goods which have demonstrably been intended for the particular contract even though those goods are unfinished.

(2) Where the goods are unfinished an aggrieved seller may in the exercise of reasonable commercial judgment for the purposes of avoiding loss and of effective realization either complete the manufacture and wholly identify the goods to the contract or cease manufacture and resell for scrap or salvage value or proceed in any other reasonable manner.

Definitional Cross References:

"Aggrieved party". Section 1-201.

"Conforming". Section 2-106.

"Contract". Section 1-201.

"Delivery". Section 2–103.

"Goods". Section 2–103.

"Rights". Section 1–201.

"Seller". Section 2–103.

§ 2–705. Seller's Stoppage of Delivery in Transit or Otherwise.

(1) The seller may stop delivery of goods in the possession of a carrier or other bailee when the seller discovers the buyer to be insolvent (Section 2–702) or when the buyer repudiates or fails to make a payment due before delivery or if for any other reason the seller has a right to withhold or reclaim the goods.

(2) As against such buyer the seller may stop delivery until

(a) receipt of the goods by the buyer; or

(b) acknowledgment to the buyer by any bailee of the goods, except a carrier, that the bailee holds the goods for the buyer; or

(c) such acknowledgment to the buyer by a carrier by reshipment or as warehouse; or

(d) negotiation to the buyer of any negotiable document of title covering the goods.

(3)

(a) To stop delivery the seller must so notify as to enable the bailee by reasonable diligence to prevent delivery of the goods.

(b) After such notification the bailee must hold and deliver the goods according to the directions of the seller but the seller is liable to the bailee for any ensuing charges or damages.

(c) If a negotiable document of title has been issued for goods, the bailee is not obliged to obey a notification to stop until surrender of the document.

(d) A carrier that has issued a non-negotiable bill of lading is not obliged to obey a notification to stop received from a person other than the consignor.

Definitional Cross References:

"Bill of lading". Section 1–201.

"Buyer". Section 1–203.

"Contract for sale". Section 2–106.

"Document of title". Section 1–201.

"Goods". Section 2–103.

"Insolvent". Section 1–201.

"Notification". Section 1–202.

"Receipt" of goods. Section 2–103.

"Rights". Section 1–201.

§ 2–706. Seller's Resale Including Contract for Resale.

(1) In an appropriate case involving breach by the buyer, the seller may resell the goods concerned or the undelivered balance thereof. Where the resale is made in good faith and in a commercially reasonable manner the seller may recover the difference between the contract price

and the resale price together with any incidental or consequential damages allowed under the provisions of this Article (Section 2–710), but less expenses saved in consequence of the buyer's breach.

(2) Except as otherwise provided in subsection (3) or unless otherwise agreed resale may be at public or private sale including sale by way of one or more contracts to sell or of identification to an existing contract of the seller. Sale may be as a unit or in parcels and at any time and place and on any terms but every aspect of the sale including the method, manner, time, place and terms must be commercially reasonable. The resale must be reasonably identified as referring to the broken contract, but it is not necessary that the goods be in existence or that any or all of them have been identified to the contract before the breach.

(3) Where the resale is at private sale the seller must give the buyer reasonable notification of an intention to resell.

(4) Where the resale is at public sale

(a) only identified goods can be sold except where there is a recognized market for a public sale of futures in goods of the kind; and

(b) it must be made at a usual place or market for public sale if one is reasonably available and except in the case of goods which are perishable or threaten to decline in value speedily the seller must give the buyer reasonable notice of the time and place of the resale; and

(c) if the goods are not to be within the view of those attending the sale the notification of sale must state the place where the goods are located and provide for their reasonable inspection by prospective bidders; and

(d) the seller may buy.

(5) A purchaser that buys in good faith at a resale takes the goods free of any rights of the original buyer even though the seller fails to comply with one or more of the requirements of this section.

(6) The seller is not accountable to the buyer for any profit made on any resale. A person in the position of a seller (Section 2–707) or a buyer that has rightfully rejected or justifiably revoked acceptance must account for any excess over the amount of the buyer's security interest, as hereinafter defined (subsection (3) of Section 2–711).

(7) Failure of a seller to resell under this section does not bar the seller from any other remedy.

Definitional Cross References:

"Buyer". Section 2–103.

"Contract". Section 1–201.

"Contract for sale". Section 2–106.

"Good faith". Section 2–103.

"Goods". Section 2–103.

"Notification". Section 1–202.

"Person in position of seller". Section 2–707.

"Purchase". Section 1–201.

"Rights". Section 1–201.

"Sale". Section 2–106.

"Security interest". Section 1–201.

"Seller". Section 2–103.

§ 2–707. "Person in the Position of a Seller".

(1) A "person in the position of a seller" includes as against a principal an agent that has paid or become responsible for the price of goods on behalf of the principal or anyone that otherwise holds a security interest or other right in goods similar to that of a seller.

(2) A person in the position of a seller has the same remedies as a seller under this Article.

Definitional Cross References:

"Goods". Section 2–103.

"Security interest". Section 1–201.

"Seller". Section 2–103.

§ 2–708. Seller's Damages for Non-acceptance or Repudiation.

(1) Subject to subsection (2) and to the provisions of this Article with respect to proof of market price (Section 2–723):

(a) the measure of damages for non-acceptance by the buyer is the difference between the contract price and the market price at the time and place for tender together with any incidental or consequential damages provided in this Article (Section 2–710), but less expenses saved in consequence of the buyer's breach; and

(b) the measure of damages for repudiation by the buyer is the difference between the contract price and the market price at the place for tender at the expiration of a commercially reasonable time after the seller learned of the repudiation, but no later than the time stated in paragraph (a), together with any incidental or consequential damages provided in this Article (Section 2–710), less expenses saved in consequence of the buyer's breach.

(2) If the measure of damages provided in subsection (1) or in Section 2–706 is inadequate to put the seller in as good a position as performance would have done then the measure of damages is the profit (including reasonable overhead) which the seller would have made from full performance by the buyer, together with any incidental or consequential damages provided in this Article (Section 2–710).

Definitional Cross References:

"Buyer". Section 2–103.

"Contract". Section 1–201.

"Reasonable time". Section 1–205.

"Seller". Section 2–103.

§ 2–709. Action for the Price.

(1) When the buyer fails to pay the price as it becomes due the seller may recover, together with any incidental or consequential damages under the next section, the price

    (a) of goods accepted or of conforming goods lost or damaged within a commercially reasonable time after risk of their loss has passed to the buyer; and

    (b) of goods identified to the contract if the seller is unable after reasonable effort to resell them at a reasonable price or the circumstances reasonably indicate that such effort will be unavailing.

(2) Where the seller sues for the price the seller must hold for the buyer any goods which have been identified to the contract and are still in the seller's control except that if resale becomes possible the seller may resell them at any time prior to the collection of the judgment. The net proceeds of any such resale must be credited to the buyer and payment of the judgment entitles the buyer to any goods not resold.

(3) After the buyer has wrongfully rejected or revoked acceptance of the goods or has failed to make a payment due or has repudiated (Section 2–610), a seller that is held not entitled to the price under this section shall nevertheless be awarded damages for non-acceptance under the preceding section.

Definitional Cross References:

"Action". Section 1–201.

"Buyer". Section 2–103.

"Conforming". Section 2–106.

"Contract". Section 1–201.

"Goods". Section 2–103.

"Reasonable time". Section 1–205.

"Seller". Section 2–103.

§ 2–710. Seller's Incidental and Consequential Damages.

(1) Incidental damages to an aggrieved seller include any commercially reasonable charges, expenses or commissions incurred in stopping delivery, in the transportation, care and custody of goods after the buyer's breach, in connection with return or resale of the goods or otherwise resulting from the breach.

(2) Consequential damages resulting from the buyer's breach include any loss resulting from general or particular requirements and needs of which the buyer at the time of contracting had reason to know and which could not reasonably be prevented by resale or otherwise.

(3) In a consumer contract, a seller may not recover consequential damages from a consumer.

Definitional Cross References:

"Aggrieved party". Section 1–201.

"Buyer". Section 2–103.

"Consumer contract". Section 2–103.

"Delivery". Section 2–103.

"Goods". Section 2–103.

"Seller". Section 2–103.

§ 2–711. Buyer's Remedies in General; Buyer's Security Interest in Rejected Goods.

(1) A breach of contract by the seller includes the seller's wrongful failure to deliver or to perform a contractual obligation, making of a nonconforming tender of delivery or performance, and repudiation.

(2) If a seller is in breach of contract under subsection (1) the buyer, to the extent provided for by this Act or other law, may:

(a) in the case of rightful cancellation, rightful rejection or justifiable revocation of acceptance recover so much of the price as has been paid;

(b) deduct damages from any part of the price still due under Section 2–717;

(c) cancel;

(d) cover and have damages under Section 2–712 as to all goods affected whether or not they have been identified to the contract;

(e) recover damages for non-delivery or repudiation under Section 2–713;

(f) recover damages for breach with regard to accepted goods or breach with regard to a remedial promise under Section 2–714;

(g) recover identified goods under Section 2–502;

(h) obtain specific performance or obtain the goods by replevin or similar remedy under Section 2–716;

(i) recover liquidated damages under Section 2–718;

(j) in other cases, recover damages in any manner that is reasonable under the circumstances.

(3) On rightful rejection or justifiable revocation of acceptance a buyer has a security interest in goods in the buyer's possession or control for any payments made on their price and any expenses reasonably incurred in their inspection, receipt, transportation, care and custody and may hold such goods and resell them in like manner as an aggrieved seller (Section 2–706).

Definitional Cross References:

"Aggrieved party". Section 1–201.

"Buyer". Section 2–103.

"Cancellation". Section 2–106.

"Conforming". Section 2–106. 2–103.

"Contract". Section 1–201.

"Cover". Section 2–712.

"Delivery". Section 2–103.

"Goods". Section 2–103.

"Notifies". Section 1–202.

"Receipt" of goods. Section 2–103.

"Remedial promise". Section

"Remedy". Section 1–201.

"Security interest". Section 1–201.

"Seller". Section 2–103.

"Tender of delivery". Sections 2–503 and 2–507.

§ 2–712. "Cover"; Buyer's Procurement of Substitute Goods.

(1) If the seller wrongfully fails to deliver or repudiates or the buyer rightfully rejects or justifiably revokes acceptance, the buyer may "cover" by making in good faith and without unreasonable delay any reasonable purchase of or contract to purchase goods in substitution for those due from the seller.

(2) The buyer may recover from the seller as damages the difference between the cost of cover and the contract price together with any incidental or consequential damages as hereinafter defined (Section 2–715), but less expenses saved in consequence of the seller's breach.

(3) Failure of the buyer to effect cover within this section does not bar the buyer from any other remedy.

Definitional Cross References:

"Buyer". Section 2–103.

"Contract". Section 1–201.

"Delivery". Section 2–103.

"Good faith". Section 2–103.

"Goods". Section 2–103.

"Purchase". Section 1–201.

"Reasonable time". Section 1–205.

"Remedy". Section 1–201.

"Seller". Section 2–103.

§ 2–713. Buyer's Damages for Non-delivery or Repudiation.

(1) Subject to the provisions of this Article with respect to proof of market price (Section 2–723), if the seller wrongfully fails to deliver or repudiates or the buyer rightfully rejects or justifiably revokes acceptance:

(a) the measure of damages in the case of wrongful failure to deliver by the seller or rightful rejection or justifiable revocation of acceptance by the buyer is the difference between the market price at the time for tender under the contract and the contract price together with any incidental or consequential damages provided in this Article (Section 2–715), but less expenses saved in consequence of the seller's breach; and

(b) the measure of damages for repudiation by the seller is the difference between the market price at the expiration of a commercially reasonable time after the buyer learned of the repudiation, but no later than the time stated in paragraph (a), and the contract price together with any incidental or consequential damages provided in this Article (Section 2–715), less expenses saved in consequence of the seller's breach.

(2) Market price is to be determined as of the place for tender or, in cases of rejection after arrival or revocation of acceptance, as of the place of arrival.

Definitional Cross References:

"Buyer". Section 2–103.

"Contract". Section 1–201.

"Delivery". Section 2–103.

"Reasonable time". Section 1–205.

"Seller". Section 2–103.

§ 2–714. Buyer's Damages for Breach in Regard to Accepted Goods.

(1) Where the buyer has accepted goods and given notification (subsection (3) of Section 2–607) the buyer may recover as damages for any non-conformity of tender the loss resulting in the ordinary course of events from the seller's breach as determined in any manner which is reasonable.

(2) The measure of damages for breach of warranty is the difference at the time and place of acceptance between the value of the goods accepted and the value they would have had if they had been as warranted, unless special circumstances show proximate damages of a different amount.

(3) In a proper case any incidental and consequential damages under the next section may also be recovered.

Definitional Cross References:

"Buyer". Section 2–103.

"Conform". Section 2–106.

"Goods". Section 2–103.

"Notification". Section 1–202.

"Seller". Section 2–103.

§ 2–715. Buyer's Incidental and Consequential Damages.

(1) Incidental damages resulting from the seller's breach include expenses reasonably incurred in inspection, receipt, transportation and care and custody of goods rightfully rejected, any commercially reasonable charges, expenses or commissions in connection with effecting cover and any other reasonable expense incident to the delay or other breach.

(2) Consequential damages resulting from the seller's breach include

(a) any loss resulting from general or particular requirements and needs of which the seller at the time of contracting had reason to know and which could not reasonably be prevented by cover or otherwise; and

(b) injury to person or property proximately resulting from any breach of warranty.

Definitional Cross References:

"Cover". Section 2–712.

"Goods". Section 2–103.

"Person". Section 1–201.

"Receipt" of goods. Section 2–103.

"Seller". Section 2–103.

§ 2–716. Specific Performance; Buyer's Right to Replevin.

(1) Specific performance may be decreed where the goods are unique or in other proper circumstances. In a contract other than a consumer contract, specific performance may be decreed if the parties have agreed to that remedy. However, even if the parties agree to specific performance, specific performance may not be decreed if the breaching party's sole remaining contractual obligation is the payment of money.

(2) The decree for specific performance may include such terms and conditions as to payment of the price, damages, or other relief as the court may deem just.

(3) The buyer has a right of replevin or similar remedy for goods identified to the contract if after reasonable effort the buyer is unable to effect cover for such goods or the circumstances reasonably indicate that such effort will be unavailing or if the goods have been shipped under reservation and satisfaction of the security interest in them has been made or tendered.

(4) The buyer's right under subsection (3) vests upon acquisition of a special property, even if the seller had not then repudiated or failed to deliver.

Definitional Cross References:

"Agreement". Section 1–201.

"Buyer". Section 2–103.

"Consumer contract". Section 2–103.

"Contract". Section 1–201.

"Deliver". Section 2–201.

"Goods". Section 2–103.

"Party". Section 1–201.

"Remedy". Section 1–201.

"Rights". Section 1–201.

§ 2–717. Deduction of Damages From the Price.

The buyer on notifying the seller of an intention to do so may deduct all or any part of the damages resulting from any breach of the contract from any part of the price still due under the same contract.

Definitional Cross References:

"Buyer". Section 2–103.

"Contract". Section 1–201.

"Seller". Section 2–103.

§ 2–718. Liquidation or Limitation of Damages; Deposits.

(1) Damages for breach by either party may be liquidated in the agreement but only at an amount which is reasonable in the light of the anticipated or actual harm caused by the breach and, in a consumer contract, the difficulties of proof of loss, and the inconvenience or nonfeasibility of otherwise obtaining an adequate remedy. Section 2–719 determines the enforceability of a term that limits but does not liquidate damages.

(2) Where the seller justifiably withholds delivery of goods or stops performance because of the buyer's breach or insolvency, the buyer is entitled to restitution of any amount by which the sum of the buyer's payments exceeds the amount to which the seller is entitled by virtue of terms liquidating the seller's damages in accordance with subsection (1).

(3) The buyer's right to restitution under subsection (2) is subject to offset to the extent that the seller establishes

> (a) a right to recover damages under the provisions of this Article other than subsection (1), and

> (b) the amount or value of any benefits received by the buyer directly or indirectly by reason of the contract.

(4) Where a seller has received payment in goods their reasonable value or the proceeds of their resale shall be treated as payments for the purposes of subsection (2); but if the seller has notice of the buyer's breach before reselling goods received in part performance, the resale is subject to the conditions laid down in this Article on resale by an aggrieved seller (Section 2-706).

Definitional Cross References:

"Aggrieved party". Section 1-201.

"Agreement". Section 1-201.

"Buyer". Section 2-103.

"Consumer contract". Section 2-103.

"Contract". Section 1-201.

"Goods". Section 2-103.

"Insolvent". Section 1-201.

"Notice". Section 1-202.

"Party". Section 1-201.

"Remedy". Section 1-201.

"Seller". Section 2-103.

"Term". Section 1-201.

§ 2-719. Contractual Modification or Limitation of Remedy.

(1) Subject to the provisions of subsections (2) and (3) of this section and of the preceding section on liquidation and limitation of damages,

> (a) the agreement may provide for remedies in addition to or in substitution for those provided in this Article and may limit or alter the measure of damages recoverable under this Article, as by limiting the buyer's remedies to return of the goods and repayment of the price or to repair and replacement of non-conforming goods or parts; and

> (b) resort to a remedy as provided is optional unless the remedy is expressly agreed to be exclusive, in which case it is the sole remedy.

(2) Where circumstances cause an exclusive or limited remedy to fail of its essential purpose, remedy may be had as provided in this Act.

(3) Consequential damages may be limited or excluded unless the limitation or exclusion is unconscionable. Limitation of consequential damages for injury to the person in the case of consumer goods is prima

facie unconscionable but limitation of damages where the loss is commercial is not.

Definitional Cross References:

"Agreement". Section 1–201.

"Buyer". Section 2–103.

"Conforming". Section 2–106.

"Contract". Section 1–201.

"Goods". Section 2–103.

"Remedy". Section 1–201.

"Seller". Section 2–103.

§ 2–720. Effect of "Cancellation" or "Rescission" on Claims for Antecedent Breach.

Unless the contrary intention clearly appears, expressions of "cancellation" or "rescission" of the contract or the like shall not be construed as a renunciation or discharge of any claim in damages for an antecedent breach.

Definitional Cross References:

"Cancellation". Section 2–106.

"Contract". Section 1–201.

§ 2–721. Remedies for Fraud.

Remedies for material misrepresentation or fraud include all remedies available under this Article for non-fraudulent breach. Neither rescission or a claim for rescission of the contract for sale nor rejection or return of the goods shall bar or be deemed inconsistent with a claim for damages or other remedy.

Definitional Cross References:

"Contract for sale". Section 2–106.

"Remedy". Section 1–201.

"Goods". Section 2–103.

§ 2–722. Who Can Sue Third Parties for Injury to Goods.

Where a third party so deals with goods which have been identified to a contract for sale as to cause actionable injury to a party to that contract

(a) a right of action against the third party is in either party to the contract for sale that has title to or a security interest or a special property or an insurable interest in the goods; and if the goods have been destroyed or converted a right of action is also in the party that either bore the risk of loss under the contract for sale or has since the injury assumed that risk as against the other;

(b) if at the time of the injury the party plaintiff did not bear the risk of loss as against the other party to the contract for sale and there is no arrangement between them for disposition of the recovery, the party plaintiff's suit or settlement is, subject to its own interest, as a fiduciary for the other party to the contract;

(c) either party may with the consent of the other sue for the benefit of which it may concern.

Definitional Cross References:

"Action". Section 1–201.

"Buyer". Section 2–103.

"Contract for sale". Section 2–106.

"Goods". Section 2–103. 1–201.

"Party". Section 1–201.

"Rights". Section 1–201.

"Security interest". Section

§ 2–723. Proof of Market: Time and Place.

(1) If evidence of a price prevailing at the times or places described in this Article is not readily available the price prevailing within any reasonable time before or after the time described or at any other place which in commercial judgment or under usage of trade would serve as a reasonable substitute for the one described may be used, making any proper allowance for the cost of transporting the goods to or from such other place.

(2) Evidence of a relevant price prevailing at a time or place other than the one described in this Article offered by one party is not admissible unless and until he has given the other party such notice as the court finds sufficient to prevent unfair surprise.

Definitional Cross References:

"Notifies". Section 1–202.

"Party". Section 1–201.

"Reasonable time". Section 1–205.

"Usage of trade". Section 1–303.

§ 2–724. Admissibility of Market Quotations.

Whenever the prevailing price or value of any goods regularly bought and sold in any established commodity market is in issue, reports in official publications or trade journals or in newspapers, periodicals or other means of communication in general circulation published as the reports of such market shall be admissible in evidence. The circumstances of the preparation of such a report may be shown to affect its weight but not its admissibility.

Definitional Cross Reference:

"Goods". Section 2–103.

§ 2–725. Statute of Limitations in Contracts for Sale.

(1) Except as otherwise provided in this section, an action for breach of any contract for sale must be commenced within the later of four years after the right of action has accrued under subsection (2) or (3) or one year after the breach was or should have been discovered, but no longer than five years after the right of action accrued. By the original agreement the parties may reduce the period of limitation to not less than one year but may not extend it. However, in a consumer contract, the period of limitation may not be reduced.

(2) Except as otherwise provided in subsection (3), the following rules apply:

(a) Except as otherwise provided in this subsection, a right of action for breach of a contract accrues when the breach occurs, even if the aggrieved party did not have knowledge of the breach.

(b) For breach of a contract by repudiation, a right of action accrues at the earlier of when the aggrieved party elects to treat the repudiation as a breach or when a commercially reasonable time for awaiting performance has expired.

(c) For breach of a remedial promise, a right of action accrues when the remedial promise is not performed when performance is due.

(d) In an action by a buyer against a person that is answerable over to the buyer for a claim asserted against the buyer, the buyer's right of action against the person answerable over accrues at the time the claim was originally asserted against the buyer.

(3) If a breach of a warranty arising under Section 2–312, 2–313(2), 2–314, or 2–315, or a breach of an obligation, other than a remedial promise, arising under Section 2–313A or 2–313B, is claimed the following rules apply:

(a) Except as otherwise provided in paragraph(c), a right of action for breach of a warranty arising under Section 2–313(2), 2–314 or 2–315 accrues when the seller has tendered delivery to the immediate buyer, as defined in Section 2–313, and has completed performance of any agreed installation or assembly of the goods.

(b) Except as otherwise provided in paragraph(c), a right of action for breach of an obligation, other than a remedial promise, arising under Section 2–313A or 2–313B accrues when the remote purchaser, as defined in sections 2–313A and 2–313B, receives the goods.

(c) Where a warranty arising under Section 2–313(2) or an obligation, other than a remedial promise, arising under Section 2–313A or 2–313B explicitly extends to future performance of the goods and discovery of the breach must await the time for performance the right of action accrues when the immediate buyer as defined in Section 2–313 or the remote purchaser as defined in Sections 2–313A and 2–313B discovers or should have discovered the breach.

(d) A right of action for breach of warranty arising under Section 2–312 accrues when the aggrieved party discovers or should have discovered the breach. However, an action for breach of the warranty of non-infringement may not be commenced more than six years after tender of delivery of the goods to the aggrieved party.

171

(4) Where an action commenced within the time limited by subsection (1) is so terminated as to leave available a remedy by another action for the same breach such other action may be commenced after the expiration of the time limited and within six months after the termination of the first action unless the termination resulted from voluntary discontinuance or from dismissal for failure or neglect to prosecute.

(5) This section does not alter the law on tolling of the statute of limitations nor does it apply to causes of action which have accrued before this Act becomes effective.

Definitional Cross References:

"Action". Section 1–201.

"Aggrieved party". Section 1–201.

"Agreement". Section 1–201. 1–205.

"Buyer". Section 2–103.

"Consumer contract". Section 2–103.

"Contract". Section 1–201.

"Contract for sale". Section 2–106.

"Delivery". Section 2–103.

"Goods". Section 2–103.

"Party". Section 1–201.

"Reasonable time". Section

"Remedial promise". Section 2–103.

"Remedy". Section 1–201.

"Tender of delivery". Sections 2–503 and 2–507.

"Term". section 1–201.

"Termination". Section 2–106.

PART 8

TRANSITION PROVISIONS

§ 2–801. Effective Date.

This [Act] takes effect on _____, 20__ .

§ 2–802. Amendment of Existing Article 2.

This [Act] amends [insert citation to existing Article 2].

§ 2–803. Applicability.

This [Act] applies to a transaction within its scope that is entered into on or after the effective date of this [Act]. . . . This [Act] does not apply to a right of action that accrued before the effective date of this [Act]. Section 2–313B of this [Act] does not apply to an advertisement or similar communication made before the effective date of this [Act].

§ 2–804. Savings Clause.

A transaction entered into before the effective date of this [Act], and the rights, obligations, and interests flowing from that transaction, are governed by any statute or other law amended or repealed by this [Act] as if amendment or repeal had not occurred and may be terminated, completed, consummated, or enforced under that statute or other law.

RESTATEMENT OF THE LAW, SECOND, OF CONTRACTS

(Selected Sections)

COMPILERS' NOTE

The American Law Institute was formed in 1923 as the outgrowth of a "Committee on the Establishment of a Permanent Organization for the Improvement of the Law." Its members were to be 400 practitioners, judges and law professors; there are now about 4,000. The idea of the Institute, and of "restating" the law, was broached by Professor William Draper Lewis and fostered by Elihu Root and others. The Carnegie Corporation supported work on the original Restatement, comprising nine subjects, which was completed by 1944.

Contracts was one of the first three subjects upon which the Institute began work, and the Restatement of Contracts was completed in 1932. Professor Samuel Williston acted as Reporter, with responsibility for preparing drafts. (Professor Arthur L. Corbin served as Reporter for the Chapter on Remedies.) Other experts in the subject were formed into a Committee of Advisers who conferred with the Reporter over the whole period in producing drafts for submission to the Council of the Institute. The plan was "that the drafts of the different chapters submitted to the Council shall be the product of the committee composed of the Reporter and his advisers; that these drafts after discussion and amendment by the Council and before revision shall be submitted as tentative drafts for criticism and suggestion with a view to their improvement to the annual meetings of the Institute and to bar associations and the profession generally." Restatement of Contracts, Introduction, p. x. Final promulgation depended on approval of the text by both the Council and the full meeting of Institute members. The same procedure was followed in making revisions and in preparing the Restatement Second.

In 1962 the Institute initiated the preparation of the Restatement (Second) of Contracts, parts of which are reproduced here. Professor Robert Braucher served as Reporter until his appointment to the Supreme Judicial Court of Massachusetts in 1971; he was succeeded by Professor E. Allan Farnsworth. The work was completed in 1980.

As originally conceived, the first Restatement was to be accompanied by treatises citing and discussing case authority, but experience proved that group production of such volumes was not feasible. As they stand, the Restatements consist of sections stating rules or principles (the so-called black letter), each followed by one or more comments with illustrations, and in the Restatement Second also by Reporter's Notes in which supporting authorities are collected. (Reproduced here are the black letter of selected sections and in a few instances their comments and illustrations.)

Assaults on the Restatement, along with sympathetic appraisals, have produced a rich literature. An eminent critic of the Restatement of Contracts immediately objected that the American Law Institute "seems constantly to be seeking the force of a statute without statutory enactment." Clark, The Restatement of the Law of Contracts, 42 Yale L.J. 643, 654 (1933).[1] To what measure of authority is the Restatement entitled, then, in the courts?

This general question can have only a general answer. The Supreme Court of Oregon has emphasized the difference between statutory and Restatement texts:[2]

> Although this court frequently quotes sections of the Restatements of the American Law Institute, it does not literally "adopt" them in the manner of a legislature enacting, for instance, a draft prepared by the Commissioners on Uniform State Laws, such as the Residential Landlord and Tenant Act. In the nature of common law, such quotations in opinions are no more than shorthand expressions of the court's view that the analysis summarized in the Restatement corresponds to Oregon law applicable to the facts of the case before the court. They do not enact the exact phrasing of the Restatement rule, complete with comments, illustrations, and caveats. Such quotations should not be relied on in briefs as if they committed his court or lower courts to track every detail of the Restatement analysis in other cases. The Restatements themselves purport to be just that, "restatements" of law found in other sources, although at times they candidly report that the law is in flux and offer a formula preferred on policy grounds.

There is agreement among those who applaud the Restatement and those who deprecate it about the persuasiveness of an ideal restatement of the law. "A restatement, then, can have no other authority than as the product of men learned in the subject who have studied and deliberated over it. It needs no other, and what could be higher?" Clark, op. cit. supra, p. 655. Judge Herbert Goodrich, for many years Director of the Institute, explained:

> If an advocate thinks the Restatement was wrong as applied to his case, he can urge the court not to follow it, but to apply some other

---

1. On occasion a legislature has given statutory backing to the Restatement. The Virgin Islands Code (Title 1, § 4) provides: "The rules of the common law, as expressed in the restatements of the law approved by the American Law Institute ... , shall be the rules of decision ... in cases to which they apply, in the absence of local laws to the contrary."

2. Brewer v. Erwin, 600 P.2d 398, 410 n. 12 (Or.1979).

rule. If the court agrees, it will do so, but it will so do with the knowledge that the rule which it rejects has been written by the people who by training and reputation are supposed to be eminently learned in the particular subject and that the specialist's conclusions have been discussed and defended before a body of very able critics. The presumption is in favor of the Restatement.... Yet it can be overthrown and that fact leaves Restatement acceptance to persuasion. It is common law "persuasive authority" with a high degree of persuasion.

Restatement and Codification, David D. Field Centenary Essays 241, 244–45 (1949).

The Restatement Second. To a substantial extent the Restatement Second reflects the thought of two men in particular: Professor Corbin and Professor Karl Llewellyn, who shared an attitude toward law sometimes described as "legal realism."[3] Professor Corbin prepared a critical review of the original Restatement, which "has been the basis for much of the work on the revision."[4] He served also as consultant for the Restatement Second in its early stages. Professor Llewellyn's efforts affected the revision less directly, largely through the impact of his contributions to the Uniform Commercial Code.

In restating the law of contracts for the second half of the twentieth century, an obvious difficulty arose from the fact that large tracts of the subject had recently been occupied by legislation such as the Code and, to a lesser extent, consumer-protection statutes. Indeed, the worth of the enterprise was questioned on the ground of an apparently diminishing importance of common law doctrine. In response, Professor Braucher made this claim:

The effort to restate the law of contracts in modern terms highlights the reliance of private autonomy in an era of expanding government activity.... Freedom of contract, refined and redefined in response to social change, has power as it always had.[5]

At the beginning of the twenty-first century, work was begun on a Restatement (Third) of Restitution and Unjust Enrichment.

A continuing theme of controversy about the Restatements is the wisdom or unwisdom of departing from rules derived from existing precedents, in the interest of a more just and more convenient regime of law. Professor Herbert Wechsler, when Director of the Institute, proposed "a working formula" that received the unanimous approval of the

3. For symposia devoted to the Restatement Second, see 81 Colum.L.Rev. 1 (1981) and 67 Cornell L.Rev. 631 (1982).

4. Braucher, Formation of Contract and the Second Restatement, 78 Yale L.J. 598 (1969). See also Perillo, Twelve Letters from Arthur L.Corbin to Robert Braucher Annotated, 50 Wash. & Lee L. Rev. 755 (1993).

5. Id. at 615–16. For another comment by Professor Braucher, see Offer and Acceptance in the Second Restatement, 74 Yale L.J. 302 (1964)

Council: "we should feel obliged in our deliberations to give weight to all of the considerations that the courts, under a proper view of the judicial function, deem it right to weigh in theirs."[6] An example of creative restating from the first Restatement of Contracts was the formulation of the doctrine of promissory estoppel, in section 90.[7]

6. Wechsler, The Course of the Restatements, 55 A.B.A.J. 147, 150 (1969).

7. The Oregon opinion quoted above refers to a section of the Torts Restatement as a "bold sally." Notwithstanding that, the section has gained widespread adherence.

RESTATEMENT (SECOND) OF CONTRACTS[1]

Table of Contents

CHAPTER 1. MEANING OF TERMS

CHAPTER 2. FORMATION OF CONTRACTS— PARTIES AND CAPACITY

CHAPTER 3. FORMATION OF CONTRACTS—MUTUAL ASSENT

TOPIC 1. IN GENERAL

TOPIC 2. MANIFESTATION OF ASSENT IN GENERAL

TOPIC 3. MAKING OF OFFERS

TOPIC 4. DURATION OF THE OFFEREE'S POWER OF ACCEPTANCE

CHAPTER 1.   MEANING OF TERMS

§ 1.   Contract Defined

A contract is a promise or a set of promises for the breach of which the law gives a remedy, or the performance of which the law in some way recognizes as a duty.

CHAPTER 2.   FORMATION OF CONTRACTS— PARTIES AND CAPACITY

§ 14.   Infants

Unless a statute provides otherwise, a natural person has the capacity to incur only voidable contractual duties until the beginning of the day before the person's eighteenth birthday.

§ 15.   Mental Illness or Defect

(1) A person incurs only voidable contractual duties by entering into a transaction if by reason of mental illness or defect

> (a) he is unable to understand in a reasonable manner the nature and consequences of the transaction, or
>
> (b) he is unable to act in a reasonable manner in relation to the transaction and the other party has reason to know of his condition.

(2) Where the contract is made on fair terms and the other party is without knowledge of the mental illness or defect, the power of avoidance under Subsection (1) terminates to the extent that the contract has been so performed in whole or in part or the circumstances have so changed that avoidance would be unjust. In such a case a court may grant relief on such equitable terms as justice requires.

CHAPTER 3.   FORMATION OF CONTRACTS—MUTUAL ASSENT

TOPIC 1.   IN GENERAL

§ 17.   Requirement of a Bargain

(1) Except as stated in Subsection (2), the formation of a contract requires a bargain in which there is a manifestation of mutual assent to the exchange and a consideration.

(2) Whether or not there is a bargain a contract may be formed under special rules applicable to formal contracts or under the rules stated in §§ 82–94.

TOPIC 2. MANIFESTATION OF ASSENT IN GENERAL

§ 20. Effect of Misunderstanding

(1) There is no manifestation of mutual assent to an exchange if the parties attach materially different meanings to their manifestations and

  (a) neither party knows or has reason to know the meaning attached by the other; or

  (b) each party knows or each party has reason to know the meaning attached by the other.

(2) The manifestations of the parties are operative in accordance with the meaning attached to them by one of the parties if

  (a) that party does not know of any different meaning attached by the other, and the other knows the meaning attached by the first party; or

  (b) that party has no reason to know of any different meaning attached by the other, and the other has reason to know the meaning attached by the first party.

TOPIC 3. MAKING OF OFFERS

§ 24. Offer Defined

An offer is the manifestation of willingness to enter into a bargain, so made as to justify another person in understanding that his assent to that bargain is invited and will conclude it.

§ 26. Preliminary Negotiations

A manifestation of willingness to enter into a bargain is not an offer if the person to whom it is addressed knows or has reason to know that the person making it does not intend to conclude a bargain until he has made a further manifestation of assent.

§ 27. Existence of Contract Where Written Memorial Is Contemplated

Manifestations of assent that are in themselves sufficient to conclude a contract will not be prevented from so operating by the fact that the parties also manifest an intention to prepare and adopt a written memorial thereof; but the circumstances may show that the agreements are preliminary negotiations.

§ 30. Form of Acceptance Invited

(1) An offer may invite or require acceptance to be made by an affirmative answer in words, or by performing or refraining from per-

forming a specified act, or may empower the offeree to make a selection of terms in his acceptance.

(2) Unless otherwise indicated by the language or the circumstances, an offer invites acceptance in any manner and by any medium reasonable in the circumstances.

§ 32. Invitation of Promise or Performance

In case of doubt an offer is interpreted as inviting the offeree to accept either by promising to perform what the offer requests or by rendering the performance, as the offeree chooses.

§ 33. Certainty

(1) Even though a manifestation of intention is intended to be understood as an offer, it cannot be accepted so as to form a contract unless the terms of the contract are reasonably certain.

(2) The terms of a contract are reasonably certain if they provide a basis for determining the existence of a breach and for giving an appropriate remedy.

(3) The fact that one or more terms of a proposed bargain are left open or uncertain may show that a manifestation of intention is not intended to be understood as an offer or as an acceptance.

TOPIC 4. DURATION OF THE OFFEREE'S POWER OF ACCEPTANCE

§ 36. Methods of Termination of the Power of Acceptance

(1) An offeree's power of acceptance may be terminated by

     (a) rejection or counter-offer by the offeree, or

     (b) lapse of time, or

     (c) revocation by the offeror, or

     (d) death or incapacity of the offeror or offeree.

(2) In addition, an offeree's power of acceptance is terminated by the non-occurrence of any condition of acceptance under the terms of the offer.

§ 37. Termination of Power of Acceptance Under Option Contract

Notwithstanding §§ 38–49, the power of acceptance under an option contract is not terminated by rejection or counter-offer, by revocation, or by death or incapacity of the offeror, unless the requirements are met for the discharge of a contractual duty.

§ 38. Rejection

(1) An offeree's power of acceptance is terminated by his rejection of the offer, unless the offeror has manifested a contrary intention.

(2) A manifestation of intention not to accept an offer is a rejection unless the offeree manifests an intention to take it under further advisement.

§ 39. Counter–Offers

(1) A counter-offer is an offer made by an offeree to his offeror relating to the same matter as the original offer and proposing a substituted bargain differing from that proposed by the original offer.

(2) An offeree's power of acceptance is terminated by his making of a counter-offer, unless the offeror has manifested a contrary intention or unless the counter-offer manifests a contrary intention of the offeree.

§ 40. Time When Rejection or Counter–Offer Terminates the Power of Acceptance

Rejection or counter-offer by mail or telegram does not terminate the power of acceptance until received by the offeror, but limits the power so that a letter or telegram of acceptance started after the sending of an otherwise effective rejection or counter-offer is only a counter-offer unless the acceptance is received by the offeror before he receives the rejection or counter-offer.

§ 42. Revocation by Communication From Offeror Received by Offeree

An offeree's power of acceptance is terminated when the offeree receives from the offeror a manifestation of an intention not to enter into the proposed contract.

§ 43. Indirect Communication of Revocation

An offeree's power of acceptance is terminated when the offeror takes definite action inconsistent with an intention to enter into the proposed contract and the offeree acquires reliable information to that effect.

§ 45. Option Contract Created by Part Performance or Tender

(1) Where an offer invites an offeree to accept by rendering a performance and does not invite a promissory acceptance, an option contract is created when the offeree tenders or begins the invited performance or tenders a beginning of it.

(2) The offeror's duty of performance under any option contract so created is conditional on completion or tender of the invited performance in accordance with the terms of the offer.

Comment:

a. *Offer limited to acceptance by performance only.* This Section is limited to cases where the offer does not invite a promissory acceptance. Such an offer has often been referred to as an "offer for a unilateral contract." Typical illustrations are found in offers of rewards or prizes and in non-commercial arrangements among relatives and friends. See Comment b to § 32. As to analogous cases arising under offers which give the offeree power to accept either by performing or by promising to perform, as he chooses, see §§ 32, 62.

b. *Manifestation of contrary intention.* The rule of this Section is designed to protect the offeree in justifiable reliance on the offeror's promise, and the rule yields to a manifestation of intention which makes reliance unjustified. A reservation of power to revoke after performance has begun means that as yet there is no promise and no offer. See §§ 2, 24. In particular, if the performance is one which requires the cooperation of both parties, such as the payment of money or the manual delivery of goods, a person who reserves the right to refuse to receive the performance has not made an offer. See § 26.

Illustrations:

1. B owes A $5000 payable in installments over a five-year period. A proposes that B discharge the debt by paying $4,500 cash within one month, but reserves the right to refuse any such payment. A has not made an offer. A tender by B in accordance with the proposal is an offer by B.

2. A, an insurance company, issues a bulletin to its agents, entitled "Extra Earnings Agreement," providing for annual bonus payments to the agents varying according to "monthly premiums in force" and "lapse ratio," but reserving the right to change or discontinue the bonus, individually or collectively, with or without notice, at any time before payment. There is no offer or promise.

c. *Tender of performance.* A proposal to receive a payment of money or a delivery of goods is an offer only if acceptance can be completed without further cooperation by the offeror. If there is an offer, it follows that acceptance must be complete at the latest when performance is tendered. A tender of performance, so bargained for and given in exchange for the offer, ordinarily furnishes consideration and creates a contract. See §§ 17, 71, 72.

This is so whether or not the tender carries with it any incidental promises. See §§ 54, 62. If no commitment is made by the offeree, the contract is an option contract. See § 25.

Illustration:

3. A promises B to sell him a specified chattel for $5, stating that B is not to be bound until he pays the money. B tenders $5 within a reasonable time, but A refuses to accept the tender. There is a breach of contract.

d. *Beginning to perform.* If the invited performance takes time, the invitation to perform necessarily includes an invitation to begin performance. In most such cases the beginning of performance carries with it an express or implied promise to complete performance. See § 62. In the less common case where the offer does not contemplate or invite a promise by the offeree, the beginning of performance nevertheless completes the manifestation of mutual assent and furnishes consideration for an option contract. See § 25. If the beginning of performance requires the cooperation of the offeror, tender of part performance has the same effect. Part performance or tender may also create an option contract in a situation where the offeree is invited to take up the option by making a promise, if the offer invites a preliminary performance before the time for the offeree's final commitment.

Illustrations:

4. A offers a reward for the return of lost property. In response to the offer, B searches for the property and finds it. A then notifies B that the offer is revoked. B makes a tender of the property to A conditional on payment of the reward, and A refuses. There is a breach of contract by A.

5. A, a magazine, offers prizes in a subscription contest. At a time when B has submitted the largest number of subscriptions, A cancels the contest. A has broken its contract with B.

6. A writes to her daughter B, living in another state, an offer to leave A's farm to B if B gives up her home and cares for A during A's life, B remaining free to terminate the arrangement at any time. B gives up her home, moves to A's farm, and begins caring for A. A is bound by an option contract.

7. A offers to sell a piece of land to B, and promises that if B incurs expense in employing experts to appraise the property the offer will be irrevocable for 30 days. B hires experts and pays for their transportation to the land. A is bound by an option contract.

8. In January A, an employer, publishes a notice to his employees, promising a stated Christmas bonus to any employee who is continuously in A's employ from January to Christmas. B, an employee hired by the week, reads the notice and continues at work beyond the expiration of the current week. A is bound by an option contract, and if B is continuously in A's employ until Christmas a notice of revocation of the bonus is ineffective.

e. Completion of performance. Where part performance or tender by the offeree creates an option contract, the offeree is not bound to complete performance. The offeror alone is bound, but his duty of performance is conditional on completion of the offeree's performance. If the offeree abandons performance, the offeror's duty to perform never arises. See § 224, defining "condition," and Illustration 4 to that Section. But the condition may be excused, for example, if the offeror prevents performance, waives it, or repudiates. See Comment b to § 225 and §§ 239, 278.

f. Preparations for performance. What is begun or tendered must be part of the actual performance invited in order to preclude revocation under this Section. Beginning preparations, though they may be essential to carrying out the contract or to accepting the offer, is not enough. Preparations to perform may, however, constitute justifiable reliance sufficient to make the offeror's promise binding under § 87(2).

In many cases what is invited depends on what is a reasonable mode of acceptance. See § 30. The distinction between preparing for performance and beginning performance in such cases may turn on many factors: the extent to which the offeree's conduct is clearly referable to the offer, the definite and substantial character of that conduct, and the extent to which it is of actual or prospective benefit to the offeror rather than the offeree, as well as the terms of the communications between the parties, their prior course of dealing, and any relevant usages of trade.

Illustration:

9. A makes a written promise to pay $5000 to B, a hospital, "to aid B in its humanitarian work." Relying upon this and other like promises, B proceeds in its humanitarian work, expending large sums of money and incurring large

liabilities. Performance by B has begun, and A's offer is irrevocable.

g. Agency contracts. This Section frequently applies to agency arrangements, particularly offers made to real estate brokers. Sometimes there is a return promise by the agent, particularly if there is an agreement for exclusive dealing, since such an agreement normally imposes an obligation on the agent to use best efforts. See Uniform Commercial Code § 2–306(2); compare Restatement, Second, Agency § 378. In other cases the agent does not promise to act, but the principal must compensate him if he does act. The rules governing the principal's duty of compensation are stated in detail in Chapter 14 of the Restatement, Second, Agency, particularly §§ 443–57.

§ 46. Revocation of General Offer

Where an offer is made by advertisement in a newspaper or other general notification to the public or to a number of persons whose identity is unknown to the offeror, the offeree's power of acceptance is terminated when a notice of termination is given publicity by advertisement or other general notification equal to that given to the offer and no better means of notification is reasonably available.

§ 48. Death or Incapacity of Offeror or Offeree

An offeree's power of acceptance is terminated when the offeree or offeror dies or is deprived of legal capacity to enter into the proposed contract.

TOPIC 5. ACCEPTANCE OF OFFERS

§ 50. Acceptance of Offer Defined; Acceptance by Performance; Acceptance by Promise

(1) Acceptance of an offer is a manifestation of assent to the terms thereof made by the offeree in a manner invited or required by the offer.

(2) Acceptance by performance requires that at least part of what the offer requests be performed or tendered and includes acceptance by a performance which operates as a return promise.

(3) Acceptance by a promise requires that the offeree complete every act essential to the making of the promise.

§ 51. Effect of Part Performance Without Knowledge of Offer

Unless the offeror manifests a contrary intention, an offeree who learns of an offer after he has rendered part of the performance requested by the offer may accept by completing the requested performance.

§ 52. Who May Accept an Offer

An offer can be accepted only by a person whom it invites to furnish the consideration.

§ 53. Acceptance by Performance; Manifestation of Intention Not to Accept

(1) An offer can be accepted by the rendering of a performance only if the offer invites such an acceptance.

(2) Except as stated in § 69, the rendering of a performance does not constitute an acceptance if within a reasonable time the offeree exercises reasonable diligence to notify the offeror of non-acceptance.

(3) Where an offer of a promise invites acceptance by performance and does not invite a promissory acceptance, the rendering of the invited performance does not constitute an acceptance if before the offeror performs his promise the offeree manifests an intention not to accept.

§ 54. Acceptance by Performance; Necessity of Notification to Offeror

(1) Where an offer invites an offeree to accept by rendering a performance, no notification is necessary to make such an acceptance effective unless the offer requests such a notification.

(2) If an offeree who accepts by rendering a performance has reason to know that the offeror has no adequate means of learning of the performance with reasonable promptness and certainty, the contractual duty of the offeror is discharged unless

  (a) the offeree exercises reasonable diligence to notify the offeror of acceptance, or

  (b) the offeror learns of the performance within a reasonable time, or

  (c) the offer indicates that notification of acceptance is not required.

§ 56. Acceptance by Promise; Necessity of Notification to Offeror

Except as stated in § 69 or where the offer manifests a contrary intention, it is essential to an acceptance by promise either that the offeree exercise reasonable diligence to notify the offeror of acceptance or that the offeror receive the acceptance seasonably.

§ 58. Necessity of Acceptance Complying With Terms of Offer

An acceptance must comply with the requirements of the offer as to the promise to be made or the performance to be rendered.

§ 59. Purported Acceptance Which Adds Qualifications

A reply to an offer which purports to accept it but is conditional on the offeror's assent to terms additional to or different from those offered is not an acceptance but is a counter-offer.

§ 60. Acceptance of Offer Which States Place, Time or Manner of Acceptance

If an offer prescribes the place, time or manner of acceptance its terms in this respect must be complied with in order to create a contract. If an offer merely suggests a permitted place, time or manner of acceptance, another method of acceptance is not precluded.

§ 61. Acceptance Which Requests Change of Terms

An acceptance which requests a change or addition to the terms of the offer is not thereby invalidated unless the acceptance is made to depend on an assent to the changed or added terms.

§ 62. Effect of Performance by Offeree Where Offer Invites Either Performance or Promise

(1) Where an offer invites an offeree to choose between acceptance by promise and acceptance by performance, the tender or beginning of the invited performance or a tender of a beginning of it is an acceptance by performance.

(2) Such an acceptance operates as a promise to render complete performance.

§ 63. Time When Acceptance Takes Effect

Unless the offer provides otherwise,

  (a) an acceptance made in a manner and by a medium invited by an offer is operative and completes the manifestation of mutual assent as soon as put out of the offeree's possession, without regard to whether it ever reaches the offeror; but

  (b) an acceptance under an option contract is not operative until received by the offeror.

§ 69. Acceptance by Silence or Exercise of Dominion

(1) Where an offeree fails to reply to an offer, his silence and inaction operate as an acceptance in the following cases only:

(a) Where an offeree takes the benefit of offered services with reasonable opportunity to reject them and reason to know that they were offered with the expectation of compensation.

(b) Where the offeror has stated or given the offeree reason to understand that assent may be manifested by silence or inaction, and the offeree in remaining silent and inactive intends to accept the offer.

(c) Where because of previous dealings or otherwise, it is reasonable that the offeree should notify the offeror if he does not intend to accept.

(2) An offeree who does any act inconsistent with the offeror's ownership of offered property is bound in accordance with the offered terms unless they are manifestly unreasonable. But if the act is wrongful as against the offeror it is an acceptance only if ratified by him.

CHAPTER 4. FORMATION OF CONTRACTS—CONSIDERATION

TOPIC 1. THE REQUIREMENT OF CONSIDERATION

§ 71. Requirement of Exchange; Types of Exchange

(1) To constitute consideration, a performance or a return promise must be bargained for.

(2) A performance or return promise is bargained for if it is sought by the promisor in exchange for his promise and is given by the promisee in exchange for that promise.

(3) The performance may consist of

(a) an act other than a promise, or

(b) a forbearance, or

(c) the creation, modification, or destruction of a legal relation.

(4) The performance or return promise may be given to the promisor or to some other person. It may be given by the promisee or by some other person.

Comment:

a. Other meanings of "consideration." The word "consideration" has often been used with meanings different from that given here. It is often used merely to express the legal conclusion that a promise is enforceable. Historically, its primary meaning may have been that the conditions were met under which an action of assumpsit would lie. It was also used as the equivalent of the quid pro quo required in an action of debt. A seal, it has been said, "imports a consideration," although the law was clear that no element of bargain was necessary to enforcement of a promise under seal. On the other hand, consideration has sometimes been used to refer to almost any reason asserted for enforcing a

191

promise, even though the reason was insufficient. In this sense we find references to promises "in consideration of love and affection," to "illegal consideration," to "past consideration," and to consideration furnished by reliance on a gratuitous promise.

Consideration has also been used to refer to the element of exchange without regard to legal consequences. Consistent with that usage has been the use of the phrase "sufficient consideration" to express the legal conclusion that one requirement for an enforceable bargain is met. Here § 17 states the element of exchange required for a contract enforceable as a bargain as "a consideration. "Thus "consideration" refers to an element of exchange which is sufficient to satisfy the legal requirement; the word "sufficient" would be redundant and is not used.

b. *"Bargained for."* In the typical bargain, the consideration and the promise bear a reciprocal relation of motive or inducement: the consideration induces the making of the promise and the promise induces the furnishing of the consideration. Here, as in the matter of mutual assent, the law is concerned with the external manifestation rather than the undisclosed mental state: it is enough that one party manifests an intention to induce the other's response and to be induced by it and that the other responds in accordance with the inducement. See § 81; compare §§ 19, 20. But it is not enough that the promise induces the conduct of the promisee or that the conduct of the promisee induces the making of the promise; both elements must be present, or there is no bargain. Moreover, a mere pretense of bargain does not suffice, as where there is a false recital of consideration or where the purported consideration is merely nominal. In such cases there is no consideration and the promise is enforced, if at all, as a promise binding without consideration under §§ 82–94. See Comments b and c to § 87.

Illustrations:

1. A offers to buy a book owned by B and to pay B $10 in exchange therefor. B accepts the offer and delivers the book to A. The transfer and delivery of the book constitute a performance and are consideration for A's promise. See Uniform Commercial Code §§ 2–106, 2–301. This is so even though A at the time he makes the offer secretly intends to pay B $10 whether or not he gets the book, or even though B at the time he accepts secretly intends not to collect the $10.

2. A receives a gift from B of a book worth $10. Subsequently A promises to pay B the value of the book. There is no consideration for A's promise. This is so even though B at the time he makes the gift secretly hopes that A will pay him for it. As to the enforcement of such promises, see § 86.

3. A promises to make a gift of $10 to B. In reliance on the promise B buys a book from C and promises to pay C $10 for it. There is no consideration for A's promise. As to the enforcement of such promises, see § 90.

4. A desires to make a binding promise to give $1000 to his son B. Being advised that a gratuitous promise is not binding, A writes out and signs a false recital that B has sold him a car for $1000 and a promise to pay that amount. There is no consideration for A's promise.

5. A desires to make a binding promise to give $1000 to his son B. Being advised that a gratuitous promise is not binding, A offers to buy from B for $1000 a book

worth less than $1. B accepts the offer knowing that the purchase of the book is a mere pretense. There is no consideration for A's promise to pay $1000.

c. *Mixture of bargain and gift.* In most commercial bargains there is a rough equivalence between the value promised and the value received as consideration. But the social functions of bargains include the provision of opportunity for free individual action and exercise of judgment and the fixing of values by private action, either generally or for purposes of the particular transaction. Those functions would be impaired by judicial review of the values so fixed. Ordinarily, therefore, courts do not inquire into the adequacy of consideration, particularly where one or both of the values exchanged are difficult to measure. See § 79. Even where both parties know that a transaction is in part a bargain and in part a gift, the element of bargain may nevertheless furnish consideration for the entire transaction.

On the other hand, a gift is not ordinarily treated as a bargain, and a promise to make a gift is not made a bargain by the promise of the prospective donee to accept the gift, or by his acceptance of part of it. This may be true even though the terms of gift impose a burden on the donee as well as the donor. See Illustration 2 to § 24. In such cases the distinction between bargain and gift may be a fine one, depending on the motives manifested by the parties. In some cases there may be no bargain so long as the agreement is entirely executory, but performance may furnish consideration or the agreement may become fully or partly enforceable by virtue of the reliance of one party or the unjust enrichment of the other. Compare § 90.

Illustrations:

6. A offers to buy a book owned by B and to pay B $10 in exchange therefor. B's transfer and delivery of the book are consideration for A's promise even though both parties know that such books regularly sell for $5 and that part of A's motive in making the offer is to make a gift to B. See §§ 79, 81.

7. A owns land worth $10,000 which is subject to a mortgage to secure a debt of $5,000. A promises to make a gift of the land to his son B and to pay off the mortgage, and later gives B a deed subject to the mortgage. B's acceptance of the deed is not consideration for A's promise to pay the mortgage debt.

8. A and B agree that A will advance $1000 to B as a gratuitous loan. B's promise to accept the loan is not consideration for A's promise to make it. But the loan when made is consideration for B's promise to repay

d. *Types of consideration.* Consideration may consist of a performance or of a return promise. Consideration by way of performance may be a specified act of forbearance, or any one of several specified acts or forbearances of which the offeree is given the choice, or such conduct as will produce a specified result. Or either the offeror or the offeree may request as consideration the creation, modification or destruction of a purely intangible legal relation. Not infrequently the consideration bargained for is an act with the added requirement that a certain legal result shall be produced. Consideration by way of return promise requires a promise as defined in § 2. Consideration may consist partly of promise and partly of other acts or forbearances, and the consideration invited may be a performance or a return promise in the alternative. Though a promise is itself an act, it is treated separately from other acts. See § 75.

Illustrations:

9. A promises B, his nephew aged 16, that A will pay B $1000 when B becomes 21 if B does not smoke before then. B's forbearance to smoke is a performance and if bargained for is consideration for A's promise.

10. A says to B, the owner of a garage, "I will pay you $100 if you will make my car run properly." The production of this result is consideration for A's promise.

11. A has B's horse in his possession. B writes to A, "If you will promise me $100 for the horse, he is yours." A promptly replies making the requested promise. The property in the horse at once passes to A. The change in ownership is consideration for A's promise.

12. A promises to pay B $1,000 if B will make an offer to C to sell C certain land for $25,000 and will leave the offer open for 24 hours. B makes the requested offer and forbears to revoke it for 24 hours, but C does not accept. The creation of a power of acceptance in C is consideration for A's promise.

13. A mails a written order to B, offering to buy specified machinery on specified terms. The order provides "Ship at once." B's prompt shipment or promise to ship is consideration for A's promise to pay the price. See § 32; Uniform Commercial Code § 2–206(1)(b).

e. Consideration moving from or to a third person. It matters not from whom the consideration moves or to whom it goes. If it is bargained for and given in exchange for the promise, the promise is not gratuitous.

Illustrations:

14. A promises B to guarantee payment of a bill of goods if B sells the goods to C. Selling the goods to C is consideration for A's promise.

15. A makes a promissory note payable to B in return for a payment by B to C. The payment is consideration for the note.

16. A, at C's request and in exchange for $1 paid by C, promises B to give him a book. The payment is consideration for A's promise.

17. A promises B to pay B $1, in exchange for C's promise to A to give A a book. The promises are consideration for one another.

18. A promises to pay $1,000 to B, a bank, in exchange for the delivery of a car by C to A's son D. The delivery of the car is consideration for A's promise.

§ 73. Performance of Legal Duty

Performance of a legal duty owed to a promisor which is neither doubtful nor the subject of honest dispute is not consideration; but a similar performance is consideration if it differs from what was required by the duty in a way which reflects more than a pretense of bargain.

§ 74. Settlement of Claims

(1) Forbearance to assert or the surrender of a claim or defense which proves to be invalid is not consideration unless

(a) the claim or defense is in fact doubtful because of uncertainty as to the facts or the law, or

(b) the forbearing or surrendering party believes that the claim or defense may be fairly determined to be valid.

(2) The execution of a written instrument surrendering a claim or defense by one who is under no duty to execute it is consideration if the execution of the written instrument is bargained for even though he is not asserting the claim or defense and believes that no valid claim or defense exists.

§ 75. Exchange of Promise for Promise

Except as stated in §§ 76 and 77, a promise which is bargained for is consideration if, but only if, the promised performance would be consideration.

§ 77. Illusory and Alternative Promises

A promise or apparent promise is not consideration if by its terms the promisor or purported promisor reserves a choice of alternative performances unless

(a) each of the alternative performances would have been consideration if it alone had been bargained for; or

(b) one of the alternative performances would have been consideration and there is or appears to the parties to be a substantial possibility that before the promisor exercises his choice events may eliminate the alternatives which would not have been consideration.

§ 79. Adequacy of Consideration; Mutuality of Obligation

If the requirement of consideration is met, there is no additional requirement of

(a) a gain, advantage, or benefit to the promisor or a loss, disadvantage, or detriment to the promisee; or

(b) equivalence in the values exchanged; or

(c) "mutuality of obligation."

§ 81. Consideration as Motive or Inducing Cause

(1) The fact that what is bargained for does not of itself induce the making of a promise does not prevent it from being consideration for the promise.

(2) The fact that a promise does not of itself induce a performance or return promise does not prevent the performance or return promise from being consideration for the promise.

TOPIC 2.   CONTRACTS WITHOUT CONSIDERATION

§ 82.   Promise to Pay Indebtedness; Effect on the Statute of Limitations

(1) A promise to pay all or part of an antecedent contractual or quasi-contractual indebtedness owed by the promisor is binding if the indebtedness is still enforceable or would be except for the effect of a statute of limitations.

(2) The following facts operate as such a promise unless other facts indicate a different intention:

> (a) A voluntary acknowledgment to the obligee, admitting the present existence of the antecedent indebtedness; or
>
> (b) A voluntary transfer of money, a negotiable instrument, or other thing by the obligor to the obligee, made as interest on or part payment of or collateral security for the antecedent indebtedness; or
>
> (c) A statement to the obligee that the statute of limitations will not be pleaded as a defense.

§ 83.   Promise to Pay Indebtedness Discharged in Bankruptcy

An express promise to pay all or part of an indebtedness of the promisor, discharged or dischargeable in bankruptcy proceedings begun before the promise is made, is binding.

§ 84.   Promise to Perform a Duty in Spite of Non-occurrence of a Condition

(1) Except as stated in Subsection (2), a promise to perform all or part of a conditional duty under an antecedent contract in spite of the non-occurrence of the condition is binding, whether the promise is made before or after the time for the condition to occur, unless

> (a) occurrence of the condition was a material part of the agreed exchange for the performance of the duty and the promisee was under no duty that it occur; or
>
> (b) uncertainty of the occurrence of the condition was an element of the risk assumed by the promisor.

(2) If such a promise is made before the time for the occurrence of the condition has expired and the condition is within the control of the promisee or a beneficiary, the promisor can make his duty again subject to the condition by notifying the promisee or beneficiary of his intention to do so if

(a) the notification is received while there is still a reasonable time to cause the condition to occur under the antecedent terms or an extension given by the promisor; and

(b) reinstatement of the requirement of the condition is not unjust because of a material change of position by the promisee or beneficiary; and

(c) the promise is not binding apart from the rule stated in Subsection (1).

§ 86. Promise for Benefit Received

(1) A promise made in recognition of a benefit previously received by the promisor from the promisee is binding to the extent necessary to prevent injustice.

(2) A promise is not binding under Subsection (1)

(a) if the promisee conferred the benefit as a gift or for other reasons the promisor has not been unjustly enriched; or

(b) to the extent that its value is disproportionate to the benefit.

Comment:

a. "Past consideration"; "moral obligation." Enforcement of promises to pay for benefit received has sometimes been said to rest on "past consideration" or on the "moral obligation" of the promisor, and there are statutes in such terms in a few states. Those terms are not used here: "past consideration" is inconsistent with the meaning of consideration stated in § 71, and there seems to be no consensus as to what constitutes a "moral obligation." The mere fact of promise has been thought to create a moral obligation, but it is clear that not all promises are enforced. Nor are moral obligations based solely on gratitude or sentiment sufficient of themselves to support a subsequent promise.

Illustrations:

1. A gives emergency care to B's adult son while the son is sick and without funds far from home. B subsequently promises to reimburse A for his expenses. The promise is not binding under this Section.

2. A lends money to B, who later dies. B's widow promises to pay the debt. The promise is not binding under this Section.

3. A has immoral relations with B, a woman not his wife, to her injury. A's subsequent promise to reimburse B for her loss is not binding under this Section.

b. Rationale. Although in general a person who has been unjustly enriched at the expense of another is required to make restitution, restitution is denied in many cases in order to protect persons who have had benefits thrust upon them. See Restatement of Restitution §§ 1, 2, 112. In other cases restitution is denied by virtue of rules designed to guard against false claims, stale claims, claims already litigated, and the like. In many such cases a subsequent promise to make restitution removes the reason for the denial of relief, and the policy against unjust enrichment then prevails. Compare Restatement, Second, Agency § 462 on ratification of the acts of a person who officiously purports to act as an agent. Enforcement of the subsequent promise sometimes makes it unnecessary to decide a difficult question as to the limits on quasi-contractual relief.

Many of the cases governed by the rules stated in §§ 82–85 are within the broader principle stated in this Section. But the broader principle is not so firmly established as those rules, and it may not be applied if there is doubt whether the objections to restitution are fully met by the subsequent promise. Facts such as the definite and substantial character of the benefit received, formality in the making of the promise, part performance of the promise, reliance on the promise or the probability of such reliance may be relevant to show that no imposition results from enforcement.

c. Promise to correct a mistake. One who makes a mistake in the conferring of a benefit is commonly entitled to restitution regardless of any promise. But restitution is often denied to avoid prejudice to the recipient of the benefit. Thus restitution of the value of services or of improvements to land or chattels may require a payment which the recipient cannot afford. See Restatement of Restitution §§ 41, 42. Where a subsequent promise shows that the usual protection is not needed in the particular case, restitution is granted to the extent promised.

Illustrations:

4. A is employed by B to repair a vacant house. By mistake A repairs the house next door, which belongs to C. A subsequent promise by C to pay A the value of the repairs is binding.

5. A pays B a debt and gets a signed receipt. Later B obtains a default judgment against A for the amount of the debt, and A pays again. B's subsequent promise to refund the second payment if A has a receipt is binding.

d. Emergency services and necessaries. The law of restitution in the absence of promise severely limits recovery for necessaries furnished to a person under disability and for emergency services. See Restatement of Restitution §§ 113–17, 139. A subsequent promise in such a case may remove doubt as to the reality of the benefit and as to its value, and may negate any danger of imposition or false claim. A positive showing that payment was expected is not then required; an intention to make a gift must be shown to defeat restitution.

Illustrations:

6. A finds B's escaped bull and feeds and cares for it. B's subsequent promise to pay reasonable compensation to A is binding.

7. A saves B's life in an emergency and is totally and permanently disabled in so doing. One month later B promises to pay A $15 every two weeks for the rest of A's life, and B makes the payments for 8 years until he dies. The promise is binding.

e. Benefit conferred as a gift. In the absence of mistake or the like, there is no element of unjust enrichment in the receipt of a gift, and the rule of this Section has no application to a promise to pay for a past gift. Similarly, when a debt is discharged by a binding agreement, the transaction is closed even though full payment is not made. But marginal cases arise in which both parties understand that what is in form a gift is intended to be reimbursed indirectly, or in which a subsequent promise to pay is expressly contemplated. See Illustration 3 to § 83. Enforcement of the subsequent promise is proper in some such cases.

Illustrations:

8. A submits to B at B's request a plan for advertising products manufactured by B, expecting payment only if the plan is adopted. Because of a change in B's selling arrangements, B rejects the plan without giving it fair consideration. B's subsequent promise to reimburse A's expenses in preparing the plan is binding.

9. A contributes capital to B, an insurance company, on the understanding that B is not liable to reimburse A but that A will be reimbursed through salary and commissions. Later A withdraws from the company and B promises to pay him ten percent of premiums received until he is reimbursed. The promise is binding.

f. Benefit conferred pursuant to contract. By virtue of the policy of enforcing bargains, the enrichment of one party as a result of an unequal exchange is not regarded as unjust, and this Section has no application to a promise to pay or perform more or to accept less than is called for by a pre-existing bargain between the same parties. Compare §§ 79, 89. Similarly, if a third person receives a benefit as a result of the performance of a bargain, this Section does not make binding the subsequent promise of the third person to pay extra compensation to the performing party. But a promise to pay in substitution for the return performance called for by the bargain may be binding under this Section.

Illustration:

10. A digs a well on B's land in performance of a bargain with B's tenant C. C is unable to pay as agreed, and B promises to pay A the reasonable value of the well. The promise is binding.

g. Obligation unenforceable under the Statute of Frauds. A promise to pay a debt unenforceable under the Statute of Frauds is very similar to the promises governed by §§ 82–85. But the problem seldom arises. Part performance often renders the Statute inapplicable; if it does not, the contract can be made enforceable by a subsequent memorandum. See § 136. In any event, the Statute does not ordinarily foreclose the remedy of restitution. See § 375. Where the question does arise, the new promise is binding if the policy of the Statute is satisfied.

Illustration:

11. By statute an agreement authorizing a real estate broker to sell land for compensation is void unless the agreement or a memorandum thereof is in writing. A, a real estate broker, procures a purchaser for B's land without any written agreement. In the written sale agreement, signed by B, B promises to pay A $200, the usual commission, "for services rendered." The promise is binding.

h. Obligation unenforceable because usurious. If a promise is unenforceable because it is usurious, an agreement in renewal or substitution for it that provides for a payment including the usurious interest is also unenforceable, even though the interest from the date of renewal or substitution is not usurious. However, a promise to pay the original debt with interest that is not usurious in substitution for the usurious interest is enforceable.

i. Partial enforcement. The rules stated in §§ 82–85 refer to promises to perform all or part of an antecedent duty, and do not make enforceable a promise to do more. Similarly, where a benefit received is a liquidated sum of money, a promise is not enforceable under this Section beyond the amount of the benefit. Where the value of the benefit is uncertain, a promise to pay the value is binding and a promise to pay a liquidated sum may serve to fix the amount due if in all the circumstances it is not disproportionate to the benefit. See Illustration 7. A promise which is excessive may sometimes be enforced to the extent of the value of the benefit, and the remedy may be thought of as quasi-contractual rather than contractual. In other cases a promise of disproportionate value may tend to show unfair pressure or other conduct by the promisee such that justice does not require any enforcement of the promise. Compare Comment c to § 72.

Illustrations:

12. A, a married woman of sixty, has rendered household services without compensation over a period of years for B, a man of eighty living alone and having no close relatives. B has a net worth of three million dollars and has often assured A that she will be well paid for her services, whose reasonable value is not in excess of $6,000. B executes and delivers to A a written promise to pay A $25,000 "to be taken from my estate." The promise is binding.

13. The facts being otherwise as stated in Illustration 12, B's promise is made orally and is to leave A his entire estate. A cannot recover more than the reasonable value of her services.

§ 87. Option Contract

(1) An offer is binding as an option contract if it

(a) is in writing and signed by the offeror, recites a purported consideration for the making of the offer, and proposes an exchange on fair terms within a reasonable time; or

(b) is made irrevocable by statute.

(2) An offer which the offeror should reasonably expect to induce action or forbearance of a substantial character on the part of the offeree before acceptance and which does induce such action or forbearance is binding as an option contract to the extent necessary to avoid injustice.

§ 89. Modification of Executory Contract

A promise modifying a duty under a contract not fully performed on either side is binding

(a) if the modification is fair and equitable in view of circumstances not anticipated by the parties when the contract was made; or

(b) to the extent provided by statute; or

(c) to the extent that justice requires enforcement in view of material change of position in reliance on the promise.

Comment:

a. Rationale. This Section relates primarily to adjustments in on-going transactions. Like offers and guaranties, such adjustments are ancillary to exchanges and have some of the same presumptive utility. See §§ 72, 87, 88. Indeed, paragraph (a) deals with bargains which are without consideration only because of the rule that performance of a legal duty to the promisor is not consideration. See § 73. This Section is also related to § 84 on waiver of conditions: it may apply to cases in which § 84 is inapplicable because a condition is material to the exchange or risk. As in cases governed by § 84, relation to a bargain tends to satisfy the cautionary and channeling functions of legal formalities. See Comment c to § 72. The Statute of Frauds may prevent enforcement in the absence of reliance. See §§ 149–50. Otherwise formal requirements are at a minimum.

b. Performance of legal duty. The rule of § 73 finds its modern justification in cases of promises made by mistake or induced by unfair pressure. Its application to cases where those elements are absent has been much criticized and is avoided if paragraph (a) of this Section is applicable. The limitation to a modification which is "fair and equitable" goes beyond absence of coercion and requires an objectively demonstrable reason for seeking a modification. Compare Uniform Commercial Code § 2–209 Comment. The reason for modification must rest in circumstances not "anticipated" as part of the context in which the contract was made, but a frustrating event may be unanticipated for this purpose if it was not adequately covered, even though it was foreseen as a remote possibility. When such a reason is present, the relative financial strength of the parties, the formality with which the modification is made, the extent to which it is performed or relied on and other circumstances may be relevant to show or negate imposition or unfair surprise.

The same result called for by paragraph (a) is sometimes reached on the ground that the original contract was "rescinded" by mutual agreement and that new promises were then made which furnished consideration for each other. That theory is rejected here because it is fictitious when the "rescission" and new agreement are simultaneous, and because if logically carried out it might uphold unfair and inequitable modifications.

Illustrations:

1. By a written contract A agrees to excavate a cellar for B for a stated price. Solid rock is unexpectedly encountered and A so notifies B. A and B then orally agree that A will remove the rock at a unit price which is reasonable but nine times that used in computing the original price, and A completes the job. B is bound to pay the increased amount.

2. A contracts with B to supply for $300 a laundry chute for a building B has contracted to build for the Government for $150,000. Later A discovers that he made an error as to the type of material to be used and should have bid $1,200. A offers to supply the chute for $1000, eliminating overhead and profit. After ascertaining that other suppliers would charge more, B agrees. The new agreement is binding.

3. A is employed by B as a designer of coats at $90 a week for a year beginning November 1 under a written contract executed September 1. A is offered $115 a week by another employer and so informs B. A and B then agree that A will be paid $100 a week and in October execute a new written contract to that effect, simultaneously tearing up the prior contract. The new contract is binding.

4. A contracts to manufacture and sell to B 2,000 steel roofs for corn cribs at $60. Before A begins manufacture a threat of a nationwide steel strike raises the cost of steel about $10 per roof, and A

and B agree orally to increase the price to $70 per roof. A thereafter manufactures and delivers 1700 of the roofs, and B pays for 1,500 of them at the increased price without protest, increasing the selling price of the corn cribs by $10. The new agreement is binding.

5. A contracts to manufacture and sell to B 100,000 castings for lawn mowers at 50 cents each. After partial delivery and after B has contracted to sell a substantial number of lawn mowers at a fixed price, A notifies B that increased metal costs require that the price be increased to 75 cents. Substitute castings are available at 55 cents, but only after several months delay. B protests but is forced to agree to the new price to keep its plant in operation. The modification is not binding.

c. Statutes. Uniform Commercial Code § 2–209 dispenses with the requirement of consideration for an agreement modifying a contract for the sale of goods. Under that section the original contract can provide against oral modification, and the requirements of the Statute of Frauds must be met if the contract as modified is within its provisions; but an ineffective modification can operate as a waiver. The Comment indicates that extortion of a modification without legitimate commercial reason is ineffective as a violation of the duty of good faith imposed by the Code. A similar limitation may be applicable under statutes which give effect to a signed writing as a substitute for the seal, or under statutes which give effect to acceptance by the promisee of the modified performance. In some States statutes or constitutional provisions flatly forbid the payment of extra compensation to Government contractors.

d. Reliance. Paragraph (c) states the application of § 90 to modification of an executory contract in language adapted from Uniform Commercial Code § 2–209. Even though the promise is not binding when made, it may become binding in whole or in part by reason of action or forbearance by the promisee or third persons in reliance on it. In some cases the result can be viewed as based either on estoppel to contradict a representation of fact or on reliance on a promise. Ordinarily reliance by the promisee is reasonably foreseeable and makes the modification binding with respect to performance by the promisee under it and any return performance owed by the promisor. But as under § 84 the original terms can be reinstated for the future by reasonable notification received by the promisee unless reinstatement would be unjust in view of a change of position on his part. Compare Uniform Commercial Code § 2–209(5).

Illustrations:

6. A defaults in payment of a premium on a life insurance policy issued by B, an insurance company. Pursuant to the terms of the policy, B notifies A of the lapse of the policy and undertakes to continue the insurance until a specified future date, but by mistake specifies a date two months later than the insured would be entitled to under the policy. On inquiry by A two years later, B repeats the mistake, offering A an option to take a cash payment. A fails to do so, and dies one month before the specified date. B is bound to pay the insurance.

7. A is the lessee of an apartment house under a 99–year lease from B at a rent of $10,000 per year. Because of war conditions many of the apartments become vacant, and in order to enable A to stay in business B agrees to reduce the

rent to $5,000. The reduced rent is paid for five years. The war being over, the apartments are then fully rented, and B notifies A that the full rent called for by the lease must be paid. A is bound to pay the full rent only from a reasonable time after the receipt of the notification.

8. A contracts with B to carry a shipment of fish under refrigeration. During the short first leg of the voyage the refrigeration equipment on the ship breaks down, and A offers either to continue under ventilation or to hold the cargo at the first port for later shipment. B agrees to shipment under ventilation but later changes his mind. A receives notification of the change before he has changed his position. A is bound to ship under refrigeration.

§ 90. Promise Reasonably Inducing Action or Forbearance

(1) A promise which the promisor should reasonably expect to induce action or forbearance on the part of the promisee or a third person and which does induce such action or forbearance is binding if injustice can be avoided only by enforcement of the promise. The remedy granted for breach may be limited as justice requires.

(2) A charitable subscription or a marriage settlement is binding under Subsection (1) without proof that the promise induced action or forbearance.

Comment:

a. *Relation to other rules.* Obligations and remedies based on reliance are not peculiar to the law of contracts. This Section is often referred to in terms of "promissory estoppel," a phrase suggesting an extension of the doctrine of estoppel. Estoppel prevents a person from showing the truth contrary to a representation of fact made by him after another has relied on the representation. See Restatement, Second, Agency § 8B; Restatement, Second, Torts §§ 872, 894. Reliance is also a significant feature of numerous rules in the law of negligence, deceit and restitution. See, e.g., Restatement, Second, Agency §§ 354, 378; Restatement, Second, Torts §§ 323, 537; Restatement of Restitution § 55. In some cases those rules and this Section overlap; in others they provide analogies useful in determining the extent to which enforcement is necessary to avoid injustice.

It is fairly arguable that the enforcement of informal contracts in the action of assumpsit rested historically on justifiable reliance on a promise. Certainly reliance is one of the main bases for enforcement of the half-completed exchange, and the probability of reliance lends support to the enforcement of the executory exchange. See Comments to §§ 72, 75. This Section thus states a basic principle which often renders inquiry unnecessary as to the precise scope of the policy of enforcing bargains. Sections 87–89 state particular applications of the same principle to promises ancillary to bargains, and it also applies in a wide variety of noncommercial situations. See, e.g., § 94.

Illustration:

1. A, knowing that B is going to college, promises B that A will give him $5,000 on completion of his course. B goes to college, and borrows and spends more than $5,000 for college expenses. When he has nearly completed his course, A notifies him of an intention to revoke

the promise. A's promise is binding and B is entitled to payment on completion of the course without regard to whether his performance was "bargained for" under § 71.

b. Character of reliance protected. The principle of this Section is flexible. The promisor is affected only by reliance which he does or should foresee, and enforcement must be necessary to avoid injustice. Satisfaction of the latter requirement may depend on the reasonableness of the promisee's reliance, on its definite and substantial character in relation to the remedy sought, on the formality with which the promise is made, on the extent to which the evidentiary, cautionary, deterrent and channeling functions of form are met by the commercial setting or otherwise, and on the extent to which such other policies as the enforcement of bargains and the prevention of unjust enrichment are relevant. Compare Comment to § 72. The force of particular factors varies in different types of cases: thus reliance need not be of substantial character in charitable subscription cases, but must in cases of firm offers and guaranties. Compare Subsection (2) with §§ 87, 88.

Illustrations:

2. A promises B not to foreclose, for a specified time, a mortgage which A holds on B's land. B thereafter makes improvements on the land. A's promise is binding and may be enforced by denial of foreclosure before the time has elapsed.

3. A sues B in a municipal court for damages for personal injuries caused by B's negligence. After the one year statute of limitations has run, B requests A to discontinue the action and start again in the superior court where the action can be consolidated with other actions against B arising out of the same accident. A does so. B's implied promise that no harm to A will result bars B from asserting the statute of limitations as a defense.

4. A has been employed by B for 40 years. B promises to pay A a pension of $200 per month when A retires. A retires and forbears to work elsewhere for several years while B pays the pension. B's promise is binding.

c. Reliance by third persons. If a promise is made to one party for the benefit of another, it is often foreseeable that the beneficiary will rely on the promise. Enforcement of the promise in such cases rests on the same basis and depends on the same factors as in cases of reliance by the promisee. Justifiable reliance by third persons who are not beneficiaries is less likely, but may sometimes reinforce the claim of the promisee or beneficiary.

Illustrations:

5. A holds a mortgage on B's land. To enable B to obtain a loan, A promises B in writing to release part of the land from the mortgage upon payment of a stated sum. As A contemplated, C lends money to B on a second mortgage, relying on A's promise. The promise is binding and may be enforced by C.

6. A executes and delivers a promissory note to B, a bank, to give B a false appearance of assets, deceive the banking authorities, and enable the bank to continue to operate. After several years B fails and is taken over by C, a representative of B's creditors. A's note is enforceable by C.

7. A and B, husband and wife, are tenants by the entirety of a tract of land. They make an oral

promise to B's niece C to give her the tract. B, C and C's husband expend money in building a house on the tract and C and her husband take possession and live there for several years until B dies. The expenditures by B and by C's husband are treated like those by C in determining whether justice requires enforcement of the promise against A.

d. Partial enforcement. A promise binding under this section is a contract, and full-scale enforcement by normal remedies is often appropriate. But the same factors which bear on whether any relief should be granted also bear on the character and extent of the remedy. In particular, relief may sometimes be limited to restitution or to damages or specific relief measured by the extent of the promisee's reliance rather than by the terms of the promise. See §§ 84, 89; compare Restatement, Second, Torts § 549 on damages for fraud. Unless there is unjust enrichment of the promisor, damages should not put the promisee in a better position than performance of the promise would have put him. See §§ 344, 349. In the case of a promise to make a gift it would rarely be proper to award consequential damages which would place a greater burden on the promisor than performance would have imposed.

Illustrations:

8. A applies to B, a distributor of radios manufactured by C, for a "dealer franchise" to sell C's products. Such franchises are revocable at will. B erroneously informs A that C has accepted the application and will soon award the franchise, that A can proceed to employ salesmen and solicit orders, and that A will receive an initial delivery of at least 30 radios. A expends $1,150 in preparing to do business, but does not receive the franchise or any radios. B is liable to A for the $1,150 but not for the lost profit on 30 radios. Compare Restatement, Second, Agency § 329.

9. The facts being otherwise as stated in Illustration 8, B gives A the erroneous information deliberately and with C's approval and requires A to buy the assets of a deceased former dealer and thus discharge C's "moral obligation "to the widow. C is liable to A not only for A's expenses but also for the lost profit on 30 radios.

10. A, who owns and operates a bakery, desires to go into the grocery business. He approaches B, a franchisor of supermarkets. B states to A that for $18,000 B will establish A in a store. B also advises A to move to another town and buy a small grocery to gain experience. A does so. Later B advises A to sell the grocery, which A does, taking a capital loss and foregoing expected profits from the summer tourist trade. B also advises A to sell his bakery to raise capital for the supermarket franchise, saying "Everything is ready to go. Get your money together and we are set." A sells the bakery taking a capital loss on this sale as well. Still later, B tells A that considerably more than an $18,000 investment will be needed, and the negotiations between the parties collapse. At the point of collapse many details of the proposed agreement between the parties are unresolved. The assurances from B to A are promises on which B reasonably should have expected A to rely, and A is entitled to his actual losses on the sales of the bakery and grocery and for his moving and temporary

living expenses. Since the proposed agreement was never made, however, A is not entitled to lost profits from the sale of the grocery or to his expectation interest in the proposed franchise from B.

11.   A is about to buy a house on a hill. Before buying he obtains a promise from B, who owns adjoining land, that B will not build on a particular portion of his lot, where a building would obstruct the view from the house. A then buys the house in reliance on the promise. B's promise is binding, but will be specifically enforced only so long as A and his successors do not permanently terminate the use of the view.

12.   A promises to make a gift of a tract of land to B, his son-in-law. B takes possession and lives on the land for 17 years, making valuable improvements. A then dispossesses B, and specific performance is denied because the proof of the terms of the promise is not sufficiently clear and definite. B is entitled to a lien on the land for the value of the improvements, not exceeding their cost.

e. Gratuitous promises to procure insurance. This Section is to be applied with caution to promises to procure insurance. The appropriate remedy for breach of such a promise makes the promisor an insurer, and thus may result in a liability which is very large in relation to the value of the promised service. Often the promise is properly to be construed merely as a promise to use reasonable efforts to procure the insurance, and reliance by the promisee may be unjustified or may be justified only for a short time. Or it may be doubtful whether he did in fact rely. Such difficulties may be removed if the proof of the promise and the reliance are clear, or if the promise is made with some formality, or if part perfor-

mance or a commercial setting or a potential benefit to the promisor provide a substitute for formality.

Illustrations:

13.   A, a bank, lends money to B on the security of a mortgage on B's new home. The mortgage requires B to insure the property. At the closing of the transaction A promises to arrange for the required insurance, and in reliance on the promise B fails to insure. Six months later the property, still uninsured, is destroyed by fire. The promise is binding.

14.   A sells an airplane to B, retaining title to secure payment of the price. After the closing A promises to keep the airplane covered by insurance until B can obtain insurance. B could obtain insurance in three days but makes no effort to do so, and the airplane is destroyed after six days. A is not subject to liability by virtue of the promise.

f. Charitable subscriptions, marriage settlements, and other gifts. One of the functions of the doctrine of consideration is to deny enforcement to a promise to make a gift. Such a promise is ordinarily enforced by virtue of the promisee's reliance only if his conduct is foreseeable and reasonable and involves a definite and substantial change of position which would not have occurred if the promise had not been made. In some cases, however, other policies reinforce the promisee's claim. Thus the promisor might be unjustly enriched if he could reclaim the subject of the promised gift after the promisee has improved it.

Subsection (2) identifies two other classes of cases in which the promisee's claim is similarly reinforced. American courts have traditionally favored charitable subscriptions and marriage settlements, and have found consideration in many cases where the element of exchange was doubtful or nonexistent. Where recovery is rested on reliance in such cases, a probability of reliance is enough, and no effort is made to sort out mixed motives or to consider whether partial enforcement would be appropriate.

Illustrations:

15. A promises B $5000, knowing that B desires that sum for the purchase of a parcel of land. Induced thereby, B secures without any payment an option to buy the parcel. A then tells B that he withdraws his promise. A's promise is not binding.

16. A orally promises to give her son B a tract of land to live on. As A intended, B gives up a homestead elsewhere, takes possession of the land, lives there for a year and makes substantial improvements. A's promise is binding.

17. A orally promises to pay B, a university, $100,000 in five annual installments for the purposes of its fund-raising campaign then in progress. The promise is confirmed in writing by A's agent, and two annual installments are paid before A dies. The continuance of the fund-raising campaign by B is sufficient reliance to make the promise binding on A and his estate.

18. A and B are engaged to be married. In anticipation of the marriage A and his father C enter into a formal written agreement by which C promises to leave certain property to A by will. A's subsequent marriage to B is sufficient reliance to make the promise binding on C and his estate.

CHAPTER 5. THE STATUTE OF FRAUDS

TOPIC 6. SATISFACTION OF THE STATUTE BY A MEMORANDUM

§ 131. General Requisites of a Memorandum

Unless additional requirements are prescribed by the particular statute, a contract within the Statute of Frauds is enforceable if it is evidenced by any writing, signed by or on behalf of the party to be charged, which

    (a) reasonably identifies the subject matter of the contract,

    (b) is sufficient to indicate that a contract with respect thereto has been made between the parties or offered by the signer to the other party, and

    (c) states with reasonable certainty the essential terms of the unperformed promises in the contract.

TOPIC 8. CONSEQUENCES OF NON-COMPLIANCE

§ 139. Enforcement by Virtue of Action in Reliance

(1) A promise which the promisor should reasonably expect to induce action or forbearance on the part of the promisee or a third

person and which does induce the action or forbearance is enforceable notwithstanding the Statute of Frauds if injustice can be avoided only by enforcement of the promise. The remedy granted for breach is to be limited as justice requires.

(2) In determining whether injustice can be avoided only by enforcement of the promise, the following circumstances are significant:

> (a) the availability and adequacy of other remedies, particularly cancellation and restitution;
>
> (b) the definite and substantial character of the action or forbearance in relation to the remedy sought;
>
> (c) the extent to which the action or forbearance corroborates evidence of the making and terms of the promise, or the making and terms are otherwise established by clear and convincing evidence;
>
> (d) the reasonableness of the action or forbearance;
>
> (e) the extent to which the action or forbearance was foreseeable by the promisor.

Comment:

a. Relation to other rules. This Section is complementary to § 90, which dispenses with the requirement of consideration if the same conditions are met, but it also applies to promises supported by consideration. Like § 90, this Section overlaps in some cases with rules based on estoppel or fraud; it states a basic principle which sometimes renders inquiry unnecessary as to the precise scope of other policies. Sections 128 and 129 state particular applications of the same principle to land contracts; §§ 125(3) and 130(2) also rest on it in part. See also Uniform Commercial Code §§ 2–201(3), 8–319(b). Where a promise is made without intention to perform, remedies under this Section may be alternative to remedies for fraud. See Comment b to § 313; Restatement, Second, Torts § 530.

b. Avoidance of injustice. Like § 90 this Section states a flexible principle, but the requirement of consideration is more easily displaced than the requirement of a writing. The reliance must be foreseeable by the promisor, and enforcement must be necessary to avoid injustice. Subsection (2) lists some of the relevant factors in applying the latter requirement. Each factor relates either to the extent to which reliance furnishes a compelling substantive basis for relief in addition to the expectations created by the promise or to the extent to which the circumstances satisfy the evidentiary purpose of the Statute and fulfill any cautionary, deterrent and channeling functions it may serve.

Illustrations:

1. A is lessee of a building for five years at $75 per month and has sublet it for three years at $100 per month. A seeks to induce B to purchase the building, and to that end orally promises to assign to B the lease and sublease and to execute a written assignment as soon as B obtains a deed. B purchases the building in reliance on the promise. B is entitled to the rentals from the sublease.

2. A is a pilot with an established airline having rights to continued

employment, and could take up to six months leave without prejudice to those rights. He takes such leave to become general manager of B, a small airline which hopes to expand if a certificate to operate over an important route is granted. When his six months leave is about to expire, A demands definite employment because of that fact, and B orally agrees to employ A for two years and on the granting of the certificate to give A an increase in salary and a written contract. In reliance on this agreement A lets his right to return to his prior employer expire. The certificate is soon granted, but A is discharged in breach of the agreement. The Statute of Frauds does not prevent recovery of damages by A.

c. Particular factors. The force of the factors listed varies in different types of cases, and additional factors may affect particular types of contracts. Thus reliance of the kinds usual in suretyship transactions is not sufficient to justify enforcement of an oral guaranty, where the evidentiary and cautionary functions performed by the statutory formalities are not fulfilled. See Comment a to § 112. In the case of a contract between prospective spouses made upon consideration of marriage, the policy of the Statute is reinforced by a policy against legal interference in the marriage relation, and reliance incident to the marriage relation does not make the contract enforceable. See Comment d to § 124. Where restitution is an unavailable remedy because to grant it would nullify the statutory purpose, a remedy based on reliance will ordinarily also be denied. See Comment a to § 375.

Illustration:

3. A orally promises to pay B a commission for services in negotiating the sale of a business opportunity, and B finds a purchaser to whom A sells the business opportunity. A statute extends the Statute of Frauds to such promises, and is interpreted to preclude recovery of the reasonable value of such services. The promise is not made enforceable by B's reliance on it.

d. Partial enforcement; particular remedies. The same factors which bear on whether any relief should be granted also bear on the character and extent of the remedy. In particular, the remedy of restitution is not ordinarily affected by the Statute of Frauds (see § 375); where restitution is an adequate remedy, other remedies are not made available by the rule stated in this Section. Again, when specific enforcement is available under the rule stated in § 129, an ordinary action for damages is commonly less satisfactory, and justice then does not require enforcement in such an action. See Comment c to § 129. In some cases it may be appropriate to measure relief by the extent of the promisee's reliance rather than by the terms of the promise. See § 90 Comment e and Illustrations.

Illustration:

4. A renders services to B under an oral contract within the Statute by which B promises to pay for the services. On discharge without cause in breach of the contract, A is entitled to the reasonable value of the services, but in the absence of additional circumstances is not entitled to damages for wrongful discharge.

§ 141. Action for Value of Performance Under Unenforceable Contract

(1) In an action for the value of performance under a contract, except as stated in Subsection (2), the Statute of Frauds does not

invalidate any defense which would be available if the contract were enforceable against both parties.

(2) Where a party to a contract which is unenforceable against him refuses either to perform the contract or to sign a sufficient memorandum, the other party is justified in suspending any performance for which he has not already received the agreed return, and such a suspension is not a defense in an action for the value of performance rendered before the suspension.

CHAPTER 6.   MISTAKE

§ 151.   Mistake Defined

A mistake is a belief that is not in accord with the facts.

§ 152.   When Mistake of Both Parties Makes a Contract Voidable

(1) Where a mistake of both parties at the time a contract was made as to a basic assumption on which the contract was made has a material effect on the agreed exchange of performances, the contract is voidable by the adversely affected party unless he bears the risk of the mistake under the rule stated in § 154.

(2) In determining whether the mistake has a material effect on the agreed exchange of performances, account is taken of any relief by way of reformation, restitution, or otherwise.

§ 153.   When Mistake of One Party Makes a Contract Voidable

Where a mistake of one party at the time a contract was made as to a basic assumption on which he made the contract has a material effect on the agreed exchange of performances that is adverse to him, the contract is voidable by him if he does not bear the risk of the mistake under the rule stated in § 154, and

> (a) the effect of the mistake is such that enforcement of the contract would be unconscionable, or
>
> (b) the other party had reason to know of the mistake or his fault caused the mistake.

§ 154.   When a Party Bears the Risk of a Mistake

A party bears the risk of a mistake when

> (a) The risk is allocated to him by agreement of the parties, or
>
> (b) he is aware, at the time the contract is made, that he has only limited knowledge with respect to the facts to which

the mistake relates but treats his limited knowledge as sufficient, or

(c) the risk is allocated to him by the court on the ground that it is reasonable in the circumstances to do so.

§ 157. Effect of Fault of Party Seeking Relief

A mistaken party's fault in failing to know or discover the facts before making the contract does not bar him from avoidance or reformation under the rules stated in this Chapter, unless his fault amounts to a failure to act in good faith and in accordance with reasonable standards of fair dealing.

§ 158. Relief Including Restitution

(1) In any case governed by the rules stated in this Chapter, either party may have a claim for relief including restitution under the rules stated in §§ 240 and 376.

(2) In any case governed by the rules stated in this Chapter, if those rules together with the rules stated in Chapter 16 will not avoid injustice, the court may grant relief on such terms as justice requires including protection of the parties' reliance interest.

CHAPTER 7. MISREPRESENTATION, DURESS AND UNDUE INFLUENCE

TOPIC 1. MISREPRESENTATION

§ 159. Misrepresentation Defined

A misrepresentation is an assertion that is not in accord with the facts.

§ 160. When Action is Equivalent to an Assertion (Concealment)

Action intended or known to be likely to prevent another from learning a fact is equivalent to an assertion that the fact does not exist.

§ 161. When Non-disclosure Is Equivalent to an Assertion

A person's non-disclosure of a fact known to him is equivalent to an assertion that the fact does not exist in the following cases only:

(a) where he knows that disclosure of the fact is necessary to prevent some previous assertion from being a misrepresentation or from being fraudulent or material.

(b) where he knows that disclosure of the fact would correct a mistake of the other party as to a basic assumption on which that party is making the contract and if non-disclosure of the fact amounts to a failure to act in good faith and in accordance with reasonable standards of fair dealing.

(c) where he knows that disclosure of the fact would correct a mistake of the other party as to the contents or effect of a writing, evidencing or embodying an agreement in whole or in part.

(d) where the other person is entitled to know the fact because of a relation of trust and confidence between them.

§ 162. When a Misrepresentation Is Fraudulent or Material

(1) A misrepresentation is fraudulent if the maker intends his assertion to induce a party to manifest his assent and the maker

(a) knows or believes that the assertion is not in accord with the facts, or

(b) does not have the confidence that he states or implies in the truth of the assertion, or

(c) knows that he does not have the basis that he states or implies for the assertion.

(2) A misrepresentation is material if it would be likely to induce a reasonable person to manifest his assent, or if the maker knows that it would be likely to induce the recipient to do so.

§ 163. When a Misrepresentation Prevents Formation of a Contract

If a misrepresentation as to the character or essential terms of a proposed contract induces conduct that appears to be a manifestation of assent by one who neither knows nor has reasonable opportunity to know of the character or essential terms of the proposed contract, his conduct is not effective as a manifestation of assent.

§ 164. When a Misrepresentation Makes a Contract Voidable

(1) If a party's manifestation of assent is induced by either a fraudulent or a material misrepresentation by the other party upon which the recipient is justified in relying, the contract is voidable by the recipient.

(2) If a party's manifestation of assent is induced by either a fraudulent or a material misrepresentation by one who is not a party to the transaction upon which the recipient is justified in relying, the contract is voidable by the recipient, unless the other party to the transaction in good faith and without reason to know of the misrepresentation either gives value or relies materially on the transaction.

§ 168. Reliance on Assertions of Opinion

(1) An assertion is one of opinion if it expresses only a belief, without certainty, as to the existence of a fact or expresses only a judgment as to quality, value, authenticity, or similar matters.

(2) If it is reasonable to do so, the recipient of an assertion of a person's opinion as to facts not disclosed and not otherwise known to the recipient may properly interpret it as an assertion

   (a) that the facts known to that person are not incompatible with his opinion, or

   (b) that he knows facts sufficient to justify him in forming it.

§ 169. When Reliance on an Assertion of Opinion Is Not Justified

To the extent that an assertion is one of opinion only, the recipient is not justified in relying on it unless the recipient

   (a) stands in such a relation of trust and confidence to the person whose opinion is asserted that the recipient is reasonable in relying on it, or

   (b) reasonably believes that, as compared with himself, the person whose opinion is asserted has special skill, judgment or objectivity with respect to the subject matter, or

   (c) is for some other special reason particularly susceptible to a misrepresentation of the type involved.

TOPIC 2. DURESS AND UNDUE INFLUENCE

§ 175. When Duress by Threat Makes a Contract Voidable

(1) If a party's manifestation of assent is induced by an improper threat by the other party that leaves the victim no reasonable alternative, the contract is voidable by the victim.

(2) If a party's manifestation of assent is induced by one who is not a party to the transaction, the contract is voidable by the victim unless the other party to the transaction in good faith and without reason to know of the duress either gives value or relies materially on the transaction.

§ 176. When a Threat Is Improper

(1) A threat is improper if

   (a) what is threatened is a crime or a tort, or the threat itself would be a crime or a tort if it resulted in obtaining property,

   (b) what is threatened is a criminal prosecution,

213

(c) what is threatened is the use of civil process and the threat is made in bad faith, or

(d) the threat is a breach of the duty of good faith and fair dealing under a contract with the recipient.

(2) A threat is improper if the resulting exchange is not on fair terms, and

(a) the threatened act would harm the recipient and would not significantly benefit the party making the threat,

(b) the effectiveness of the threat in inducing the manifestation of assent is significantly increased by prior unfair dealing by the party making the threat, or

(c) what is threatened is otherwise a use of power for illegitimate ends.

§ 177. When Undue Influence Makes a Contract Voidable

(1) Undue influence is unfair persuasion of a party who is under the domination of the person exercising the persuasion or who by virtue of the relation between them is justified in assuming that that person will not act in a manner inconsistent with his welfare.

(2) If a party's manifestation of assent is induced by undue influence by the other party, the contract is voidable by the victim.

(3) If a party's manifestation of assent is induced by one who is not a party to the transaction, the contract is voidable by the victim unless the other party to the transaction in good faith and without reason to know of the undue influence either gives value or relies materially on the transaction.

CHAPTER 8. UNENFORCEABILITY ON GROUNDS OF PUBLIC POLICY

TOPIC 1. UNENFORCEABILITY IN GENERAL

§ 178. When a Term Is Unenforceable on Grounds of Public Policy

(1) A promise or other term of an agreement is unenforceable on grounds of public policy if legislation provides that it is unenforceable or the interest in its enforcement is clearly outweighed in the circumstances by a public policy against the enforcement of such terms.

(2) In weighing the interest in the enforcement of a term, account is taken of

(a) the parties' justified expectations,

(b) any forfeiture that would result if enforcement were denied, and

    (c) any special public interest in the enforcement of the particular term.

    (3) In weighing a public policy against enforcement of a term, account is taken of

        (a) the strength of that policy as manifested by legislation or judicial decisions,

        (b) the likelihood that a refusal to enforce the term will further that policy,

        (c) the seriousness of any misconduct involved and the extent to which it was deliberate, and

        (d) the directness of the connection between that misconduct and the term.

§ **181.** Effect of Failure to Comply With Licensing or Similar Requirement

    If a party is prohibited from doing an act because of his failure to comply with a licensing, registration or similar requirement, a promise in consideration of his doing that act or of his promise to do it is unenforceable on grounds of public policy if

        (a) the requirement has a regulatory purpose, and

        (b) the interest in the enforcement of the promise is clearly outweighed by the public policy behind the requirement.

TOPIC 2.   RESTRAINT OF TRADE

§ **187.** Non-ancillary Restraints on Competition

    A promise to refrain from competition that imposes a restraint that is not ancillary to an otherwise valid transaction or relationship is unreasonably in restraint of trade.

§ **188.** Ancillary Restraints on Competition

    (1) A promise to refrain from competition that imposes a restraint that is ancillary to an otherwise valid transaction or relationship is unreasonably in restraint of trade if

        (a) the restraint is greater than is needed to protect the promisee's legitimate interest, or

        (b) the promisee's need is outweighed by the hardship to the promisor and the likely injury to the public.

    (2) Promises imposing restraints that are ancillary to a valid transaction or relationship include the following:

        (a) a promise by the seller of a business not to compete with the buyer in such a way as to injure the value of the business sold;

    (b) a promise by an employee or other agent not to compete with his employer or other principal;

    (c) a promise by a partner not to compete with the partnership.

CHAPTER 9.   THE SCOPE OF CONTRACTUAL OBLIGATIONS

TOPIC 1.   THE MEANING OF AGREEMENTS

§ 201.   Whose Meaning Prevails

(1) Where the parties have attached the same meaning to a promise or agreement or a term thereof, it is interpreted in accordance with that meaning.

(2) Where the parties have attached different meanings to a promise or agreement or a term thereof, it is interpreted in accordance with the meaning attached by one of them if at the time the agreement was made

    (a) that party did not know of any different meaning attached by the other, and the other knew the meaning attached by the first party; or

    (b) that party had no reason to know of any different meaning attached by the other, and the other had reason to know the meaning attached by the first party.

(3) Except as stated in this Section, neither party is bound by the meaning attached by the other, even though the result may be a failure of mutual assent.

§ 202.   Rules in Aid of Interpretation

(1) Words and other conduct are interpreted in the light of all the circumstances, and if the principal purpose of the parties is ascertainable it is given great weight.

(2) A writing is interpreted as a whole, and all writings that are part of the same transaction are interpreted together.

(3) Unless a different intention is manifested,

    (a) where language has a generally prevailing meaning, it is interpreted in accordance with that meaning;

    (b) technical terms and words of art are given their technical meaning when used in a transaction within their technical field.

(4) Where an agreement involves repeated occasions for performance by either party with knowledge of the nature of the performance and opportunity for objection to it by the other, any course of performance accepted or acquiesced in without objection is given great weight in the interpretation of the agreement.

(5) Wherever reasonable, the manifestations of intention of the parties to a promise or agreement are interpreted as consistent with each other and with any relevant course of performance, course of dealing, or usage of trade.

§ 203. Standards of Preference in Interpretation

In the interpretation of a promise or agreement or a term thereof, the following standards of preference are generally applicable:

(a) an interpretation which gives a reasonable, lawful, and effective meaning to all the terms is preferred to an interpretation which leaves a part unreasonable, unlawful, or of no effect;

(b) express terms are given greater weight than course of performance, course of dealing, and usage of trade, course of performance is given greater weight than course of dealing or usage of trade, and course of dealing is given greater weight than usage of trade;

(c) specific terms and exact terms are given greater weight than general language;

(d) separately negotiated or added terms are given greater weight than standardized terms or other terms not separately negotiated.

§ 204. Supplying an Omitted Essential Term

When the parties to a bargain sufficiently defined to be a contract have not agreed with respect to a term which is essential to a determination of their rights and duties, a term which is reasonable in the circumstances is supplied by the court.

TOPIC 2. CONSIDERATIONS OF FAIRNESS AND THE PUBLIC INTEREST

§ 205. Duty of Good Faith and Fair Dealing

Every contract imposes upon each party a duty of good faith and fair dealing in its performance and its enforcement.

§ 208. Unconscionable Contract or Term

If a contract or term thereof is unconscionable at the time the contract is made a court may refuse to enforce the contract, or may enforce the remainder of the contract without the unconscionable term, or may so limit the application of any unconscionable term as to avoid any unconscionable result.

TOPIC 3. EFFECT OF ADOPTION OF A WRITING

§ 209. Integrated Agreements

(1) An integrated agreement is a writing or writings constituting a final expression of one or more terms of an agreement.

(2) Whether there is an integrated agreement is to be determined by the court as a question preliminary to determination of a question of interpretation or to application of the parol evidence rule.

(3) Where the parties reduce an agreement to a writing which in view of its completeness and specificity reasonably appears to be a complete agreement, it is taken to be an integrated agreement unless it is established by other evidence that the writing did not constitute a final expression.

§ 210. Completely and Partially Integrated Agreements

(1) A completely integrated agreement is an integrated agreement adopted by the parties as a complete and exclusive statement of the terms of the agreement.

(2) A partially integrated agreement is an integrated agreement other than a completely integrated agreement.

(3) Whether an agreement is completely or partially integrated is to be determined by the court as a question preliminary to determination of a question of interpretation or to application of the parol evidence rule.

§ 211. Standardized Agreements

(1) Except as stated in Subsection (3), where a party to an agreement signs or otherwise manifests assent to a writing and has reason to believe that like writings are regularly used to embody terms of agreements of the same type, he adopts the writing as an integrated agreement with respect to the terms included in the writing.

(2) Such a writing is interpreted wherever reasonable as treating alike all those similarly situated, without regard to their knowledge or understanding of the standard terms of the writing.

(3) Where the other party has reason to believe that the party manifesting such assent would not do so if he knew that the writing contained a particular term, the term is not part of the agreement.

§ 213. Effect of Integrated Agreement on Prior Agreements (Parol Evidence Rule)

(1) A binding integrated agreement discharges prior agreements to the extent that it is inconsistent with them.

(2) A binding completely integrated agreement discharges prior agreements to the extent that they are within its scope.

(3) An integrated agreement that is not binding or that is voidable and avoided does not discharge a prior agreement. But an integrated agreement, even though not binding, may be effective to render inoperative a term which would have been part of the agreement if it had not been integrated.

§ 214. Evidence of Prior or Contemporaneous Agreements and Negotiations

Agreements and negotiations prior to or contemporaneous with the adoption of a writing are admissible in evidence to establish

(a) that the writing is or is not an integrated agreement;

(b) that the integrated agreement, if any, is completely or partially integrated;

(c) the meaning of the writing, whether or not integrated;

(d) illegality, fraud, duress, mistake, lack of consideration, or other invalidating cause;

(e) ground for granting or denying rescission, reformation, specific performance, or other remedy.

§ 215. Contradiction of Integrated Terms

Except as stated in the preceding Section, where there is a binding agreement, either completely or partially integrated, evidence of prior or contemporaneous agreements or negotiations is not admissible in evidence to contradict a term of the writing.

§ 216. Consistent Additional Terms

(1) Evidence of a consistent additional term is admissible to supplement an integrated agreement unless the court finds that the agreement was completely integrated.

(2) An agreement is not completely integrated if the writing omits a consistent additional agreed term which is

(a) agreed to for separate consideration, or

(b) such a term as in the circumstances might naturally be omitted from the writing.

§ 217. Integrated Agreement Subject to Oral Requirement of a Condition

Where the parties to a written agreement agree orally that performance of the agreement is subject to the occurrence of a stated condition, the agreement is not integrated with respect to the oral condition.

TOPIC 5. CONDITIONS AND SIMILAR EVENTS

§ 224. Condition Defined

A condition is an event, not certain to occur, which must occur, unless its non-occurrence is excused, before performance under a contract becomes due.

§ 225. Effects of the Non-occurrence of a Condition

(1) Performance of a duty subject to a condition cannot become due unless the condition occurs or its non-occurrence is excused.

(2) Unless it has been excused, the non-occurrence of a condition discharges the duty when the condition can no longer occur.

(3) Non-occurrence of a condition is not a breach by a party unless he is under a duty that the condition occur.

§ 227. Standards of Preference With Regard to Conditions

(1) In resolving doubts as to whether an event is made a condition of an obligor's duty, and as to the nature of such an event, an interpretation is preferred that will reduce the obligee's risk of forfeiture, unless the event is within the obligee's control or the circumstances indicate that he has assumed the risk.

(2) Unless the contract is of a type under which only one party generally undertakes duties, when it is doubtful whether

>   (a) a duty is imposed on an obligee that an event occur, or

>   (b) the event is made a condition of the obligor's duty, or

>   (c) the event is made a condition of the obligor's duty and a duty is imposed on the obligee that the event occur,

the first interpretation is preferred if the event is within the obligee's control.

(3) In case of doubt, an interpretation under which an event is a condition of an obligor's duty is preferred over an interpretation under which the non-occurrence of the event is a ground for discharge of that duty after it has become a duty to perform.

§ 228. Satisfaction of the Obligor as a Condition

When it is a condition of an obligor's duty that he be satisfied with respect to the obligee's performance or with respect to something else, and it is practicable to determine whether a reasonable person in the position of the obligor would be satisfied, an interpretation is preferred under which the condition occurs if such a reasonable person in the position of the obligor would be satisfied.

§ 229. Excuse of a Condition to Avoid Forfeiture

To the extent that the non-occurrence of a condition would cause disproportionate forfeiture, a court may excuse the non-occurrence of that condition unless its occurrence was a material part of the agreed exchange.

CHAPTER 10.   PERFORMANCE AND NON–PERFORMANCE

TOPIC 1.   PERFORMANCES TO BE EXCHANGED UNDER AN EXCHANGE OF PROMISES

§ 231. Criterion for Determining When Performances Are to Be Exchanged Under an Exchange of Promises

Performances are to be exchanged under an exchange of promises if each promise is at least part of the consideration for the other and the performance of each promise is to be exchanged at least in part for the performance of the other.

§ 232. When it is Presumed That Performances Are to Be Exchanged Under an Exchange of Promises

Where the consideration given by each party to a contract consists in whole or in part of promises, all the performances to be rendered by each party taken collectively are treated as performances to be exchanged under an exchange of promises, unless a contrary intention is clearly manifested.

§ 234. Order of Performances

(1) Where all or part of the performances to be exchanged under an exchange of promises can be rendered simultaneously, they are to that extent due simultaneously, unless the language or the circumstances indicate the contrary.

(2) Except to the extent stated in Subsection (1), where the performance of only one party under such an exchange requires a period of time, his performance is due at an earlier time than that of the other party, unless the language or the circumstances indicate the contrary.

TOPIC 2.   EFFECT OF PERFORMANCE AND NON–PERFORMANCE

§ 236. Claims for Damages for Total and for Partial Breach

(1) A claim for damages for total breach is one for damages based on all of the injured party's remaining rights to performance.

(2) A claim for damages for partial breach is one for damages based on only part of the injured party's remaining rights to performance.

§ 237. Effect on Other Party's Duties of a Failure to Render Performance

Except as stated in § 240, it is a condition of each party's remaining duties to render performances to be exchanged under an exchange of promises that there be no uncured material failure by the other party to render any such performance due at an earlier time.

§ 238. Effect on Other Party's Duties of a Failure to Offer Performance

Where all or part of the performances to be exchanged under an exchange of promises are due simultaneously, it is a condition of each party's duties to render such performance that the other party either render or, with manifested present ability to do so, offer performance of his part of the simultaneous exchange.

§ 240. Part Performances as Agreed Equivalents

If the performances to be exchanged under an exchange of promises can be apportioned into corresponding pairs of part performances so that the parts of each pair are properly regarded as agreed equivalents, a party's performance of his part of such a pair has the same effect on the other's duties to render performance of the agreed equivalent as it would have if only that pair of performances had been promised.

§ 241. Circumstances Significant in Determining Whether a Failure Is Material

In determining whether a failure to render or to offer performance is material, the following circumstances are significant:

    (a) the extent to which the injured party will be deprived of the benefit which he reasonably expected;

    (b) the extent to which the injured party can be adequately compensated for the part of that benefit of which he will be deprived;

    (c) the extent to which the party failing to perform or to offer to perform will suffer forfeiture;

    (d) the likelihood that the party failing to perform or to offer to perform will cure his failure, taking account of all the circumstances including any reasonable assurances;

    (e) the extent to which the behavior of the party failing to perform or to offer to perform comports with standards of good faith and fair dealing.

Comment:

a. Nature of significant circumstances. The application of the rules stated in §§ 237 and 238 turns on a standard of materiality that is necessarily imprecise and flexible. (Contrast the situation where the parties have, by their agreement, made an event a condition. See § 226 and Comments a and c thereto and § 229.) The standard of materiality applies to contracts of all types and without regard to whether the whole performance of either party is to be rendered at one time or part performances are to be rendered at different times. See Uniform Commercial Code § 2–612. It also applies to pairs of agreed equivalents under § 240. See Illustration 2. It is to be applied in the light of the facts of each case in such a way as to further the purpose of securing for each party his expectation of an exchange of performances. This Section therefore states circumstances, not rules, which are to be considered in determining whether a particular failure is material. A determination that a failure is not material means only that it does not have the effect of the non-occurrence of a condition under §§ 237 and 238. Even if not material, the failure may be a breach and give rise to a claim for damages for partial breach (§§ 236, 243).

Illustrations:

1. A, a subcontractor, contracts to do excavation and earth moving on a housing subdivision project for B, the owner and general contractor, and to do all work "in a workmanlike manner." B is to make monthly progress payments for the work performed during the preceding month less a retainer of ten percent. A negligently damages a building with his bulldozer causing serious damage and denies any liability for B's loss. When B refuses to make further progress payments until A repairs the damage or admits liability, A notifies B that he cancels the contract. If the court determines that A's breach is material, A has no claim against

B. B has a claim against A for damages for breach of contract.

2. The facts being otherwise as stated in Illustration 6 to § 240, A completes the part concerned with the excavation and grading of lots and streets but fails in a minor respect to comply with the specifications. If a court determines that the failure is not material, A has a claim against B for $75,000 under the contract for the excavation and grading. B has a claim for damages against A for his failure fully to perform as to excavation and grading and also for his unjustified refusal to make street improvements.

b. Loss of benefit to injured party. Since the purpose of the rules stated in §§ 237 and 238 is to secure the parties' expectation of an exchange of performances, an important circumstance in determining whether a failure is material is the extent to which the injured party will be deprived of the benefit which he reasonably expected from the exchange (Subsection (a)). If the consideration given by either party consists partly of some performance and only partly of a promise (see Comment a to § 232), regard must be had to the entire exchange, including that performance, in applying this criterion. Although the relationship between the monetary loss to the injured party as a result of the failure and the contract price may be significant, no simple rule based on the ratio of the one to the other can be laid down, and here, as elsewhere under this Section, all relevant circumstances must be considered. In construction contracts, for example, defects affecting structural soundness are ordinarily regarded as particularly significant. In the sale of goods a particularly exacting standard has evolved. There it has long been established that, in the absence of a showing of a contrary intention, a buyer is entitled to expect strict performance of the contract, and Uniform Commercial Code § 2–601 carries forward this expectation by allowing the buyer to reject "if the goods or the tender of delivery fail in any respect to conform to the contract."The Code, however, compensates to some extent for the severity of this standard by extending the seller's right to cure beyond the point when the time for performance has expired in some instances (§ 2–508(2)), by allowing revocation of acceptance only if a nonconformity "substantially impairs" the value of the goods to the buyer (§ 2–608(1)), and by allowing the injured party to treat a nonconformity or default as to one installment under an installment contract as a breach of the whole only if it "substantially impairs" the value of the whole (§ 2–612(3)).

c. Adequacy of compensation for loss. The second circumstance, the extent to which the injured party can be adequately compensated for his loss of benefit (Subsection (b)), is a corollary of the first. Difficulty that he may have in proving with sufficient certainty the amount of that loss will affect the adequacy of compensation. If the failure is a breach, the injured party always has a claim for damages, and the question becomes one of the adequacy of that claim to compensate him for the lost benefit. Where the failure is not a breach, the question becomes one of the adequacy of any claim, such as one in restitution, to which the injured party may be entitled. This is a particularly important circumstance when the party in breach seeks specific performance. Such relief may be granted if damages can adequately compensate the injured party for the defect in performance. See Comment c to § 242.

d. Forfeiture by party who fails. Because a material failure acts as the non-occurrence of a condition, the same risk of forfeiture obtains as in the case of conditions generally if the party who fails to perform or tender has relied substantially on the expectation of the exchange, as through preparation or performance. Therefore a third circumstance is the extent to which the party failing to perform or to make an offer to perform will suffer forfeiture if the failure is treated as material. For this reason a failure is less likely to be regarded as material if it occurs late, after substantial preparation or performance, and more likely to be regarded as material if it occurs early, before such reliance. For the same reason the failure is more likely to be regarded as material if such preparation or performance as has taken place can be returned to and salvaged by the party failing to perform or tender, and less likely to be regarded as material if it cannot. These factors argue against a finding of material failure and in favor of one of substantial performance where a builder has completed performance under a construction contract and, because the building is on the owner's land, can salvage nothing if he is denied recovery of the balance of the price. Even in such a case, however, the potential forfeiture may be mitigated if the builder has a claim in restitution (§§ 370–77, especially § 374) or if he has already received progress payments under a provision of the contract. The same factors argue for a finding of material failure where a seller tenders goods and can salvage them by resale to others if they are rejected and he is denied recovery of the price. This helps to explain the severity of the rule as applied to the sale of goods. See Comment b. Even in such a case, however, the potential forfeiture may be aggravated if the seller has manufactured the goods specially for the buyer or has spent substantial sums in shipment.

Illustrations:

   3. A contracts to sell and B to buy 300 crates of Australian on-

ions, shipment to be from Australia in March. A has 300 crates ready for shipment in March, but government requisitions prevent him from loading more than 240 crates on the only ship available in March. B refuses to accept or pay for the onions when they are tendered. Under the circumstances stated in Subsections (a) and (c), A's failure is material and A has no claim against B. If A's failure is unjustified, B has a claim against A for damages for partial breach because of the delay even if A cures his failure, and has a claim against A for damages for total breach if A does not cure his failure (§ 243).

4. The facts being otherwise as stated in Illustration 2 to § 232, B can have the part of the street in front of his own lot paved for $500, but this will not give him the expected access to his lot because the rest of the street is not paved. Under the circumstances stated in Subsections (a), (b), and (c), the failure of performance is material and A has no claim against B. If A's failure is unjustified, B has a claim against A for damages for partial breach because of the delay even if A cures his failure, and has a claim against A for damages for total breach if A does not cure his failure (§ 243).

e. Uncertainty. A material failure by one party gives the other party the right to withhold further performance as a means of securing his expectation of an exchange of performances. To the extent that that expectation is already reasonably secure, in spite of the failure, there is less reason to conclude that the failure is material. The likelihood that the failure will be cured is therefore a significant circumstance in determining whether it is material (Subsection (d)). The fact that the injured party already has some security for the other party's performance argues against a determination that the failure is material. So do reasonable assurances of performance given by the other party after his failure. So does a shift in the market that makes performance of the contract more favorable to the other party. On the other hand, defaults by the other party under other contracts or as to other installments under the same contract argue for a determination of materiality. So does such financial weakness of the other party as suggests an inability to cure. This circumstance differs from the notion of reasonable grounds for insecurity (§ 251), in that the former can become relevant only after there has been an actual failure to perform or to tender. On discharge by repudiation, see § 253(2).

Illustration:

5. A contracts to sell and B to buy land for $25,000. B is to make a $5,000 down payment and pay the balance in four annual installments of $5,000 each. A is to proceed immediately to have abstracts of title prepared showing a marketable title and to deliver them prior to the time for payment of the first annual installment. Without explanation, A fails to have abstracts prepared for delivery prior to the time for payment of the first annual installment. B refuses to pay that installment. Under the circumstances stated in Subsections (a)-(d), the failure of performance is material and A has no claim against B. B has a claim against A for damages for partial breach based on the delay if A cures his failure and a claim for damages for total breach if he does not (§ 243).

f. Absence of good faith or fair dealing. A party's adherence to standards of good faith and fair dealing (§ 205) will not prevent his failure to perform a duty from amounting to a breach (§ 236(2)). Nor will his adherence to such standards necessarily prevent his failure from having the effect of the non-occurrence of a condition (§ 237; cf. § 238). The extent to which the behavior of the party failing to perform or to offer to perform comports with standards of good faith and fair dealing is, however, a significant circumstance in determining whether the failure is material (Subsection (e)). In giving weight to this factor courts have often used such less precise terms as "wilful. "Adherence to the standards stated in Subsection (e) is not conclusive, since other circumstances may cause a failure to be material in spite of such adherence. Nor is nonadherence conclusive, and other circumstances may cause a failure not to be material in spite of such non-adherence.

Illustrations:

6. A contracts to build a house for B, using pipe of Reading manufacture. In return, B agrees to pay $75,000, with provision for progress payments. Without B's knowledge, a subcontractor mistakenly uses pipe of Cohoes manufacture which is identical in quality and is distinguishable only by the name of the manufacturer which is stamped on it. The substitution is not discovered until the house is completed, when replacement of the pipe will require destruction of substantial parts of the house. B refuses to pay the unpaid balance of $10,000. Under the circumstances stated in Subsections (a), (c), and (e), the failure of performance is not material and A has a claim against B for the unpaid balance of $10,000, subject to a claim by B against A for damages for A's breach of his duty to use Reading pipe. See Illustration 1 to § 229.

7. A contracts to build a supermarket for B. In return B agrees to pay $250,000, with provision for progress payments. A completes performance except that, angered by a dispute over an unrelated transaction, he refuses to build a cover over a compressor. B can have the cover built by another builder for $300. B refuses to pay the unpaid balance of $40,000. In spite of the circumstances stated in Subsection (e), under the circumstances stated in Subsections (a), (b), and (c), the failure of performance is not material and A has a claim against B for the unpaid balance of $40,000, subject to a claim by B against A for damages for A's breach of his duty to build a cover over the compressor.

§ 242. Circumstances Significant in Determining When Remaining Duties Are Discharged

In determining the time after which a party's uncured material failure to render or to offer performance discharges the other party's remaining duties to render performance under the rules stated in §§ 237 and 238, the following circumstances are significant:

(a) those stated in § 241;

(b) the extent to which it reasonably appears to the injured party that delay may prevent or hinder him in making reasonable substitute arrangements;

(c) the extent to which the agreement provides for performance without delay, but a material failure to perform or to offer to perform on a stated day does not of itself discharge the other party's remaining duties unless the circumstances, including the language of the agreement, indicate that performance or an offer to perform by that day is important.

Comment:

a. Cure. Under §§ 237 and 238, a party's uncured material failure to perform or to offer to perform not only has the effect of suspending the other party's duties (§ 225(1)) but, when it is too late for the performance or the offer to perform to occur, the failure also has the effect of discharging those duties (§ 225(2)). Ordinarily there is some period of time between suspension and discharge, and during this period a party may cure his failure. Even then, since any breach gives rise to a claim, a party who has cured a material breach has still committed a breach, by his delay, for which he is liable in damages. Furthermore, in some instances timely performance is so essential that any delay immediately results in discharge and there is no period of time during which the injured party's duties are merely suspended and the other party can cure his failure.

b. Significant circumstances. This Section states circumstances which are to be considered in determining whether there is still time to cure a particular failure, or whether the period of time for discharge has expired. They are similar to the circumstances stated in the preceding section. The importance of delay to the injured party will depend on the extent to which it will deprive him of the benefit which he reasonably expected (§ 241(a)) and on the extent to which he can be adequately compensated (§ 241(b)). The extent of the forfeiture by the party failing to perform or to offer to perform (§ 241(c)) is also significant in determining the importance of delay.

The likelihood that the injured party's withholding of performance will induce the other party to cure his failure is particularly important (§ 241(d)), because the very reason for suspending rather than immediately discharging the injured party's duties is that this will induce cure. The reasonableness of the injured party's conduct in communicating his grievances and in seeking satisfaction is a factor to be considered in this connection. Where performance is to extend over a period of time, as where delivery of goods is to be in installments, so that a continuing relationship between the parties is contemplated, the injured party may be expected to give more opportunity for cure than in the case of an isolated exchange. On discharge by repudiation, see § 253(2). Finally, the nature of the behavior of the party failing to perform or to offer to perform may be considered here as under the preceding section (§ 241(e)).

Illustration:

1. The facts being otherwise as stated in Illustration 1 to § 237, B tenders the progress payment after a two-day delay along with damages for the delay. A refuses to accept the payment and resume work and notifies B that he cancels the contract. B's tender cured his breach before A's remaining duties to render performance were discharged, and B has a claim against A for total breach of contract, subject to a claim by A against B for damages for partial breach because of the delay.

c. Substitute arrangements. It is often said that in commercial transactions, notably those for the sale of goods, prompt performance by a party is essential if he is to be allowed to require the other to perform or, as it is sometimes put, "time is of the essence." The importance of prompt delivery by a seller of goods generally derives from the circumstance that goods, as contrasted for example with land, are particularly likely to be subject to rapid fluctuations in market price. Therefore, even a relatively short delay in a rising market may adversely affect the buyer by causing a sharp increase in the cost of "cover." See Uniform Commercial Code §§ 2–712, 2–713. A less rigid standard applies to contracts for the sale of goods to be delivered in installments or to be specially manufactured for the buyer. On the other hand, considerable delay does not preclude enforcement of a contract for the sale of land if damages are adequate to compensate for the delay and there are no special circumstances indicating that prompt performance was essential and no express provision requiring such performance. But these are all merely particular applications of a more general principle. Subsection (b) states that principle. Under any contract, the extent to which it reasonably appears to the injured party that delay may prevent or hinder him from making reasonable substitute arrangements is a consideration in determining the effect of delay. Cf. § 241(a), (b). As in the case of § 241 (see Comment c), a party in breach who seeks specific performance may be granted relief with compensation for the delay, in circumstances where he would have no claim for damages.

Illustrations:

2. A, a theater manager, contracts with B, an actress, for her performance for six months in a play that A is about to present. B becomes ill during the second month of the performance, and A immediately engages another actress to fill B's place during the remainder of the six months. B recovers at the end of ten days and offers to perform the remainder of the contract, but A refuses. Whether B's failure to render performance due to illness immediately discharges A's remaining duties of performance, instead of merely suspending them, depends on the circumstances stated in Subsection (b) and in § 241(b) and (d), and in particular on the possibility as it reasonably appears to A when B becomes ill of the illness being only temporary and of A's obtaining an adequate temporary substitute.

3. A contracts to sell and B to buy 1,000 shares of stock traded on a national securities exchange, delivery and payment to be on February 1. B offers to pay the price on February 1, but A unjustifiably and without explanation fails to offer to deliver the stock until February 2. B then refuses to accept the stock or pay the price. Under the circumstances stated in Subsection (b) and in § 241(a) and (c), the period of time has passed after which B's remaining duties to render performance are discharged because of A's material breach and A therefore has no claim against B. B has a claim against A for breach.

4. A contracts to sell and B to buy land, the transfer to be on February 1. B tenders the price on February 1, but A does not tender a deed until February 2. B then refuses to accept the deed or pay the price. Under the circumstances stated in Subsections (b) and (c) and in § 241(a), in the

absence of special circumstances, the period of time has not passed after which B's remaining duties to render performance are discharged. Although A's breach is material, it has been cured. A has a claim against B for damages for total breach of contract, subject to a claim by B against A for damages for partial breach because of the delay.

5. A agrees to sell and B to buy land, the transfer to be on February 1. A tenders a sufficient deed on February 1, but B explains that although he wants to carry out the contract he would like to have a few weeks more to raise the amount of the price. A replies that unless B tenders the price immediately he will not deliver the deed. On February 15, B sues for specific performance, offering in his pleading to pay the agreed price with interest to compensate A for the delay. In the circumstances stated in Subsection (b) and in § 241(a), (b), and (d), the period of time has not passed after which A's remaining duties to render performance are discharged. Although B's breach is material, the court may decree specific performance subject to B's tender of the price and payment by B of damages for partial breach to compensate A for the delay.

6. A contracts to sell and B to buy 5,000 tons of iron at a stated price, delivery to be in five monthly installments of 1,000 tons each on the first of each month and payment for each installment to be made on the tenth of that month. A makes the first three deliveries on the first of the month but, although the market price for iron is falling, he delays twelve days in making the fourth delivery, explaining to B that tempo-

rary labor troubles have caused the delay. B notifies A that he refuses to take or pay for the fourth delivery and that he cancels the contract. Whether the period of time has passed after which B's remaining duties to render performance are discharged, so that B's notification is not a repudiation, depends on the circumstances stated in Subsection (b) and in § 241(a), (b), (d), and (e). See Uniform Commercial Code § 2–612.

7. A contracts to sell and B to buy 5,000 tons of iron at a stated price, delivery to be in five monthly installments of 1,000 tons each on the first of each month and payment for each installment to be made on the tenth of that month. A makes the first four deliveries on the first of the month, and B makes the first three payments by the tenth but does not make the fourth payment. The market price for iron is falling and B gives no assurances or explanation for the delay. On the twentieth of the month A notifies B that he will make no further deliveries and that he cancels the contract. Whether the period of time has passed after which A's remaining duties to render performance are discharged, so that A's notification is not a repudiation, depends on the circumstances stated in Subsection (b) and in § 241(a), (b), (d), and (e). See Uniform Commercial Code § 2–612.

d. Effect of agreement. The agreement of the parties often contains a provision for the time of performance or tender. It may simply provide for performance on a stated date. In that event, a material breach on that date entitles the injured party to withhold his performance and gives him a claim for damages for delay, but it does not of itself discharge the other party's remaining duties. Only if the circumstances, viewed as of the time of the breach, indicate that performance or tender on that day is of genuine importance are the injured party's remaining duties discharged immediately, with no period of time during which they are merely suspended. It is, of course, open to the parties to make performance or tender by a stated date a condition by their agreement, in which event, absent excuse (see Comment b to § 225 and Comment c to § 229), delay beyond that date results in discharge (§ 225(2)). Such stock phrases as "time is of the essence" do not necessarily have this effect, although under Subsection (c) they are to be considered along with other circumstances in determining the effect of delay.

Illustrations:

8. A contracts to charter a vessel belonging to B and to pay stipulated freight "on condition that the vessel arrive in New York ready for loading by March 1." B promises that the vessel will arrive by that date and carry A's cargo. B unjustifiably fails to have the vessel in New York to be loaded until March 2. A refuses to load the vessel. Whether or not the period of time has passed after which B's uncured material failure would discharge A's remaining duties to render performance, A's duties are discharged under § 225(2) by the non-occurrence of an event that is made a condition by the agreement of the parties. B has no claim against A. A has a claim against B for damages for total breach.

9. The facts being otherwise as stated in Illustration 4, the parties use a printed form contract that provides that "time is of the essence." Absent other circumstances indicating that performance by February 1 is of genuine importance, A has a claim against B for damages for total breach of contract.

10. The facts being otherwise as stated in Illustration 4, the contract provides that A's rights are "conditional on his tendering a deed on or before February 1." A has no claim against B. But cf. Illustration 4 to § 229.

e. *Excuse and reinstatement.* Just as a party may under § 84 promise to perform in spite of the complete non-occurrence of a condition, he may under that section promise to perform in spite of a delay in its occurrence. If he places no limit on the delay, his power to impose a time limit by later notification of the other party is subject to the rules on reinstatement stated in § 84(2).

§ 243. Effect of a Breach by Non-performance as Giving Rise to a Claim for Damages for Total Breach

(1) With respect to performances to be exchanged under an exchange of promises, a breach by non-performance gives rise to a claim for damages for total breach only if it discharges the injured party's remaining duties to render such performance, other than a duty to render an agreed equivalent under § 240.

(2) Except as stated in Subsection (3), a breach by nonperformance accompanied or followed by a repudiation gives rise to a claim for damages for total breach.

(3) Where at the time of the breach the only remaining duties of performance are those of the party in breach and are for the payment of

money in installments not related to one another, his breach by non-performance as to less than the whole, whether or not accompanied or followed by a repudiation, does not give rise to a claim for damages for total breach.

(4) In any case other than those stated in the preceding subsections, a breach by non-performance gives rise to a claim for total breach only if it so substantially impairs the value of the contract to the injured party at the time of the breach that it is just in the circumstances to allow him to recover damages based on all his remaining rights to performance.

§ 245. Effect of a Breach by Non–Performance as Excusing the Non-occurrence of a Condition

Where a party's breach by non-performance contributes materially to the non-occurrence of a condition of one of his duties, the non-occurrence is excused.

§ 248. Effect of Insufficient Reason for Rejection as Excusing the Non-occurrence of a Condition

Where a party rejecting a defective performance or offer of performance gives an insufficient reason for rejection, the non-occurrence of a condition of his duty is excused only if he knew or had reason to know of that non-occurrence and then only to the extent that the giving of an insufficient reason substantially contributes to a failure by the other party to cure.

TOPIC 3. EFFECT OF PROSPECTIVE NON–PERFORMANCE

§ 250. When a Statement or an Act Is a Repudiation

A repudiation is

    (a) a statement by the obligor to the obligee indicating that the obligor will commit a breach that would of itself give the obligee a claim for damages for total breach under § 243, or

    (b) a voluntary affirmative act which renders the obligor unable or apparently unable to perform without such a breach.

§ 251. When a Failure to Give Assurance May Be Treated as a Repudiation

(1) Where reasonable grounds arise to believe that the obligor will commit a breach by non-performance that would of itself give the obligee a claim for damages for total breach under § 243, the obligee may demand adequate assurance of due performance and may, if reasonable, suspend any performance for which he has not already received the agreed exchange until he receives such assurance.

(2) The obligee may treat as a repudiation the obligor's failure to provide within a reasonable time such assurance of due performance as is adequate in the circumstances of the particular case.

§ 253. Effect of a Repudiation as a Breach and on Other Party's Duties

(1) Where an obligor repudiates a duty before he has committed a breach by non-performance and before he has received all of the agreed exchange for it, his repudiation alone gives rise to a claim for damages for total breach.

(2) Where performances are to be exchanged under an exchange of promises, one party's repudiation of a duty to render performance discharges the other party's remaining duties to render performance.

§ 256. Nullification of Repudiation or Basis for Repudiation

(1) The effect of a statement as constituting a repudiation under § 250 or the basis for a repudiation under § 251 is nullified by a retraction of the statement if notification of the retraction comes to the attention of the injured party before he materially changes his position in reliance on the repudiation or indicates to the other party that he considers the repudiation to be final.

(2) The effect of events other than a statement as constituting a repudiation under § 250 or the basis for a repudiation under § 251 is nullified if, to the knowledge of the injured party, those events have ceased to exist before he materially changes his position in reliance on the repudiation or indicates to the other party that he considers the repudiation to be final.

§ 257. Effect of Urging Performance in Spite of Repudiation

The injured party does not change the effect of a repudiation by urging the repudiator to perform in spite of his repudiation or to retract his repudiation.

CHAPTER 11. IMPRACTICABILITY OF PERFORMANCE AND FRUSTRATION OF PURPOSE

§ 261. Discharge by Supervening Impracticability

Where, after a contract is made, a party's performance is made impracticable without his fault by the occurrence of an event the non-occurrence of which was a basic assumption on which the contract was made, his duty to render that performance is discharged, unless the language or the circumstances indicate the contrary.

Comment:

a. Scope. Even though a party, in assuming a duty, has not qualified the language of his undertaking, a court may relieve him of that duty if performance has unexpectedly become impracticable as a result of a supervening event (see Introductory Note to this Chapter). This Section states the general principle under which a party's duty may be so discharged. The following three sections deal with the three categories of cases where this general principle has traditionally been applied: supervening death or incapacity of a person necessary for performance (§ 262), supervening destruction of a specific thing necessary for performance (§ 263), and supervening prohibition or prevention by law (§ 264). But, like Uniform Commercial Code § 2–615(a), this Section states a principle broadly applicable to all types of impracticability and it "deliberately refrains from any effort at an exhaustive expression of contingencies" (Comment 2 to Uniform Commercial Code § 2–615). The principle, like others in this Chapter, yields to a contrary agreement by which a party may assume a greater as well as a lesser obligation. By such an agreement, for example, a party may undertake to achieve a result irrespective of supervening events that may render its achievement impossible, and if he does so his non-performance is a breach even if it is caused by such an event. See Comment c. The rule stated in this Section applies only to discharge a duty to render a performance and does not affect a claim for breach that has already arisen. The effect of events subsequent to a breach on the amount of damages recoverable is governed by the rules on remedies stated in Chapter 16. See Comment e to § 347. Their effect on a claim for breach by anticipatory repudiation is governed by the rules on discharge stated in Chapter 12. Cases of existing, as opposed to supervening, impracticability are governed by § 266 rather than this Section.

b. Basic assumption. In order for a supervening event to discharge a duty under this Section, the non-occurrence of that event must have been a "basic assumption" on which both parties made the contract (see Introductory Note to this Chapter). This is the criterion used by Uniform Commercial Code § 2–615(a). Its application is simple enough in the cases of the death of a person or destruction of a specific thing necessary for performance. The continued existence of the person or thing (the non-occurrence of the death of destruction) is ordinarily a basic assumption on which the contract was made, so that death or destruction effects a discharge. Its application is also simple enough in the cases of market shifts or the financial inability of one of the parties. The continuation of existing market conditions and of the financial situation of the parties are ordinarily not such assumptions, so that mere market shifts or financial inability do not usually effect discharge under the rule stated in this Section. In borderline cases this criterion is sufficiently flexible to take account of factors that bear on a just allocation of risk. The fact that the event was foreseeable, or even foreseen, does not necessarily compel a conclusion that its non-occurrence was not a basic assumption. See Comment c to this Section and Comment a to § 265.

Illustrations:

1. On June 1, A agrees to sell and B to buy goods to be delivered in October at a designated port. The port is subsequently closed by quarantine regulations during the entire month of October, no commercially reasonable substitute

performance is available (see Uniform Commercial Code § 2–614(1)), and A fails to deliver the goods. A's duty to deliver the goods is discharged, and A is not liable to B for breach of contract.

2. A contracts to produce a movie for B. As B knows, A's only source of funds is a $100,000 deposit in C bank. C bank fails, and A does not produce the movie. A's duty to produce the movie is not discharged, and A is liable to B for breach of contract.

3. A and B make a contract under which B is to work for A for two years at a salary of $50,000 a year. At the end of one year, A discontinues his business because governmental regulations have made it unprofitable and fires B. A's duty to employ B is not discharged, and A is liable to B for breach of contract.

4. A contracts to sell and B to buy a specific machine owned by A to be delivered on July 30. On July 29, as a result of a creditor's suit against A, a receiver is appointed and takes charge of all of A's assets, and A does not deliver the goods on July 30. A's duty to deliver the goods is not discharged, and A is liable to B for breach of contract.

c. Contrary indication. A party may, by appropriate language, agree to perform in spite of impracticability that would otherwise justify his nonperformance under the rule stated in this Section. He can then be held liable for damages although he cannot perform. Even absent an express agreement, a court may decide, after considering all the circumstances, that a party impliedly assumed such a greater obligation. In this respect the rule stated in this Section parallels that of Uniform Commercial Code § 2–615, which applies "Except so far as a seller may have assumed a greater obligation. . . . " Circumstances relevant in deciding whether a party has assumed a greater obligation include his ability to have inserted a provision in the contract expressly shifting the risk of impracticability to the other party. This will depend on the extent to which the agreement was standardized (cf. § 211), the degree to which the other party supplied the terms (cf. § 206), and, in the case of a particular trade or other group, the frequency with which language so allocating the risk is used in that trade or group (cf. § 219). The fact that a supplier has not taken advantage of his opportunity expressly to shift the risk of a shortage in his supply by means of contract language may be regarded as more significant where he is middleman, with a variety of sources of supply and an opportunity to spread the risk among many customers on many transactions by slight adjustment of his prices, than where he is a producer with a limited source of supply, few outlets, and no comparable opportunity. A commercial practice under which a party might be expected to insure or otherwise secure himself against a risk also militates against shifting it to the other party. If the supervening event was not reasonably foreseeable when the contract was made, the party claiming discharge can hardly be expected to have provided against its occurrence. However, if it was reasonably foreseeable, or even foreseen, the opposite conclusion does not necessarily follow. Factors such as the practical difficulty of reaching agreement on the myriad of conceivable terms of a complex agreement may excuse a failure to deal with improbable contingencies. See Comment b to this Section and Comment a to § 265.

Illustration:

5. A, who has had many years of experience in the field of salvage,

contracts to raise and float B's boat, which has run aground. The contract, prepared by A, contains no clause limiting A's duty in the case of unfavorable weather, unforeseen circumstances, or otherwise. The boat then slips into deep water and fills with mud, making it impracticable for A to raise it. If the court concludes, on the basis of such circumstances as A's experience and the absence of any limitation in the contract that A prepared, that A assumed an absolute duty, it will decide that A's duty to raise and float the boat is not discharged and that A is liable to B for breach of contract.

d. Impracticability. Events that come within the rule stated in this Section are generally due either to "acts of God" or to acts of third parties. If the event that prevents the obligor's performance is caused by the obligee, it will ordinarily amount to a breach by the latter and the situation will be governed by the rules stated in Chapter 10, without regard to this Section. See Illustrations 4–7 to § 237. If the event is due to the fault of the obligor himself, this Section does not apply. As used here "fault" may include not only "willful" wrongs, but such other types of conduct as that amounting to breach of contract or to negligence. See Comment 1 to Uniform Commercial Code § 2–613. Although the rule stated in this Section is sometimes phrased in terms of "impossibility," it has long been recognized that it may operate to discharge a party's duty even though the event has not made performance absolutely impossible. This Section, therefore, uses "impracticable," the term employed by Uniform Commercial Code § 2–615(a), to describe the required extent of the impediment to performance. Performance may be impracticable because extreme and unreasonable difficulty, expense, injury, or loss to one of the

parties will be involved. A severe shortage of raw materials or of supplies due to war, embargo, local crop failure, unforeseen shutdown of major sources of supply, or the like, which either causes a marked increase in cost or prevents performance altogether may bring the case within the rule stated in this Section. Performance may also be impracticable because it will involve a risk of injury to person or to property, of one of the parties or of others, that is disproportionate to the ends to be attained by performance. However, "impracticability" means more than "impracticality." A mere change in the degree of difficulty or expense due to such causes as increased wages, prices of raw materials, or costs of construction, unless well beyond the normal range, does not amount to impracticability since it is this sort of risk that a fixed-price contract is intended to cover. Furthermore, a party is expected to use reasonable efforts to surmount obstacles to performance (see § 205), and a performance is impracticable only if it is so in spite of such efforts.

Illustrations:

6. A contracts to repair B's grain elevator. While A is engaged in making repairs, a fire destroys the elevator without A's fault, and A does not finish the repairs. A's duty to repair the elevator is discharged, and A is not liable to B for breach of contract. See Illustration 3 to § 263.

7. A contracts with B to carry B's goods on his ship to a designated foreign port. A civil war then unexpectedly breaks out in that country and the rebels announce that they will try to sink all vessels bound for that port. A refuses to perform. Although A did not contract to sail on the vessel, the risk of injury to others is sufficient

to make A's performance impracticable. A's duty to carry the goods to the designated port is discharged, and A is not liable to B for breach of contract. Compare Illustration 5 to § 262.

8. The facts being otherwise as stated in Illustration 7, the rebels announce merely that they will confiscate all vessels found in the designated port. The goods can be bought and sold on markets throughout the world. A refuses to perform. Although there is no risk of injury to persons, the court may conclude that the risk of injury to property is disproportionate to the ends to be attained. A's duty to carry the goods to the designated port is then discharged, and A is not liable to B for breach of contract. If, however, B is a health organization and the goods are scarce medical supplies vital to the health of the population of the designated port, the court may conclude that the risk is not disproportionate to the ends to be attained and may reach a contrary decision.

9. Several months after the nationalization of the Suez Canal, during the international crisis resulting from its seizure, A contracts to carry a cargo of B's wheat on A's ship from Galveston, Texas to Bandar Shapur, Iran for a flat rate. The contract does not specify the route, but the voyage would normally be through the Straits of Gibraltar and the Suez Canal, a distance of 10,000 miles. A month later, and several days after the ship has left Galveston, the Suez Canal is closed by an outbreak of hostilities, so that the only route to Bandar Shapur is the longer 13,000 mile voyage around the Cape of Good Hope. A refuses to complete the voyage unless B

pays additional compensation. A's duty to carry B's cargo is not discharged, and A is liable to B for breach of contract.

10. The facts being otherwise as in Illustration 9, the Suez Canal is closed while A's ship is in the Canal, preventing the completion of the voyage. A's duty to carry B's cargo is discharged, and A is not liable to B for breach of contract.

11. A contracts to construct and lease to B a gasoline service station. A valid zoning ordinance is subsequently enacted forbidding the construction of such a station but permitting variances in appropriate cases. A, in breach of his duty of good faith and fair dealing (§ 205), makes no effort to obtain a variance, although variances have been granted in similar cases, and fails to construct the station. A's performance has not been made impracticable. A's duty to construct is not discharged, and A is liable to B for breach of contract.

e. *"Subjective" and "objective" impracticability.* It is sometimes said that the rule stated in this Section applies only when the performance itself is made impracticable, without regard to the particular party who is to perform. The difference has been described as that between "the thing cannot be done" and "I cannot do it," and the former has been characterized as "objective "and the latter as "subjective." This Section recognizes that if the performance remains practicable and it is merely beyond the party's capacity to render it, he is ordinarily not discharged, but it does not use the terms "objective" and "subjective" to express this. Instead, the rationale is that a party generally assumes the risk of his own inability to perform his duty. Even if a party contracts to render a performance that depends on some act by a third party, he is not ordinarily discharged because of a failure by that party because this is also a risk that is commonly understood to be on the obligor. See Comment c. But see Comment a to § 262.

Illustrations:

12. A, a milkman, and B, a dairy farmer, make a contract under which B is to sell and A to buy all of A's requirements of milk, but not less than 200 quarts a day, for one year. B may deliver milk from any source but expects to deliver milk from his own herd. B's herd is destroyed because of hoof and mouth disease and he fails to deliver any milk. B's duty to deliver milk is not discharged, and B is liable to A for breach of contract. See Illustration 1 to § 263; compare Illustration 7 to § 263.

13. A contracts to sell and B to buy on credit 1,500,000 gallons of molasses "of the usual run from the C sugar refinery." C delivers molasses to others but fails to deliver any to A, and A fails to deliver any to B. A's duty to deliver molasses is not discharged, and A is liable to B for breach of contract. If A has a contract with C, C may be liable to A for breach of contract.

14. A, a general contractor, is bidding on a construction contract with B which gives B the right to disapprove the choice of subcontractors. A makes a contract with C, a subcontractor, under which, if B awards A the contract, A will obtain B's approval of C and C will do the excavation for A. A is awarded the contract by B, but B disapproves A's choice of C, and A has the excavation work done by another subcontractor. A's duty to have C do the excavation is not

discharged, and A is liable to C for breach of contract.

f. Alternative performances. A contract may permit a party to choose to perform in one of several different ways, any of which will discharge his duty. Where the duty is to render such an alternative performance, the fact that one or more of the alternatives has become impracticable will not discharge the party's duty to perform if at least one of them remains practicable. The form of the promise is not controlling, however, and not every promise that is expressed in alternative form gives rise to a duty to render an alternative performance. For example, a surety's undertaking that either the principal will perform or the surety will compensate the creditor does not ordinarily impose such a duty. See Restatement of Security § 117. Nor does a promise either to render a performance or pay liquidated damages impose such a duty. Furthermore, a duty that is originally one to render alternative performances ceases to be such a duty if all but one means of performance have been foreclosed, as by the lapse of time or the occurrence of a condition including election by the obligor, or on the grounds of public policy (Chapter 8) or unconscionability (§ 208).

Illustrations:

15. On June 1, A contracts to sell and B to buy whichever of three specified machines A chooses to deliver on October 1. Two of the machines are destroyed by fire on July 1, and A fails to deliver the third on October 1. A's duty to deliver a machine is not discharged, and A is liable to B for breach of contract. If all three machines had been destroyed, A's duty to deliver a machine would have been discharged, and A would not have been liable to B

for breach of contract. See Uniform Commercial Code § 2–613.

16. A contracts to repair B's building. The contract contains a valid provision requiring A to pay liquidated damages if he fails to make any of the repairs. S is surety for A's performance. Before A is able to begin, B's building is destroyed by fire. Neither A's nor S's duty is one to render an alternative performance. A's duty to repair the building is discharged, and A is not liable to B for liquidated damages or otherwise for breach of contract. S's duty as surety for A is also discharged, and S is not liable to B for breach of contract.

§ 265. Discharge by Supervening Frustration

Where, after a contract is made, a party's principal purpose is substantially frustrated without his fault by the occurrence of an event the non-occurrence of which was a basic assumption on which the contract was made, his remaining duties to render performance are discharged, unless the language or the circumstances indicate the contrary.

§ 272. Relief Including Restitution

(1) In any case governed by the rules stated in this Chapter, either party may have a claim for relief including restitution under the rules stated in §§ 240 and 377.

(2) In any case governed by the rules stated in this Chapter, if those rules together with the rules stated in Chapter 16 will not avoid injustice, the court may grant relief on such terms as justice requires including protection of the parties' reliance interests.

CHAPTER 14. CONTRACT BENEFICIARIES

§ 302. Intended and Incidental Beneficiaries

(1) Unless otherwise agreed between promisor and promisee, a beneficiary of a promise is an intended beneficiary if recognition of a right to performance in the beneficiary is appropriate to effectuate the intention of the parties and either

>   (a) the performance of the promise will satisfy an obligation of the promisee to pay money to the beneficiary; or

>   (b) the circumstances indicate that the promisee intends to give the beneficiary the benefit of the promised performance.

(2) An incidental beneficiary is a beneficiary who is not an intended beneficiary.

§ 309. Defenses Against the Beneficiary

(1) A promise creates no duty to a beneficiary unless a contract is formed between the promisor and the promisee; and if a contract is

voidable or unenforceable at the time of its formation the right of any beneficiary is subject to the infirmity.

(2) If a contract ceases to be binding in whole or in part because of impracticability, public policy, non-occurrence of a condition, or present or prospective failure of performance, the right of any beneficiary is to that extent discharged or modified.

(3) Except as stated in Subsections (1) and (2) and in § 311 or as provided by the contract, the right of any beneficiary against the promisor is not subject to the promisor's claims or defenses against the promisee or to the promisee's claims or defenses against the beneficiary.

(4) A beneficiary's right against the promisor is subject to any claim or defense arising from his own conduct or agreement.

§ 311. Variation of a Duty to a Beneficiary

(1) Discharge or modification of a duty to an intended beneficiary by conduct of the promisee or by a subsequent agreement between promisor and promisee is ineffective if a term of the promise creating the duty so provides.

(2) In the absence of such a term, the promisor and promisee retain power to discharge or modify the duty by subsequent agreement.

(3) Such a power terminates when the beneficiary, before he receives notification of the discharge or modification, materially changes his position in justifiable reliance on the promise or brings suit on it or manifests assent to it at the request of the promisor or promisee.

(4) If the promisee receives consideration for an attempted discharge or modification of the promisor's duty which is ineffective against the beneficiary, the beneficiary can assert a right to the consideration so received. The promisor's duty is discharged to the extent of the amount received by the beneficiary.

§ 313. Government Contracts

(1) The rules stated in this Chapter apply to contracts with a government or governmental agency except to the extent that application would contravene the policy of the law authorizing the contract or prescribing remedies for its breach.

(2) In particular, a promisor who contracts with a government or governmental agency to do an act for or render a service to the public is not subject to contractual liability to a member of the public for consequential damages resulting from performance or failure to perform unless

    (a) the terms of the promise provide for such liability; or

    (b) the promisee is subject to liability to the member of the public for the damages and a direct action against the promisor is consistent with the terms of the contract and with the policy of the law authorizing the contract and prescribing remedies for its breach.

CHAPTER 15.   ASSIGNMENT AND DELEGATION

TOPIC 1.   WHAT CAN BE ASSIGNED OR DELEGATED

§ 317. Assignment of a Right

(1) An assignment of a right is a manifestation of the assignor's intention to transfer it by virtue of which the assignor's right to performance by the obligor is extinguished in whole or in part and the assignee acquires a right to such performance.

(2) A contractual right can be assigned unless

   (a) the substitution of a right of the assignee for the right of the assignor would materially change the duty of the obligor, or materially increase the burden or risk imposed on him by his contract, or materially impair his chance of obtaining return performance, or materially reduce its value to him, or

   (b) the assignment is forbidden by statute or is otherwise inoperative on grounds of public policy, or

   (c) assignment is validly precluded by contract.

§ 318. Delegation of Performance of Duty

(1) An obligor can properly delegate the performance of his duty to another unless the delegation is contrary to public policy or the terms of his promise.

(2) Unless otherwise agreed, a promise requires performance by a particular person only to the extent that the obligee has a substantial interest in having that person perform or control the acts promised.

(3) Unless the obligee agrees otherwise, neither delegation of performance nor a contract to assume the duty made with the obligor by the person delegated discharges any duty or liability of the delegating obligor.

§ 322. Contractual Prohibition of Assignment

(1) Unless the circumstances indicate the contrary, a contract term prohibiting assignment of "the contract" bars only the delegation to an assignee of the performance by the assignor of a duty or condition.

(2) A contract term prohibiting assignment of rights under the contract, unless a different intention is manifested,

(a) does not forbid assignment of a right to damages for breach of the whole contract or a right arising out of the assignor's due performance of his entire obligation;

(b) gives the obligor a right to damages for breach of the terms forbidding assignment but does not render the assignment ineffective;

(c) is for the benefit of the obligor, and does not prevent the assignee from acquiring rights against the assignor or the obligor from discharging his duty as if there were no such prohibition.

TOPIC 4.   EFFECT ON THE OBLIGOR'S DUTY

§ 336. Defenses Against an Assignee

(1) By an assignment the assignee acquires a right against the obligor only to the extent that the obligor is under a duty to the assignor; and if the right of the assignor would be voidable by the obligor or unenforceable against him if no assignment had been made, the right of the assignee is subject to the infirmity.

(2) The right of an assignee is subject to any defense or claim of the obligor which accrues before the obligor receives notification of the assignment, but not to defenses or claims which accrue thereafter except as stated in this Section or as provided by statute.

(3) Where the right of an assignor is subject to discharge or modification in whole or in part by impossibility, illegality, non-occurrence of a condition, or present or prospective failure of performance by an obligee, the right of the assignee is to that extent subject to discharge or modification even after the obligor receives notification of the assignment.

(4) An assignee's right against the obligor is subject to any defense or claim arising from his conduct or to which he was subject as a party or a prior assignee because he had notice.

CHAPTER 16.   REMEDIES

TOPIC 1. IN GENERAL

§ 344. Purposes of Remedies

Judicial remedies under the rules stated in this Restatement serve to protect one or more of the following interests of a promisee:

(a) his "expectation interest," which is his interest in having the benefit of his bargain by being put in as good a position as he would have been in had the contract been performed,

(b) his "reliance interest," which is his interest in being reimbursed for loss caused by reliance on the contract by being put in as good a position as he would have been in had the contract not been made, or

(c) his "restitution interest," which is his interest in having restored to him any benefit that he has conferred on the other party.

TOPIC 2.   ENFORCEMENT BY AWARD OF DAMAGES

§ 347.   Measure of Damages in General

Subject to the limitations stated in §§ 350–53, the injured party has a right to damages based on his expectation interest as measured by

(a) the loss in the value to him of the other party's performance caused by its failure or deficiency, plus

(b) any other loss, including incidental or consequential loss, caused by the breach, less

(c) any cost or other loss that he has avoided by not having to perform.

§ 348.   Alternatives to Loss in Value of Performance

(1) If a breach delays the use of property and the loss in value to the injured party is not proved with reasonable certainty, he may recover damages based on the rental value of the property or on interest on the value of the property.

(2) If a breach results in defective or unfinished construction and the loss in value to the injured party is not proved with sufficient certainty, he may recover damages based on

(a) the diminution in the market price of the property caused by the breach, or

(b) the reasonable cost of completing performance or of remedying the defects if that cost is not clearly disproportionate to the probable loss in value to him.

(3) If a breach is of a promise conditioned on a fortuitous event and it is uncertain whether the event would have occurred had there been no breach, the injured party may recover damages based on the value of the conditional right at the time of breach.

§ 349.   Damages Based on Reliance Interest

As an alternative to the measure of damages stated in § 347, the injured party has a right to damages based on his reliance interest, including expenditures made in preparation for performance or in performance, less any loss that the party in breach can prove with reasonable certainty the injured party would have suffered had the contract been performed.

§ 350. Avoidability as a Limitation on Damages

(1) Except as stated in Subsection (2), damages are not recoverable for loss that the injured party could have avoided without undue risk, burden or humiliation.

(2) The injured party is not precluded from recovery by the rule stated in Subsection (1) to the extent that he has made reasonable but unsuccessful efforts to avoid loss.

§ 351. Unforeseeability and Related Limitations on Damages

(1) Damages are not recoverable for loss that the party in breach did not have reason to foresee as a probable result of the breach when the contract was made.

(2) Loss may be foreseeable as a probable result of a breach because it follows from the breach

>   (a) in the ordinary course of events, or

>   (b) as a result of special circumstances beyond the ordinary course of events, that the party in breach had reason to know.

(3) A court may limit damages for foreseeable loss by excluding recovery for loss of profits, by allowing recovery only for loss incurred in reliance, or otherwise if it concludes that in the circumstances justice so requires in order to avoid disproportionate compensation.

Comment:

a. Requirement of foreseeability. A contracting party is generally expected to take account of those risks that are foreseeable at the time he makes the contract. He is not, however, liable in the event of breach for loss that he did not at the time of contracting have reason to foresee as a probable result of such a breach. The mere circumstance that some loss was foreseeable, or even that some loss of the same general kind was foreseeable, will not suffice if the loss that actually occurred was not foreseeable. It is enough, however, that the loss was foreseeable as a probable, as distinguished from a necessary, result of his breach. Furthermore, the party in breach need not have made a "tacit agreement" to be liable for the loss. Nor must he have had the loss in mind when making the contract, for the test is an objective one based on what he had reason to foresee. There is no requirement of foreseeability with respect to the injured party. In spite of these qualifications, the requirement of foreseeability is a more severe limitation of liability than is the requirement of substantial or "proximate" cause in the case of an action in tort or for breach of warranty. Compare Restatement, Second, Torts § 431; Uniform Commercial Code § 2–715(2)(b). Although the recovery that is precluded by the limitation of foreseeability is usually based on the expectation interest and takes the form of lost profits (see Illustration 1), the limitation may also preclude recovery based on the reliance interest (see Illustration 2).

Illustrations:

1. A, a carrier, contracts with B, a miller, to carry B's broken crankshaft to its manufacturer for repair. B tells A when they make the contract that the crankshaft is part of B's milling machine and that it must be sent at once, but not that the mill is stopped because B has no replacement. Because A delays in carrying the crankshaft, B loses profit during an additional period while the mill is stopped because of the delay. A is not liable for B's loss of profit. That loss was not foreseeable by A as a probable result of the breach at the time the contract was made because A did not know that the broken crankshaft was necessary for the operation of the mill.

2. A contracts to sell land to B and to give B possession on a stated date. Because A delays a short time in giving B possession, B incurs unusual expenses in providing for cattle that he had already purchased to stock the land as a ranch. A had no reason to know when they made the contract that B had planned to purchase cattle for this purpose. A is not liable for B's expenses in providing for the cattle because that loss was not foreseeable by A as a probable result of the breach at the time the contract was made.

b. "General" and "special" damages. Loss that results from a breach in the ordinary course of events is foreseeable as the probable result of the breach. See Uniform Commercial Code § 2–714(1). Such loss is sometimes said to be the "natural" result of the breach, in the sense that its occurrence accords with the common experience of ordinary persons. For example, a seller of a commodity to a wholesaler usually has reason to foresee that his failure to deliver the commodity as agreed will probably cause the wholesaler to lose a reasonable profit on it. See Illustrations 3 and 4. Similarly, a seller of a machine to a manufacturer usually has reason to foresee that his delay in delivering the machine as agreed will probably cause the manufacturer to lose a reasonable profit from its use, although courts have been somewhat more cautious in allowing the manufacturer recovery for loss of such profits than in allowing a middleman recovery for loss of profits on an intended resale. See Illustration 5. The damages recoverable for such loss that results in the ordinary course of events are sometimes called "general" damages.

If loss results other than in the ordinary course of events, there can be no recovery for it unless it was foreseeable by the party in breach because of special circumstances that he had reason to know when he made the contract. See Uniform Commercial Code § 2–715(2)(a). For example, a seller who fails to deliver a commodity to a wholesaler is not liable for the wholesaler's loss of profit to the extent that it is extraordinary nor for his loss due to unusual terms in his resale contracts unless the seller had reason to know of these special circumstances. See Illustration 6. Similarly, a seller who delays in delivering a machine to a manufacturer is not liable for the manufacturer's loss of profit to the extent that it results from an intended use that was abnormal unless the seller had reason to know of this special circumstance. See Illustration 7. In the case of a written agreement, foreseeability is sometimes established by the use of recitals in the agreement itself. The parol evidence rule (§ 213) does not, however, preclude the use of negotiations prior to the making of the contract to show for this purpose circumstances that were then known to a party. The damages recoverable for loss that results other than in the ordinary course of events are sometimes called "special" or "consequential "damages. These terms are often misleading, however, and it is not necessary to distinguish between "general" and "special" or "consequential" damages for the purpose of the rule stated in this Section.

Illustrations:

3. A and B make a written contract under which A is to recondition by a stated date a used machine owned by B so that it will be suitable for sale by B to C. A knows when they make the contract that B has contracted to sell the machine to C but knows nothing of the terms of B's contract with C. Because A delays in returning the machine to B, B is unable to sell it to C and loses the profit that he would have made on that sale. B's loss of reasonable profit was foreseeable by A as a probable result of the breach at the time the contract was made.

4. A, a manufacturer of machines, contracts to make B his exclusive selling agent in a specified area for the period of a year. Because A fails to deliver any machines, B loses the profit on contracts that he would have made for their resale. B's loss of reasonable profit was foreseeable by A as a probable result of the breach at the time the contract was made.

5. A and B make a contract under which A is to recondition by a stated date a used machine owned by B so that it will be suitable for use in B's canning factory. A knows that the machine must be reconditioned by that date if B's factory is to operate at full capaci-

ty during the canning season, but nothing is said of this in the written contract. Because A delays in returning the machine to B, B loses its use for the entire canning season and loses the profit that he would have made had his factory operated at full capacity. B's loss of reasonable profit was foreseeable by A as a probable result of the breach at the time the contract was made.

6. The facts being otherwise as stated in Illustration 3, the profit that B would have made under his contract with A was extraordinarily large because C promised to pay an exceptionally high price as a result of a special need for the machine of which A was unaware. A is not liable for B's loss of profit to the extent that it exceeds what would ordinarily result from such a contract. To that extent the loss was not foreseeable by A as a probable result of the breach at the time the contract was made

7. The facts being otherwise as stated in Illustration 5, the profit that B would have made from the use of the machine was unusually large because of an abnormal use to which he planned to put it of which A was unaware. A is not liable for B's loss of profit to the extent that it exceeds what would ordinarily result from the use of such a machine. To that extent the loss was not foreseeable by A at the time the contract was made as a probable result of the breach.

c. Litigation or settlement caused by breach. Sometimes a breach of contract results in claims by third persons against the injured party. The party in breach is liable for the amount of any judgment against the injured party together with his reasonable expenditures in the litigation, if the party in breach had reason to foresee such expenditures as the probable result of his breach at the time he made the contract. See Illustrations 8, 10, 11 and 12. This is so even if the judgment in the litigation is based on a liquidated damage clause in the injured party's contract with the third party. See Illustration 8. A failure to notify the party in breach in advance of the litigation may prevent the result of the litigation from being conclusive as to him. But to the extent that the injured party's loss resulting from litigation is reasonable, the fact that the party in breach was not notified does not prevent the inclusion of that loss in the damages assessed against him. In furtherance of the policy favoring private settlement of disputes, the injured party is also allowed to recover the reasonable amount of any settlement made to avoid litigation, together with the costs of settlement. See Illustration 9.

Illustrations:

8. The facts being otherwise as stated in Illustration 3, B not only loses the profit that he would have made on sale of the machine to C, but is held liable for damages in an action brought by C for breach of contract. The damages paid to C and B's reasonable expenses in defending the action were also foreseeable by A as a probable result of the breach at the time he made the contract with B. The result is the same even though they were based on a liquidated damage clause in the contract between B and C if A knew of the clause or if the use of such a clause in the contract between B and C was foreseeable by A at the time he made the contract with B.

9. The facts being otherwise as stated in Illustration 3, B not only loses the profit that he would have made on sale of the machine to C, but settles with C by paying C a reasonable sum of money to avoid litigation. The amount of the settlement paid to C and B's reasonable expenses in settling were also foreseeable by A at the time he made the contract with B as a probable result of the breach.

10. A contracts to supply B with machinery for unloading cargo. A, in breach of contract, furnishes defective machinery, and C, an employee of B, is injured. C sues B and gets a judgment, which B pays. The amount of the judgment and B's reasonable expenditures in defending the action were foreseeable by A at the time the contract was made as a probable result of the breach.

11. A contracts to procure a right of way for B, for a railroad. Because A, in breach of contract, fails to do this, B has to acquire the right of way by condemnation proceedings. B's reasonable expenditures in those proceedings were foreseeable by A at the time the contract was made as a probable result of the breach.

12. A leases land to B with a covenant for quiet enjoyment. C brings an action of ejectment against B and gets judgment. B's reasonable expenditures in defending the action were foreseeable by A as the probable result of the breach at the time the contract was made.

d. Unavailability of substitute. If several circumstances have contributed to cause a loss, the party in breach is not liable for it unless he had reason to foresee all of them. Sometimes a loss would not have occurred if the injured party had been able to make substitute arrangements after breach, as, for example, by "cover" through purchase of substitute goods in the case of a buyer of goods (see Uniform Commercial Code § 2–712). If the inability of the injured party to make such arrangements was foreseeable by the party in breach at the time he made the contract, the resulting loss was foreseeable. See Illustration 13. On the impact of this principle on contracts to lend money, see Comment e.

Illustration:

> 13. A contracts with B, a farmer, to lease B a machine to be used harvesting B's crop, delivery to be made on July 30. A knows when he makes the contract that B's crop will be ready on that date and that B cannot obtain another machine elsewhere. Because A delays delivery until August 10, B's crop is damaged and he loses profit. B's loss of profit was foreseeable by A at the time the contract was made as a probable result of the breach.

e. Breach of contract to lend money. The limitation of foreseeability is often applied in actions for damages for breach of contracts to lend money. Because credit is so widely available, a lender often has no reason to foresee at the time the contract is made that the borrower will be unable to make substitute arrangements in the event of breach. See Comment d. In most cases, then, the lender's liability will be limited to the relatively small additional amount that it would ordinarily cost to get a similar loan from another lender. However, in the less common situation in which the lender has reason to foresee that the borrower will be unable to borrow elsewhere or will be delayed in borrowing elsewhere, the lender may be liable for much heavier damages based on the borrower's inability to take advantage of a specific opportunity (see Illustration 14), his having to postpone or abandon a profitable project (see Illustration 15), or

his forfeiture of security for failure to make prompt payment (see Illustration 16).

Illustrations:

> 14. A contracts to lend B $100,000 for one year at eight percent interest for the stated purpose of buying a specific lot of goods for resale. B can resell the goods at a $20,000 profit. A delays in making the loan, and although B can borrow money on the market at ten percent interest, he is unable to do so in time and loses the opportunity to buy the goods. Unless A had reason to foresee at the time that he made the contract that such a delay in making the loan would probably cause B to lose the opportunity, B can only recover damages based on two percent of the amount of the loan.
>
> 15. A contracts to lend $1,000,000 to B for the stated purpose of enabling B to build a building and takes property of B as security. After construction is begun, A refuses to make the loan or release the security. Because B lacks further security, he is unable to complete the building, which becomes a total loss. B's loss incurred in partial construction of the building was foreseeable by A at the time of the contract as a probable result of the breach.
>
> 16. A, who holds B's land as security for a loan, contracts to lend B a sum of money sufficient to pay off other liens on the land at the current rate of interest. A repudiates and informs B in time to obtain money elsewhere on the market, but B is unable to do so. The liens are foreclosed and the land sold at a loss. Unless A knew when he made the contract that B would probably be unable to borrow the money elsewhere, B's loss

on the foreclosure sale was not foreseeable as a probable result of A's breach.

f. Other limitations on damages. It is not always in the interest of justice to require the party in breach to pay damages for all of the foreseeable loss that he has caused. There are unusual instances in which it appears from the circumstances either that the parties assumed that one of them would not bear the risk of a particular loss or that, although there was no such assumption, it would be unjust to put the risk on that party. One such circumstance is an extreme disproportion between the loss and the price charged by the party whose liability for that loss is in question. The fact that the price is relatively small suggests that it was not intended to cover the risk of such liability. Another such circumstance is an informality of dealing, including the absence of a detailed written contract, which indicates that there was no careful attempt to allocate all of the risks. The fact that the parties did not attempt to delineate with precision all of the risks justifies a court in attempting to allocate them fairly. The limitations dealt with in this Section are more likely to be imposed in connection with contracts that do not arise in a commercial setting. Typical examples of limitations imposed on damages under this discretionary power involve the denial of recovery for loss of profits and the restriction of damages to loss incurred in reliance on the contract. Sometimes these limits are covertly imposed, by means of an especially demanding requirement of foreseeability or of certainty. The rule stated in this Section recognizes that what is done in such cases is the imposition of a limitation in the interests of justice.

Illustrations:

17. A, a private trucker, contracts with B to deliver to B's factory a machine that has just been repaired and without which B's factory, as A knows, cannot re-open. Delivery is delayed because A's truck breaks down. In an action by B against A for breach of contract the court may, after taking into consideration such factors as the absence of an elaborate written contract and the extreme disproportion between B's loss of profits during the delay and the price of the trucker's services, exclude recovery for loss of profits.

18. A, a retail hardware dealer, contracts to sell B an inexpensive lighting attachment, which, as A knows, B needs in order to use his tractor at night on his farm. A is delayed in obtaining the attachment and, since no substitute is available, B is unable to use the tractor at night during the delay. In an action by B against A for breach of contract, the court may, after taking into consideration such factors as the absence of an elaborate written contract and the extreme disproportion between B's loss of profits during the delay and the price of the attachment, exclude recovery for loss of profits.

19. A, a plastic surgeon, makes a contract with B, a professional entertainer, to perform plastic surgery on her face in order to improve her appearance. The result of the surgery is, however, to disfigure her face and to require a second operation. In an action by B against A for breach of contract, the court may limit damages by allowing recovery only for loss incurred by B in reliance on the contract, including the fees paid by B and expenses for hospitalization, nursing care and medicine for both operations, together with any damages for the worsening of

B's appearance if these can be proved with reasonable certainty, but not including any loss resulting from the failure to improve her appearance.

§ 352. Uncertainty as a Limitation on Damages

Damages are not recoverable for loss beyond an amount that the evidence permits to be established with reasonable certainty.

§ 353. Loss Due to Emotional Disturbance

Recovery for emotional disturbance will be excluded unless the breach also caused bodily harm or the contract or the breach is of such a kind that serious emotional disturbance was a particularly likely result.

§ 355. Punitive Damages

Punitive damages are not recoverable for a breach of contract unless the conduct constituting the breach is also a tort for which punitive damages are recoverable.

§ 356. Liquidated Damages and Penalties

(1) Damages for breach by either party may be liquidated in the agreement but only at an amount that is reasonable in the light of the anticipated or actual loss caused by the breach and the difficulties of proof of loss. A term fixing unreasonably large liquidated damages is unenforceable on grounds of public policy.

(2) A term in a bond providing for an amount of money as a penalty for non-occurrence of the condition of the bond is unenforceable on grounds of public policy to the extent that the amount exceeds the loss caused by such non-occurrence.

TOPIC 3. ENFORCEMENT BY SPECIFIC PERFORMANCE AND INJUNCTION

§ 359. Effect of Adequacy of Damages

(1) Specific performance or an injunction will not be ordered if damages would be adequate to protect the expectation interest of the injured party.

(2) The adequacy of the damage remedy for failure to render one part of the performance due does not preclude specific performance or injunction as to the contract as a whole.

(3) Specific performance or an injunction will not be refused merely because there is a remedy for breach other than damages, but such a remedy may be considered in exercising discretion under the rule stated in § 357.

§ 360. Factors Affecting Adequacy of Damages

In determining whether the remedy in damages would be adequate, the following circumstances are significant:

>   (a) the difficulty of proving damages with reasonable certainty,
>
>   (b) the difficulty of procuring a suitable substitute performance by means of money awarded as damages, and
>
>   (c) the likelihood that an award of damages could not be collected.

TOPIC 4.   RESTITUTION

§ 370. Requirement That Benefit Be Conferred

A party is entitled to restitution under the rules stated in this Restatement only to the extent that he has conferred a benefit on the other party by way of part performance or reliance.

§ 371. Measure of Restitution Interest

If a sum of money is awarded to protect a party's restitution interest, it may as justice requires be measured by either

>   (a) the reasonable value to the other party of what he received in terms of what it would have cost him to obtain it from a person in the claimant's position, or
>
>   (b) the extent to which the other party's property has been increased in value or his other interests advanced.

§ 373. Restitution When Other Party Is in Breach

(1) Subject to the rule stated in Subsection (2), on a breach by nonperformance that gives rise to a claim for damages for total breach or on a repudiation, the injured party is entitled to restitution for any benefit that he has conferred on the other party by way of part performance or reliance.

(2) The injured party has no right to restitution if he has performed all of his duties under the contract and no performance by the other party remains due other than payment of a definite sum of money for that performance.

§ 374. Restitution in Favor of Party in Breach

(1) Subject to the rule stated in Subsection (2), if a party justifiably refuses to perform on the ground that his remaining duties of performance have been discharged by the other party's breach, the party in breach is entitled to restitution for any benefit that he has conferred by way of part performance or reliance in excess of the loss that he has caused by his own breach.

(2) To the extent that, under the manifested assent of the parties, a party's performance is to be retained in the case of breach, that party is not entitled to restitution if the value of the performance as liquidated damages is reasonable in the light of the anticipated or actual loss caused by the breach and the difficulties of proof of loss.

§ 375. Restitution When Contract Is Within Statute of Frauds

A party who would otherwise have a claim in restitution under a contract is not barred from restitution for the reason that the contract is unenforceable by him because of the Statute of Frauds unless the Statute provides otherwise or its purpose would be frustrated by allowing restitution.

§ 376. Restitution When Contract Is Voidable

A party who has avoided a contract on the ground of lack of capacity, mistake, misrepresentation, duress, undue influence or abuse of a fiduciary relation is entitled to restitution for any benefit that he has conferred on the other party by way of part performance or reliance.

§ 377. Restitution in Cases of Impracticability, Frustration, Non-occurrence of Condition or Disclaimer by Beneficiary

A party whose duty of performance does not arise or is discharged as a result of impracticability of performance, frustration of purpose, non-occurrence of a condition or disclaimer by a beneficiary is entitled to restitution for any benefit that he has conferred on the other party by way of part performance or reliance.

*

UNITED NATIONS CONVENTION ON CONTRACTS FOR THE INTERNATIONAL SALE OF GOODS

COMPILERS' NOTE

Since January 1, 1988 American exporters and importers have been subject to the Convention on Contracts for the International Sale of Goods (CISG). With respect to transactions within its scope, it displaces much of Article 2, Sales, of the Uniform Commercial Code—including, for example, the requirements of the statute of frauds (CISG 11).[1]

The Convention "applies to contracts for the sale of goods between parties whose places of business are in different States ... when the States are Contracting States" (CISG 1).[2] The Convention preserves the autonomy of the parties by allowing them to "exclude the application of this Convention or ... derogate from or vary the effect of any of its provisions" (CISG 6). The Convention does not displace rules of national law that relate to "the validity of the contract or of any of its provisions or of any usages." (CISG 4(a)).[3]

Work on the Convention began in the 1930s when the Institute for the Unification of Private Law in Rome, then under the auspices of the League of Nations, set up a drafting committee of European scholars to work on a uniform law for international sales. By the outbreak of the Second World War, the committee had prepared a first draft, solicited comments from governments, and prepared a revised draft taking account of these comments.

After the War the Dutch Government appointed a commission to do further work, solicited comments from governments and, in 1964, convened a diplomatic conference at The Hague. The conference approved a uniform law on the international sale of goods (ULIS) and a shorter companion uniform law on the formation of contracts for the international sale of goods.

1. The United States did not make the declaration described in CISG 12.

2. In this context "States" means nations and "Contracting" means adopting. The United States did not accept CISG 1(b), which would have given the Convention a broader application.

3. For a definitive treatment of the Convention, see J. Honnold, Uniform Law for International Sales under the 1980 U.N. Convention (3d ed. 1999). See also C. Bianca, M. Bonell et al., Commentary on the International Sales Law: The 1980 Vienna Convention (1987); P. Schlechtriem et al., Commentary on the UN Convention on the International Sale of Goods (CISG) (G. Thomas trans. 2d ed. 1998).

Although the United States had quickly put together a delegation to The Hague to consider a draft prepared by a group of exclusively European scholars, that delegation's influence was not pervasive enough to produce a final text that justified United States ratification.[4] Nevertheless, ULIS did receive eight adoptions by other countries, enough for it to take effect.

Even before ULIS had taken effect, however, efforts were afoot under United Nations auspices to produce a revised international sales law that would be more widely acceptable. In 1966, the United Nations General Assembly established the United Nations Commission on International Trade Law (UNCITRAL). The Commission has "for its object the promotion of the progressive harmonization and unification of the law of international trade." Its thirty-six members include common law as well as civil law countries, developing as well as industrialized countries, and countries with centrally planned economics as well as those with free-market economies.

In 1969, UNCITRAL appointed a fourteen-member Working Group on Sales to consider what changes in ULIS would make it more acceptable to countries of varied legal, social, and economic systems. The United States was an active member of this Working Group from its inception. In 1977 UNCITRAL revised and approved a text of CISG prepared by the Working Group on Sales, and in 1978 it integrated into CISG additional provisions on formation and interpretation. In 1980, the United Nations held in Vienna a diplomatic conference to propose a final text of CISG. After five weeks of intensive effort by the sixty-two countries represented, CISG—often referred to as "the Vienna Convention"—was adopted.

The final product of this half-century of work consists of eighty-eight substantive articles (what we in the United States would call "sections") plus thirteen more articles on effective date, reservations, and the like. Only the eighty-eight substantive articles are set out below. CISG took effect following adoption by ten countries. It has now be adopted by about sixty.[5]

---

4. The traditional scheme for international unification results in a multilateral treaty, put in final form at a diplomatic conference and then adopted by ratification or accession. One important difference between this scheme and that used for unification within the United States is that a country ratifying or acceding to a treaty cannot make changes in its text, except for a few variations that the diplomatic conference has allowed countries to make by means of reservations.

5. Countries that have ratified the Convention include Argentina, Australia, Austria, Belgium, Bulgaria, Belarus, Canada, Chile, China, Cuba, Czechoslovakia, Denmark, Equador, Egypt, Finland, France, Germany, Greece, Guinea, Hungary, Iraq, Italy, Mexico, Netherlands, New Zealand, Norway, Poland, Romania, Russian Federation, Singapore, Spain, Syrian Arab Republic, Sweden, Switzerland, Ukraine, United States, Uruguay, Yugoslavia, Zambia.

CONVENTION ON CONTRACTS FOR THE INTERNATIONAL SALE OF GOODS

THE STATES PARTIES TO THIS CONVENTION,

Bearing in mind the broad objectives in the resolutions adopted by the sixth special session of the General Assembly of the United Nations on the establishment of a New International Economic Order,

Considering that the development of international trade on the basis of equality and mutual benefit is an important element in promoting friendly relations among States,

Being of the opinion that the adoption of uniform rules which govern contracts for the international sale of goods and take into account the different social, economic and legal systems would contribute to the removal of legal barriers in international trade and promote the development of international trade,

Have agreed as follows:

Part I. Sphere of application and general provisions

CHAPTER I. SPHERE OF APPLICATION

Article 1

(1) This Convention applies to contracts of sale of goods between parties whose places of business are in different States:

>   (a) When the States are Contracting States; or

>   (b) When the rules of private international law lead to the application of the law of a Contracting State.

(2) The fact that the parties have their places of business in different States is to be disregarded whenever this fact does not appear either from the contract or from any dealings between, or from information disclosed by, the parties at any time before or at the conclusion of the contract.

(3) Neither the nationality of the parties nor the civil or commercial character of the parties or of the contract is to be taken into consideration in determining the application of this Convention.

Article 2

This Convention does not apply to sales:

(a) Of goods bought for personal, family or household use, unless the seller, at any time before or at the conclusion of the contract, neither knew nor ought to have known that the goods were bought for any such use;

(b) By auction;

(c) On execution or otherwise by authority of law;

(d) Of stocks, shares, investment securities, negotiable instruments or money;

(e) Of ships, vessels, hovercraft or aircraft;

(f) Of electricity.

Article 3

(1) Contracts for the supply of goods to be manufactured or produced are to be considered sales unless the party who order the goods undertakes to supply a substantial part of the materials necessary for such manufacture or production.

(2) This Convention does not apply to contracts in which the preponderant part of the obligations of the party who furnishes the goods consists in the supply of labour or other services.

Article 4

This Convention governs only the formation of the contract of sale and the rights and obligations of the seller and the buyer arising from such a contract. In particular, except as otherwise expressly provided in this Convention, it is not concerned with:

(a) The validity of the contract or of any of its provisions or of any usage;

(b) The effect which the contract may have on the property in the goods sold.

Article 5

This Convention does not apply to the liability of the seller for death or personal injury caused by the goods to any person.

Article 6

The parties may exclude the application of this Convention or, subject to article 12, derogate from or vary the effect of any of its provisions.

CHAPTER II. GENERAL PROVISIONS

Article 7

(1) In the interpretation of this Convention, regard is to be had to its international character and to the need to promote uniformity in its application and the observance of good faith in international trade.

(2) Questions concerning matters governed by this Convention which are not expressly settled in it are to be settled in conformity with the general principles on which it is based or, in the absence of such principles, in conformity with the law applicable by virtue of the rules of private international law.

Article 8

(1) For the purposes of this Convention statements made by and other conduct of a party are to be interpreted according to his intent where the other party knew or could not have been unaware what that intent was.

(2) If the preceding paragraph is not applicable, statements made by and other conduct of a party are to be interpreted according to the understanding that a reasonable person of the same kind as the other party would have had in the same circumstances.

(3) In determining the intent of a party or the understanding a reasonable person would have had, due consideration is to be given to all relevant circumstances of the case including the negotiations, any practices which the parties have established between themselves, usages and any subsequent conduct of the parties.

Article 9

(1) The parties are bound by any usages to which they have agreed and by any practices which they have established between themselves.

(2) The parties are considered, unless otherwise agreed, to have impliedly made applicable to their contract or its formation a usage of which the parties knew or ought to have known and which in international trade is widely known to, and regularly observed by, parties to contracts of the type involved in the particular trade concerned.

Article 10

For the purposes of this Convention:

(a) If a party has more than one place of business, the place of business is that which has the closest relationship to the contract and its performance, having regard to the circumstances known to or contemplated by the parties at any time before or at the conclusion of the contract;

(b) If a party does not have a place of business, reference is to be made to his habitual residence.

Article 11

A contract of sale need not be concluded in or evidenced by writing and is not subject to any other requirement as to form. It may be proved by any means, including witnesses.

Article 12

Any provision of article 11, article 29 or Part II of this Convention that allows a contract of sale or its modification or termination by agreement or any offer, acceptance or other indication of intention to be made in any form other than in writing does not apply where any party has his place of business in a Contracting State which has made a declaration under article 96 of this Convention. The parties may not derogate from or vary the effect of this article.

Article 13

For the purposes of this Convention "writing" includes telegram and telex.

Part II. Formation of the contract

Article 14

(1) A proposal for concluding a contract addressed to one or more specific persons constitutes an offer if it is sufficiently definite and indicates the intention of the offeror to be bound in case of acceptance. A proposal is sufficiently definite if it indicates the goods and expressly or implicitly fixes or makes provision for determining the quantity and the price.

(2) A proposal other than one addressed to one or more specific persons is to be considered merely as an invitation to make offers, unless the contrary is clearly indicated by the person making the proposal.

Article 15

(1) An offer becomes effective when it reaches the offeree.

(2) An offer, even if it is irrevocable, may be withdrawn if the withdrawal reaches the offeree before or at the same time as the offer.

Article 16

(1) Until a contract is concluded an offer may be revoked if the revocation reaches the offeree before he has dispatched an acceptance.

(2) However, an offer cannot be revoked:

  (a) If it indicates, whether by stating a fixed time for acceptance or otherwise, that it is irrevocable; or

  (b) If it was reasonable for the offeree to rely on the offer as being irrevocable and the offeree has acted in reliance on the offer.

Article 17

An offer, even if it is irrevocable, is terminated when a rejection reaches the offeror.

Article 18

(1) A statement made by or other conduct of the offeree indicating assent to an offer is an acceptance. Silence or inactivity does not in itself amount to acceptance.

(2) An acceptance of an offer becomes effective at the moment the indication of assent reaches the offeror. An acceptance is not effective if the indication of assent does not reach the offeror within the time he has fixed or, if no time is fixed, within a reasonable time, due account being taken of the circumstances of the transaction, including the rapidity of the means of communication employed by the offeror. An oral offer must be accepted immediately unless the circumstances indicate otherwise.

(3) However, if, by virtue of the offer or as a result of practices which the parties have established between themselves or of usage, the offeree may indicate assent by performing an act, such as one relating to the dispatch of the goods or payment of the price, without notice to the offeror, the acceptance is effective at the moment the act is performed, provided that the act is performed within the period of time laid down in the preceding paragraph.

Article 19

(1) A reply to an offer which purports to be an acceptance but contains additions, limitations or other modifications is a rejection of the offer and constitutes a counter-offer.

(2) However, a reply to an offer which purports to be an acceptance but contains additional or different terms which do not materially alter the terms of the offer constitutes an acceptance, unless the offeror, without undue delay, objects orally to the discrepancy or dispatches a notice to that effect. If he does not so object, the terms of the contract are the terms of the offer with the modifications contained in the acceptance.

(3) Additional or different terms relating, among other things, to the price, payment, quality and quantity of the goods, place and time of delivery, extent of one party's liability to the other or the settlement of disputes are considered to alter the terms of the offer materially.

Article 20

(1) A period of time for acceptance fixed by the offeror in a telegram or a letter begins to run from the moment the telegram is handed in for dispatch or from the date shown on the letter or, if no such date is shown, from the date shown on the envelope. A period of time for acceptance fixed by the offeror by telephone, telex or other means of instantaneous communication, begins to run from the moment that the offer reaches the offeree.

(2) Official holidays or non-business days occurring during the period for acceptance are included in calculating the period. However, if a notice of acceptance cannot be delivered at the address of the offeror on the last day of the period because that day falls on an official holiday or a non-business day at the place of business of the offeror, the period is extended until the first business day which follows.

Article 21

(1) A late acceptance is nevertheless effective as an acceptance if without delay the offeror orally so informs the offeree or dispatches a notice to that effect.

(2) If a letter or other writing containing a late acceptance shows that it has been sent in such circumstances that if its transmission had been normal it would have reached the offeror in due time, the late acceptance is effective as an acceptance unless, without delay, the offeror orally informs the offeree that he considers his offer as having lapsed or dispatches a notice to that effect.

Article 22

An acceptance may be withdrawn if the withdrawal reaches the offeror before or at the same time as the acceptance would have become effective.

Article 23

A contract is concluded at the moment when an acceptance of an offer becomes effective in accordance with the provisions of this Convention.

Article 24

For the purposes of this Part of the Convention, an offer, declaration of acceptance or any other indication of intention "reaches" the addressee when it is made orally to him or delivered by any other means to him personally, to his place of business or mailing address or, if he does not have a place of business or mailing address, to his habitual residence.

Part III. Sale of goods

CHAPTER I. GENERAL PROVISIONS

Article 25

A breach of contract committed by one of the parties is fundamental if it results in such detriment to the other party as substantially to deprive him of what he is entitled to expect under the contract, unless the party in breach did not foresee, and a reasonable person of the same kind in the same circumstances would not have foreseen, such a result.

Article 26

A declaration of avoidance of the contract is effective only if made by notice to the other party.

Article 27

Unless otherwise expressly provided in this Part of the Convention, if any notice, request or other communication is given or made by a party in accordance with this Part, and by means appropriate in the circumstances, a delay or error in the transmission of the communication or its failure to arrive does not deprive that party of the right to rely on the communication.

Article 28

If, in accordance with the provisions of this Convention, one party is entitled to require performance of any obligation by the other party, a court is not bound to enter a judgment for specific performance unless the court would do so under its own law in respect of similar contracts of sale not governed by this Convention.

Article 29

(1) A contract may be modified or terminated by the mere agreement of the parties.

(2) A contract in writing which contains a provision requiring any modification or termination by agreement to be in writing may not be otherwise modified or terminated by agreement. However, a party may be precluded by his conduct from asserting such a provision to the extent that the other party has relied on that conduct.

CHAPTER II.   OBLIGATIONS OF THE SELLER

Article 30

The seller must deliver the goods, hand over any documents relating to them and transfer the property in the goods, as required by the contract and this Convention.

Section I.   Delivery of the goods and handing over of documents

Article 31

If the seller is not bound to deliver the goods at any other particular place, his obligation to deliver consists:

(a) If the contract of sale involves carriage of the goods—in handing the goods over to the first carrier for transmission to the buyer;

(b) If, in cases not within the preceding subparagraph, the contract relates to specific goods, or unidentified goods to be drawn from a specific stock or to be manufactured or produced, and at the time of the conclusion of the contract the parties knew that the goods were at, or were to be manufactured or produced at, a particular place—in placing the goods at the buyer's disposal at that place;

(c) In other cases—in placing the goods at the buyer's disposal at the place where the seller had his place of business at the time of the conclusion of the contract.

Article 32

(1) If the seller, in accordance with the contract or this Convention, hands the goods over to a carrier and if the goods are not clearly identified to the contract by markings on the goods, by shipping documents or otherwise, the seller must give the buyer notice of the consignment specifying the goods.

(2) If the seller is bound to arrange for carriage of the goods, he must make such contracts as are necessary for carriage to the place fixed by means of transportation appropriate in the circumstances and according to the usual terms for such transportation.

(3) If the seller is not bound to effect insurance in respect of the carriage of the goods, he must, at the buyer's request, provide him with all available information necessary to enable him to effect such insurance.

Article 33

The seller must deliver the goods:

(a) If a date is fixed by or determinable from the contract, on that date;

(b) If a period of time is fixed by or determinable from the contract, at any time within that period unless circumstances indicate that the buyer is to choose a date; or

(c) In any other case, within a reasonable time after the conclusion of the contract.

Article 34

If the seller is bound to hand over documents relating to the goods, he must hand them over at the time and place and in the form required by the contract. If the seller has handed over documents before that time, he may, up to that time, cure any lack of conformity in the documents, if the exercise of this right does not cause the buyer unreasonable inconvenience or unreasonable expense. However, the buyer retains any right to claim damages as provided for in this Convention.

Section II. Conformity of the goods and third party claims

Article 35

(1) The seller must deliver goods which are of the quantity, quality and description required by the contract and which are contained or packaged in the manner required by the contract.

(2) Except where the parties have agreed otherwise, the goods do not conform with the contract unless they:

(a) Are fit for the purposes for which goods of the same description would ordinarily be used;

(b) Are fit for any particular purpose expressly or impliedly made known to the seller at the time of the conclusion of the contract, except where the circumstances show that the buyer did not rely, or that it was unreasonable for him to rely, on the seller's skill and judgment;

(c) Possess the qualities of goods which the seller has held out to the buyer as a sample or model;

(d) Are contained or packaged in the manner usual for such goods or, where there is no such manner, in a manner adequate to preserve and protect the goods.

(3) The seller is not liable under subparagraphs (a) to (d) of the preceding paragraph for any lack of conformity of the goods if at the time of the conclusion of the contract the buyer knew or could not have been unaware of such lack of conformity.

Article 36

(1) The seller is liable in accordance with the contract and this Convention for any lack of conformity which exists at the time when the risk passes to the buyer, even though the lack of conformity becomes apparent only after that time.

(2) The seller is also liable for any lack of conformity which occurs after the time indicated in the preceding paragraph and which is due to a breach of any of his obligations, including a breach of any guarantee that for a period of time the goods will remain fit for their ordinary purpose or for some particular purpose or will retain specified qualities or characteristics.

Article 37

If the seller has delivered goods before the date for delivery, he may, up to that date, deliver any missing part or make up any deficiency in the quantity of the goods delivered, or deliver goods in replacement of any nonconforming goods delivered or remedy any lack of conformity in the goods delivered, provided that the exercise of this right does not cause the buyer unreasonable inconvenience or unreasonable expense.

However, the buyer retains any right to claim damages as provided for in this Convention.

Article 38

(1) The buyer must examine the goods, or cause them to be examined, within as short a period as is practicable in the circumstances.

(2) If the contract involves carriage of the goods, examination may be deferred until after the goods have arrived at their destination.

(3) If the goods are redirected in transit or redispatched by the buyer without a reasonable opportunity for examination by him and at the time of the conclusion of the contract the seller knew or ought to have known of the possibility of such redirection or redispatch, examination may be deferred until after the goods have arrived at the new destination.

Article 39

(1) The buyer loses the right to rely on a lack of conformity of the goods if he does not give notice to the seller specifying the nature of the lack of conformity within a reasonable time after he has discovered it or ought to have discovered it.

(2) In any event, the buyer loses the right to rely on a lack of conformity of the goods if he does not give the seller notice thereof at the latest within a period of two years from the date on which the goods were actually handed over to the buyer, unless this time-limit is inconsistent with a contractual period of guarantee.

Article 40

The seller is not entitled to rely on the provisions of articles 38 and 39 if the lack of conformity relates to facts of which he knew or could not have been unaware and which he did not disclose to the buyer.

Article 41

The seller must deliver goods which are free from any right or claim of a third party, unless the buyer agreed to take the goods subject to that right or claim. However, if such right or claim is based on industrial property or other intellectual property, the seller's obligation is governed by article 42.

Article 42

(1) The seller must deliver goods which are free from any right or claim of a third party based on industrial property or other intellectual property, of which at the time of the conclusion of the contract the seller knew or could not have been unaware, provided that the right or claim is based on industrial property or other intellectual property:

    (a) Under the law of the State where the goods will be resold or otherwise used, if it was contemplated by the parties at the time of the conclusion of the contract that the goods would be resold or otherwise used in that State; or

    (b) In any other case, under the law of the State where the buyer has his place of business.

(2) The obligation of the seller under the preceding paragraph does not extend to cases where:

    (a) At the time of the conclusion of the contract the buyer knew or could not have been unaware of the right or claim; or

    (b) The right or claim results from the seller's compliance with technical drawings, designs, formulae or other such specifications furnished by the buyer.

Article 43

(1) The buyer loses the right to rely on the provisions of article 41 or article 42 if he does not give notice to the seller specifying the nature of the right or claim of the third party within a reasonable time after he has become aware or ought to have become aware of the right or claim.

(2) The seller is not entitled to rely on the provisions of the preceding paragraph if he knew of the right or claim of the third party and the nature of it.

Article 44

Notwithstanding the provisions of paragraph (1) of article 39 and paragraph (1) of article 43, the buyer may reduce the price in accordance with article 50 or claim damages, except for loss of profit, if he has a reasonable excuse for his failure to give the required notice.

Section III.   Remedies for breach of contract by the seller

Article 45

(1) If the seller fails to perform any of his obligations under the contract or this Convention, the buyer may:

    (a) Exercise the rights provided in articles 46 to 52;

    (b) Claim damages as provided in articles 74 to 77.

(2) The buyer is not deprived of any right he may have to claim damages by exercising his right to other remedies.

(3) No period of grace may be granted to the seller by a court or arbitral tribunal when the buyer resorts to a remedy for breach of contract.

Article 46

(1) The buyer may require performance by the seller of his obligations unless the buyer has resorted to a remedy which is inconsistent with this requirement.

(2) If the goods do not conform with the contract, the buyer may require delivery of substitute goods only if the lack of conformity constitutes a fundamental breach of contract and a request for substitute goods is made either in conjunction with notice given under article 39 or within a reasonable time thereafter.

(3) If the goods do not conform with the contract, the buyer may require the seller to remedy the lack of conformity by repair, unless this is unreasonable having regard to all the circumstances. A request for repair must be made either in conjunction with notice given under article 39 or within a reasonable time thereafter.

Article 47

(1) The buyer may fix an additional period of time of reasonable length for performance by the seller of his obligations.

(2) Unless the buyer has received notice from the seller that he will not perform within the period so fixed, the buyer may not, during that period, resort to any remedy for breach of contract. However, the buyer is not deprived thereby of any right he may have to claim damages for delay in performance.

Article 48

(1) Subject to article 49, the seller may, even after the date for delivery, remedy at his own expense any failure to perform his obligations, if he can do so without unreasonable delay and without causing the buyer unreasonable inconvenience or uncertainty of reimbursement by the seller of expenses advanced by the buyer. However, the buyer retains any right to claim damages as provided for in this Convention.

(2) If the seller requests the buyer to make known whether he will accept performance and the buyer does not comply with the request within a reasonable time, the seller may perform within the time indicated in his request. The buyer may not, during that period of time, resort to any remedy which is inconsistent with performance by the seller.

(3) A notice by the seller that he will perform within a specified period of time is assumed to include a request, under the preceding paragraph, that the buyer make known his decision.

(4) A request or notice by the seller under paragraph (2) or (3) of this article is not effective unless received by the buyer.

Article 49

(1) The buyer may declare the contract avoided:

(a) If the failure by the seller to perform any of his obligations under the contract or this Convention amounts to a fundamental breach of contract; or

(b) In case of non-delivery, if the seller does not deliver the goods within the additional period of time fixed by the buyer in accordance with paragraph (1) of article 47 or declares that he will not deliver within the period so fixed.

(2) However, in cases where the seller has delivered the goods, the buyer loses the right to declare the contract avoided unless he does so:

(a) In respect of late delivery, within a reasonable time after he has become aware that delivery has been made;

(b) In respect of any breach other than late delivery, within a reasonable time:

(i) After he knew or ought to have known of the breach;

(ii) After the expiration of any additional period of time fixed by the buyer in accordance with paragraph (1) of article 47, or after the seller has declared that he will not perform his obligations within such an additional period; or

(iii) After the expiration of any additional period of time indicated by the seller in accordance with paragraph (2) of article 48, or after the buyer has declared that he will not accept performance.

Article 50

If the goods do not conform with the contract and whether or not the price has already been paid, the buyer may reduce the price in the same proportion as the value that the goods actually delivered had at the time of the delivery bears to the value that conforming goods would have had at that time. However, if the seller remedies any failure to perform his obligations in accordance with article 37 or article 48 or if the buyer refuses to accept performance by the seller in accordance with those articles, the buyer may not reduce the price.

Article 51

(1) If the seller delivers only a part of the goods or if only a part of the goods delivered is in conformity with the contract, articles 46 to 50 apply in respect of the part which is missing or which does not conform.

(2) The buyer may declare the contract avoided in its entirety only if the failure to make delivery completely or in conformity with the contract amounts to a fundamental breach of the contract.

Article 52

(1) If the seller delivers the goods before the date fixed, the buyer may take delivery or refuse to take delivery.

(2) If the seller delivers a quantity of goods greater than that provided for in the contract, the buyer may take delivery or refuse to take delivery of the excess quantity. If the buyer takes delivery of all or part of the excess quantity, he must pay for it at the contract rate.

CHAPTER III. OBLIGATIONS OF THE BUYER

Article 53

The buyer must pay the price for the goods and take delivery of them as required by the contract and this Convention.

Section I. Payment of the price

Article 54

The buyer's obligation to pay the price includes taking such steps and complying with such formalities as may be required under the contract or any laws and regulations to enable payment to be made.

Article 55

Where a contract has been validly concluded but does not expressly or implicitly fix or make provision for determining the price, the parties are considered, in the absence of any indication to the contrary, to have impliedly made reference to the price generally charged at the time of the conclusion of the contract for such goods sold under comparable circumstances in the trade concerned.

Article 56

If the price is fixed according to the weight of the goods, in case of doubt it is to be determined by the net weight.

Article 57

(1) If the buyer is not bound to pay the price at any other particular place, he must pay it to the seller:

    (a) At the seller's place of business; or

    (b) If the payment is to be made against the handing over of the goods or of documents, at the place where the handing over takes place.

(2) The seller must bear any increase in the expenses incidental to payment which is caused by a change in his place of business subsequent to the conclusion of the contract.

Article 58

(1) If the buyer is not bound to pay the price at any other specific time, he must pay it when the seller places either the goods or documents controlling their disposition at the buyer's disposal in accordance with the contract and this Convention. The seller may make such payment a condition for handing over the goods or documents.

(2) If the contract involves carriage of the goods, the seller may dispatch the goods on terms whereby the goods, or documents controlling their disposition, will not be handed over to the buyer except against payment of the price.

(3) The buyer is not bound to pay the price until he has had an opportunity to examine the goods, unless the procedures for delivery or payment agreed upon by the parties are inconsistent with his having such an opportunity.

Article 59

The buyer must pay the price on the date fixed by or determinable from the contract and this Convention without the need for any request or compliance with any formality on the part of the seller.

Section II.   Taking delivery

Article 60

The buyer's obligation to take delivery consists:

  (a) In doing all the acts which could reasonably be expected of him in order to enable the seller to make delivery; and

  (b) In taking over the goods.

Section III.   Remedies for breach of contract by the buyer

Article 61

(1) If the buyer fails to perform any of his obligations under the contract or this Convention, the seller may:

  (a) Exercise the rights provided in articles 62 to 65;

  (b) Claim damages as provided in articles 74 to 77.

(2) The seller is not deprived of any right he may have to claim damages by exercising his right to other remedies.

(3) No period of grace may be granted to the buyer by a court or arbitral tribunal when the seller resorts to a remedy for breach of contract.

Article 62

The seller may require the buyer to pay the price, take delivery or perform his other obligations, unless the seller has resorted to a remedy which is inconsistent with this requirement.

Article 63

(1) The seller may fix an additional period of time of reasonable length for performance by the buyer of his obligations.

(2) Unless the seller has received notice from the buyer that he will not perform within the period so fixed, the seller may not, during that period, resort to any remedy for breach of contract. However, the seller is not deprived thereby of any right he may have to claim damages for delay in performance.

Article 64

(1) The seller may declare the contract avoided:

(a) If the failure by the buyer to perform any of his obligations under the contract or this Convention amounts to a fundamental breach of contract; or

(b) If the buyer does not, within the additional period of time fixed by the seller in accordance with paragraph (1) of article 63, perform his obligation to pay the price or take delivery of the goods, or declares that he will not do so within the period so fixed.

(2) However, in cases where the buyer has paid the price, the seller loses the right to declare the contract avoided unless he does so:

(a) In respect of late performance by the buyer, before the seller has become aware that performance has been rendered; or

(b) In respect of any breach other than late performance by the buyer, within a reasonable time:

(i) After the seller knew or ought to have known of the breach; or

(ii) After the expiration of any additional period of time fixed by the seller in accordance with paragraph (1) of article 63, or after the buyer has declared that he will not perform his obligations within such an additional period.

Article 65

(1) If under the contract the buyer is to specify the form, measurement or other features of the goods and he fails to make such specification either on the date agreed upon or within a reasonable time after receipt of a request from the seller, the seller may, without prejudice to any other rights he may have, make the specification himself in accordance with the requirements of the buyer that may be known to him.

(2) If the seller makes the specification himself, he must inform the buyer of the details thereof and must fix a reasonable time within which the buyer may make a different specification. If, after receipt of such a

communication, the buyer fails to do so within the time so fixed, the specification made by the seller is binding.

CHAPTER IV. PASSING OF RISK
Article 66

Loss of or damage to the goods after the risk has passed to the buyer does not discharge him from his obligation to pay the price, unless the loss or damage is due to an act or omission of the seller.

Article 67

(1) If the contract of sale involves carriage of the goods and the seller is not bound to hand them over at a particular place, the risk passes to the buyer when the goods are handed over to the first carrier for transmission to the buyer in accordance with the contract of sale. If the seller is bound to hand the goods over to a carrier at a particular place, the risk does not pass to the buyer until the goods are handed over to the carrier at that place. The fact that the seller is authorized to retain documents controlling the disposition of the goods does not affect the passage of the risk.

(2) Nevertheless, the risk does not pass to the buyer until the goods are clearly identified to the contract, whether by markings on the goods, by shipping documents, by notice given to the buyer or otherwise.

Article 68

The risk in respect of goods sold in transit passes to the buyer from the time of the conclusion of the contract. However, if the circumstances so indicate, the risk is assumed by the buyer from the time the goods were handed over to the carrier who issued the documents embodying the contract of carriage. Nevertheless, if at the time of the conclusion of the contract of sale the seller knew or ought to have known that the goods had been lost or damaged and did not disclose this to the buyer, the loss or damage is at the risk of the seller.

Article 69

(1) In cases not within articles 67 and 68, the risk passes to the buyer when he takes over the goods or, if he does not do so in due time, from the time when the goods are placed at his disposal he commits a breach of contract by failing to take delivery.

(2) However, if the buyer is bound to take over the goods at a place other than a place of business of the seller, the risk passes when delivery is due and the buyer is aware of the fact that the goods are placed at his disposal at that place.

(3) If the contract relates to goods not then identified, the goods are considered not to be placed at the disposal of the buyer until they are clearly identified to the contract.

Article 70

If the seller has committed a fundamental breach of contract, articles 67, 68, and 69 do not impair the remedies available to the buyer on account of the breach.

CHAPTER V.   PROVISIONS COMMON TO THE OBLIGATIONS OF THE SELLER AND OF THE BUYER

Section I.   Anticipatory breach and installment contracts

Article 71

(1) A party may suspend the performance of his obligations if, after the conclusion of the contract, it becomes apparent that the other party will not perform a substantial part of his obligations as a result of:

(a) A serious deficiency in his ability to perform or in his creditworthiness; or

(b) His conduct in preparing to perform or in performing the contract.

(2) If the seller has already dispatched the goods before the grounds described in the preceding paragraph become evident, he may prevent the handing over of the goods to the buyer even though the buyer holds a document which entitles him to obtain them.   The present paragraph relates only to the rights in the goods as between the buyer and the seller.

(3) A party suspending performance, whether before or after dispatch of the goods, must immediately give notice of the suspension to the other party and must continue with performance if the other party provides adequate assurance of his performance.

Article 72

(1) If prior to the date for performance of the contract it is clear that one of the parties will commit a fundamental breach of contract, the other party may declare the contract avoided.

(2) If time allows, the party intending to declare the contract avoided must give reasonable notice to the other party in order to permit him to provide adequate assurance of his performance.

(3) The requirements of the preceding paragraph do not apply if the other party has declared that he will not perform his obligations.

Article 73

(1) In the case of a contract for delivery of goods by instalments, if the failure of one party to perform any of his obligations in respect of any instalment constitutes a fundamental breach of contract with re-

spect to that instalment, the other party may declare the contract avoided with respect to that instalment.

(2) If one party's failure to perform any of his obligations in respect of any instalment gives the other party good grounds to conclude that a fundamental breach of contract will occur with respect to future instalments, he may declare the contract avoided for the future, provided that he does so within a reasonable time.

(3) A buyer who declares the contract avoided in respect of any delivery may, at the same time, declare it avoided in respect of deliveries already made or of future deliveries if, by reason of their interdependence, those deliveries could not be used for the purpose contemplated by the parties at the time of the conclusion of the contract.

Section II. Damages
Article 74

Damages for breach of contract by one party consist of a sum equal to the loss, including loss of profit, suffered by the other party as a consequence of the breach. Such damages may not exceed the loss which the party in breach foresaw or ought to have foreseen at the time of the conclusion of the contract, in the light of the facts and matters of which he then knew or ought to have known, as a possible consequence of the breach of contract.

Article 75

If the contract is avoided and if, in a reasonable manner and within a reasonable time after avoidance, the buyer has bought goods in replacement or the seller has resold the goods, the party claiming damages may recover the difference between the contract price and the price in the substitute transaction as well as any further damages recoverable under article 74.

Article 76

(1) If the contract is avoided and there is a current price for the goods, the party claiming damages may, if he has not made a purchase or resale under article 75, recover the difference between the price fixed by the contract and the current price at the time of avoidance as well as any further damages recoverable under article 74. If, however, the party claiming damages has avoided the contract after taking over the goods, the current price at the time of such taking over shall be applied instead of the current price at the time of avoidance.

(2) For the purposes of the preceding paragraph, the current price is the price prevailing at the place where delivery of the goods should have been made or, if there is no current price at that place, the price at such other place as serves as a reasonable substitute, making due allowance for differences in the cost of transporting the goods.

Article 77

A party who relies on a breach of contract must take such measures as are reasonable in the circumstances to mitigate the loss, including loss of profit, resulting from the breach. If he fails to take such measures, the party in breach may claim a reduction in the damages in the amount by which the loss should have been mitigated.

Section III.   Interest

Article 78

If a party fails to pay the price or any other sum that is in arrears, the other party is entitled to interest on it, without prejudice to any claim for damages recoverable under article 74.

Section IV.   Exemptions

Article 79

(1) A party is not liable for a failure to perform any of his obligations if he proves that the failure was due to an impediment beyond his control and that he could not reasonably be expected to have taken the impediment into account at the time of the conclusion of the contract or to have avoided or overcome it or its consequences.

(2) If the party's failure is due to the failure by a third person whom he has engaged to perform the whole or a party of the contract, that party is exempt from liability only if:

(a) He is exempt under the preceding paragraph; and

(b) The person whom he has so engaged would be so exempt if the provisions of that paragraph were applied to him.

(3) The exemption provided by this article has effect for the period during which the impediment exists.

(4) The party who fails to perform must give notice to the other party of the impediment and its effect on his ability to perform. If the notice is not received by the other party within a reasonable time after the party who fails to perform knew or ought to have known of the impediment, he is liable for damages resulting from such non-receipt.

(5) Nothing in this article prevents either party from exercising any right other than to claim damages under this Convention.

Article 80

A party may not rely on a failure of the other party to perform, to the extent that such failure was caused by the first party's act or omission.

Section V. Effects of avoidance

Article 81

(1) Avoidance of the contract releases both parties from their obligations under it, subject to any damages which may be due. Avoidance does not affect any provision of the contract for the settlement of disputes or any other provision of the contract governing the rights and obligations of the parties consequent upon the avoidance of the contract.

(2) A party who has performed the contract either wholly or in part may claim restitution from the other party of whatever the first party has supplied or paid under the contract. If both parties are bound to make restitution, they must do so concurrently.

Article 82

(1) The buyer loses the right to declare the contract avoided or to require the seller to deliver substitute goods if it is impossible for him to make restitution of the goods substantially in the condition in which he received them.

(2) The preceding paragraph does not apply:

(a) If the impossibility of making restitution of the goods or of making restitution of the goods substantially in the condition in which the buyer received them is not due to his act or omission;

(b) If the goods or part of the goods have perished or deteriorated as a result of the examination provided for in article 38; or

(c) If the goods or part of the goods have been sold in the normal course of business or have been consumed or transformed by the buyer in the course of normal use before he discovered or ought to have discovered the lack of conformity.

Article 83

A buyer who has lost the right to declare the contract avoided or to require the seller to deliver substitute goods in accordance with article 82 retains all other remedies under the contract and this Convention.

Article 84

(1) If the seller is bound to refund the price, he must also pay interest on it, from the date on which the price was paid.

(2) The buyer must account to the seller for all benefits which he has derived from the goods or part of them:

(a) If he must make restitution of the goods or part of them; or

(b) If it is impossible for him to make restitution of all or part of the goods or to make restitution of all or part of the goods substantially in the condition in which he received them, but he has nevertheless declared the contract avoided or required the seller to deliver substitute goods.

Section VI.   Preservation of the goods

Article 85

If the buyer is in delay in taking delivery of the goods or, where payment of the price and delivery of the goods are to be made concurrently, if he fails to pay the price, and the seller is either in possession of the goods or otherwise able to control their disposition, the seller must take such steps as are reasonable in the circumstances to preserve them. He is entitled to retain them until he has been reimbursed his reasonable expenses by the buyer.

Article 86

(1) If the buyer has received the goods and intends to exercise any right under the contract or this Convention to reject them, he must take such steps to preserve them as are reasonable in the circumstances. He is entitled to retain them until he has been reimbursed his reasonable expenses by the seller.

(2) If goods dispatched to the buyer have been placed at his disposal at their destination and he exercises the right to reject them, he must take possession of them on behalf of the seller, provided that this can be done without payment of the price and without unreasonable inconvenience or unreasonable expense. This provision does not apply if the seller or a person authorized to take charge of the goods on his behalf is present at the destination. If the buyer takes possession of the goods under this paragraph, his rights and obligations are governed by the preceding paragraph.

Article 87

A party who is bound to take steps to preserve the goods may deposit them in a warehouse of a third person at the expense of the other party provided that the expense incurred is not unreasonable.

Article 88

(1) A party who is bound to preserve the goods in accordance with article 85 or 86 may sell them by any appropriate means if there has been an unreasonable delay by the other party in taking possession of the goods or in taking them back or in paying the price or the cost of preservation, provided that reasonable notice of the intention to sell has been given to the other party.

(2) If the goods are subject to rapid deterioration or their preservation would involve unreasonable expense, a party who is bound to preserve the goods in accordance with article 85 or 86 must take reasonable measures to sell them. To the extent possible he must give notice to the other party of this intention to sell.

(3) A party selling the goods has the right to retain out of the proceeds of sale an amount equal to the reasonable expenses of preserving the goods and of selling them. He must account to the other party for the balance.

*

UNIDROIT PRINCIPLES OF INTERNATIONAL COMMERCIAL CONTRACTS

COMPILERS' NOTE[1]

In 1994, there appeared an important body of rules for international contracts, the UNIDROIT Principles of International Commercial Contracts.[2] Like the Restatements, the Principles are not designed for legislative enactment. What is the source of these Principles? "For the most part," their Introduction explains, they "reflect concepts to be found in many, if not all, legal systems," though "they also embody what are perceived to be the best solutions, even if still not yet generally adopted." These concepts are drawn from a variety of sources such as the United Nations Convention on Contracts for the International Sale of Goods (CISG), generally recognized principles of civil law systems, and generally recognized principles of common law systems—including the Uniform Commercial Code and the Restatement (Second) of Contracts.

Since the Principles have not been enacted by a legislature, parties that want them to apply should incorporate them, either by name or generally. According to their Preamble, they "set forth general rules for international commercial contracts" to be applied "when the parties have agreed that their contract be governed by [them or by] 'general principles of law,' the 'lex mercatoria' or the like." It is likely that their impact will be largely in international arbitration, and their Preamble suggests that arbitrators apply them if "it proves impossible to establish the relevant rule of the applicable law." This might be the case if it is uncertain what law is applicable or if, though this is certain, that law lacks a clear rule. Because CISG covers international sales of goods, it is likely that the Principles will be significant in disputes arising under other types of contracts, notably contracts for services.

The Principles are the product of the same organization that began the work on the unification of the law of international sales, the International Institute for the Unification of Private Law (UNIDROIT)

---

1. Copyright by E. Farnsworth. This Note is adapted from Farnsworth on Contracts § 1.8a (2d ed. 1998) and is used with permission.

2. For discussion by the chair of the working group that drafted the Principles, see M. Bonell, An International Restatement of Contract Law: The UNIDROIT Principles of International Commercial Contracts (2d ed.1997) (includes bibliography and the text in eight languages). See generally Perillo, UNIDROIT Principles of International Commercial Contracts: The Black Letter Text and a Review, 63 Fordham L.Rev. 281 (1994); Symposium, 69 Tul. L.Rev. 1121 (1995); Symposium, 3 Tul. J.Intl. & Comp.L. 45 (1995); Symposium, 40 Am.J.Comp.L. 541 (1992).

in Rome. Founded in 1926 under the auspices of the League of Nations, it has continued as an independent governmental organization of which the United States is a member. The idea of drafting the Principles dates back to 1971, when the topic was put on the Institute's work program, but it was not until 1980 that the Institute set up a working group, which the United States joined toward the end of that decade. After more than a decade of semiannual meetings of the working group, the Institute's Governing Council approved publication of the Principles in 1994. Like the Restatement and the Uniform Commercial Code, they are accompanied by comments, illustrations, and section captions. Their initial success was such that an expanded set of Principles is now in preparation. A similar effort, under different auspices, has prepared a set of Principles of European Contract Law.[3]

The Principles contain some hundred and twenty articles and deal with such matters as contract formation, performance, excuse from performance, and remedies. As to many of these matters they track the provisions of CISG. On some matters, however, the Principles break fresh ground. These include precontractual liability, hardship as an excuse for nonperformance, specific performance, and stipulated damages.

The Principles also break fresh ground by stating a number of general principles. One is freedom of contract: "parties are free to enter into a contract and to determine its contents"[4] and "may exclude the application of these Principles ... or vary [their] effect."[5] A second is *pacta sunt servanda* (agreements are to be observed): if "performance becomes more onerous for one of the parties, that party is nevertheless bound to perform its obligations."[6] A third is fairness: a party may avoid a contract or term "if, at the time of the conclusion of the contract, the contract or term unjustifiably gave the other party an excessive advantage,"[7] and a term "contained in standard terms" that "is of such a character that the other party could not reasonably have expected it" is not effective unless expressly accepted by that party.[8] A fourth is good faith and fair dealing: a "party must act in accordance with good faith and fair dealing in international trade."[9]

The Principles raise troublesome questions concerning mandatory rules—rules that the parties are not free to change by agreement. Given that the Principles are generally applicable only as a result of agreement of the parties, one might make two assumptions as to mandatory rules. The first is that the parties would be completely free to exclude or

3. Principles of European Contract Law (Parts I & II) (2000) (includes comments, illustrations, and citations to largely European national sources).

4. Art. 1.1 ("Freedom of contract").

5. Art. 1.5 ("Exclusion or modification by the parties").

6. Art. 6.2.1 ("Contract to be observed").

7. Art. 3.10 ("Gross disparity").

8. Art. 2.20 ("Surprising terms").

9. Art. 1.7 ("Good faith and fair dealing").

modify the Principles, an assumption that seems to be confirmed by the principle of freedom of contract mentioned above. The second is that the parties could not themselves exclude or modify mandatory rules of the applicable law, an assumption that seems to be confirmed by a provision that the Principles do not "restrict the application of mandatory rules . . . which are applicable in accordance with the relevant rules of private international law."[10]

Perhaps surprisingly, the Principles qualify both assumptions. As to the first assumption, despite the general principle of freedom of contract, the Principles subject their declaration that they may be excluded or varied by the parties to an exception where "otherwise provided in the Principles."[11] These exceptions include the rules on good faith and fair dealing[12] and on gross disparity.[13] It is, to be sure, unlikely that parties would include in their contracts explicit provisions derogating from either of these rules, but if they were to do so it might be difficult explain why such provisions should not be given effect. As to the second assumption, despite the statement that the Principles cannot affect mandatory rules, the Principles seem to contemplate exceptions as to the requirement of a writing, the requirement for modification of an agreement, the availability of specific performance, and the enforceability of a provision for stipulated damages. As to all of these, the Principles state rules that change common law rules that the parties cannot change by agreement—common law mandatory rules.

10.	Art. 1.4 ("Mandatory rules").	**12.**	Art. 1.7.
11.	Art. 1.5.	**13.**	Art. 3.10

*

281

UNIDROIT PRINCIPLES
OF
INTERNATIONAL COMMERCIAL
CONTRACTS

Table of Contents

283

285

PREAMBLE

(Purpose of the Principles)

These Principles set forth general rules for international commercial contracts.

They shall be applied when the parties have agreed that their contract be governed by them.

They may be applied when the parties have agreed that their contract be governed by general principles of law, the lex mercatoria or the like.

They may provide a solution to an issue raised when it proves impossible to establish the relevant rule of the applicable law.

They may be used to interpret or supplement international uniform law instruments.

They may serve as a model for national and international legislators.

CHAPTER 1—GENERAL PROVISIONS

ARTICLE 1.1

(Freedom of contract)

The parties are free to enter into a contract and to determine its content.

ARTICLE 1.2

(No form required)

Nothing in these Principles requires a contract to be concluded in or evidenced by writing. It may be proved by any means, including witnesses.

ARTICLE 1.3

(Binding character of contract)

A contract validly entered into is binding upon the parties. It can only be modified or terminated in accordance with its terms or by agreement or as otherwise provided in these Principles.

ARTICLE 1.4

(Mandatory rules)

Nothing in these Principles shall restrict the application of mandatory rules, whether of national, international or supranational origin, which are applicable in accordance with the relevant rules of private international law.

ARTICLE 1.5

(Exclusion or modification by the parties)

The parties may exclude the application of these Principles or derogate from or vary the effect of any of their provisions, except as otherwise provided in the Principles.

ARTICLE 1.6

(Interpretation and supplementation of the Principles)

(1) In the interpretation of these Principles, regard is to be had to their international character and to their purposes including the need to promote uniformity in their application.

(2) Issues within the scope of these Principles but not expressly settled by them are as far as possible to be settled in accordance with their underlying general principles.

ARTICLE 1.7

(Good faith and fair dealing)

(1) Each party must act in accordance with good faith and fair dealing in international trade.

(2) The parties may not exclude or limit this duty.

COMMENT

1. "Good faith and fair dealing" as a fundamental idea underlying the Principles.

There are a number of provisions throughout the different chapters of the Principles which constitute a direct or indirect application of the principle of good faith and fair dealing. See, for instance, Articles 2.4(2)(b), 2.15, 2.16, 2.18, 2.20, 3.5, 3.8, 3.10, 4.1(2), 4.2(2), 4.6, 4.8, 5.2, 5.3, 6.1.3, 6.1.5, 6.1.16(2), 6.1.17(1), 6.2.3(3)(4), 7.1.2, 7.1.6, 7.1.7, 7.2.2(b)(c), 7.4.8 and 7.4.13. This means that good faith and fair dealing may be considered to be one of the fundamental ideas underly-ing the Principles. By stating in general terms that each party must act in accordance with good faith and fair dealing para. (1) of this articles makes it clear that even in the absence of special provisions in the Principles the parties' behaviour throughout the life of the contract, including the negotia-tion process, must conform to good faith and fair dealing.

Illustrations

1. A grants B forty-eight hours as the time within which B may accept its offer. When B, shortly before the expiry of the deadline,

287

decides to accept, it is unable to do so: it is the weekend, the fax at A's office is disconnected and there is no telephone answering machine which can take the message. When on the following Monday A refuses B's acceptance A acts contrary to good faith since when it fixed the time-limit for acceptance it was for A to ensure that messages could be received at its office throughout the forty-eight hour period.

2. A contract for the supply and installation of a special production line contains a provision according to which A, the seller, is obliged to communicate to B, the purchaser, any improvements made by A to the technology of that line. After a year B learns of an important improvement of which it had not been informed. A is not excused by the fact that the production of that particular type of production line is no longer its responsibility but that of C, a wholly-owned affiliated company of A. It would be against good faith for A to invoke the separate entity of C, which was specifically set up to take over this production in order to avoid A's contractual obligations vis-à-vis B.

3. A, an agent, undertakes on behalf of B, the principal, to promote the sale of B's goods in a given area. Under the contract A's right to compensation arises only after B's approval of the contracts procured by A. While B is free to decide whether or not to approve the contracts procured by A, a systematic and unjustified refusal to approve any contract procured by A would be against good faith.

4. Under a line of credit agreement between A, a bank, and B, a customer, A suddenly and inexplicably refuses to make further advances to B whose business suffers heavy losses as a consequence. Notwithstanding the fact that the agreement contains a term permitting A to accelerate payment "at will", A's demand for payment in full without prior warning and with no justification would be against good faith.

2. "Good faith and fair dealing in international trade"

The reference to "good faith and fair dealing in international trade" first makes it clear that in the context of the Principles the two concepts are not to be applied according to the standards ordinarily adopted within the different national legal systems. In other words, such domestic standards may be taken into account only to the extent that they are shown to be generally accepted among the various legal systems. A further implication of the formula used is that good faith and fair dealing must be construed in the light of the special conditions of international trade. Standards of business practice may indeed vary considerably from one trade sector to another, and even within a given trade sector they may be more or less stringent depending on the socio-economic environment in which the enterprises operate, their size and technical skill, etc.

It should be noted that the provisions of the Principles and/or the comments thereto at times refer only to "good faith" or to "good faith and fair dealing". Such references should always be understood as a reference to "good faith and fair dealing in international trade" as specified in this article.

Illustrations

5. Under a contract for the sale of high-technology equipment the purchaser loses the right to rely on any defect in the goods if it

does not give notice to the seller specifying the nature of the defect without undue delay after it has discovered or ought to have discovered the defect. A, a buyer operating in a country where such equipment is commonly used, discovers a defect in the equipment after having put it into operation, but in its notice to B, the seller of the equipment, A gives misleading indications as to the nature of the defect. A loses its right to rely on the defect since a more careful examination of the defect would have permitted it to give B the necessary specifications.

6. The facts are the same as in Illustration 5, the difference being that A operates in a country where this type of equipment is so far almost unknown. A does not lose its right to rely on the defect be-cause B, being aware of A's lack of technical knowledge, could not reasonably have expected A properly to identify the nature of the defect.

3. The mandatory nature of the principle of good faith and fair dealing

The parties' duty to act in accordance with good faith and fair dealing is of such a fundamental nature that the parties may not contractually exclude or limit it (para. (2)). As to specific applications of the general prohibition to exclude or limit the principle of good faith and fair dealing between the parties, see Arts. 3.19, 7.1.6 and 7.4.13.

On the other hand, nothing prevents parties from providing in their contract for a duty to observe more stringent standards of behaviour.

ARTICLE 1.8

(Usages and practices)

(1) The parties are bound by any usage to which they have agreed and by any practices which they have established between themselves.

(2) The parties are bound by a usage that is widely known to and regularly observed in international trade by parties in the particular trade concerned except where the application of such a usage would be unreasonable.

ARTICLE 1.9

(Notice)

(1) Where notice is required it may be given by any means appropriate to the circumstances.

(2) A notice is effective when it reaches the person to whom it is given.

(3) For the purpose of paragraph (2) a notice "reaches" a person when given to that person orally or delivered at that person's place of business or mailing address.

(4) For the purpose of this article "notice" includes a declaration, demand, request or any other communication of intention.

289

ARTICLE 1.10

(Definitions)

In these Principles

—"court" includes an arbitral tribunal;

—where a party has more than one place of business the relevant "place of business" is that which has the closest relationship to the contract and its performance, having regard to the circumstances known to or contemplated by the parties at any time before or at the conclusion of the contract;

—"obligor" refers to the party who is to perform an obligation and "obligee" refers to the party who is entitled to performance of that obligation.

—"writing" means any mode of communication that preserves a record of the information contained therein and is capable of being reproduced in tangible form.

CHAPTER 2—FORMATION

ARTICLE 2.1

(Manner of formation)

A contract may be concluded either by the acceptance of an offer or by conduct of the parties that is sufficient to show agreement.

ARTICLE 2.2

(Definition of offer)

A proposal for concluding a contract constitutes an offer if it is sufficiently definite and indicates the intention of the offeror to be bound in case of acceptance.

ARTICLE 2.3

(Withdrawal of offer)

(1) An offer becomes effective when it reaches the offeree.

(2) An offer, even if it is irrevocable, may be withdrawn if the withdrawal reaches the offeree before or at the same time as the offer.

ARTICLE 2.4

(Revocation of offer)

(1) Until a contract is concluded an offer may be revoked if the revocation reaches the offeree before it has dispatched an acceptance.

(2) However, an offer cannot be revoked

(a) if it indicates, whether by stating a fixed time for acceptance or otherwise, that it is irrevocable; or

(b) if it was reasonable for the offeree to rely on the offer as being irrevocable and the offeree has acted in reliance on the offer.

ARTICLE 2.5

(Rejection of offer)

An offer is terminated when a rejection reaches the offeror.

ARTICLE 2.6

(Mode of acceptance)

(1) A statement made by or other conduct of the offeree indicating assent to an offer is an acceptance. Silence or inactivity does not in itself amount to acceptance.

(2) An acceptance of an offer becomes effective when the indication of assent reaches the offeror.

(3) However, if, by virtue of the offer or as a result of practices which the parties have established between themselves or of usage, the offeree may indicate assent by performing an act without notice to the offeror, the acceptance is effective when the act is performed.

ARTICLE 2.7

(Time of acceptance)

An offer must be accepted within the time the offeror has fixed or, if no time is fixed, within a reasonable time having regard to the circumstances, including the rapidity of the means of communication employed by the offeror. An oral offer must be accepted immediately unless the circumstances indicate otherwise.

ARTICLE 2.8

(Acceptance within a fixed period of time)

(1) A period of time for acceptance fixed by the offeror in a telegram or a letter begins to run from the moment the telegram is handed in for dispatch or from the date shown on the letter or, if no such date is shown, from the date shown on the envelope. A period of time for acceptance fixed by the offeror by means of instantaneous communication begins to run from the moment that the offer reaches the offeree.

(2) Official holidays or non-business days occurring during the period for acceptance are included in calculating the period. However, if a notice of acceptance cannot be delivered at the address of the offeror on the last day of the period because that day falls on an official holiday or a non-business day at the place of business of the offeror, the period is extended until the first business day which follows.

ARTICLE 2.9

(Late acceptance. Delay in transmission)

(1) A late acceptance is nevertheless effective as an acceptance if without undue delay the offeror so informs the offeree or gives notice to that effect.

(2) If a letter or other writing containing a late acceptance shows that it has been sent in such circumstances that if its transmission had been normal it would have reached the offeror in due time, the late acceptance is effective as an acceptance unless, without undue delay, the offeror informs the offeree that it considers the offer as having lapsed.

ARTICLE 2.10

(Withdrawal of acceptance)

An acceptance may be withdrawn if the withdrawal reaches the offeror before or at the same time as the acceptance would have become effective.

ARTICLE 2.11

(Modified acceptance)

(1) A reply to an offer which purports to be an acceptance but contains additions, limitations or other modifications is a rejection of the offer and constitutes a counter-offer.

(2) However, a reply to an offer which purports to be an acceptance but contains additional or different terms which do not materially alter the terms of the offer constitutes an acceptance, unless the offeror, without undue delay, objects to the discrepancy. If the offeror does not object, the terms of the contract are the terms of the offer with the modifications contained in the acceptance.

ARTICLE 2.12

(Writings in confirmation)

If a writing which is sent within a reasonable time after the conclusion of the contract and which purports to be a confirmation of the contract contains additional or different terms, such terms become part of the contract, unless they materially alter the contract or the recipient, without undue delay, objects to the discrepancy.

ARTICLE 2.13

*(Conclusion of contract dependent on agreement
on specific matters or in a specific form)*

Where in the course of negotiations one of the parties insists that the contract is not concluded until there is agreement on specific matters or in a specific form, no contract is concluded before agreement is reached on those matters or in that form.

ARTICLE 2.14

(Contract with terms deliberately left open)

(1) If the parties intend to conclude a contract, the fact that they intentionally leave a term to be agreed upon in further negotiations or to be determined by a third person does not prevent a contract from coming into existence.

(2) The existence of the contract is not affected by the fact that subsequently

(a) the parties reach no agreement on the term; or

(b) the third person does not determine the term,

provided that there is an alternative means of rendering the term definite that is reasonable in the circumstances, having regard to the intention of the parties.

ARTICLE 2.15

(Negotiations in bad faith)

(1) A party is free to negotiate and is not liable for failure to reach an agreement.

(2) However, a party who negotiates or breaks off negotiations in bad faith is liable for the losses caused to the other party.

(3) It is bad faith, in particular, for a party to enter into or continue negotiations when intending not to reach an agreement with the other party.

COMMENT

1. Freedom of negotiation

As a rule, parties are not only free to decide when and with whom to enter into negotiations with a view to concluding a contract, but also if, how and for how long to proceed with their efforts to reach an agreement. This follows from the basic principle of freedom of contract enunciated in Art. 1.1, and is essential in order to guarantee healthy competition among business people engaged in international trade.

2. Liability for negotiating in bad faith

A party's right freely to enter into negotiations and to decide on the terms to be negotiated is, however, not unlimited, and must not conflict with the principle of good faith and fair dealing laid down in Art. 1.7. One particular instance of negotiating in bad faith which is expressly indicated in para. (3) of this article is that where a party enters into negotiations or continues to negotiate without any intention of concluding an agreement with the other party. Other instances are where one party has deliberately or by negligence misled the other party as to the nature or terms of the proposed contract, either by actually misrepresenting facts, or by not disclosing facts which, given the nature of the parties and/or the contract, should have been disclosed. As to the duty of confidentiality, see Art. 2.16.

A party's liability for negotiating in bad faith is limited to the losses caused to the other party (para. (2)). In other words, the aggrieved party may recover the expenses incurred in the negotiations and may also be compensated for the lost opportunity to conclude another contract with a third person (so-called reliance or negative interest), but may generally not recover the profit which would have resulted had the original contract been concluded (so-called expectation or positive interest).

Illustrations

1. A learns of B's intention to sell its restaurant. A, who has no intention whatsoever of buying the restaurant, nevertheless enters into lengthy negotiations with B for the sole purpose of preventing B from selling the restaurant to C, a competitor of A's. A, who breaks off negotiations when C has bought another restaurant, is liable to B, who ultimately succeeds in selling the restaurant at a lower price than offered by C, for the difference in price.

2. A, who is negotiating with B for the promotion of the purchase of military equipment by the armed forces of B's country, learns that B will not receive the necessary export license from its own government authorities, a pre-requisite for permission to pay B's fees. A does not reveal this fact to B and finally concludes the contract, which, however, cannot be enforced by reason of the missing licenses. A is liable to B for the costs incurred after A had learned of the impossibility of obtaining the required licenses.

3. A enters into lengthy negotiations for a bank loan from B's

branch office. At the last minute the branch office discloses that it had no authority to sign and that its head office had decided not to approve the draft agreement. A, who could in the meantime have obtained the loan from another bank, is entitled to recover the expenses entailed by the negotiations and the profits it would have made during the delay before obtaining the loan from the other bank.

3. Liability for breaking off negotiations in bad faith

The right to break off negotiations also is subject to the principle of good faith and fair dealing. Once an offer has been made, it may be revoked only within the limits provided for in Art. 2.4. Yet even before this stage is reached, or in a negotiation process with no ascertainable sequence of offer and acceptance, a party may no longer be free to break off negotiations abruptly and without justification. When such a point of no return is reached depends of course on the circumstances of the case, in particular the extent to which the other party, as a result of the conduct of the first party, had reason to rely on the positive outcome of the negotiations, and on the number of issues relating to the future contract on which the parties have already reached agreement.

Illustration

4. A assures B of the grant of a franchise if B takes steps to gain experience and is prepared to invest US$ 150,000. During the next two years B makes extensive preparations with a view to concluding the contract, always with A's assurance that B will be granted the franchise. When all is ready for the signing of the agreement, A informs B that the latter must in-

vest a substantially higher sum. B, who refuses, is entitled to recover from A the expenses incurred with a view to the conclusion of the contract.

ARTICLE 2.16

(Duty of confidentiality)

Where information is given as confidential by one party in the course of negotiations, the other party is under a duty not to disclose that information or to use it improperly for its own purposes, whether or not a contract is subsequently concluded. Where appropriate, the remedy for breach of that duty may include compensation based on the benefit received by the other party.

ARTICLE 2.17

(Merger clauses)

A contract in writing which contains a clause indicating that the writing completely embodies the terms on which the parties have agreed cannot be contradicted or supplemented by evidence of prior statements or agreements. However, such statements or agreements may be used to interpret the writing.

ARTICLE 2.18

(Written modification clauses)

A contract in writing which contains a clause requiring any modification or termination by agreement to be in writing may not be otherwise modified or terminated. However, a party may be precluded by its conduct from asserting such a clause to the extent that the other party has acted in reliance on that conduct.

ARTICLE 2.19

(Contracting under standard terms)

(1) Where one party or both parties use standard terms in concluding a contract, the general rules on formation apply, subject to Articles 2.20–2.22.

(2) Standard terms are provisions which are prepared in advance for general and repeated use by one party and which are actually used without negotiation with the other party.

ARTICLE 2.20

(Surprising terms)

(1) No term contained in standard terms which is of such a character that the other party could not reasonably have expected it, is effective unless it has been expressly accepted by that party.

(2) In determining whether a term is of such a character regard is to be had to its content, language and presentation.

ARTICLE 2.21

(Conflict between standard terms and non-standard terms)

In case of conflict between a standard term and a term which is not a standard term the latter prevails.

ARTICLE 2.22

(Battle of forms)

Where both parties use standard terms and reach agreement except on those terms, a contract is concluded on the basis of the agreed terms and of any standard terms which are common in substance unless one party clearly indicates in advance, or later and without undue delay informs the other party, that it does not intend to be bound by such a contract.

CHAPTER 3—VALIDITY

ARTICLE 3.1

(Matters not covered)

These Principles do not deal with invalidity arising from

(a) lack of capacity;

(b) lack of authority;

(c) immorality or illegality.

ARTICLE 3.2

(Validity of mere agreement)

A contract is concluded, modified or terminated by the mere agreement of the parties, without any further requirement.

ARTICLE 3.3

(Initial impossibility)

(1) The mere fact that at the time of the conclusion of the contract the performance of the obligation assumed was impossible does not affect the validity of the contract.

(2) The mere fact that at the time of the conclusion of the contract a party was not entitled to dispose of the assets to which the contract relates does not affect the validity of the contract.

ARTICLE 3.4

(Definition of mistake)

Mistake is an erroneous assumption relating to facts or to law existing when the contract was concluded.

ARTICLE 3.5

(Relevant mistake)

(1) A party may only avoid the contract for mistake if, when the contract was concluded, the mistake was of such importance that a reasonable person in the same situation as the party in error would only have concluded the contract on materially different terms or would not have concluded it at all if the true state of affairs had been known, and

(a) the other party made the same mistake, or caused the mistake, or knew or ought to have known of the mistake and it was contrary to reasonable commercial standards of fair dealing to leave the mistaken party in error; or

(b) the other party had not at the time of avoidance acted in reliance on the contract.

(2) However, a party may not avoid the contract if

(a) it was grossly negligent in committing the mistake; or

(b) the mistake relates to a matter in regard to which the risk of mistake was assumed or, having regard to the circumstances, should be borne by the mistaken party.

ARTICLE 3.6

(Error in expression or transmission)

An error occurring in the expression or transmission of a declaration is considered to be a mistake of the person from whom the declaration emanated.

ARTICLE 3.7

(Remedies for non-performance)

A party is not entitled to avoid the contract on the ground of mistake if the circumstances on which that party relies afford, or could have afforded, a remedy for non-performance.

ARTICLE 3.8

(Fraud)

A party may avoid the contract when it has been led to conclude the contract by the other party's fraudulent representation, including language or practices, or fraudulent non-disclosure of circumstances which, according to reasonable commercial standards of fair dealing, the latter party should have disclosed.

ARTICLE 3.9

(Threat)

A party may avoid the contract when it has been led to conclude the contract by the other party's unjustified threat which, having regard to the circumstances, is so imminent and serious as to leave the first party no reasonable alternative. In particular, a threat is unjustified if the act or omission with which a party has been threatened is wrongful in itself, or it is wrongful to use it as a means to obtain the conclusion of the contract.

ARTICLE 3.10
(Gross disparity)

(1) A party may avoid the contract or an individual term of it if, at the time of the conclusion of the contract, the contract or term unjustifiably gave the other party an excessive advantage. Regard is to be had, among other factors, to

(a) the fact that the other party has taken unfair advantage of the first party's dependence, economic distress or urgent needs, or of its improvidence, ignorance, inexperience or lack of bargaining skill; and

(b) the nature and purpose of the contract.

(2) Upon the request of the party entitled to avoidance, a court may adapt the contract or term in order to make it accord with reasonable commercial standards of fair dealing.

(3) A court may also adapt the contract or term upon the request of the party receiving notice of avoidance, provided that that party informs the other party of its request promptly after receiving such notice and before the other party has acted in reliance on it. The provisions of Article 3.13(2) apply accordingly.

ARTICLE 3.11
(Third persons)

(1) Where fraud, threat, gross disparity or a party's mistake is imputable to, or is known or ought to be known by, a third person for whose acts the other party is responsible, the contract may be avoided under the same conditions as if the behaviour or knowledge had been that of the party itself.

(2) Where fraud, threat or gross disparity is imputable to a third person for whose acts the other party is not responsible, the contract may be avoided if that party knew or ought to have known of the fraud, threat or disparity, or has not at the time of avoidance acted in reliance on the contract.

ARTICLE 3.12
(Confirmation)

If the party entitled to avoid the contract expressly or impliedly confirms the contract after the period of time for giving notice of avoidance has begun to run, avoidance of the contract is excluded.

ARTICLE 3.13

(Loss of right to avoid)

(1) If a party is entitled to avoid the contract for mistake but the other party declares itself willing to perform or performs the contract as it was understood by the party entitled to avoidance, the contract is considered to have been concluded as the latter party understood it. The other party must make such a declaration or render such performance promptly after having been informed of the manner in which the party entitled to avoidance had understood the contract and before that party has acted in reliance on a notice of avoidance.

(2) After such a declaration or performance the right to avoidance is lost and any earlier notice of avoidance is ineffective.

ARTICLE 3.14

(Notice of avoidance)

The right of a party to avoid the contract is exercised by notice to the other party.

ARTICLE 3.15

(Time limits)

(1) Notice of avoidance shall be given within a reasonable time, having regard to the circumstances, after the avoiding party knew or could not have been unaware of the relevant facts or became capable of acting freely.

(2) Where an individual term of the contract may be avoided by a party under Article 3.10, the period of time for giving notice of avoidance begins to run when that term is asserted by the other party.

ARTICLE 3.16

(Partial avoidance)

Where a ground of avoidance affects only individual terms of the contract, the effect of avoidance is limited to those terms unless, having regard to the circumstances, it is unreasonable to uphold the remaining contract.

ARTICLE 3.17

(Retroactive effect of avoidance)

(1) Avoidance takes effect retroactively.

(2) On avoidance either party may claim restitution of whatever it has supplied under the contract or the part of it avoided, provided that it concurrently makes restitution of whatever it has received under the contract or the part of it avoided or, if it cannot make restitution in kind, it makes an allowance for what it has received.

ARTICLE 3.18

(Damages)

Irrespective of whether or not the contract has been avoided, the party who knew or ought to have known of the ground for avoidance is liable for damages so as to put the other party in the same position in which it would have been if it had not concluded the contract.

ARTICLE 3.19

(Mandatory character of the provisions)

The provisions of this Chapter are mandatory, except insofar as they relate to the binding force of mere agreement, initial impossibility or mistake.

ARTICLE 3.20

(Unilateral declarations)

The provisions of this Chapter apply with appropriate adaptations to any communication of intention addressed by one party to the other.

CHAPTER 4—INTERPRETATION

ARTICLE 4.1

(Intention of the parties)

(1) A contract shall be interpreted according to the common intention of the parties.

(2) If such an intention cannot be established, the contract shall be interpreted according to the meaning that reasonable persons of the same kind as the parties would give to it in the same circumstances.

ARTICLE 4.2

(Interpretation of statements and other conduct)

(1) The statements and other conduct of a party shall be interpreted according to that party's intention if the other party knew or could not have been unaware of that intention.

(2) If the preceding paragraph is not applicable, such statements and other conduct shall be interpreted according to the meaning that a reasonable person of the same kind as the other party would give to it in the same circumstances.

ARTICLE 4.3

(Relevant circumstances)

In applying Articles 4.1 and 4.2, regard shall be had to all the circumstances, including

(a) preliminary negotiations between the parties;

(b) practices which the parties have established between themselves;

(c) the conduct of the parties subsequent to the conclusion of the contract;

(d) the nature and purpose of the contract;

(e) the meaning commonly given to terms and expressions in the trade concerned;

(f) usages.

ARTICLE 4.4

(Reference to contract or statement as a whole)

Terms and expressions shall be interpreted in the light of the whole contract or statement in which they appear.

ARTICLE 4.5

(All terms to be given effect)

Contract terms shall be interpreted so as to give effect to all the terms rather than to deprive some of them of effect.

ARTICLE 4.6

(Contra proferentem rule)

If contract terms supplied by one party are unclear, an interpretation against that party is preferred.

ARTICLE 4.7

(Linguistic discrepancies)

Where a contract is drawn up in two or more language versions which are equally authoritative there is, in case of discrepancy between the versions, a preference for the interpretation according to a version in which the contract was originally drawn up.

ARTICLE 4.8

(Supplying an omitted term)

(1) Where the parties to a contract have not agreed with respect to a term which is important for a determination of their rights and duties, a term which is appropriate in the circumstances shall be supplied.

(2) In determining what is an appropriate term regard shall be had, among other factors, to

(a) the intention of the parties;

(b) the nature and purpose of the contract;

(c) good faith and fair dealing;

(d) reasonableness.

CHAPTER 5—CONTENT

ARTICLE 5.1

(Express and implied obligations)

The contractual obligations of the parties may be express or implied.

ARTICLE 5.2

(Implied obligations)

Implied obligations stem from

(a) the nature and purpose of the contract;

(b) practices established between the parties and usages;

(c) good faith and fair dealing;

(d) reasonableness.

ARTICLE 5.3

(Co-operation between the parties)

Each party shall co-operate with the other party when such co-operation may reasonably be expected for the performance of that party's obligations.

ARTICLE 5.4

(Duty to achieve a specific result Duty of best efforts)

(1) To the extent that an obligation of a party involves a duty to achieve a specific result, that party is bound to achieve that result.

(2) To the extent that an obligation of a party involves a duty of best efforts in the performance of an activity, that party is bound to make such efforts as would be made by a reasonable person of the same kind in the same circumstances.

ARTICLE 5.5

(Determination of kind of duty involved)

In determining the extent to which an obligation of a party involves a duty of best efforts in the performance of an activity or a duty to achieve a specific result, regard shall be had, among other factors, to

(a) the way in which the obligation is expressed in the contract;

(b) the contractual price and other terms of the contract;

(c) the degree of risk normally involved in achieving the expected result;

(d) the ability of the other party to influence the performance of the obligation.

ARTICLE 5.6

(Determination of quality of performance)

Where the quality of performance is neither fixed by, nor determinable from, the contract a party is bound to render a performance of a quality that is reasonable and not less than average in the circumstances.

ARTICLE 5.7

(Price determination)

(1) Where a contract does not fix or make provision for determining the price, the parties are considered,in the absence of any indication to the contrary, to have made reference to the price generally charged at the time of the conclusion of the contract for such performance in comparable circumstances in the trade concerned or, if no such price is available, to a reasonable price.

(2) Where the price is to be determined by one party and that determination is manifestly unreasonable, a reasonable price shall be substituted notwithstanding any contract term to the contrary.

(3) Where the price is to be fixed by a third person, and that person cannot or will not do so, the price shall be a reasonable price.

(4) Where the price is to be fixed by reference to factors which do not exist or have ceased to exist or to be accessible, the nearest equivalent factor shall be treated as a substitute.

ARTICLE 5.8

(Contract for an indefinite period)

A contract for an indefinite period may be ended by either party by giving notice a reasonable time in advance.

CHAPTER 6—PERFORMANCE

SECTION 1: PERFORMANCE IN GENERAL

ARTICLE 6.1.1

(Time of performance)

A party must perform its obligations:

(a) if a time is fixed by or determinable from the contract, at that time;

(b) if a period of time is fixed by or determinable from the contract, at any time within that period unless circumstances indicate that the other party is to choose a time;

(c) in any other case, within a reasonable time after the conclusion of the contract.

ARTICLE 6.1.2

(Performance at one time or in instalments)

In cases under Article 6.1.1(b) or (c), a party must perform its obligations at one time if that performance can be rendered at one time and the circumstances do not indicate otherwise.

ARTICLE 6.1.3

(Partial performance)

(1) The obligee may reject an offer to perform in part at the time performance is due, whether or not such offer is coupled with an assurance as to the balance of the performance, unless the obligee has no legitimate interest in so doing.

(2) Additional expenses caused to the obligee by partial performance are to be borne by the obligor without prejudice to any other remedy.

ARTICLE 6.1.4

(Order of performance)

(1) To the extent that the performances of the parties can be rendered simultaneously, the parties are bound to render them simultaneously unless the circumstances indicate otherwise.

(2) To the extent that the performance of only one party requires a period of time, that party is bound to render its performance first, unless the circumstances indicate otherwise.

ARTICLE 6.1.5

(Earlier performance)

(1) The obligee may reject an earlier performance unless it has no legitimate interest in so doing.

(2) Acceptance by a party of an earlier performance does not affect the time for the performance of its own obligations if that time has been fixed irrespective of the performance of the other party's obligations.

(3) Additional expenses caused to the obligee by earlier performance are to be borne by the obligor, without prejudice to any other remedy.

ARTICLE 6.1.6

(Place of performance)

(1) If the place of performance is neither fixed by, nor determinable from, the contract, a party is to perform:

(a) a monetary obligation, at the obligee's place of business;

(b) any other obligation, at its own place of business.

(2) A party must bear any increase in the expenses incidental to performance which is caused by a change in its place of business subsequent to the conclusion of the contract.

ARTICLE 6.1.7

(Payment by cheque or other instrument)

(1) Payment may be made in any form used in the ordinary course of business at the place for payment.

(2) However, an obligee who accepts, either by virtue of paragraph (1) or voluntarily, a cheque, any other order to pay or a promise to pay, is presumed to do so only on condition that it will be honoured.

ARTICLE 6.1.8

(Payment by funds transfer)

(1) Unless the obligee has indicated a particular account, payment may be made by a transfer to any of the financial institutions in which the obligee has made it known that it has an account.

(2) In case of payment by a transfer the obligation of the obligor is discharged when the transfer to the obligee's financial institution becomes effective.

ARTICLE 6.1.9

(Currency of payment)

(1) If a monetary obligation is expressed in a currency other than that of the place for payment, it may be paid by the obligor in the currency of the place for payment unless

(a) that currency is not freely convertible; or

(b) the parties have agreed that payment should be made only in the currency in which the monetary obligation is expressed.

(2) If it is impossible for the obligor to make payment in the currency in which the monetary obligation is expressed, the obligee may require payment in the currency of the place for payment, even in the case referred to in paragraph (1)(b).

(3) Payment in the currency of the place for payment is to be made according to the applicable rate of exchange prevailing there when payment is due.

(4) However, if the obligor has not paid at the time when payment is due, the obligee may require payment according to the applicable rate of exchange prevailing either when payment is due or at the time of actual payment.

ARTICLE 6.1.10

(Currency not expressed)

Where a monetary obligation is not expressed in a particular currency, payment must be made in the currency of the place where payment is to be made.

ARTICLE 6.1.11

(Costs of performance)

Each party shall bear the costs of performance of its obligations.

ARTICLE 6.1.12

(Imputation of payments)

(1) An obligor owing several monetary obligations to the same obligee may specify at the time of payment the debt to which it intends the payment to be applied. However, the payment discharges first any expenses, then interest due and finally the principal.

(2) If the obligor makes no such specification, the obligee may, within a reasonable time after payment, declare to the obligor the obligation to which it imputes the payment, provided that the obligation is due and undisputed.

(3) In the absence of imputation under paragraphs (1) or (2), payment is imputed to that obligation which satisfies one of the following criteria and in the order indicated:

(a) an obligation which is due or which is the first to fall due;

(b) the obligation for which the obligee has least security;

(c) the obligation which is the most burdensome for the obligor;

(d) the obligation which has arisen first.

If none of the preceding criteria applies, payment is imputed to all the obligations proportionally.

ARTICLE 6.1.13

(Imputation of non-monetary obligations)

Article 6.1.12 applies with appropriate adaptations to the imputation of performance of non-monetary obligations.

ARTICLE 6.1.14

(Application for public permission)

Where the law of a State requires a public permission affecting the validity of the contract or its performance and neither that law nor the circumstances indicate otherwise

(a) if only one party has its place of business in that State, that party shall take the measures necessary to obtain the permission:

(b) in any other case the party whose performance requires permission shall take the necessary measures.

ARTICLE 6.1.15

(Procedure in applying for permission)

(1) The party required to take the measures necessary to obtain the permission shall do so without undue delay and shall bear any expenses incurred.

(2) That party shall whenever appropriate give the other party notice of the grant or refusal of such permission without undue delay.

ARTICLE 6.1.16

(Permission neither granted nor refused)

(1) If, notwithstanding the fact that the party responsible has taken all measures required, permission is neither granted nor refused within an agreed period or, where no period has been agreed, within a reasonable time from the conclusion of the contract, either party is entitled to terminate the contract.

(2) Where the permission affects some terms only, paragraph (1) does not apply if, having regard to the circumstances, it is reasonable to uphold the remaining contract even if the permission is refused.

ARTICLE 6.1.17

(Permission refused)

(1) The refusal of a permission affecting the validity of the contract renders the contract void. If the refusal affects the validity of some terms only, only such terms are void if, having regard to the circumstances, it is reasonable to uphold the remaining contract.

(2) Where the refusal of a permission renders the performance of the contract impossible in whole or in part, the rules on non-performance apply.

SECTION 2: HARDSHIP

ARTICLE 6.2.1

(Contract to be observed)

Where the performance of a contract becomes more onerous for one of the parties, that party is nevertheless bound to perform its obligations subject to the following provisions on hardship.

COMMENT

1. Binding character of the contract the general rule

The purpose of this article is to make it clear that as a consequence of the general principle of the binding character of the contract (see Art. 1.3) performance must be rendered as long as it is possible and regardless of the burden it may impose on the performing party. In other words, even if a party experiences heavy losses instead of the expected profits or the performance has become meaningless for that party the terms of the contract must nevertheless be respected.

Illustration

In January 1990 A, a forwarding agent, enters into a two-year shipping contract with B, a carrier. Under the contract B is bound to ship certain goods from Hamburg to New York at a fixed price, on a monthly basis throughout the two-year period. Alleging a substantial increase in the price of fuel in the aftermath of the 1990 Gulf crisis, B requests a five per cent increase in the rate for August 1990. B is not entitled to such an increase because B bears the risk of its performance becoming more onerous.

2. Change in circumstances relevant only in exceptional cases

The principle of the binding character of the contract is not however an absolute one. When supervising circumstances are such that they lead to a fundamental alteration of the equilibrium of the contract, they create an exceptional situation referred to in these Principles as "hardship" and dealt with in the following articles of this section.

The phenomenon of hardship has been acknowledged by various legal systems under the guise of other concepts such as frustration of purpose, *Wegfall der Geschäftsgrundlage, imprévision, eccessiva onerositá sopravvenuta*, etc. The term "hardship" was chosen because it is widely known in international trade practice as confirmed by the inclusion in many international contracts of so-called "hardship clauses".

ARTICLE 6.2.2

(Definition of hardship)

There is hardship where the occurrence of events fundamentally alters the equilibrium of the contract either because the cost of a party's performance has increased or because the value of the performance a party receives has diminished, and

(a) the events occur or become known to the disadvantaged party after the conclusion of the contract;

(b) the events could not reasonably have been taken into account by the disadvantaged party at the time of the conclusion of the contract;

(c) the events are beyond the control of the disadvantaged party; and

(d) the risk of the events was not assumed by the disadvantaged party.

COMMENT

1. Hardship defined

This article defines hardship as a situation where the occurrence of events fundamentally alters the equilibrium of the contract, provided that those events meet the requirements which are laid down in sub-paras. (a) to (d).

2. Fundamental alteration of equilibrium of the contract

Since the general principle is that change in circumstances does not affect the obligation to perform (see Art. 6.2.1), it follows that hardship may not be invoked unless the alteration of the equilibrium of the contract is fundamental. Whether an alteration is "fundamental" in a given case will of course depend upon the circumstances. If, however, the performances are capable of precise measurement in monetary terms, an alteration amounting to 50% or more of the cost or value of the performance is likely to amount to a "fundamental" alteration.

Illustration

1. In September 1989 A, a dealer in electronic goods situated in the former German Democratic Republic, purchases stocks from B, situated in country X, also a former socialist country. The goods are to be delivered by B in December 1990. In November 1990, A informs B that the goods are no longer of any use to it, claiming that after the unification of the German Democratic Republic and the Federal Republic of Germany there is no longer any market for such goods imported from country X. Unless the circumstances indicate otherwise, A is entitled to invoke hardship.

a. Increase in cost of performance

In practice a fundamental alteration in the equilibrium of the contract may manifest itself in two different but related ways. The first is characterised by a substantial increase in the cost for one party of performing its obligation. This party will normally be the one who is to perform the non-monetary obligation. The substantial increase in the cost may, for instance, be due to a dramatic rise in the price of the raw materials necessary for the production of the goods or the rendering of the services, or to the introduction of new safety regulations requiring far more expensive production procedures.

b. Decrease in value of the performance received by one party

The second manifestation of hardship is characterised by a substantial decrease in the value of the performance received by one party, including cases where the performance no longer has any value at all for the receiving party. The performance may be that either of a monetary or of a non-monetary obligation. The substantial decrease in the value or the total loss of any value of the performance may be due either to drastic changes in market conditions (e.g. the effect of a dramatic increase in inflation on a contractually agreed price) or the frustration of the purpose for which the performance was required (e.g. the effect of a prohibition to build on a plot of land acquired for building purposes or the effect of an export embargo on goods acquired with a view to their subsequent export).

Naturally the decrease in value of the performance must be capable of objective measurement: a mere change in the personal opinion of the receiving party as to the value of the performance is of no relevance. As to the frustration of the purpose of the performance, this can only be taken into account when the purpose in question was known or at least ought to have been known to both parties.

3. Additional requirements for hardship to arise

a. Events occur or become known after conclusion of the contract

According to sub-para. (a) of this article, the events causing hardship must take place or become known to the disadvantaged party after the conclusion of the contract. If that party had known of those events when entering into the contract, it would have been able to take them into account at that time and may not subsequently rely on hardship.

b. Events could not reasonably have been taken into account by disadvantaged party

Even if the change in circumstances occurs after the conclusion of the contract, sub-para. (b) of this article makes it clear that such circumstances cannot cause hardship if they could reasonably have been taken into account by the disadvantaged party at the time the contract was concluded.

Illustration

2. A agrees to supply B with crude oil from country X at a fixed price for the next five years, notwithstanding the acute political tensions in the region. Two years after the conclusion of the contract, a war erupts between contending factions in neighbouring countries. The war results in a world energy crisis and oil prices increase drastically. A is not entitled to invoke hardship because such a rise in the price of crude oil was not unforeseeable.

Sometimes the change in circumstances is gradual, but the final result of those gradual changes may constitute a case of hardship. If the change began before the contract was concluded, hardship will not arise unless the pace of change increases dramatically during the life of the contract.

Illustration

3. In a sales contract between A and B the price is expressed in the currency of country X, a currency whose value was already depreciating slowly against other major currencies before the conclusion of the contract. One month afterwards a political crisis in country X leads to a massive devaluation of the order of 80% of its currency. Unless the circumstances indicate otherwise, this constitutes a case of hardship, since such a dramatic acceleration of the loss of value of the currency of country X was not foreseeable.

c. Events beyond the control of disadvantaged party

Under sub-para. (c) of this article a case of hardship can only arise if the events causing the hardship are beyond the control of the disadvantaged party.

d. Risks must not have been assumed by disadvantaged party

Under sub-para (d) there can be no hardship if the disadvantaged party had assumed the risk of the change in circumstances. The word "assumption" makes it clear that the risks need not have been taken over expressly, but that this may follow from the very nature of the contract. A party who enters into a speculative transaction is deemed to accept a certain degree of risk, even though it may not have been fully aware of that risk at the time it entered into the contract.

Illustration

4. A, an insurance company specialised in the insurance of shipping risks, requests an additional premium from those of its custom-

ers who have contracts which include the risks of war and civil insurrection, so as to meet the substantially greater risk to which it is exposed following upon the simultaneous outbreak of war and civil insurrection in three countries in the same region. A is not entitled to such an adaptation of the contract, since by the war and civil insurrection clause insurance companies assume these risks even if three countries are affected at the same time.

4. Hardship relevant only to performance not yet rendered

By its very nature hardship can only become of relevance with respect to performances still to be rendered: once a party has performed, it is no longer entitled to invoke a substantial increase in the costs of its performance or a substantial decrease in the value of the performance it receives as a consequence of a change in circumstances which occurs after such performance.

If the fundamental alteration in the equilibrium of the contract occurs at a time when performance has been only partially rendered, hardship can be of relevance only to the parts of the performance still to be rendered.

Illustration

5. A enters into a contract with B, a waste disposal company in country X, for the purpose of arranging the storage of its waste. The contract provides for a four-year term and a fixed price per ton of waste. Two years after the conclusion of the contract, the environmental movement in country X gains ground and the Government of country X prescribes prices for

storing waste which are ten times higher than before. B may successfully invoke hardship only with respect to the two remaining years of the life of the contract.

5. Hardship normally relevant to long-term contracts

Although this article does not expressly exclude the possibility of hardship being invoked in respect of other kinds of contracts, hardship will normally be of relevance to long-term contracts, i.e. those where the performance of at least one party extends over a certain period of time.

6. Hardship and force majeure

In view of the respective definitions of hardship and force majeure (see Art. 7.1.7) under these Principles there may be factual situations which can at the same time be considered as cases of hardship and of force majeure. If this is the case, it is for the party affected by these events to decide which remedy to pursue. If it invokes force majeure, it is with a view to its non-performance being excused. If, on the other hand, a party invokes hardship, this is in the first instance for the purpose of renegotiating the terms of the contract so as to allow the contract to be kept alive although on revised terms.

7. Hardship and contract practice

The definition of hardship in this article is necessarily of a rather general character. International commercial contracts often contain much more precise and elaborate provisions in this regard. The parties may therefore find it appropriate to adapt the content of this article so as to take account of the particular features of the specific transaction.

ARTICLE 6.2.3

(Effects of hardship)

(1) In case of hardship the disadvantaged party is entitled to request renegotiations. The request shall be made without undue delay and shall indicate the grounds on which it is based.

(2) The request for renegotiation does not in itself entitle the disadvantaged party to withhold performance.

(3) Upon failure to reach agreement within a reasonable time either party may resort to the court.

(4) If the court finds hardship it may, if reasonable,

(a) terminate the contract at a date and on terms to be fixed; or

(b) adapt the contract with a view to restoring its equilibrium.

COMMENT

1. Disadvantaged party entitled to request renegotiations

Since hardship consists in a fundamental alteration of the equilibrium of the contract, para. (1) of this article in the first instance entitles the disadvantaged party to request the other party to enter into renegotiation of the original terms of the contract with a view to adapting them to the changed circumstances.

Illustration

1. A, a construction company situation in country X, enters into a lump sum contract with B, a governmental agency, for the erection of a plant in country Y. Most of the sophisticated machinery has to be imported from abroad. Due to an unexpected devaluation of the currency of country Y, which is the currency of payment, the cost of the machinery increases by more than 50%. A is entitled to request B to renegotiate the original contract price so as to adapt it to the changed circumstances.

A request for renegotiations is not admissible where the contract itself already incorporates a clause providing for the automatic adaptation of the contract (e.g. a clause providing for automatic indexation of the price if certain events occur).

Illustration

2. The facts are the same as in Illustration 1, the difference being that the contract contains a price indexation clause relating to variations in the cost of materials and labour. A is not entitled to request a renegotiation of the price.

However, even in such a case renegotiation on account of hardship would not be precluded if the adaptation clause incorporated in the contract did not contemplate the events giving rise to hardship.

Illustration

3. The facts are the same as in Illustration 2, the difference being that the substantial increase in A's costs is due to the adoption of new safety regulations in country Y. A is entitled to request B to renegotiate the original contract price so as to adapt it to the changed circumstances.

2. Request for renegotiations without undue delay

The request for renegotiations must be made as quickly as possible after the time at which hardship is alleged to have occurred (para. (1)). The precise time for requesting renegotiations will depend upon the circumstances of the case: it may, for instance, be longer when the change in circumstances takes place gradually (see comment 3(b) on Art. 6.2.2).

The disadvantaged party does not lose its right to request renegotiations simply because it fails to act without undue delay. The delay in making the request may however affect the finding as to whether hardship actually existed and, if so, its consequences for the contract.

3. Grounds for request for renegotiations

Para. (1) of this article also imposes on the disadvantaged party a duty to indicate the grounds on which the request for renegotiations is based so as to permit the other party to better assess whether or not the request for renegotiations is justified. An incomplete request is to be considered as not being raised in time, unless the grounds of the alleged hardship are so obvious that they need not be spelt out in the request.

Failure to set forth the grounds on which the request for renegotiations is based may have similar effects to those resulting from undue delay in making the request (see comment 2 on this article).

4. Request for renegotiations and withholding of performance

Para. (2) of this article provides that the request for renegotiations does not of itself entitle the disadvantaged party to withhold performance. The reason for this lies in the exceptional character of hardship and in the risk of possible abuses of the remedy. With-

holding performance may be justified only in extraordinary circumstances.

Illustration

4. A enters into a contract with B for the construction of a plant. The plant is to be built in country X, which adopts new safety regulations after the conclusion of the contract. The new regulations require additional apparatus and thereby fundamentally alter the equilibrium of the contract making A's performance substantially more onerous. A is entitled to request negotiations and may withhold performance in view of the time it needs to implement the new safety regulations, but it may also withhold the delivery of the additional apparatus, for as long as the corresponding price adaptation is not agreed.

5. Renegotiations in good faith

Although nothing is said in this article to that effect, both the request for renegotiations by the disadvantaged party and the conduct of both parties during the renegotiation process are subject to the general principle of good faith (Art. 1.7) and to the duty of cooperation (Art. 5.3). Thus the disadvantaged party must honestly believe that a case of hardship actually exists and not request renegotiations as a purely tactical manoeuvre. Similarly, once the request has been made, both parties must conduct the renegotiations in a constructive manner, in particular by refraining from any forms of obstruction and by providing all the necessary information.

6. Resort to the court upon failure to reach an agreement

If the parties fail to reach an agreement on the adaptation of the contract to the changed circumstances within a reasonable time, para. (3) of the present article authorises either party to resort to the court. Such a situation may arise either because the non-disadvantaged party completely ignored the request for renegotiations or because the renegotiations, although conducted by both parties in good faith, did not achieve a positive outcome.

How long a party must wait before resorting to the court will depend on the complexity of the issues to be settled and the particular circumstances of the case.

7. *Court measures in case of hardship*

According to para. (4) of this article a court which finds that a hardship situation exists may react in a number of different ways.

A first possibility is for it to terminate the contract. However, since termination in this case does not depend on a non-performance by one of the parties, its effects on the performances already rendered might be different from those provided for by the rules governing termination in general (Arts. 7.3.1. et seq.). Accordingly, para. (4)(a) provides that termination shall take place "at a date and on terms to be fixed" by the court.

Another possibility would be for a court to adapt the contract with a view to restoring its equilibrium (para. (4)(b)). In so doing the court will seek to make a fair distribution of the losses between the parties. This may or may not, depending on the nature of the hardship, involve a price adaptation. However, if it does, the adaptation will not necessarily reflect in full the loss entailed by the change in circumstances, since the court will, for instance, have to consider the extent to which one of the parties has taken a risk and the extent to which the party

is entitled to receive a performance may still benefit from that performance.

Para. (4) of this article expressly states that the court may terminate or adapt the contract only when this is reasonable. The circumstances may even be such that neither termination nor adaptation is appropriate and in consequence the only reasonable solution will be for the court either to direct the parties to resume negotiations with a view to reaching agreement on the adaptation of the contract, or to confirm the terms of the contract as they stand.

Illustration

5. A, an exporter, undertakes to supply B, an importer in country X, with beer for three years. Two years after the conclusion of the contract new legislation is introduced in country X prohibiting the sale and consumption of alcoholic drinks. B immediately invokes hardship and requests A to renegotiate the contract. A recognises that hardship has occurred, but refuses to accept the modifications of the contract proposed by B. After one month of fruitless discussions B resorts to the court.

If B has the possibility to sell the beer in a neighbouring country, although at a substantially lower price, the court may decide to uphold the contract but to reduce the agreed price.

If on the contrary B has no such possibility, it may be reasonable for the court to terminate the contract, at the same time however requiring B to pay A for the last consignment still en route.

CHAPTER 7—NON–PERFORMANCE

SECTION 1: NON–PERFORMANCE IN GENERAL

ARTICLE 7.1.1

(Non-performance defined)

Non-performance is failure by a party to perform any of its obligations under the contract, including defective performance or late performance.

ARTICLE 7.1.2

(Interference by the other party)

A party may not rely on the non-performance of the other party to the extent that such non-performance was caused by the first party's act or omission or by another event as to which the first party bears the risk.

ARTICLE 7.1.3

(Withholding performance)

(1) Where the parties are to perform simultaneously, either party may withhold performance until the other party tenders its performance.

(2) Where the parties are to perform consecutively, the party that is to perform later may withhold its performance until the first party has performed.

ARTICLE 7.1.4

(Cure by non-performing party)

(1) The non-performing party may, at its own expense, cure any non-performance, provided that

(a) without undue delay, it gives notice indicating the proposed manner and timing of the cure;

(b) cure is appropriate in the circumstances;

(c) the aggrieved party has no legitimate interest in refusing cure; and

(d) cure is effected promptly.

(2) The right to cure is not precluded by notice of termination.

(3) Upon effective notice of cure, rights of the aggrieved party that are inconsistent with the non-performing party's performance are suspended until the time for cure has expired.

(4) The aggrieved party may withhold performance pending cure.

(5) Notwithstanding cure, the aggrieved party retains the right to claim damages for delay as well as for any harm caused or not prevented by the cure.

ARTICLE 7.1.5

(Additional period for performance)

(1) In a case of non-performance the aggrieved party may by notice to the other party allow an additional period of time for performance.

(2) During the additional period the aggrieved party may withhold performance of its own reciprocal obligations and may claim damages but may not resort to any other remedy. If it receives notice from the other party that the latter will not perform within that period, or if upon expiry of that period due performance has not been made, the aggrieved party may resort to any of the remedies that may be available under this Chapter.

(3) Where in a case of delay in performance which is not fundamental the aggrieved party has given notice allowing an additional period of time of reasonable length, it may terminate the contract at the end of that period. If the additional period allowed is not of reasonable length it shall be extended to a reasonable length. The aggrieved party may in its notice provide that if the other party fails to perform within the period allowed by the notice the contract shall automatically terminate.

(4) Paragraph (3) does not apply where the obligation which has not been performed is only a minor part of the contractual obligation of the non-performing party.

ARTICLE 7.1.6

(Exemption clauses)

A clause which limits or excludes one party's liability for non-performance or which permits one party to render performance substantially different from what the other party reasonably expected may not be invoked if it would be grossly unfair to do so, having regard to the purpose of the contract.

ARTICLE 7.1.7

(Force majeure)

(1) Non-performance by a party is excused if that party proves that the non-performance was due to an impediment beyond its control and that it could not reasonably be expected to have taken the impediment into account at the time of the conclusion of the contract or to have avoided or overcome it or its consequences.

(2) When the impediment is only temporary, the excuse shall have effect for such period as is reasonable having regard to the effect of the impediment on the performance of the contract.

(3) The party who fails to perform must give notice to the other party of the impediment and its effect on its ability to perform. If the notice is not received by the other party within a reasonable time after the party who fails to perform knew or ought to have known of the impediment, it is liable for damages resulting from such non-receipt.

(4) Nothing in this article prevents a party from exercising a right to terminate the contract or to withhold performance or request interest on money due.

SECTION 2: RIGHT TO PERFORMANCE
ARTICLE 7.2.1
(Performance of monetary obligation)

Where a party who is obliged to pay money does not do so, the other party may require payment.

ARTICLE 7.2.2
(Performance of non-monetary obligation)

Where a party who owes an obligation other than one to pay money does not perform, the other party may require performance, unless

(a) performance is impossible in law or in fact;

(b) performance or, where relevant, enforcement is unreasonably burdensome or expensive;

(c) the party entitled to performance may reasonably obtain performance from another source;

(d) performance is of an exclusively personal character; or

(e) the party entitled to performance does not require performance within a reasonable time after it has, or ought to have, become aware of the non-performance.

ARTICLE 7.2.3
(Repair and replacement of defective performance)

The right to performance includes in appropriate cases the right to require repair, replacement, or other cure of defective performance. The provisions of Articles 7.2.1 and 7.2.2 apply accordingly.

ARTICLE 7.2.4
(Judicial penalty)

(1) Where the court orders a party to perform, it may also direct that this party pay a penalty if it does not comply with the order.

(2) The penalty shall be paid to the aggrieved party unless mandatory provisions of the law of the forum provide otherwise. Payment of the penalty to the aggrieved party does not exclude any claim for damages.

ARTICLE 7.2.5

(Change of remedy)

(1) An aggrieved party who has required performance of a non-monetary obligation and who has not received performance within a period fixed or otherwise within a reasonable period of time may invoke any other remedy.

(2) Where the decision of a court for performance of a non-monetary obligation cannot be enforced, the aggrieved party may invoke any other remedy.

SECTION 3: TERMINATION

ARTICLE 7.3.1

(Right to terminate the contract)

(1) A party may terminate the contract where the failure of the other party to perform an obligation under the contract amounts to a fundamental non-performance.

(2) In determining whether a failure to perform an obligation amounts to a fundamental non-performance regard shall be had, in particular, to whether

(a) the non-performance substantially deprives the aggrieved party of what it was entitled to expect under the contract unless the other party did not foresee and could not reasonably have foreseen such result;

(b) strict compliance with the obligation which has not been performed is of essence under the contract;

(c) the non-performance is intentional or reckless;

(d) the non-performance gives the aggrieved party reason to believe that it cannot rely on the other party's future performance;

(e) the non-performing party will suffer disproportionate loss as a result of the preparation or performance if the contract is terminated.

(3) In the case of delay the aggrieved party may also terminate the contract if the other party fails to perform before the time allowed it under Article 7.1.5 has expired.

ARTICLE 7.3.2

(Notice of termination)

(1) The right of a party to terminate the contract is exercised by notice to the other party.

(2) If performance has been offered late or otherwise does not conform to the contract the aggrieved party will lose its right to

terminate the contract unless it gives notice to the other party within a reasonable time after it has or ought to have become aware of the offer or of the non-conforming performance.

ARTICLE 7.3.3
(Anticipatory non-performance)

Where prior to the date for performance by one of the parties it is clear that there will be a fundamental non-performance by that party, the other party may terminate the contract.

ARTICLE 7.3.4
(Adequate assurance of due performance)

A party who reasonably believes that there will be a fundamental non-performance by the other party may demand adequate assurance of due performance and may meanwhile withhold its own performance. Where this assurance is not provided within a reasonable time the party demanding it may terminate the contract.

ARTICLE 7.3.5
(Effects of termination in general)

(1) Termination of the contract releases both parties from their obligation to effect and to receive future performance.

(2) Termination does not preclude a claim for damages for non-performance.

(3) Termination does not affect any provision in the contract for the settlement of disputes or any other term of the contract which is to operate even after termination.

ARTICLE 7.3.6
(Restitution)

(1) On termination of the contract either party may claim restitution of whatever it has supplied, provided that such party concurrently makes restitution of whatever it has received. If restitution in kind is not possible or appropriate allowance should be made in money whenever reasonable.

(2) However, if performance of the contract has extended over a period of time and the contract is divisible, such restitution can only be claimed for the period after termination has taken effect.

SECTION 4: DAMAGES
ARTICLE 7.4.1
(Right to damages)

Any non-performance gives the aggrieved party a right to damages either exclusively or in conjunction with any other remedies except where the non-performance is excused under these Principles.

319

ARTICLE 7.4.2

(Full compensation)

(1) The aggrieved party is entitled to full compensation for harm sustained as a result of the non-performance. Such harm includes both any loss which it suffered and any gain of which it was deprived, taking into account any gain to the aggrieved party resulting from its avoidance of cost or harm.

(2) Such harm may be non-pecuniary and includes, for instance, physical suffering or emotional distress.

ARTICLE 7.4.3

(Certainty of harm)

(1) Compensation is due only for harm, including future harm, that is established with a reasonable degree of certainty.

(2) Compensation may be due for the loss of a chance in proportion to the probability of its occurrence.

(3) Where the amount of damages cannot be established with a sufficient degree of certainty, the assessment is at the discretion of the court.

ARTICLE 7.4.4

(Foreseeability of harm)

The non-performing party is liable only for harm which it foresaw or could reasonably have foreseen at the time of the conclusion of the contract as being likely to result from its non-performance.

ARTICLE 7.4.5

(Proof of harm in case of replacement transaction)

Where the aggrieved party has terminated the contract and has made a replacement transaction within a reasonable time and in a reasonable manner it may recover the difference between the contract price and the price of the replacement transaction as well as damages for any further harm.

ARTICLE 7.4.6

(Proof of harm by current price)

(1) Where the aggrieved party has terminated the contract and has not made a replacement transaction but there is a current price for the performance contracted for, it may recover the difference between the contract price and the price current at the time the contract is terminated as well as damages for any further harm.

(2) Current price is the price generally charged for goods delivered or services rendered in comparable circumstances at the place where the contract should have been performed or, if there is no current price at that place, the current price at such other place that appears reasonable to take as a reference.

ARTICLE 7.4.7

(Harm due in part to aggrieved party)

Where the harm is due in part to an act or omission of the aggrieved party or to another event as to which that party bears the risk, the amount of damages shall be reduced to the extent that these factors have contributed to the harm, having regard to the conduct of each of the parties.

ARTICLE 7.4.8

(Mitigation of harm)

(1) The non-performing party is not liable for harm suffered by the aggrieved party to the extent that the harm could have been reduced by the latter party's taking reasonable steps.

(2) The aggrieved party is entitled to recover any expenses reasonably incurred in attempting to reduce the harm.

ARTICLE 7.4.9

(Interest for failure to pay money)

(1) If a party does not pay a sum of money when it falls due the aggrieved party is entitled to interest upon that sum from the time when payment is due to the time of payment whether or not the non-payment is excused.

(2) The rate of interest shall be the average bank short-term lending rate to prime borrowers prevailing for the currency of payment at the place for payment, or where no such rate exists at that place, then the same rate in the State of the currency of payment. In the absence of such a rate at either place the rate of interest shall be the appropriate rate fixed by the law of the State of the currency of payment.

(3) The aggrieved party is entitled to additional damages if the non-payment caused it a greater harm.

ARTICLE 7.4.10

(Interest on damages)

Unless otherwise agreed, interest on damages for non-performance of non-monetary obligations accrues as from the time of non-performance.

ARTICLE 7.4.11

(Manner of monetary redress)

(1) Damages are to be paid in a lump sum. However, they may be payable in instalments where the nature of the harm makes this appropriate.

(2) Damages to be paid in instalments may be indexed.

ARTICLE 7.4.12

(Currency in which to assess damages)

Damages are to be assessed either in the currency in which the monetary obligation was expressed or in the currency in which the harm was suffered, whichever is more appropriate.

ARTICLE 7.4.13

(Agreed payment for non-performance)

(1) Where the contract provides that a party who does not perform is to pay a specified sum to the aggrieved party for such non-performance, the aggrieved party is entitled to that sum irrespective of its actual harm.

(2) However, notwithstanding any agreement to the contrary the specified sum may be reduced to a reasonable amount where it is grossly excessive in relation to the harm resulting from the non-performance and to the other circumstances.

SELECTED FORMS

Acknowledgment

Thanks are due to the following, among others, for their willingness to permit reproduction of their standard forms: American Institute of Architects, American Textile Manufacturers Institute, General Electric Company, National Football League, and North American Export Grain Association. In the process of reproduction some forms have been substantially altered in size.

NFL PLAYER CONTRACT

THIS CONTRACT is between _____ _, hereinafter "Player," and

_____ , a _____ _____

____ corporation (limited partnership) (partnership), hereinafter "Club" operating under the name of the _____ _____

_____ as a member of the National Football League, hereinafter "League." In consideration of the promises made by each to the other, Player and Club agree as follows:

    1.   TERM. This contract covers _____ football season(s), and will begin on the date of execution or March 1, _____, whichever is later, and end on February 28 or 29, _____, unless extended, terminated, or renewed as specified elsewhere in this contract.

    2.   EMPLOYMENT AND SERVICES. Club employs Player as a skilled football player. Player accepts such employment. He agrees to give his best efforts and loyalty to the Club, and to conduct himself on and off the field with appropriate recognition of the fact that the success of professional football depends largely on public respect for and approval of those associated with the game. Player will report promptly for and participate fully in Club's official mandatory mini-camp(s), official preseason training camp, all Club meetings and practice sessions, and all pre-season, regular season, and post-season football games scheduled for or by Club. If invited, Player will practice for and play in any all-star football game sponsored by the League. Player will not participate in any football game not sponsored by the League unless the game is first approved by the League.

    3.   OTHER ACTIVITIES. Without prior written consent of the Club, Player will not play football or engage in activities related to football otherwise than for Club or engage in any activity other than football which may involve a significant risk of personal injury. Player represents that he has special, exceptional and unique knowledge, skill, ability, and experience as a football player, the loss of which cannot be estimated with any certainty and cannot be fairly or adequately compensated by damages. Player therefore agrees that Club will have the right, in addition to any other right which Club may possess, to enjoin Player by appropriate proceedings from playing football or engaging in football-related activities other than for Club or from engaging in any activity other than football which may involve a significant risk of personal injury.

    4.   PUBLICITY AND NFLPA GROUP LICENSING PROGRAM. (a) Player grants to Club and the League, separately and together, the authority to use his name and picture for publicity and the promotion of NFL Football, the League or any of its member clubs in newspapers, magazines, motion pictures, game programs and roster manuals, broadcasts and telecasts, and all other publicity and advertising media, provided such publicity and promotion does not constitute an endorsement by Player of a commercial product. Player will cooperate with the news media, and will participate upon request in reasonable activities to promote the Club and the League. Player and National Football League Players Association, hereinafter "NFLPA," will not contest the rights of the League and its member clubs to telecast, broadcast, or otherwise transmit NFL Football or the right of NFL Films to produce, sell, market, or distribute football game film footage, except insofar as such broadcast, telecast, or transmission of footage is used in any commercially marketable game or interactive use. The League and its member clubs, and Player and the NFLPA, reserve their respective rights as to the use of such broadcasts, telecasts or transmissions of footage in such games or interactive uses, which shall be unaffected by this subparagraph.

    (b)   Player hereby assigns to the NFLPA and its licensing affiliates, if any, the exclusive right to use and to grant to persons, firms, or corporations (collectively "licensees") the right to use his name, signature facsimile, voice, picture, photograph, likeness, and/or biographical information (collectively "image") in group licensing programs. Group licensing programs are defined as those licensing programs in which a licensee utilizes a total of six (6) or more NFL player images on products that are sold at retail or used as promotional or premium items. Player retains the right to grant permission to a licensee to utilize his image if that licensee is not concurrently utilizing the images of five (5) or more other NFL players on products that are sold at retail or are used as promotional or premium items. . . .

    5.   COMPENSATION. For performance of Player's services and all other promises of Player, Club will pay Player a yearly salary as follows:

. . .

In addition, Club will pay Player such earned performance bonuses as may be called for in this contract; Player's necessary traveling expenses from his residence to training camp; Player's reasonable board and lodging expenses during pre-season training and in connection with playing pre-season, regular season, and post-season football games outside Club's home city; Player's necessary traveling expenses to and from pre-season, regular season, and post-season football games outside Club's home city; Player's necessary traveling expenses to his residence if this contract is terminated by Club; and such additional compensation, benefits, and reimbursement of expenses as may be called for in any collective bargaining agreement in existence during the term of this contract. (For purposes of this contract, a collective bargaining agreement will be deemed to be "in existence" during its stated term or during any period for which the parties to that agreement agree to extend it.)

PROFESSIONAL FOOTBALL PLAYER'S CONTRACT

6. PAYMENT. Unless this contract or any collective bargaining agreement in existence during the term of this contract specifically provides otherwise, Player will be paid 100% of his yearly salary under this contract in equal weekly or bi-weekly installments over the course of the applicable regular season period, commencing with the first regular season game played by Club in each season. Unless this contract specifically provides otherwise, if this contract is executed or Player is activated after the beginning of the regular season, the yearly salary payable to Player will be reduced proportionately and Player will be paid the weekly or bi-weekly portion of his yearly salary becoming due and payable after he is activated. Unless this contract specifically provides otherwise, if this contract is terminated after the beginning of the regular season, the yearly salary payable to Player will be reduced proportionately and Player will be paid the weekly or bi-weekly portions of his yearly salary having become due and payable up to the time of termination.

7. DEDUCTIONS. Any advance made to Player will be repaid to Club, and any properly levied Club fine or Commissioner fine against Player will be paid, in cash on demand or by means of deductions from payments coming due to the Player under this contract, the amount of such deductions to be determined by Club unless this contract or any collective bargaining agreement in existence during the term of this contract specifically provides otherwise.

8. PHYSICAL CONDITION. Player represents to Club that he is and will maintain himself in excellent physical condition. Player will undergo a complete physical examination by the Club physician upon Club request, during which physical examination Player agrees to make full and complete disclosure of any physical or mental condition known to him which might impair his performance under this contract and to respond fully and in good faith when questioned by the Club physician about such condition. If Player fails to establish or maintain his excellent physical condition to the satisfaction of the Club physician, or make the required full and complete disclosure and good faith responses to the Club physician, then Club may terminate this contract.

9. INJURY. Unless this contract specifically provides otherwise, if Player is injured in the performance of his services under this contract and promptly reports such injury to the Club physician or trainer, then Player will receive such medical and hospital care during the term of this contract as the Club physician may deem necessary, and will continue to receive his yearly salary for so long, during the season of injury only and for no subsequent period covered by this contract, as Player is physically unable to perform the services required of him by this contract because of such injury. If Player's injury in the performance of his services under this contract results in his death, the unpaid balance of his yearly salary for the season of injury will be paid to his stated beneficiary, or in the absence of a stated beneficiary, to his estate.

10. WORKERS' COMPENSATION. Any compensation paid to Player under this contract or under any collective bargaining agreement in existence during the term of this contract for a period during which he is entitled to workers' compensation benefits by reason of temporary total, permanent total, temporary partial, or permanent partial disability will be deemed an advance payment of workers' compensation benefits due Player, and Club will be entitled to be reimbursed the amount of such payment out of any award of workers' compensation.

11. SKILL, PERFORMANCE AND CONDUCT. Player understands that he is competing with other players for a position on Club's roster within the applicable player limits. If at any time, in the sole judgement of Club, Player's skill or performance has been unsatisfactory as compared with that of other players competing for positions on Club's roster, or if Player has engaged in personal conduct reasonably judged by Club to adversely affect or reflect on Club, then Club may terminate this contract. In addition, during the period any salary cap is legally in effect, this contract may be terminated if, in Club's opinion, Player is anticipated to make less of a contribution to Club's ability to compete on the playing field than another player or players who Club intends to sign or attempts to sign, or another player or players who is or are already on Club's roster, and for whom Club needs room.

12. TERMINATION. The rights of termination set forth in this contract will be in addition to any other rights of termination allowed either party by law. Termination will be effective upon the giving of written notice, except that Player's death, other than as a result of injury incurred in the performance of his services under this contract, will automatically terminate this contract. If this contract is terminated by Club and either Player or Club so requests, Player will promptly undergo a complete physical examination by the Club physician.

13. INJURY GRIEVANCE. Unless a collective bargaining agreement in existence at the time of termination of this contract by Club provides otherwise, the following injury grievance procedure will apply: If Player believes that at the time of termination of this contract by Club he was physically unable to perform the services required of him by this contract because of an injury incurred in the performance of his services under this contract, Player may, within 60 days after examination by the Club physician, submit at his own expense to examination by a physician of his choice. If the opinion of Player's physician with respect to his physical ability to perform the services required of him by this contract is contrary to that of the Club's physician, the dispute will be submitted within a reasonable time to final and binding arbitration by an arbitrator selected by Club and Player or, if they are unable to agree, one selected in accordance with the procedures of the American Arbitration Association on application by either party.

14. RULES. Player will comply with and be bound by all reasonable Club rules and regulations in effect during the term of this contract which are not inconsistent with the provisions of this contract or of any collective bargaining agreement in existence during the term of this contract. Player's attention is also called to the fact that the League functions with certain rules and procedures expressive of its operation as a joint venture among its member clubs and that these rules and practices may affect Player's relationship to the League and its member clubs independently of the provisions of this contract.

15. INTEGRITY OF GAME. Player recognizes the detriment to the League and professional football that would result from impairment of public confidence in the honest and orderly conduct of NFL games or the integrity and good character of NFL players. Player therefore acknowledges his awareness that if he accepts a bribe or agrees to throw or fix an NFL game; fails to promptly report a bribe offer or an attempt to throw or fix an NFL game; bets on an NFL game; knowingly associates with gamblers or gambling activity; uses or provides

SELECTED FORMS

other players with stimulants or other drugs for the purpose of attempting to enhance on-field performance; or is guilty of any other form of conduct reasonably judged by the League Commissioner to be detrimental to the League or professional football, the Commissioner will have the right, but only after giving Player the opportunity for a hearing at which he may be represented by counsel of his choice, to fine Player in a reasonable amount; to suspend Player for a period certain or indefinitely; and/or to terminate this contract.

16. EXTENSION. Unless this contract specifically provides otherwise, if Player becomes a member of the Armed Forces of the United States or any other country, or retires from professional football as an active player, or otherwise fails or refuses to perform his services under this contract, then this contract will be tolled between the date of Player's induction into the Armed Forces, or his retirement, or his failure or refusal to perform, and the later date of his return to professional football. During the period this contract is tolled, Player will not be entitled to any compensation or benefits. On Player's return to professional football, the term of this contract will be extended for a period of time equal to the number of seasons (to the nearest multiple of one) remaining at the time the contract was tolled. The right of renewal, if any, contained in this contract will remain in effect until the end of any such extended term.

17. ASSIGNMENT. Unless this contract specifically provides otherwise, Club may assign this contract and Player's services under this contract to any successor to Club's franchise or to any other Club in the League. Player will report to the assignee Club promptly upon being informed of the assignment of his contract and will faithfully perform his services under this contract. The assignee club will pay Player's necessary traveling expenses in reporting to it and will faithfully perform this contract with Player.

18. FILING. This contract will be valid and binding upon Player and Club immediately upon execution. A copy of this contract, including any attachment to it, will be filed by Club with the League Commissioner within 10 days after execution. The Commissioner will have the right to disapprove this contract on reasonable grounds, including but not limited to an attempt by the parties to abridge or impair the rights of any other club, uncertainty or incompleteness in expression of the parties' respective rights and obligations, or conflict between the terms of this contract and any collective bargaining agreement then in existence. Approval will be automatic unless, within 10 days after receipt of this contract in his office, the Commissioner notifies the parties either of disapproval or of extension of this 10-day period for purposes of investigation or clarification pending his decision. On the receipt of notice of disapproval and termination, both parties will be relieved of their respective rights and obligations under this contract.

19. DISPUTES. During the term of any collective bargaining agreement, any dispute between Player and Club involving the interpretation or application of any provision of this contract will be submitted to final and binding arbitration in accordance with the procedure called for in any collective bargaining agreement in existence at the time the event giving rise to any such dispute occurs.

20. NOTICE. Any notice, request, approval or consent under this contract will be sufficiently given if in writing and delivered in person or mailed (certified or first class) by one party to the other at the address set forth in this contract or to such other address as the recipient may subsequently have furnished in writing to the sender.

21. OTHER AGREEMENTS. This contract, including any attachment to it, sets forth the entire agreement between Player and Club and cannot be modified or supplemented orally. Player and Club represent that no other agreement, oral or written, except as attached to or specifically incorporated in this contract, exists between them. The provisions of this contract will govern the relationship between Player and Club unless there are conflicting provisions in any collective bargaining agreement in existence during the term of this contract, in which case the provisions of the collective bargaining agreement will take precedence over conflicting provisions of this contract relating to the rights or obligations of either party.

22. LAW. This contract is made under and shall be governed by the laws of the State of _____

23. WAIVER AND RELEASE. . . .[1]

24. OTHER PROVISIONS. (a) Each of the undersigned hereby confirms that (i) this Contract, renegotiation, extension or amendment sets forth all components of the player's remuneration for playing professional football (whether such compensation is being furnished directly by the Club or by a related or affiliated entity); and (ii) there are not undisclosed agreements of any kind, whether expressed or implied, oral or written, and there are no promises, undertakings, representations, commitments, inducements, assurances of intent, or understandings of any kind that have not been disclosed to the NFL involving consideration of any kind to be paid, furnished or made available to Player or any entity or person owned or controlled by, affiliated with, or related to Player, either during the term of this contract or thereafter.

25. SPECIAL PROVISIONS.

・ ・ ・

THIS CONTRACT is executed in six (6) copies. Player acknowledges that before signing this contract he was given the opportunity to seek advice from or be represented by persons of his own selection.

_____   _____
PLAYER   CLUB

・ ・ ・

_____
PLAYER'S CERTIFIED AGENT

・ ・ ・

1. Of claims arising out of litigation. [Eds.]

(PUBLISHING AGREEMENT)

Name:

(the "Author") shall prepare and deliver to the
(the "Publisher") a manuscript for a work entitled

(the "Work") or such other title as may be mutually agreeable to the Publisher and the Author, and the Publisher shall publish the Work, in accordance with and subject to the provisions of this Agreement dated   , 19

1 RIGHTS CONVEYED TO PUBLISHER AND PAYMENTS TO AUTHOR
a. Rights and Royalties. The Author grants and assigns exclusively to the Publisher the following rights, for which the Publisher shall pay to the Author the royalties indicated:

* * *

b. Other Matters Relating to Grant of Rights

* * *

c. Other Matters Relating to Royalties and Payments

* * *

(2) *Advances.* The Publisher shall pay the Author, or the Author's duly authorized representative, an advance of $, which shall be a charge against all sums accruing to the Author under this Agreement, payable to the Author as follows:

* * *

2 MANUSCRIPT PREPARATION AND DELIVERY
a. The Author shall prepare and deliver to the Publisher on or before   ,19   , two complete, clean copies of a manuscript for the Work in double-spaced typewritten form on 8½- by 11-inch or metric size A4 sheets or as may otherwise be specified by the Publisher. The manuscript for the Work must be acceptable to the Publisher in both form and content for publication. It shall be between   and   words in length and shall include such materials as the Publisher may reasonably specify for the Work, including but not limited to copy for the title page, table of contents, index, tables, and bibliographies, and copy for drawings, illustrations, and charts. The Author shall supply these in finished form to the Publisher within a reasonable time after the delivery of the completed manuscript; if the Author shall fail to do so, the Publisher may supply them and charge the expense to the Author.

b. The Author shall obtain, without expense to the Publisher, written permission to include in the Work any copyrighted material which is not in the public domain as well as any other material for which permission is necessary in connection with the Author's warranty in Section 3 of this Agreement. These permissions must be consistent with the rights granted to the Publisher in this Agreement so that they may cover all the uses to

BOOK PUBLISHER'S CONTRACT

which the material may eventually be put. The Author shall deliver to the Publisher a copy of all these permissions with the complete manuscript.

c. If the Work or any subdivision of it contains a significant portion of material taken from documents prepared and published by the United States government and therefore not subject to copyright, the Author shall notify the Publisher in writing of the existence and location of all such material in the Work.

d. If the Author fails to deliver the complete manuscript within 90 days after the delivery date specified in this Agreement, or if the Author fails or refuses to perform any correction or revision of the manuscript within the time or as otherwise specified by the Publisher, the Publisher shall have the right in its discretion: (1) to give the Author written notice of its intention to terminate this Agreement, in which event the Author shall promptly reimburse the Publisher for all sums advanced to the Author against royalties under this Agreement, and upon such reimbursement this Agreement shall terminate; or (2) to make such other arrangements in connection with this Agreement as the Publisher deems advisable to complete, correct, or revise the manuscript, in which event the reasonable cost of such arrangements may be charged against any sums accruing to the Author under this Agreement.

e. If requested by the Publisher, the Author shall correct proof of the Work and return it promptly to the Publisher. If the Author makes or causes to be made any alterations in the type, illustrations, or film which are not typographical, drafting, or Publisher's errors and which exceed 15 percent of the original cost of composition and artwork independent of the cost of these Author's alterations, the cost of the excess alterations shall be charged against any sums accruing to the Author under this Agreement.

f. The Author shall retain one copy of the manuscript submitted to the Publisher until the Work is published. The Publisher shall have no liability of any kind to the Author by reason of the loss, destruction, or mutilation of the manuscript delivered to the Publisher. This provision shall also be applicable to the original artwork, illustrations, and photographs, unless such loss, destruction, or mutilation is covered by insurance of the Publisher, in which case the Author shall look only to the insurance carrier for replacement or reimbursement.

3 AUTHOR'S WARRANTY

a. The Author represents and warrants to the Publisher that the Author has full power and authority to enter into this Agreement and to grant the rights granted in this Agreement; that the Work is original except for material in the public domain and those excerpts from other works as may be included with the written permission of the copyright owners; that the Work does not contain any libelous or obscene material or injurious formulas, recipes, or instructions; that it does not infringe any trade name, trademark, or copyright; and that it does not invade or violate any right of privacy, personal or proprietary right, or other common law or statutory right.

b. The Author agrees to indemnify the Publisher and its licensees and assignees under this Agreement and hold them harmless from any and all losses, damages, liabilities, costs, charges, and expenses, including reasonable attorneys' fees, arising out of any breach of any of the Author's representations and warranties contained in this Agreement or third-party claims relating to the matters covered by the representations and warranties in this Section 3, which are finally sustained in a court of original jurisdiction. If any action or proceeding is brought against the Publisher with respect to the matters covered by the representations and warranties in this Section 3, the Publisher shall have the right, in its sole discretion, to select counsel to defend against this action or proceeding. In addition to other remedies available to the Publisher, the Publisher may charge the amount of these losses, damages, liabilities, costs, charges, and expenses against any sums accruing to the Author under this Agreement or any other agreement currently existing between Author and Publisher.

c. If there is an infringement of any rights granted to the Publisher or rights which the Publisher is authorized to license or in which the Publisher is to share in the proceeds, the Publisher shall have the right, in its sole discretion, to select counsel to bring an action to enforce those rights, and the Author and the Publisher shall have the right to participate jointly in the action. If both participate, they shall share equally the expenses of and any sums recovered in the action, except that if the Author retains separate legal counsel, the Author shall be solely responsible for the legal expenses of the Author's counsel. If either party declines to participate in the action, the other may proceed, and the party maintaining the action shall bear all expenses and shall retain all sums recovered.

The provisions of this Section 3 shall survive any termination of this Agreement.

4 COMPETING WORKS

While this Agreement is in effect, the Author shall not, without the prior written consent of the Publisher, write, edit, print, or publish, or cause to be written, edited, printed, or published, any other edition of the Work, whether revised, supplemented, corrected, enlarged, abridged, or otherwise, or any other work of a nature which might interfere with or injure the sales of the Work or any grant of rights or licenses permitted under this Agreement by the Publisher, or permit the use of the Author's name or likeness in connection with any such work.

5 PUBLICATION OF THE WORK

After giving written notice to the Author that it has accepted the Work for publication, the Publisher shall within 12 months of written acceptance of the manuscript publish the Work at its own expense and in such style and manner and with such trademarks, service marks, and imprints of Publisher, and sell the Work at such prices, as it shall deem suitable. The Publisher shall publish the Work with a copyright notice and register the Work in accordance with the United States copyright laws in the name of the Publisher or Author as the Author may elect.

6 AUTHOR'S COPIES

The Publisher shall give the Author ten copies of the Work upon publication, free of charge, and sell to the Author as many additional copies as the Author may wish for personal use and not for resale, at a discount of 40 percent of the Publisher's then list price, f.o.b. the Publisher's warehouse.

7 DISCONTINUANCE OF PUBLICATION

a. When in the judgment of the Publisher the demand for the Work is no longer sufficient to warrant its continued publication, the Publisher shall have the right to discontinue the publication and declare the Work out of print, in which event the Author shall be so advised in writing.

b. If the Work is not for sale in at least one edition (including any revised edition or reprint edition) published by the Publisher or under license from the Publisher and, within eight months after written demand by the Author, the Publisher or its licensee fails to offer it again for sale, then this Agreement shall terminate and all rights granted to the Publisher in it shall revert to the Author (except for material prepared by or obtained at the expense of the Publisher which shall remain the property of the Publisher).

c. The termination of this Agreement under this Section 7 or otherwise shall be subject to (1) any license, contract, or option granted to third parties by the Publisher before the termination and the Publisher's right to its share of the proceeds from these agreements after the termination and (2) the Publisher's continuing right to sell all remaining bound copies and sheets of the Work and all derivative works which are on hand at the time of termination.

8 RIGHTS OF REFUSAL

a. Other Rights. The Author grants the Publisher the "right of first refusal" to exercise or license any dramatization, video, audiovisual, and commercial rights in the Work to the extent that any of these rights have not been granted to the Publisher. The Author shall not enter into an agreement with another party relating to such rights upon terms equal to or less favorable than the last offered by the Publisher.

b. Author's Next Work. The Author grants to the Publisher the "right of first refusal" to publish the Author's next full-length book and shall submit the manuscript for it to the Publisher before submitting it to any other publisher. In no case shall the Publisher be required to exercise this option before publication or within three months following publication of the Work. The Author shall not enter into a contract for the publication of this next work with any publisher upon terms less favorable than any offered by the Publisher.

9 AGENT
The Author hereby authorizes as agent:

10 OTHER MATTERS

a. Assignments. No assignment of this Agreement, voluntary or by operation of law, shall be binding upon either of the parties without the prior written consent of the other, provided, however, that the Author may assign or transfer any sums due or to become due under this Agreement without the Publisher's consent.

b. Law to Govern. This Agreement shall be interpreted and governed by the laws of the State of New York and the United States of America.

c. Bankruptcy. In the event of bankruptcy, receivership, or liquidation of the Publisher, this Agreement shall terminate without further procedure and all rights granted in this Agreement to the Publisher by the Author shall revert to the Author.

d. Notices. Any written notice required under any of the provisions of this Agreement shall be deemed to have been properly served by delivery in person or by first-class mail, postage prepaid, to the last known address.

e. Binding Agreement. This Agreement shall be binding upon the parties signing it and on all their heirs, personal representatives, successors, and permitted assignees.

f. Complete Agreement. This Agreement constitutes the complete understanding of the parties and supersedes all prior agreements of the parties relating to the Work. No amendment or waiver of any provision of this Agreement shall be valid unless in writing and signed by all parties affected by the amendment or waiver.

11 SUPPLEMENTARY PROVISIONS (IF ANY)

By _____

_____
TAX OR SOCIAL SECURITY NUMBER

AUTHOR _____

_____
CITIZENSHIP

330

Worth Street
Textile Market Rules

Approved and Promulgated by

American Textile Manufacturers Institute, Inc.

Knitted Textile Association

Textile Distributors Association, Inc.

Standard Textile Salesnote

Revision of July 1, 1986

This present revision is effective with respect to any contract of subsequent date, which incorporates the Standard Textile Salesnote by reference, expressly giving notice that it provides for arbitration of disputes.

Arbitration

(a) Any controversy or claim arising out of or relating to this contract, or the interpretation or breach thereof, including any modification or extension thereof, shall be settled by arbitration in the City of New York in accordance with the rules then obtaining of the General Arbitration Council of the Textile and Apparel Industries, a division of the American Arbitration Association or its successor.

(b) Arbitrators shall be bound by the terms and conditions of this contract and shall have no power to alter or in rendering their award to depart from any express provision of this contract, and their failure to observe this limitation shall constitute grounds for vacating their award.

(c) The fees and expenses of such arbitration proceedings, including reasonable counsel fees, may be allocated between the parties or charged to any one of the parties by the arbitrators as part of their award.

Jurisdiction

The parties consent to the jurisdiction of the Supreme Court of the State of New York or the United States District Court for the Southern District of New York for all purposes relating to this contract, whether in connection with arbitration or otherwise. The parties consent that any process or notice of motion or other application to either of said courts, and any paper in connection with such proceedings may be served within or outside of the State of New York by certified mail or registered mail or by personal service or by such other manner as may be permissible under the rules of the applicable court or arbitration tribunal.

(E22311)

STANDARD TEXTILE SALESNOTE

Assortments

If buyer does not furnish specifications for assortments, patterns or other particulars within the time specified or, if not specified, within five (5) business days after Seller's demand in writing therefore, or forty-five (45) days prior to the initial delivery date, whichever is earlier, Seller may at its option either (1) treat the contract as substantially breached and claim damages for such breach, or (2) hold the goods for Buyer's account and invoice the Buyer therefore at finished goods contract price, in which case the Seller shall be deemed to have fully performed and to be entitled to payment from the Buyer and risk shall be upon the Buyer when goods are so set aside and invoiced. If Seller permits the Buyer to complete assortments or specifications subsequent to the time required hereunder, Seller may delay delivery for such period of time as may be then reasonably necessary.

Warranties

Seller warrants that merchandise delivered shall conform with the description on the face of the contract between the parties.

Buyer agrees that the Seller makes no warranty in fact or in law that the merchandise which is the subject of this sale is suitable for any particular use or purpose and that the suitability of the merchandise for any use is the sole responsibility of the Buyer.

Seller shall not be liable for normal manufacturing, processing or finishing defects nor for customary variations from quantities or specifications. Whether the goods are first quality shall be determined in accordance with the applicable quality standards of the Worth Street Textile Market Rules.

However, performance and other physical or chemical characteristics of the merchandise are not guaranteed unless and except to such extent as is otherwise specifically provided herein or in any other writing signed by the seller.

Deliveries

(a) Unless otherwise expressly provided herein, any shipment or tender made within fifteen (15) days after any date specified for delivery shall constitute timely delivery hereunder.

(b) Delivery to a carrier, or in the absence of shipping instructions, the mailing of a covering invoice after completion of manufacture shall constitute good delivery or tender of delivery, subject to Seller's right of stoppage in transit, and subject to Seller's security interest therein as elsewhere herein provided. Goods invoiced and held by the Seller for whatever reason shall be at Buyer's risk.

(c) In the event that delivery under this contract is prevented or delayed by strikes, lockouts, embargoes, force majeure or act of God, or any cause or circumstance not limited to the above, which is beyond the Seller's reasonable control, Seller shall not be held liable for the consequences thereof. (E2232)

Credit and Payment

(a) In case any invoice shall not be paid when due or upon Buyer's breach or default with respect to any term or condition of this or any other contract with Seller, all sums owing under this and other contracts between Buyer and Seller, shall at the option of Seller or its factor, at once become due irrespective of the terms of sale, and the Seller may defer delivery under this and such other contracts until such sums shall be paid and for a reasonable time thereafter. If the total amount due or to become due under the contracts between the Buyer and Seller exceeds the credit limit for Buyer, which may be fixed or varied from time to time at and in accordance with the sole discretion and opinion of Seller, or its factor, Buyer agrees to pay cash before delivery or anticipate payment for any future shipment in excess of such credit limit. Upon failure by Buyer to make any such payment within five (5) days after demand in writing, Seller shall have the option to cancel this and other contracts between Buyer and Seller or to sell all or part of the merchandise undelivered thereunder without notice, at public or private sale, holding Buyer responsible for any deficiency, or to bill Buyer as of the date of such demand for all or any part of the merchandise undelivered thereunder on terms of cash before delivery. Approval or credit for one delivery or more shall not be deemed a waiver of this provision.

(b) Any property of the Buyer, at any time in Seller's possession, including but not limited to merchandise paid for by the Buyer, shall be deemed held as security (with a security interest therein granted by Buyer to Seller) for Buyer's obligation under this and any other contract with the Seller. Such property, to the extent of the value thereof, may be applied by the Seller as a credit against such obligations of the Buyer, or such property or any part thereof may be sold by the Seller at public or private sale with the proceeds thereof applied as a credit against such obligations of the Buyer.

Claims

If Buyer claims goods are defective, they must be promptly and properly offered to Seller for examination. If Buyer fails to make such goods available for examination, Buyer shall not be entitled to make any claim with respect to such goods. Seller may within fifteen (15) days after such examination replace any merchandise which is found to be not in accordance with the contract, and in such event no claim may be made by Buyer. Buyer may cancel only that portion of the order pertaining to goods found to be defective in quality and not replaced by Seller.

With respect to greige goods, claims for patent defects are barred unless made in writing within twenty (20) days of discovery or within ninety (90) days after the date dyeing instructions were first issued for all or part of the goods by the Buyer, or within six (6) months after the Seller's invoice date, whichever is earliest. Buyer may make no claim for any quantity of greige goods with patent defects which have already been cut or otherwise processed beyond dyeing and finishing.   (E2233)

With respect to dyed or finished goods, claims for patent defects are barred unless made in writing within twenty (20) days after discovery or within sixty (60) days from shipment by the Seller or ninety (90) days from Seller's invoice date, whichever is earliest, but prior to the cutting or processing of the goods beyond the original condition as shipped by the Seller.

Claims for greige or finished goods with latent defects are barred unless made in writing within twenty (20) days after discovery, or ninety (90) days after shipment of the goods by the Seller to the Buyer, or within nine (9) months after the Seller's invoice date, whichever is the earliest.

The limit of liability of Seller for late delivery or nondelivery or any other breach shall be the difference, if any, between the contract price and the fair market price on the contract date of delivery of the goods delivered or to be delivered. In no event shall Buyer be entitled to claim any consequential damages or any other damages of any nature whatsoever, and in no instances shall damages include profit on contemplated use or profit of any description. Without limiting the foregoing, if Buyer exports the goods, Seller shall not be liable whatsoever for freight charges outside of the continental United States, or for customs duties, or for insurance or for forwarding costs or any other costs connected with the export of the goods.

Amendments

This contract cannot be changed, modified, amended, canceled or discharged in whole or in part unless so done in writing and signed by the party to be charged therewith.

Applicable Law

The laws of the State of New York shall apply to this contract and shall control its interpretation.

[The Salesnote is accompanied by many pages of standardized Specifications, Definitions and Trade Customs, and Quality Standards.]

[E2234]

NORTH AMERICAN EXPORT GRAIN ASSOCIATION, INC.
FREE ON BOARD EXPORT CONTRACT U.S.A./CANADA

Revised as of May 1, 2000

NO. 2

Contract No. _____

New York, N.Y. _____ 20_____ .

1 Sold by _____

2. Purchased by _____

3. Broker/Agent _____

4. Quantity

in bulk, including dockage, 5% more or less at buyer's option, and at market price (per Clause 10) as follows: If the first delivery under this contract is for a quantity between contract minimum and contract maximum (both inclusive), no further deliveries shall be made. If this contract is to be executed by more than one vessel, the loading tolerance of 5% more or less shall apply on the difference between the mean contract quantity and the quantity that has been delivered on all prior vessels. Any delivery which falls within this difference, plus or minus 5%, shall complete the contract.

5. Weight

Quantity to be final at port of loading in accordance with customary weight certificates. 1,016 kilos shall be equal to 2,240 lbs.

6. Commodity

_____

in accordance with the official grain standards of the United States or Canada, whichever applicable, in effect on the date of this contract.

7. Quality

Quality and condition to be final at port of loading in accordance with official inspection certificates.

In case of delivery at St. Lawrence ports, quality and condition to be final in accordance with Lake and/or loading ports official inspection certificates; Lake inspection certificates to be properly identified at ports of shipment.

Each party hereby authorizes the other party to request in both parties' names an appeal inspection under the U.S. Grain Standards Act at any time prior to or during the loading of the vessel, and whether or not such request was filed before commencement of loading. The cost of such appeal inspection, unless otherwise stipulated in this contract, shall be borne by the party requesting it.

Delivery of higher grades of grain of the same type and description is permissible. The commodity is not warranted free from defect, rendering same unmerchantable, which would not be apparent on reasonable examination, any statute or rule of law to the contrary notwithstanding.

8. Delivery

Delivery shall be made between _____ and _____ , both inclusive (the "delivery period"), at discharge end of loading spout, to buyer's tonnage in readiness to load, in accordance with custom of the port and subject to the elevator tariff to the extent that it does not conflict with the terms of this contract. Incorporation of a loading rate guaranty in this contract shall not entitle seller to delay delivery.

Buyer shall give vessel nominations ("preadvice") in accordance with Clause 15, in time for seller to receive minimum _____ days notice of probable readiness of tonnage and quantities required (the "preadvice period"). Buyer to keep seller informed of changes in expected date of vessel readiness.

Time for the preadvice shall be deemed to commence to count at 1200 noon, local time at place of receipt, on the business day of receipt by seller and shall be counted in consecutive periods of 24 hours.

Seller shall, if applicable, declare port and berth of loading within a reasonable time (but not later than _____ days) after receipt by seller of the preadvice, except that seller shall not be obligated to make such declaration earlier than (a) the 8th day prior to commencement of the delivery period for port declaration and (b) the 5th day prior to commencement of the delivery period for berth declaration.

The vessel shall not be prevented from filing and from taking its place in the vessel line-up at the designated port/berth during the preadvice period or before commencement of the delivery period, notwithstanding which, seller shall not be obliged to effect delivery to the vessel before the expiration of the preadvice period or before commencement of the delivery period. For the purposes of this contract a vessel shall be considered filed when it (a) has tendered valid notice of readiness to load to the charterer or its agent, at the port of loading, (b) has given written advice of such tender to the loading elevator, complete with all customarily required documents, such advice having been presented between the hours of 0900 and 1600 local time on a business day or between the hours of 0900 and 1200 noon on Saturday (provided not a holiday) and (c) is ready to receive grain in the compartments required for loading under this contract.

Buyer shall be allowed to make one substitution of a vessel, provided the substituting vessel is of the same type and approximately the same size and position. If the original or the substituting vessel is unable to lift the commodity by reason of the vessel having sunk or having suffered incapacitating physical damage, an additional substitution shall be made of a vessel of the same type and approximately the same size, and with a position agreeable to buyer and seller. Such agreement shall not be unreasonably withheld. The nomination of the substituting vessel shall be subject to the preadvice requirements of this clause, regardless of any preadvice previously given, unless the estimated time of arrival of the substituting vessel is the same as the estimated time of arrival of the original vessel when nominated. No substitution of vessels other than as provided in this clause shall be made. If this is a "named vessel" contract, no substitution other than after a casualty as described above shall be permitted.

Bills of lading and/or mate's receipts to be considered proof of date of delivery in the absence of evidence to the contrary. Any delivery in part fulfillment of this contract shall be considered as if made under a separate contract.

9. Days

In any month containing an odd number of days, the middle day shall be reckoned as belonging to both halves of the month.

COMMODITY EXPORTER'S STANDARD FORM

SELECTED FORMS

10. Price

_____ per _____

free on board buyer's tonnage at _____

If this contract is for a flat price, any variance in quantity from the mean contract quantity shall be settled basis the FOB market value (as defined in paragraph (a) and (b) below).

If the contract price is to be established on an exchange of futures, futures shall be exchanged prior to delivery of the commodity or at least 5 calendar days prior to the last trading day of the applicable futures month, whichever is earlier, to the nearest 5,000 bushels of the mean contract quantity. If deliveries under this contract result in a variance from the mean contract quantity, there shall be another exchange of futures as soon as possible after the last date of loading to bring the resulting amount of futures exchanged to the nearest 5,000 bushels of the quantity delivered. All exchanges of futures shall be made within the range of prices prevailing on the futures market on the date of the exchange. The variance from the mean contract quantity shall be settled basis the market value of the premium (as defined in paragraph (a) and (b) below).

(a) The FOB (flat price) market value, or the market value of the premium, as the case may be, shall be that prevailing on the close of the appropriate market in the country of origin of the commodity on the last date of loading, if such be a business day, otherwise on the close of such market on the previous business day.

(b) In the event the parties do not agree on the market value by the time the shipping documents are ready to be transmitted to buyer, seller shall invoice the entire shipment provisionally at contract price. Thereafter, final invoice for the difference between contract price and market value shall be presented as soon as possible and payment shall be made immediately.

11. Payment

*(a) Net cash by irrevocable divisible letters of credit issued or confirmed by a prime U.S. bank in New York (or _____ by mutual agreement), available by sight drafts accompanied by shipping documents per Clause 12 (or warehouse receipts if option (c) of Clause 18 is exercised). Such letters of credit, in a form acceptable to seller, shall be established not later than 5 days prior to the beginning of the delivery period, and shall be valid at least until the 30th day after expiration of the delivery period. Should delivery be delayed beyond the delivery period, buyer, if requested by seller, shall amend letters of credit accordingly and buyer shall increase the amount of the letter of credit to provide for carrying charges, if applicable. All bank charges shall be for buyer's account.

—or—

*(b) Net cash in U.S. Dollars, by telegraphic transfer to the bank designated by seller, against presentation of and in exchange for shipping documents per Clause 12 (or warehouse receipts if option (c) of Clause 18 is exercised). Such presentation shall be made in the city of _____

All bank charges in connection with payment shall be for buyer's account.

—or—

*(c) _____

_____

_____

*Delete paragraphs which are not applicable.

12. Shipping Documents

Payment to be made against bills of lading or mate's receipts (at seller's option), and weight and inspection certificates. However, if practicable, seller shall follow instructions of buyer in establishing bills of lading containing such clauses as buyer's/vessel's agents or owners usually endorse or attach. Buyer shall accept such bills of lading but seller assumes no responsibility for their correctness.

13. Notice of Delivery

Notice of delivery stating vessel's name, dates of bills of lading (or mate's receipts), quantities and qualities loaded (including percentage of dockage if applicable) shall be given or passed on by seller to buyer without undue delay. Notices of delivery shall be subject to correction of any errors.

14. Insurance

Marine and war risk (plus strikes, riots, civil commotions and mine risk) insurance, covering seller's/buyer's interests as they may appear, is to be covered by buyer with first-class approved companies and/or underwriters and to be confirmed by such companies and/or underwriters to seller at least 5 days prior to the expected readiness of the vessel. If this confirmation is not received by seller by such time, seller may place such insurance for buyer's account and at buyer's risk and expense.

15. Communications

All notices under this contract shall be given by letter, if delivered by hand on the day of writing, or by cable, telex or other method of rapid written communication. Any notice received after 1600 hours (local time at place of receipt) on a business day shall be deemed to have been received on the following business day, except that for notices given and received by parties which are both located in the Continental United States and/or Canada, the reference herein to 1600 hours shall signify 1600 hours New York City time (E.S.T. or E.D.T., as in effect on date of receipt of the notice).

16. Circles

(a) For the purposes of this clause, a circle shall consist of a series of contracts in which each seller is also a buyer of a commodity of the same description and quality, for delivery at the same ports and with compatible delivery periods.

(b) If this contract forms part of a circle, each party may agree with the other parties in the circle to forego actual delivery and to participate in a clearing agreement for the settlement of contract price differences. Monies due and owed to parties in the circle shall be payable on the middle day of the contract delivery period.

(c) If a circle can be shown to exist but no clearing agreement has been reached by the 10th calendar day following the last day of the delivery period, actual delivery shall not be made and payment shall be made by each buyer to its seller of the excess of seller's invoice amount over the lowest invoice amount in the circle. Such payments shall be made promptly after the 10th calendar day following the last day of the delivery period.

(d) Should any party in a circle fail to make payment on the due date as required under paragraph (b) or (c) above for reasons cited in Clause 23 or for any other reason, payment shall be made between each buyer and its seller of the difference between the seller's invoice amount at contract price and the market value of the commodity on date of insolvency or default, as the case may be. Such payment shall be made latest on the 2nd business day after the due date under paragraph (b) or (c) above.

Payments already made under paragraph (b) or (c) above shall be refunded.

(e) All circle settlements shall be based on the mean contract quantity.

If a circle under paragraph (b), (c) or (d) above exists, Clause 21 shall not apply and Clauses 18 and 20 shall not be invoked.

Payments due on a non-business day shall be made not later than the following business day.

All payments made after the delivery period shall include carrying charges from the day following the last day of the delivery period, to the date of payment, at the rates stipulated in this contract. These carrying charges shall be settled individually between each buyer and its seller.

(f) The parties agree that any dispute arising out of the voluntary clearing agreement entered into in accordance with paragraph (b) above shall be subject to arbitration as to any party thereto. Such arbitration shall be conducted in accordance with the provisions of Clause 30.

336

17. U.S./Canadian Government Rules and Regulations   Buyer and seller agree to comply with the U.S. and Canadian regulatory prerequisites applicable to this contract, including, but not limited to, those governing any export subsidy, destination controls, government financing of agricultural commodities and the monitoring of export purchases and sales. Any losses, fines, penalties, expenses, costs or damages incurred as a result of failure to perform in accordance with this provision shall be borne by the party responsible for such failure.

18. Failure to Take Delivery   If vessel fails to file before the end of the delivery period, buyer shall be in breach of contract and seller shall carry the grain for buyer's account and risk as provided in Clause 19. In the event that buyer has not given vessel nominations conforming to the applicable provisions of Clause 8 by the 15th calendar day following the last day of the delivery period, or if the vessels having been nominated within such time, fail to file by the 35th calendar day following the last day of the delivery period, seller may, in its discretion: (a) continue to carry the commodity for buyer's account and risk, (b) declare buyer in default, or (c) tender to buyer proper warehouse receipts in a quantity equal to the mean quantity open under this contract, in exchange for which buyer shall pay at contract price plus accrued carrying charges, but less out-elevation and outbound weighing and inspection charges. Such tender of warehouse receipts shall be deemed due performance of the contract by seller.

SPECIAL PROVISIONS FOR CONTRACTS PROVIDING FOR DELIVERY AT ST. LAWRENCE, GREAT LAKES OR HUDSON BAY PORTS:

(1) Seller shall be barred from declaring option (b) above while the navigation in the designated delivery area is officially closed for the ice season, and for 20 days thereafter.

(2) However, if options (a), (b) and (c) above become available to seller only while the navigation is officially closed, the seller may declare option (b) during the first 10 days it becomes available to him; thereafter, he shall be barred from declaring it, until the 21st day after the official opening of navigation.

(3) If seller carries the grain into the new season for buyer's account, buyer shall have the right to nominate vessels per Clause 8, regardless of whether vessels were already nominated during the delivery period.

19. Carrying Charges   If the commodity is being carried for buyer's account and risk as provided in Clause 18, it is mutually agreed that carrying charges, consisting of storage, insurance and interest, shall accrue as follows:

(a) Storage and insurance from the day following the last day of the delivery period up to and including the dates of delivery (or if seller exercises option (b) or (c) of Clause 18, the date applicable thereto), both dates inclusive, at the following rates:

_____ U.S. cents per bushel per day _____

_____ U.S. cents per bushel per day _____

(b) Interest from the day following the last day of the delivery period up to and including the last day of delivery (or if seller exercises option (b) or (c) of Clause 18, the date applicable thereto), both dates inclusive, at the following rates:

_____ _____

_____ _____

Carrying charges for the delivery completing this contract shall be computed on the mean contract quantity less the amounts previously delivered (if any), irrespective of whether or not buyer has availed himself of the loading tolerance option under Clause 4. It is further expressly agreed that carrying charges as provided herein are to be construed in the nature of liquidated damages and, as such, that no further proof of damages shall be required in substantiation thereof.

20. Strikes or Other Causes of Delay in Delivery

(a) This clause shall apply if delivery by seller of the commodity, or any part thereof, is prevented or delayed at the port(s) of delivery and/or elevator(s) of delivery or elsewhere, or if the forwarding of the commodity to such port(s) and/or elevator(s) is prevented, by reason of the causes enumerated in paragraph (b) below; PROVIDED that seller shall have sent notice to buyer not later than 2 business days after the date of commencement of the causes, or not later than 2 business days after the 1st day of the delivery period, whichever occurs later (except that subsequent sellers shall not be bound by these deadlines, provided they pass along the notice to their buyer, without delay); and PROVIDED further that seller shall, at buyer's request, furnish a certificate of the North American Export Grain Association, Inc., certifying the existence and the duration of the causes. Such certificate shall be final.

(b) The causes of delay and/or prevention ("causes") referred to in paragraph (a) above shall be:

(1) Riots, strikes, lockouts, interruptions in or stoppages of the normal course of labor,

(2) Embargoes or exceptional impediments to transportation,

(3) Action by Federal, State or local government or authority.

(c) The obligation of seller to make delivery shall be suspended while the causes are in effect, until the termination of the causes and/or the resumption of work after the termination of the causes, whichever is later. Seller shall not be responsible for further delays after resumption of work (whether such termination or resumption of work occurs prior to, during or after the delivery period) except that, if a vessel nominated under this contract is not loaded in the proper rotation but is bypassed by vessels (other than liners) which had filed after the vessel nominated under this contract, seller shall pay to buyer damages equal to the actual working time lost (weather working days, Saturdays, Sundays and holidays excluded) to buyer's vessel during the loading of the bypassing vessels, at the demurrage rate in the Charter Party for the vessel nominated under this contract.

If the Charter Party of the vessel under this contract does not indicate a demurrage rate, the damages are to be calculated at a reasonable demurrage rate predicated on the then current market, to be agreed upon amicably or to be determined by arbitration.

(d) (1) If the causes commence before or during the delivery period and terminate during or after delivery period, then the delivery period shall be deemed to be extended by a number of days equivalent to the period starting with the commencement of the causes or the commencement of the delivery period, whichever is later, and ending with the termination of the causes, and/or the resumption of work after the termination of the causes, whichever is later.

(2) If the causes commence during the additional time afforded to buyer under Clause 18 with respect to vessel nominations and filings, then the right of seller to exercise option (b) or (c) under Clause 18 shall be deemed to be delayed by a number of days equivalent to the period starting with the commencement of the causes and ending with the termination of the causes and/or the resumption of work after the termination of the causes, whichever is later.

(e) Carrying charges, if due under Clauses 18/19, shall begin to accrue on the day following the last day of the delivery period, as extended by paragraph (d)(1) above, however, if this clause becomes operative while carrying charges are already accruing, then such charges shall continue to accrue as they would in the absence of the causes.

21. Prohibition

In case of prohibition of export, blockade or hostilities or in case of any executive or legislative act done by or on behalf of the government of the country of origin or of the territory where the ports of shipment named herein are situate, restricting export, whether partially or otherwise, any such restriction shall be deemed by both parties to apply to this contract and to the extent of such total or partial restriction to prevent fulfillment and to that extent this contract or any unfulfilled portion thereof shall be cancelled without prejudice to seller's entitlement to carrying charges. Seller shall advise buyer without delay of the reasons therefor, and if required by buyer, seller shall provide certification of the North American Export Grain Association, Inc., as sufficient evidence for cancellation under this clause.

22. Default

In case of default by either party, the other party shall be at liberty, after giving notice, to resell or repurchase, as the case may be, without undue delay and the defaulting party shall make good the loss, if any, to the other party but the defaulting party shall not be entitled to any profit. If the non-defaulting party has not repurchased or resold the commodity by the 10th calendar day after the giving of notice of default, the market value on the said 10th day shall be used for settlement purposes. If such 10th day falls on a non-business day, the market value on the previous business day shall govern. In the event of a default by buyer, the sale price under this contract shall automatically be increased by the value of carrying charges calculated up to the date of resale, or the 10th calendar day after the giving of notice of default, whichever is applicable.

23. Insolvency

Either party shall, at any time after sending notice, have the right to terminate this contract and to recover the loss (if any) in the event that:

(a) the other party suspends payment or commits an act of bankruptcy;

--or--

(b) reasonable grounds for insecurity having arisen with respect to the financial capacity of the other party to perform under this contract, and a written demand for adequate assurance of due performance having been made, such assurance is not received within a period of time not exceeding 5 days.

24. Construction

For the purposes of this contract, except as otherwise expressly provided or unless the context otherwise requires, plural terms include the singular.

25. Passage of Title

Anything in this contract to the contrary notwithstanding, seller shall retain title to the commodity until seller has been paid in full (per Clause 11), it being understood that risk of loss shall pass to buyer on delivery at discharge end of loading spout (per Clause 8).

26. Limitation of Liability

The liability of the seller under the contract, except as expressly stated herein, shall be limited to its actions in delivering the commodity at discharge end of loading spout and to presentation of the contractually required documentation. Any claims, losses, costs, damages, etc. arising from events or actions thereafter shall be the responsibility of the buyer, who shall indemnify seller for all costs (including attorney fees) and damages thereby incurred.

27. International Conventions

The following shall not apply to this contract:

(a) the Uniform Law on the International Sale of Goods and the Uniform Law on the Formation of Contracts for the International Sale of Goods;

(b) the United Nations Convention on Contracts for the International Sale of Goods of 1980; and

(c) the United Nations Convention on the Limitation Period in the International Sale of Goods, concluded at New York on 14 June 1974, and the Protocol Amending the Convention on the Limitation Period in the International Sale of Goods, concluded at Vienna on 11 April 1980.

28. Governing Law

The parties agree that this contract shall be governed by the laws of the State of New York, notwithstanding any choice of law provision to the contrary.

29. Other Conditions

30. Arbitration

Buyer and seller expressly agree that any controversy or claim arising out of, in connection with or relating to this contract, or the interpretation, performance or breach thereof, shall be settled by arbitration in the City of New York before the American Arbitration Association (AAA), or its successors, in accordance with the International Arbitration Rules of the American Arbitration Association, as those Rules may be in effect at the time of such arbitration proceeding, which Rules are hereby deemed incorporated herein and made a part hereof, and under the laws of the State of New York. The number of arbitrators shall be three. Each party shall designate one arbitrator, and those two shall name a third, with the AAA making appointments if the tribunal is not formed by this procedure. The arbitrator named by the party-appointed arbitrators shall be from the list of grain arbitrators maintained by the AAA. Any arbitrator appointed by the AAA may be from the list of grain arbitrators maintained by the AAA or the AAA Commercial Arbitration Panel. The language of the arbitration shall be English. In disputes involving a "string" of contracts, two or more arbitrations may be consolidated before the same tribunal, at the written request of any party. The tribunal in consolidated arbitrations shall be mindful of differences in terms between the various contracts and in the action of the parties, and vary the award from contract to contract, if indicated. The arbitration award shall be final and binding on the parties and judgment upon such arbitration award may be entered in the Supreme Court of the State of New York or any other court having jurisdiction thereof. Buyer and seller hereby recognize and expressly consent to the jurisdiction over each of them of the American Arbitration Association or its successors, and all of the courts of the State of New York. The parties agree that arbitration awards may be released by the AAA to the North American Export Grain Association, Inc., for distribution to the interested public. Buyer and seller agree that this contract shall be deemed to have been made in New York State and be deemed to be performed there, any reference herein or elsewhere to the contrary notwithstanding.

_____   _____

BUYER   SELLER

GENERAL ELECTRIC COMPANY
CONDITIONS OF EXPORT SALE

NOTICE: THE OFFER, ORDER ACKNOWLEDGMENT, ORDER ACCEPTANCE OR SALE OF ANY PRODUCTS COVERED HEREIN IS CONDITIONED UPON APPLICATION TO SUCH TRANSACTION OF THE TERMS CONTAINED IN THIS INSTRUMENT. ANY ADDITIONAL OR DIFFERENT TERMS PROPOSED BY BUYER ARE OBJECTED TO AND WILL NOT BE BINDING UPON SELLER UNLESS SPECIFICALLY ASSENTED TO IN WRITING BY THE SELLER.

ARTICLE I - PRICES

Prices include the cost of (i) Seller's usual inspection and factory tests, (ii) Seller's usual packing (or containerizing, if applicable) for export, and (iii) freight by Seller's usual means to alongside vessel at the point of export designated by Seller (but not the cost of insurance, or charges for pier handling, marshalling, lighterage and heavy lifts). Insurance to cover the inland shipment shall be arranged by Seller at Buyer's expense if Seller is arranging for the export shipment pursuant to Article III.

ARTICLE II - DELIVERY, TITLE AND RISK OF LOSS

A. Except as stated in Paragraph B below, Seller shall deliver the Products to Buyer F.O.B. factory. Partial deliveries shall be permitted. Upon delivery, title to the Products and all risk of loss or damage shall pass to Buyer. Delivery times are approximate and are dependent upon prompt receipt by Seller of all material and information necessary to proceed with work without interruption. Any claim for shortages will not be considered unless Seller receives written notice thereof within 120 days of delivery F.O.B. factory.

B. If any part of the Products cannot be shipped from the point of inland shipment to alongside vessel when ready due to any cause referred to in Article V, Seller may place such Products in storage (which may be at the place of manufacture). In such event, (i) Seller shall notify Buyer of the placement of any Products in storage, (ii) Seller's delivery obligations shall be deemed fulfilled and title and all risk of loss or damage shall thereupon pass to Buyer, (iii) any amounts otherwise payable to Seller upon delivery shall be payable upon presentation of Seller's invoices therefor and its certification as to such cause, (iv) promptly upon submission of Seller's invoices, Buyer shall reimburse Seller for all expenses incurred by Seller, such as preparation for and placement into storage, handling, storage, inspection, preservation and insurance, and (v) when conditions permit, and upon payment of all amounts due hereunder, Seller shall assist and cooperate with Buyer in any reasonable manner with respect to the removal of any Products which have been placed in storage.

MACHINERY EXPORTER'S STANDARD FORM

ARTICLE III - EXPORT SHIPMENT

A. In the event Buyer wishes to arrange for export shipment, Buyer shall inform Seller by so indicating on the order. In the absence of such indication, or if Seller exercises its rights under Paragraph B of Article VI, Seller shall arrange for (i) export shipment to Buyer's country and (ii) marine warehouse-to-warehouse insurance (including war risk, if available). Buyer shall pay Seller for all fees and expenses, including, but not limited to, those covering preparation of consular documents, consular fees, ocean freight, storage, insurance and Seller's then current fee for such services. Notwithstanding any extension of credit to Buyer, all such charges shall be promptly reimbursed by Buyer in U.S. Dollars upon submission of Seller's invoices therefor.

B. Seller shall take reasonable precautions to assure that quantities, weights and identification, as stated on packing lists, are correct, but Seller shall have no liability to Buyer for any fines, penalties or other costs associated in any way with packing list errors.

C. In performing any of the foregoing services, Seller shall comply with any reasonable instructions of Buyer or, in the absence thereof, shall act according to its best judgment. In so acting on Buyer's behalf, neither Seller nor its agents shall be liable for negligence or for any special, consequential, incidental, indirect or exemplary damages to Buyer resulting therefrom.

ARTICLE IV - GOVERNMENTAL AUTHORIZATIONS

A. The party that arranges for export shipment (or Buyer's designated export agent) shall be responsible for the timely application in its own name for any required U.S.A. export license. Buyer shall be responsible for timely obtaining and maintaining any required import license, exchange permit or any other governmental authorization. Buyer and Seller shall assist each other when such help is reasonably possible. Seller shall not be liable if any authorization of any government is delayed, denied, revoked, restricted or not renewed, and Buyer shall not be relieved thereby of its obligations to pay Seller for the Products or any other charges which are the obligation of Buyer hereunder.

B. All shipments hereunder shall at all times be subject to the export control laws and regulations of the U.S.A. and any amendments thereto. Buyer agrees that it shall not make any disposition of U.S.A.-origin Products purchased from Seller, by way of trans-shipment, re-export, diversion or otherwise, other than in and to the ultimate country of destination specified

GE 43H (10/92)

-2-

on Buyer's order or declared as the country of ultimate destination on Seller's invoices, except as said laws and regulations may expressly permit.

ARTICLE V - EXCUSABLE DELAYS

A. Seller shall not be liable for delays in delivery or failure to perform due directly or indirectly to (i) causes beyond Seller's reasonable control, (ii) acts of God, acts (including failure to act) of any governmental authority (de jure or de facto), wars (declared or undeclared), governmental priorities, port congestion, riots, revolutions, strikes or other labor disputes, fires, floods, sabotage, nuclear incidents, earthquakes, storms, epidemics, or (iii) inabilities due to causes beyond Seller's reasonable control timely to obtain either necessary and proper labor, materials, components, facilities, energy, fuel, transportation, governmental authorizations or instructions, material or information required from Buyer. The foregoing shall apply even though any of such causes exists at the time of the order or occurs after Seller's performance of its obligations is delayed for other causes.

B. Seller shall notify Buyer of any delay or failure excused by this Article and shall specify the revised delivery date as soon as practicable. In the event of such delay, subject to Paragraph C of this Article, there shall be no termination of the transaction, and the time of delivery or of performance shall be extended for a period equal to the time lost by Seller by reason of the delay.

C. If delay excused by this Article extends for more than sixty (60) days and the parties have not agreed upon a revised basis for continuing the work at the end of the delay, including adjustment of the price, then either party (except where delay is caused by Buyer, in which event only Seller), upon thirty (30) days written notice, may terminate the order with respect to the unexecuted portion of the work, whereupon Buyer shall promptly pay Seller its termination charges determined in accordance with Seller's standard accounting practices upon submission of Seller's invoices therefor.

ARTICLE VI - PAYMENT

A. Payment shall be made in U.S. Dollars in New York as follows:

    (i)   On an order of fifteen thousand U.S. Dollars (U.S. $15,000) or under, payment shall be made simultaneously with the placing of the order where the laws of the Buyer's country permit.

    (ii)   On an order over fifteen thousand U.S. Dollars (U.S. $15,000), or if the laws of the Buyer's country forbid compliance with Paragraph (i) above, payment shall be made through a letter of credit to be established by Buyer at its expense. All costs, including any bank confirmation charges, relating to such letter of credit are for the account of the Buyer. All letters of credit shall a) be in favor of and acceptable to Seller, b) be consistent with the terms set forth herein, c) be maintained in sufficient amounts and for the period necessary to meet all payment obligations, d) be irrevocable and issued, or confirmed by a bank in New York acceptable to Seller within fifteen 15 days after acceptance of the order, e) permit partial deliveries, f) provide for pro rata payments upon presentation of Seller's invoices therefor and either Seller's certificate of delivery FOB factory or of delivery into storage with certification of cause therefor, and g) provide for the payment of any charges for storage, export shipment, price adjustments, and cancellation or termination.

B. In the event Seller agrees to any deviation from the cash or letter of credit requirements set forth above, Seller reserves the right to arrange for export shipment of the Products.

C. If Buyer fails to fulfill any condition of its payment obligations, Seller may (i) withhold deliveries and suspend performance, or (ii) continue performance if Seller deems it reasonable to do so, or (iii) place the Products in storage pursuant to the provisions of Article II hereof. In any event, the costs incurred by Seller as a result of Buyer's non-fulfillment shall be payable by Buyer upon submission of Seller's invoices therefor. Seller shall be entitled to an extension of time for performance of its obligations equaling the period of Buyer's non-fulfillment whether or not Seller elects to suspend performance. If such non-fulfillment is not rectified by Buyer promptly upon notice thereof, Seller may cancel the transaction, and Buyer shall pay Seller its charges for cancellation upon submission of Seller's invoices therefor.

ARTICLE VII - TAXES AND DUTIES

A. All U.S.A. taxes are included in the price except sales, use, excise, value-added and similar taxes which have been excluded based upon the

GE 43H (10/92)

-4-

assumption that the transaction involves exportation. All rights to drawback of U.S.A. customs duties paid by Seller with respect to Products (or material or components thereof) belong to and shall remain in Seller. If Buyer arranges for export shipment, Buyer agrees to furnish without charge evidence of exportation or other evidence of tax or duty exemption acceptable to the taxing or customs authorities when requested by Seller, failing which the amount of any U.S.A. taxes or duties imposed on Seller in connection with the transaction shall be promptly reimbursed in U.S. Dollars by Buyer to Seller upon submission of Seller's invoices therefor.

B. Any taxes (including income, stamp and turnover or value-added taxes), duties, fees, charges or assessments of any nature levied by any governmental authority other than of the U.S.A. in connection with this transaction, whether levied against Buyer, against Seller or its employees, or against any of Seller's subcontractors or their employees, shall be the responsibility of Buyer and shall be paid directly by Buyer to the governmental authority concerned. If Seller or its subcontractors, or the employees of either, are required to pay any such levies and/or fines, penalties or assessments in the first instance, or as a result of Buyer's failure to comply with any applicable laws or regulations governing the payment of such levies by Buyer, the amount of any payments so made, plus the expense of currency conversion, shall be promptly reimbursed in U.S. Dollars by Buyer upon submission of Seller's invoices therefor.

ARTICLE VIII - WARRANTIES

A. Seller warrants that Products manufactured by Seller shall be free from defects in material, workmanship and title, and shall be of the kind and quality specified or designated by Seller. Seller's obligations, set forth below, shall apply only to failures to meet the foregoing warranties (except as to title) occurring within fifteen (15) months from date of delivery pursuant to Article II of which Seller is given written notice within thirty (30) days of such occurrence and provided the Product or part thereof is made available to Seller as specified by Seller.

B. If any Product or part thereof fails to meet the foregoing warranties (except as to title), Seller shall repair same or, at its option, replace same, in either case F.O.B. factory, on the same basis as described in Article I. Any such failure shall not be cause for the extension of the duration of the warranty specified in this Article VIII. If such failure or defect cannot be corrected by Seller's reasonable efforts, the parties shall negotiate an equitable adjustment.

C. Seller's obligations under Paragraph B above shall not apply to any Product or part thereof which (i) is normally consumed in operation, or (ii) has a normal life inherently shorter than the warranty period specified in

GE 43H (10/92)

Paragraph A, or (iii) is not properly stored, installed, used, maintained or repaired, or is modified other than pursuant to Seller's instructions or approval, or (iv) has been subjected to any other kind of misuse or detrimental exposure, or has been involved in an accident.

D. With respect to any Products not manufactured by Seller (except for integral parts of Seller's Products to which the warranties set forth above shall apply), Seller gives no warranty, and only the warranty, if any, given by the manufacturer shall apply.

E. Subject to Article X, this Article sets forth the exclusive remedies for claims based upon defects in or nonconformity of the Products, whether the claim is in contract, warranty, tort (including negligence) or otherwise. Except as set forth in Article IX, the foregoing warranties are in lieu of all other warranties, whether oral, written, express, implied or statutory. NO IMPLIED OR STATUTORY WARRANTIES OF MERCHANTABILITY OR FITNESS FOR PARTICULAR PURPOSE SHALL APPLY.

ARTICLE IX - PATENTS

A. Seller warrants that any Product (or part thereof) manufactured by Seller and furnished hereunder shall be free of any rightful claim of any third party for infringement of any U.S.A. patent. If Buyer notifies Seller promptly of the receipt of any claim that such Product infringes a U.S.A. patent and gives Seller information, assistance and exclusive authority to settle and defend such claim, Seller shall, at its own expense and option, either (i) settle or defend such claim or any suit or proceeding arising therefrom and pay all damages and costs awarded therein against Buyer, or (ii) procure for Buyer the right to continue using such Product, or (iii) modify the Product so that it becomes non-infringing, or (iv) replace the Product with a non-infringing Product, or (v) remove the Product and refund the purchase price (less reasonable depreciation) and any transportation or installation costs which have been separately paid by Buyer. If, in any such suit arising from such claim, the continued use of the Product for the purpose intended is enjoined by any court of competent jurisdiction, Seller shall, at its option, take one or more of the actions under (ii), (iii), (iv) or (v) above. The foregoing states the entire liability of Seller for patent infringement of any Product and is subject to the limitation of total liability set forth in Article X.

B. The preceding Paragraph shall not apply to: (i) any Product (or part thereof) which is manufactured to Buyer's design or (ii) the use of any Product (or any part thereof) furnished hereunder in conjunction with any other apparatus or material. As to any Product, part or use described in the preceding sentence, Seller assumes no liability whatsoever for patent infringement.

GE 43H (10/92)

-6-

344

C. With respect to any Product (or part thereof) furnished hereunder which is not manufactured by Seller, only the patent indemnity of the manufacturer, if any, shall apply.

D. The patent warranty and indemnity obligations recited above are in lieu of all other patent warranties and indemnities whatsoever, whether oral, written, express, implied or statutory.

ARTICLE X - LIMITATIONS OF LIABILITY

A. The total liability of Seller, including its subcontractors or suppliers, on any and all claims, whether in contract, warranty, tort (including negligence or patent infringement) or otherwise, arising out of, connected with, or resulting from the performance or non-performance of any agreement resulting herefrom or from the manufacture, sale, delivery resale, repair, replacement or use of any Product or the furnishing of any service, shall not exceed the price allocable to the Product or service which gives rise to the claim. Except as to title, any such liability shall terminate upon the expiration of the warranty period specified in Article VIII.

B. In no event, whether as a result of breach of contract, warranty, tort (including negligence or patent infringement) or otherwise, shall Seller, or its subcontractors or suppliers, be liable for any special, consequential, incidental, indirect or exemplary damages, including, but not limited to, loss of profit or revenue, loss of use of the Products or any associated equipment, cost of capital, cost of substitute goods, facilities, services or replacement power, downtime costs or claims of Buyer's customers for such damages. If Buyer transfers title to, or leases the Products sold hereunder to, or otherwise permits or suffers use by, any third party, Buyer shall obtain from such third party a provision affording Seller and its subcontractors and suppliers the protection of the preceding sentence.

C. If Seller furnishes Buyer with advice or other assistance which concerns any Product supplied hereunder, or any system or equipment in which any such Product may be installed, and which is not required by the terms of this instrument or pursuant to any agreement resulting herefrom, the furnishing of such advice or assistance shall not subject Seller to any liability, whether in contract, warranty, tort (including negligence or patent infringement) or otherwise.

ARTICLE XI - NUCLEAR USE

A. Products and services sold hereunder are not intended for application (and shall not be used) in connection with the use or handling of nuclear material

GE 43H (10/92)

-7-

345

or the construction or operation of a nuclear installation. Buyer warrants that it shall not use such Products or services for such purposes, or permit others to use such Products or services for such purposes, unless such use is agreed to in writing by Seller.

B. If, in breach of the foregoing, any such use occurs, Seller disclaims all liability for any nuclear or other damages, injury or contamination, and Buyer covenants to indemnify Seller against any such liability, whether as a result of breach of contract, warranty, tort (including negligence) or otherwise.

ARTICLE XII - GENERAL

A. Any Products furnished by Seller hereunder shall comply with federal, state and local laws and regulations of the U.S.A. applicable to the manufacture, packing, sale and shipment of such Products as of the date of Seller's quotation and shall comply with any amendments thereto which may have come into effect prior to the time such Products are furnished, provided that the price and, if necessary, delivery shall be equitably adjusted to compensate Seller for the effect of compliance with any such amendments. Seller shall not comply with any law, regulation or requirement which would subject Seller to criminal or civil penalties or loss of tax benefits under any federal, state or local law or regulation of the U.S.A., and the furnishing of any quotation or acknowledgment of any order does not constitute the furnishing of or an agreement to furnish any information which would subject Seller to any of the above mentioned penalties or loss of tax benefits. Seller shall not comply with any other law, regulation or requirement which would increase Seller's costs, unless there is an appropriate adjustment in price.

B. The delegation or assignment by Buyer of any or all of its duties or rights hereunder without Seller's prior written consent shall be void.

C. Any representation, understanding, proposal, agreement, warranty, course of dealing or trade usage not contained or referenced herein shall not be binding on Seller. No modification, amendment, rescission, waiver or other change to these Conditions shall be binding on Seller unless assented to in writing by Seller.

D. The validity, performance and all matters relating to the interpretation and effect of any agreement resulting herefrom and any amendment thereto shall be governed by the internal substantive law of the State of New York, U.S.A.

E. The provisions of any agreement resulting herefrom are for the benefit of the parties hereto and not for any other person except as specifically provided herein.

GE 43H (10/92)

-8-

F. Unless otherwise specified by Seller, any quotation of Seller shall expire thirty (30) days from the date of issuance and may be modified or withdrawn at any time prior to the date of Buyer's order.

G. Buyer may terminate an order only upon paying Seller its termination charges determined in accordance with Seller's standard accounting practices upon submission of Seller's invoices therefor. Termination of an order shall not relieve either party of any obligation arising out of work performed prior to termination.

H. As used throughout this instrument (i) the term Product (or Products) is defined to include all equipment, materials, supplies, components, services, engineering, design and data, or other work which Seller has contracted to supply, and (ii) the term Seller is defined to mean General Electric Company, U.S.A. and (iii) the term Buyer is defined to mean the party other than Seller to any transaction or agreement resulting herefrom.

I. The invalidity, in whole or in part, of any Article or Paragraph hereof shall not affect the validity of the remainder of such Article or Paragraph or of any agreement resulting herefrom.

GE 43H (10/92)

-9-

347

FORD

CRABTREE FORD, Inc.

D/B/A CRABTREE FORD, AMC, RENAULT. JEEP
1435 Boston Post Rd. LARCHMONT, N.Y. 10538
SALES (914) 834-7000
SERVICE (914) 834-7025
PARTS (914) 834-7010

AMC RENAULT Jeep

16007

THIS AGREEMENT IS NOT BINDING UNLESS SIGNED BY THE SELLER AND THE BUYER

BUYER _____ SALESMAN _____

STREET _____ PHONE _____ BUS _____

CITY _____ STATE _____ ZIP _____

THE TRANSACTION

I ORDER AND AGREE TO PURCHASE FROM YOU, ON THE TERMS CONTAINED ON BOTH SIDES OF THIS AGREEMENT, THE FOLLOWING VEHICLE:
(READ OTHER SIDE)

THE VEHICLE

YEAR	☐ NEW ☐ USED ☐ DEMONSTRATOR	MAKE	MODEL	SERIES
TYPE	COLOR	TRIM	V.I.N.	
TO BE DELIVERED ON OR ABOUT:		MILEAGE	STOCK NO. (IF RESERVED)	

THE PRICE

VEHICLE PRICE	(+)	$			
TRANSPORTATION (IF NOT INCLUDED IN VEHICLE PRICE)	(+)				
FACTORY INSTALLED EQUIPMENT	(+)		PROTECTION PACKAGE	(+)	
			DEALER INSTALLED EQUIPMENT AND SERVICES	(+)	
LIEN HOLDER INFORMATION					
				TOTAL	$

THE TRADE-IN

DESCRIPTION OF TRADE				LESS TRADE-IN CREDIT	(−)	
YEAR	MILEAGE	MAKE	MODEL	(BUYER SEE 1 AND 8b ON BACK)		
PLATE NO.	EXP. DATE	COLOR	V.I.N.			$
TRADE-IN IS CLEAR OF ALL LIENS EXCEPT:			AMOUNT OWED	$	CASH PRICE	

IF YOU AGREE TO ASSIST ME IN OBTAINING FINANCING FOR ANY PART OF THE PURCHASE PRICE, THIS ORDER SHALL NOT BE BINDING UPON YOU OR ME UNTIL ALL OF THE CREDIT TERMS ARE PRESENTED TO ME IN ACCORDANCE WITH REGULATION "Z" (TRUTH-IN-LENDING) AND ARE ACCEPTED BY ME. IF I DO NOT ACCEPT THE CREDIT TERMS WHEN PRESENTED, I MAY CANCEL THIS ORDER AND MY DEPOSIT WILL BE REFUNDED.

SPECIAL NOTICE TO CONSUMER

IF, UNDER THE LAW OF THE STATE OF NEW YORK CONTROLLING THE SALE OF USED MOTOR VEHICLES, YOU SHOULD BE ENTITLED TO A REFUND IN CONNECTION WITH THIS TRANSACTION. THE VALUE OF ANY VEHICLE YOU MAY HAVE TRADED-IN IF THE SELLER CHOOSES NOT TO RETURN IT TO YOU SHALL NOT BE THE VALUE LISTED IN THIS DOCUMENT INSTEAD, THE VALUE WILL BE DETERMINED BASED ON THE NATIONAL AUTO DEALERS ASSOCIATION USED CAR GUIDE WHOLESALE VALUE OR OTHER GUIDE APPROVED BY THE COMMISSIONER OF MOTOR VEHICLES, AND ADJUSTED FOR MILEAGE, IMPROVE-MENTS AND ANY MAJOR PHYSICAL OR MECHANICAL DEFECTS

CONTRACTUAL DISCLOSURE STATEMENT FOR USED VEHICLE ONLY

"The information you see on the window form for this vehicle is part of this contract. Information on the window form overrides any contrary provisions in the contract of sale."

DEPOSITS ARE NON-REFUNDABLE ON ALL APPROVED DEALS.
ALL BALANCES MUST BE PAID IN CASH OR CERTIFIED CHECK ON DELIVERY.

TAXES AND OTHER FEES

SALES TAX	%	(+)		
TITLE FEE $2.50	N.Y.S. INSPECTION	New Car $6.00 Used Car $15.00		
REGISTRATION FEE (ESTIMATE)		(+)		
Dealer's Fee for Obtaining Registration and/or Certificate of Title (Fee May Not Exceed $10)		(+)	10	00
		(+)		
TOTAL CASH PRICE DELIVERED			$	
LESS DEPOSIT CHECK NO. _____ SUBMITTED WITH ORDER		(−)		
PLUS BALANCE OWING ON TRADE-IN		(+)		
CASH DUE ON DELIVERY			$	

I have read the terms on the back of this agreement and have received a completed copy of this agreement.

BUYER'S SIGNATURE _____ DATE: _____

CO-BUYER'S SIGNATURE _____ DATE: _____

SELLER APPROVED BY: _____ DATE: _____

Reynolds+Reynolds (JPM) © U.S.A. 5/4/93

(E2235)

<u>SEE OTHER SIDE FOR ADDITIONAL TERMS</u>

AUTOMOBILE PURCHASE ORDER

ADDITIONAL TERMS OF AGREEMENT

"I", "me", and "my" refer to the Buyer and Co-Buyer "You" and "your" refer to the Seller.

I agree this order is subject to the following terms:

1. **Trade-in Credit May Change.** If I do not deliver the trade-in vehicle to you when this Agreement is signed, I agree, that at the time the trade-in vehicle is delivered to you, should the value of my trade-in be materially diminished as a result of physical damage, alteration or deterioration in mechanical condition other than normal wear and tear, YOU HAVE THE RIGHT TO REAPPRAISE THE VEHICLE AS A RESULT OF SUCH REAPPARAISAL. I UNDERSTAND THAT THE TRADE-IN ALLOWANCE ON MY VEHICLE MAY BE REDUCED AND THAT THIS WILL IN TURN INCREASE THE NET PRICE WHICH I WILL HAVE TO PAY FOR THE VEHICLE IF I DECIDE TO PURCHASE THE VEHICLE. If the trade-in credit is reduced and I am not satisfied, I understand that I can cancel this agreement IF the purchased vehicle has not been registered in my name or delivered to me or you have not accepted delivery of the trade-in vehicle.

2. **Trade-in; Buyer's Obligations.** At the time I deliver the trade-in vehicle to you, I promise to sign a Bill of Sale and a mileage certification statement and give you satisfactory proof that I own the vehicle. I warrant (guarantee) (a) that there are no liens on the trade-in vehicle and that I owe no one any money for the vehicle or repairs to the vehicle, except as may be shown on the face of this agreement; (b) that the trade-in vehicle does not have a welded or bent frame and that the motor block is not cracked, welded or repaired, and (c) that the vehicle has not been flood damaged or declared a total loss for insurance purposes; and (d) that emission control devices have not been altered and/or removed, and nothing has been removed from the trade, including all seat belts, that was originally seen The engine and/or transmission has not been tampered with to pass your inspection

3. **Buyer's Refusal to Purchase.** Unless this agreement is non-binding because you are arranging credit for me, I understand that the cash deposit I have given to you can be retained, in accordance with your refund policy, to offset your damages if I refuse to complete my purchase. I also understand that I may be responsible for any other damages which you may incur as a result of my failure to perform my obligations under the terms of this agreement.

4. **Delays in Delivery.** I understand that you shall not be liable for delays caused by the manufacturer, accidents, sureties, fires or other causes beyond your control. Provided you promptly place my order with the manufacturer and the manufacturer refuses to accept the order or fails to deliver the vehicle after accepting the order, upon your prompt notification and refund of my deposit, I will not hold you liable and this agreement shall be cancelled. Dealer shall honor deposit on stock unit for no longer than 24 hrs. after contract date at which time unit will be placed back into inventory and deposit forfeited.

5. **Disclaimer of Warranties.** I UNDERSTAND THAT YOU EXPRESSLY DISCLAIM ALL WARRANTIES, EXPRESS OR IMPLIED, INCLUDING ANY IMPLIED WARRANTY OF MERCHANTABILITY OR FITNESS FOR A PARTICULAR PURPOSE, AND THAT YOU NEITHER ASSUME NOR AUTHORIZE ANY OTHER PERSON TO ASSUME FOR YOU ANY LIABILITY IN CONNECTION WITH THE SALE OF THE VEHICLE. except as otherwise provided in writing by YOU in an attachment to this Agreement or in a document delivered to ME when the vehicle is delivered.

   Limitation on Implied Warranties. Some States do not allow either (1) Limitations on how long an implied warranty lasts or (2) the exclusion or limitation of incidental or consequential damages, so these limitations may not apply

6. **Price Changes.**

(a) THE TOTAL CASH PRICE DELIVERED LESS THE TRADE-IN ALLOWANCE SHOWN ON THE FRONT OF THIS AGREEMENT IS THE FINAL CONTRACT PRICE TO WHICH YOU AND I HAVE AGREED. AND, IF THE VEHICLE IS A NEW MOTOR VEHICLE, NO ADDITIONAL FEE OR CHARGE WILL BE IMPOSED OR COLLECTED DUE TO CHANGES IN THE MANUFACTURER'S LIST PRICE, OR CHANGES IN THE COST OF FREIGHT OR SERVICES PROVIDED BY YOU.

(b) A REDUCTION IN THE VALUE OF THE TRADE-IN MAY RESULT IN AN INCREASE IN THE CASH PRICE DELIVERED I WILL HAVE TO PAY AS PROVIDED IN PARAGRAPH 1 OF THIS AGREEMENT

(c) IF THE BALANCE I OWE ON MY TRADE-IN AT THE TIME OF DELIVERY OF THE TRADE-IN TO YOU IS DIFFERENT THAN THE AMOUNT I HAVE TOLD YOU AND WHICH AMOUNT IS SHOWN ON THE FRONT OF THIS AGREEMENT, THEN THE CASH PRICE DELIVERED OF THE VEHICLE I AM PURCHASING SHALL CHANGE ACCORDINGLY

(d) IF THE REGISTRATION FEE VARIES FROM THE AMOUNT YOU HAVE ESTIMATED ON THE FRONT OF THIS AGREEMENT, THEN THE CASH PRICE DELIVERED SHALL CHANGE ACCORDINGLY

(e) I AGREE THAT I WILL PAY THE FINAL CASH PRICE DELIVERED AS SHOWN ON THE FRONT OF THIS AGREEMENT. IF THERE HAVE BEEN ANY CHANGES IN THE TOTAL CASH PRICE DELIVERED FOR REASONS STATED IN THIS PARAGRAPH 6 THEN I WILL PAY THE CASH PRICE DELIVERED AS CHANGED BY ANY SUCH ADJUSTMENT MY PAYMENT WILL BE EITHER IN CASH, BANK, OR CERTIFIED CHECK AT THE TIME OF DELIVERY OF THE VEHICLE I HAVE PURCHASED.

7. **Change of Design.** I understand that the manufacturer has the right to change the design of the vehicle, its chassis, accessories or any parts at any time without notice to YOU or ME In the event of such a change by the manufacturer, YOU shall have no duty to ME except to deliver the vehicle as made by the manufacturer

8. **No Other Agreements.** There are no understandings or agreements between you and me other than those set forth in this Agreement and attachments to this Agreement, if there are any such attachments"

9. **New York Law Applies.** You and I agree that this Agreement is governed by New York State Law

WET 5851
(E223%)

94-291-5289 (1/00) NY

RETAIL INSTALLMENT CONTRACT
NEW YORK - SIMPLE INTEREST

BUYER (AND CO-BUYER) NAME AND ADDRESS	CREDITOR (SELLER) NAME AND ADDRESS	DATE	ACCOUNT NUMBER

Creditor (collectively "us" and "we") agrees to sell, and buyer and co-buyer, if any, (collectively "Buyer", "you" and "your") after being quoted both a cash and credit price, agrees to buy from Creditor on a credit price basis ("Total Sale Price"), subject to the terms and conditions set forth on both the front and back of this contract, the vehicle ("Vehicle") described below. You acknowledge delivery and acceptance of the Vehicle.

DESCRIPTION OF VEHICLE— [ ] NEW [ ] USED	YEAR	MAKE	MODEL	VEHICLE IDENTIFICATION NUMBER	Description of Trade-in	YEAR & MAKE	MODEL

FEDERAL TRUTH-IN-LENDING DISCLOSURES

ANNUAL PERCENTAGE RATE	FINANCE CHARGE	Amount Financed	Total of Payments	Total Sale Price
The cost of your credit as a yearly rate.	E* The dollar amount the credit will cost you.	E* The amount of credit provided to you or on your behalf.	E* The amount you will have paid after you have made all payments as scheduled.	E* The total price of your purchase on credit, including your down-payment of
% $	$	$	$	$

Payment Schedule - Your payment schedule will be ...

NO. OF PAYMENTS	AMOUNT OF EACH PAYMENT	WHEN PAYMENTS ARE DUE [ ] MONTHLY [ ] (BEGINNING DATE OF PAYMENT)	NO. OF PAYMENTS	AMOUNT OF EACH PAYMENT	WHEN PAYMENTS ARE DUE [ ] MONTHLY [ ] (BEGINNING DATE OF PAYMENT)
	$			$	

Prepayment. If you pay off early, you will not have to pay a penalty.

Late Charge. If a payment or part thereof is more than 10 days late, you will be charged 5% of such unpaid amount.

Security Interest. You are giving us a security interest in the Vehicle being purchased.

Filing Fees $

Contract Provisions. See the back of this contract for any additional information about security interests, nonpayment, default, any required repayment in full before the scheduled date, and prepayment refunds and penalties.

*E means Estimate

LIABILITY INSURANCE COVERAGE FOR BODILY INJURY AND PROPERTY DAMAGE CAUSED TO OTHERS IS NOT INCLUDED IN THIS CONTRACT. YOU MAY OBTAIN VEHICLE INSURANCE FROM A PERSON OF YOUR CHOICE.

CREDIT LIFE, CREDIT DISABILITY, GUARANTEED AUTOMOTIVE PROTECTION COVERAGE AND OTHER OPTIONAL INSURANCE ARE NOT REQUIRED TO OBTAIN CREDIT AND WILL NOT BE PROVIDED UNLESS YOU SIGN AND AGREE TO PAY THE PREMIUM.

[ ] CREDIT LIFE PREMIUM $	[ ] MECHANICAL BREAKDOWN
INSURER	TERM PREMIUM $
INSURED(S)	INSURER
BUYER'S SIGNATURE	BUYER'S SIGNATURE
CO-BUYER'S SIGNATURE	CO-BUYER'S SIGNATURE
[ ] CREDIT DISABILITY PREMIUM $	[ ] TYPE TERM
INSURER	PREMIUM $
INSURED(S)	INSURER
BUYER'S SIGNATURE	BUYER'S SIGNATURE
CO-BUYER'S SIGNATURE	CO-BUYER'S SIGNATURE

1. Cash Price
  a. Vehicle (including accessories, delivery, installation charges, if any) .....
  b. Sales Tax .....
  c. Documentary Fee .....
  d. Service Contract (optional) ..
  e. Cash Price (1a + 1b + 1c + 1d) ..... $

2. Downpayment
  a. Downpayment .....
  b. Manufacturer's Rebate .....
  c. Gross Allowance on Trade-in
    $
  d. Pay-off on Trade-in
    $
  e. Net Allowance on Trade-in (2c – 2d) .....
  f. Downpayment (2a + 2b + 2e) ..... $
    If less than $0, disclose on Line 3a and enter $0 for the Downpayment

3. Unpaid Balance of Cash Price (1e – 2f) ..... $
  a. Unpaid Trade-in Lien Amount to be Financed **. $
    ** Paid to:

4. Other Charges Including Amounts Paid to Others on Your Behalf*
  a. Paid to Public Officials for:*
    (i) Other Taxes .....
    (ii) Filing Fees .....
    (iii) License Fees .....
    (iv) Certificate of Title Fees .
    (v) Registration Fees .....
  b. Paid to:
    *
    For:
  c. Paid to:
    *
    For:
  d. Paid to:
    *
    For:
  e. Paid to:
    *
    For:
  f. Paid to Insurance Companies for Insurance for:*
    (i) Optional Mechanical Breakdown .....
    (ii) Optional Credit Life .....
    (iii) Optional Credit Accident & Health .....
  g. Subtotal (4a + 4b + 4c + 4d + 4e + 4f) ..... $

5. Amount Financed (3 + 3a + 4g) ..... $

*Seller may receive and retain a portion of certain of these amounts.

NOTICE TO THE BUYER: 1. Do not sign this contract before you read it or if it contains any blank spaces. 2. You are entitled to a completely filled-in copy of this contract when you sign it. 3. Under the law, you have the following rights, among others: (a) To pay off in advance the full amount due and to obtain a partial refund of the credit service charge (finance charge); (b) To redeem the property if repossessed for default; (c) To require, under certain conditions, a resale of the property if repossessed. 4. According to law you have the privilege of purchasing the insurance on the motor vehicle provided for in this contract from an agent or broken of your own selection.

YOU AGREE THAT YOU SIGNED THIS CONTRACT AND RECEIVED A COMPLETELY FILLED-IN COPY ON _____ , (YR.) _____ .

RETAIL INSTALLMENT CONTRACT

BUYER'S SIGNATURE	CO-BUYER'S SIGNATURE	CO-BUYER'S SIGNATURE

THIS CONTRACT IS ACCEPTED BY THE CREDITOR (SELLER) AND ASSIGNED TO _____ ("ASSIGNEE") IN ACCORDANCE WITH THE TERMS OF THE ASSIGNMENT SET FORTH ON THE REVERSE HEREOF.

CREDITOR (SELLER)	BY	TITLE

AUTOMOBILE RETAIL INSTALLMENT CONTRACT

84-291-5289 (1/00) NY SIMPLE INTEREST (BACK)

TERMS AND CONDITIONS

1. **PAYMENT:** You agree to make all payments when they are due. Accepting a late payment or late charge does not change your payment due date. You may prepay your debt without penalty. This is a simple interest contract. **Your final payment may be larger or smaller, depending on whether you make payments late or early.** Your payment will be applied first to the earned and unpaid part of the Finance Charge, then to the unpaid Amount Financed and then to any other amounts due. The Finance Charge is **earned by applying the** Annual Percentage Rate divided by 365 to the unpaid Amount Financed for the number of days outstanding.

2. **ADDITIONAL CHARGES:** You agree to pay a late charge if any payment or part thereof is received by the Creditor more than ten days after the scheduled due date. The late charge is shown on the front of this contract. You agree to pay a charge in the amount of $20 for each check, draft, or other similar instrument presented to Creditor that is returned to Creditor due to non-sufficient funds or dishonored for any other reason.

3. **SECURITY AGREEMENT:** You give us a security interest in the Vehicle and all parts or other goods put on the Vehicle; all money or goods received for the Vehicle; and all insurance policies and service contracts financed by you in this contract, and any rebate or refunds which relate to those policies or contracts. This secures payment of all amounts you owe in this contract.

4. **USE OF VEHICLE:** You agree to maintain the Vehicle in good condition and obey all laws; keep the Vehicle free from the claims of others; and obtain our written consent prior to transferring your equity in the Vehicle, subleasing or renting the Vehicle, or taking the Vehicle outside the United States for more than thirty (30) days.

5. **WARRANTIES: If the Vehicle is for personal use and we, or the Vehicle's manufacturer, extend a written warranty or service contract covering the Vehicle within 90 days from the date of the contract, you get implied warranties of merchantability and fitness for a particular purpose covering the Vehicle. Otherwise, you agree that there are no such implied warranties.**

6. **INSURANCE:** You must insure yourself and us against loss or damage to the Vehicle and provide us proof of that insurance. We must approve the type and amount of insurance. Whether or not the Vehicle is insured, you must pay for it if it is lost, damaged or destroyed. You agree that we may endorse your name upon any check or draft representing payment made by an insurance company for a loss related to the Vehicle.

   If you fail to procure or maintain such Vehicle insurance, we may procure Vehicle insurance that covers our interest only. In such event, you agree to pay a charge consisting of the insurance premium and a Finance Charge thereon at the Annual Percentage Rate shown on the front of this contract. You agree to pay the charge in equal installments along with the installments of the unpaid balance then remaining on the contract.

   If the Vehicle is stolen, confiscated or damaged beyond repair, you will not be responsible for the "gap amount." The Gap Amount is the difference between the amount that is owing under the contract as of the date of the loss and the sum (a) of any unpaid payments and other unpaid charges owing as of the date of the loss, and (b) the actual cash value of the Vehicle as of the date of the loss.

7. **DEFAULT:** You will be in default if you do not make a payment when it is due, you do not keep any promise in this contract; you file a bankruptcy petition or one is filed against you; your Vehicle is seized by any local, state or federal authority; you provided information on the credit application which was not true and accurate; or you breach any promise, representation or warranty you have made in this contract.

   If we repossess your Vehicle, we may:

   Require you to pay the unpaid Amount Financed, the earned and unpaid part of the Finance Charge and all other amounts due; sue you to collect the amount you owe; **without the use of force or other breach of the peace, enter the premises where the Vehicle may be, and lawfully repossess (take back) the Vehicle**; take goods found in the Vehicle and hold them for you; and cancel any Credit Life, Credit Disability, Guaranteed Automotive Protection Coverage, Extended Warranty or other optional insurance financed by you under this contract, and apply the refunded premium to your outstanding balance.

   If we repossess the Vehicle, we will send you a notice. It will state that you may redeem the Vehicle and the amount needed to redeem. You may redeem the Vehicle until we sell it. The money from the sale, less allowed expenses, will be applied to the amount you owe. If there is any money left, we will pay it to you. If the money from the sale is not enough, you will pay what is still owed to us plus interest. Allowed expenses are those which we are entitled to by law in any lawful activity to obtain possession of, recondition, and dispose of the Vehicle after default. In a suit to collect the amount you owe under this contract, if we hire an attorney who is not our salaried employee to collect what you owe, you agree to pay reasonable attorney fees not to exceed fifteen percent (15%) of the unpaid balance of this contract after default, plus court costs.

8. **ASSIGNMENT:** You understand that this contract will be assigned to Assignee. Assignee will acquire all of our interest in this contract and in the Vehicle, including the right to receive all payments.

9. **GENERAL:** Notice to you is sufficient if mailed to your last address known by us. If the law does not allow a part of this contract, that part will be void. The remaining parts will be enforceable. If there is more than one Buyer, their obligation shall be joint and several. Any delay or omission by us in enforcing our rights shall not act as a waiver.

10. **DEFERRED PAYMENTS:** Any change in this contract must be in writing and signed by all the parties, however, if permitted by law, extensions, deferrals and due date changes may be agreed to orally by you and us, and we will send you a written confirmation of our agreement. Interest will continue to accrue until the next payment is received. Any deferral would not extend any purchased insurance coverage you have.

11. **POWER OF ATTORNEY:** You appoint us, through our appointed officer or employee, as your attorney-in-fact. Your grant of this power of attorney is coupled with an interest, and is irrevocable until all obligations you owe under this contract are paid in full. As your attorney-in-fact, we can: sign on your behalf all Certificates of Ownership, Registration Cards, applications, affidavits or any other documents required to register and properly perfect our security interest in the Vehicle; transfer your entire interest in the Vehicle to any other person as part of a repossession and sale; act on your behalf in any insurance matter relating to the Vehicle, including, but not limited to, the power to endorse insurance proceeds checks or drafts on your behalf; and cancel any Credit Life, Credit Disability, Guaranteed Automotive Protection Coverage, Extended Warranty or other optional insurance financed by you under this contract, and apply the refunded premium to your outstanding balance if you are in default.

12. **GOVERNING LAW:** This contract shall be governed by the laws of the State of New York except, if the Vehicle is repossessed, then the law of the state where the Vehicle is repossessed will govern the repossession. Repossession effected through legal process will be governed by the laws of the state in which such process is brought.

NOTICE: THE INFORMATION YOU SEE ON THE WINDOW FORM FOR THIS VEHICLE IS PART OF THIS CONTRACT. INFORMATION ON THE WINDOW FORM OVERRIDES ANY CONTRARY PROVISIONS IN THE CONTRACT OF SALE.

The preceding NOTICE applies if the Vehicle is a used vehicle as shown on the front of this contract and if this contract is a contract of sale under the FTC Used Motor Vehicle Trade Regulation Rule.

NOTICE: ANY HOLDER OF THIS CONSUMER CREDIT CONTRACT IS SUBJECT TO ALL CLAIMS AND DEFENSES WHICH THE DEBTOR COULD ASSERT AGAINST THE SELLER OF GOODS OR SERVICES OBTAINED PURSUANT HERETO OR WITH THE PROCEEDS HEREOF. RECOVERY HEREUNDER BY THE DEBTOR SHALL NOT EXCEED AMOUNTS PAID BY THE DEBTOR HEREUNDER.

The preceding NOTICE applies to goods or services obtained primarily for personal, family or household use.

ARBITRATION CLAUSE

IMPORTANT ARBITRATION DISCLOSURES
The following Arbitration Clause significantly affects your rights in any dispute with us.
Please read these disclosures and the Arbitration Clause carefully before you sign this contract.

1. **If either of us chooses, any dispute between us will be decided by arbitration and not in court.**
2. **If a dispute is arbitrated, each of us will give up our right to a trial by the court or a jury trial.**
3. **If a dispute is arbitrated, you will give up your right to participate as a class representative or class member on any class claim you may have against us.**
4. **The information that can be obtained in discovery from each other in an arbitration is generally more limited than in a lawsuit.**
5. **Other rights that each of us would have in court may not be available in arbitration.**
6. **Even if a dispute is arbitrated, your vehicle may still be repossessed if you do not honor your contract and either of us may seek provisional remedies from a court.**

Any claim or dispute, whether in contract, tort or otherwise (including the interpretation and scope of this clause and the arbitrability of any issue), between you and us or our employees, agents, successors or assigns, which arise out of or relate to this contract or any resulting transaction or relationship (including any such relationship with third parties who do not sign this contract) shall, at your or our election (or the election of any such third party), be resolved by a neutral, binding arbitration and not by a court action. Any claim or dispute is to be arbitrated on an individual basis and not as a class action. Whoever first demands arbitration may choose the applicable rules of the American Arbitration Association ("AAA"), which may be obtained by calling 1-800-778-7879, or the applicable rules of J.A.M.S./Endispute, which may be obtained by calling 1-800-448-1660.

Whichever rules are chosen, the arbitrators shall be attorneys or retired judges and shall be selected in accordance with the applicable rules. The arbitration award shall be in writing, but without a supporting opinion. The arbitration hearing shall be conducted in the federal district in which you reside. If you demand arbitration first, you will pay one half of any arbitration filing fee. We will pay the rest of the filing fee, and the whole filing fee if we demand arbitration first. We will pay the arbitration costs and fees for the first day of arbitration, up to a maximum of eight hours. The arbitrator shall decide who shall pay any additional costs and fees.

This contract evidences a transaction involving interstate commerce. Any arbitration under this Arbitration Clause shall be governed by the Federal Arbitration Act (9 U.S.C. § 1 et. seq.).

Notwithstanding this provision, both you and we retain the right to exercise self-help remedies and to seek provisional remedies from a court. Neither you nor we waive the right to arbitrate by exercising self-help remedies, filing suit, or seeking or obtaining provisional remedies from a court. Judgment upon the award rendered by the arbitrator may be entered in any court having jurisdiction.

ASSIGNMENT

In return for purchase of this Contract, the Seller sells to Assignee: the entire interest in this Contract; and authorizes Assignee to collect and discharge obligations of the Contract and its assignment.

Seller represents and warrants to Assignee that: (a) this Contract arose out of the sale of the disclosed Vehicle; (b) this Contract is legally enforceable against the Buyer; (c) the Buyer has the capacity to contract and paid the downpayment; (d) the Buyer is purchasing the Vehicle for the Buyer's use; (e) the Contract contains an accurate representation of statements made by the Buyer; there is no inaccuracy or misrepresentation in any statement made by or on behalf of the Buyer, including those in the credit application, furnished to Assignee by Seller; (f) all disclosures required by law were made to the Buyer before signing the Contract; (g) no material fact relating to the Vehicle was misrepresented; (h) all insurance documentation will be delivered by the Buyer within legal time limits; (i) there is no fact which invalidates or reduces the value of the Contract; (j) Buyer obtained Physical Damage insurance on the Vehicle per Assignee's requirements; (k) Assignee has a first lien on the Vehicle title; (l) title will be applied for within 10 days of the delivery of the Vehicle; (m) any co-buyers were provided notices required by law; (n) Seller will perform all warranty work that was agreed to with Buyer; and (o) the Seller is licensed as required by law.

Should any of the above representations and warranties prove to be false or incorrect in any respect, and without regard to Seller's knowledge or lack of knowledge, or Assignee's reliance, Seller unconditionally, and with waiver of all defenses, agrees to pay to Assignee immediately on demand the full unpaid balance of this Contract, in principal, interest, costs, expenses, and attorney's fees. Seller further agrees under all circumstances to indemnify, and to save and to hold Assignee, and its parent and affiliates, and its and their officers, employees, agents and attorneys, harmless from any and all liability, costs, and expense (including without limitation, reimbursement of attorney's fees and court costs), resulting from the assertion of any claim, counter-claim, defense, or recoupment by Buyer with respect to the Vehicle, the purchase of the Vehicle, the compliance, content, completion and execution of this Contract, or in any way related thereto.

Seller agrees to the initialed paragraph below. If none are initialed, the assignment is made on a "Full Repurchase Obligation" basis.

________ Without Recourse or Payment Obligation, except in the circumstances noted above.

________ Full Payment Obligation - Should Buyer default under this Contract at any time, Seller unconditionally, and with waiver of all defenses, agrees to pay to Assignee immediately on demand the full unpaid balance owing under this Contract, in principal, interest, costs, expenses, and attorney's fees.

________ Limited Payment Obligation - Should Buyer default under this Contract at any time, Seller unconditionally, and with waiver of all defenses and rights of subrogation, agrees to pay Assignee immediately on demand the unpaid principal balance then owed under this Contract up to a maximum of $____________, together with all interest, costs, expenses, and attorney's fees that may then be owed by Buyer.

________ Full Repurchase Obligation - Should Buyer default under this Contract at any time and Assignee obtains possession of the Vehicle by any means, Seller unconditionally, and with waiver of all defenses, agrees to purchase the Vehicle from Assignee at private sale for an amount equal to the full unpaid balance then owed under this Contract, in principal, interest, costs, expenses, and attorney's fees.

________ Limited Repurchase Obligation - Should Buyer default under this Contract during the first ______ months of the Contract term, and Assignee obtains possession of the Vehicle by any means, Seller unconditionally, and with waiver of all defenses, agrees to purchase the Vehicle from Assignee at private sale for an amount equal to the then unpaid balance under the Contract, in principal, interest, costs, expenses and attorney's fees.

EXCLUSIVE RIGHT TO SELL AGREEMENT

THIS AGREEMENT is effective _____, 2001, and confirms that _____ has (have) appointed Burbank/Whittemore Inc. to act as Agent for the sale of property known as _____, New York.

In return for the Agent's agreement to use Agent's best efforts to sell the above property, the Owner(s) agree(s) to grant the Agent the exclusive right to sell this property under the following terms and conditions:

PERIOD OF AGREEMENT

1. This agreement shall be effective from the above date and shall expire at midnight on _____, 2001.

PRICE AT WHICH PROPERTY WILL BE OFFERED AND AUTHORITY

2. The property will be offered for sale at a list price of _____ and shall be sold, subject to negotiation, at such price and upon such terms to which Owner(s) may agree. The word Owner refers to each and ALL parties who have ownership interest in the property and the undersigned represent(s) they are the sole and exclusive owners and are fully authorized to enter into this agreement.

COMMISSION TO BE PAID TO AGENT

3. The Agent shall be entitled to and Owner shall pay to Agent one commission of _____% of the selling price. Both the Owner(s) and the Agent acknowledge that the above commission rate was not suggested nor influenced by anyone other than the parties to this Agreement. Owner(s) hereby authorizes Agent to make an offer of cooperation to any other licensed real estate broker with whom Agent wishes to cooperate. Any commission due for a sale brought about by a Sub-Agent (another broker who is authorized by Agent to assist in the sale of Owner(s) property) or to an authorized Buyer(s) Agent shall be paid by the Agent from the commission received by the Agent pursuant to this Paragraph.

The commission offered by Agent to Sub-Agents shall be _____% of the gross selling price. The commission offered by Agent to Buyer(s) Agents shall be _____% of the gross selling price.

In the event that Owner(s) authorizes Agent to compensate a Buyer('s) Agent, Owner(s) acknowledges Owner's(s') understanding that such Buyer's Agent is not representing Owner(s) as Sub-Agent and that the Buyer's Agent will be representing only the interests of the prospective purchaser.

OWNER(S) OBLIGATIONS AFTER THE EXPIRATION OF THIS AGREEMENT

4. Owner(s) understands and agrees to pay the commission referred to in paragraph 3, if this property is sold or transferred or is the subject of a contract of sale within _____ months after the expiration date of this agreement involving a person with whom the Agent or a Cooperating Broker or the Owner(s) negotiated or to whom the property is offered, quoted or shown during the period of this listing agreement. Owner(s) will not, however, be obligated to pay such commission if Owner(s) enters into a valid Exclusive Listing Agreement with another New York State licensed real estate broker after the expiration of this agreement.

WHO MAY NEGOTIATE FOR OWNER(S)

5. Owner(s) agree(s) to direct all inquiries to the Agent. Owner(s) elect(s) to have all offers submitted through Agent ☒ or Cooperating Agent ☐

SUBMISSION OF LISTING TO MULTIPLE LISTING SERVICE

6. Both Owner(s) and Agent agree that the Agent immediately is to submit this listing agreement to the Westchester-Putnam Multiple Listing Service, Inc. ("W-PMLS"), for dissemination to its Participants. No provision of this agreement is intended to nor shall be understood to establish or imply any contractual relationship between the Owner(s) and W-PMLS nor has W-PMLS in any way participated in any of the terms of this agreement, including the commission to be paid. Owner(s) acknowledge(s) that the Agent's ability to submit this listing to W-PMLS or to maintain such listing amongst those included in any compilation of listing information made available by W-PMLS, is subject to Agent's continued status as a Participant in good standing of W-PMLS.

FAIR HOUSING

7. Agent and Owner agree to comply fully with local, state and federal fair housing laws against discrimination on the basis of race, color, religion, sex, national origin, handicap, age, marital status and/or familial status, children or other prohibited factors.

AUTHORIZATION FOR "FOR SALE" SIGN AND OTHER SERVICES

8. Agent ☐ is (☐ is not) authorized to place a "For Sale" sign on the property. Owner acknowledges that Agent has fully explained to Owner(s) the services and marketing activities which Agent has agreed to provide.

REQUIREMENTS FOR PUBLICATION IN W-PMLS COMPILATION

9. This listing agreement is not acceptable for publication by W-PMLS unless and until the Owner(s) has duly signed this agreement and an acknowledgement reflecting receipt of the definitions of "Exclusive Right to Sell" and "Exclusive Agency" required by the New York State Department of State - Division of Licensing Services.

RENTAL OF PROPERTY

10. Should the Owner(s) desire to rent the property during the period of this agreement, Agent is hereby granted the sole and exclusive right to rent the property, exclusive "FOR RENT" sign privilege and the Owner(s) agrees to pay Agent a rental commission of Not Applicable. The applicable commission for the lease term is due and will be paid ☐ upon the execution of the lease ☐ upon the date of occupancy. The commission for each and any subsequent renewal there of, is due and will be paid upon the commencement of each renewal term.

COMMISSION PAYMENT

11. (a) Escrow. If, for any reason, Agent is not paid the compensation set forth herein on the due date, Owner shall establish an escrow account with a party mutually agreeable to Agent and Owner or a title insurance agent or company, and shall place into said escrow account an amount equal to the compensation set forth herein. The escrow monies shall be paid by Owner to said escrow agent and shall be held in escrow until the parties' rights to the escrow monies have been determined (i) by the written agreement of the parties;(ii) pursuant to an arbitration award; (iii) by order of a court of competent jurisdiction; or (iv) some other process to which the parties agree to in writing.

(b) Attorneys Fees. In any action, proceeding or arbitration to enforce any provision of this Agreement, or for damages caused by default, the prevailing party shall be entitled to reasonable attorney's fees, costs and related expenses, such as expert witness fees and fees paid to investigators. In the event Agent hires an attorney to enforce the collection of any brokerage commission due hereunder and is successful in collecting all or any portion thereof with or without commencing a legal action or proceeding, Owner agrees to pay the reasonable attorney's fees, costs and related expenses incurred by Agent.

(c) Arbitration. All claims, disputes or other matters in question between Agent (or any cooperating subagent or buyer's agent) and Owner,

6-28-99 / EXCL.Right.To.Sell.BLANK.doc

Page 1 of _

REAL ESTATE BROKER'S AGREEMENT

SELECTED FORMS

arising out of or relating to this Agreement shall be determined by arbitration before the American Arbitration Association in White Plains, New York, pursuant to its Commercial Arbitration Rules. The award rendered by the arbitrator shall be final, and judgment may be entered upon it in accordance with applicable law in any court of competent jurisdiction.

TERMINATION

12. Owner(s) understands that if Owner(s) terminates the Agent's authority prior to the expiration of its term, Agent shall retain its contract rights (including but not limited to recovery of its commission, advertising expenses and/or any other damages) incurred by reason of an early termination of this agreement.

ADDITIONAL POINTS

13. Additional Points of Agreement, if any. _____

_____

ALL MODIFICATIONS TO BE MADE IN WRITING

14. Owner(s) and Agent agree that no change, amendment, modification or termination of this agreement shall be binding on any party unless the same shall be in writing and signed by the parties.

Burbank/Whittemore, Inc., Better Homes and Gardens

_____ _____   _____
(Owner)   (Date)   (Agent)

                                    By: _____

_____ _____   _____ _____
(Owner)   (Date)   (Authorized Representative)   (Date)

Owner's Mailing Address: Agent's Address
                                    2179 Boston Post Road
_____   Larchmont, NY

Owner's Telephone: _____ Agent's Phone: 914 834 1070

DEFINITIONS

In accordance with the requirements of the New York State Department of State the undersigned Owner(s) does (do) hereby acknowledge receipt of the following:

1. Explanation of "Exclusive Right to Sell" listing;
2. Explanation of "Exclusive Agency" listing;
3. A list of Participants of Westchester-Putnam Multiple Listing Service, Inc.

EXPLANATION OF EXCLUSIVE RIGHT TO SELL: (As worded verbatim by the Department of State)

An "exclusive right to sell" listing means that if you, the owner of the property find a buyer for your house, or if another broker finds a buyer, you must pay the agreed commission to the present broker.

EXPLANATION OF EXCLUSIVE AGENCY: (As worded verbatim by the Department of State)

An "exclusive agency" listing means that if you, the owner of the property find a buyer, you will not have to pay a commission to the broker. However, if another broker finds a buyer, you will owe a commission to both the selling broker and your present broker.

"THE FAIR HOUSING ACT"

The Civil Rights Act of 1968 known as the Federal Fair Housing Law makes illegal any discrimination based on race, color, religion, sex or national origin in connection with the sale or rental of housing. The 1988 amendment to this Act (The Fair Housing Amendments Act of 1988) expands the coverage of this law to handicapped persons and families with children. Agent and Owner agree to comply fully with State and local statutes and Federal Fair Housing laws.

Article 10 of the REALTOR Code of Ethics states:

"REALTORS shall not deny equal professional services to any person for reasons of race, color, religion, sex, handicap, familial status, or national origin. REALTORS shall not be parties to any plan or agreement to discriminate against a person or persons on the basis of race, color, religion, sex, handicap, familial status, or national origin."

_____
                                    Owner

_____
                                    Owner

6-28-99 / EXCL.Right.To.Sell.BLANK.doc   Page 2 of _

353

STANDARD CONSTRUCTION AGREEMENT

The following form, supplied by the American Institute of Architects, appears also in the "AIA Handbook," or Architect's Handbook of Professional Practice. The forms appearing there have been revised periodically, and the Institute cautions that "when using AIA forms, the user should ascertain the latest edition." The one presented here is AIA Document A107—1997.

Beginning with Article 7 of the form, the material consists largely of text, considerably abbreviated and rearranged, from the "General Conditions of the Contract for Construction" (AIA Document A203). The AIA Handbook traces the history of this document to its origin in a Uniform Contract of 1888. It is said to be "a recognized standard of the American construction industry." In its 1987 edition, it represents a consensus of leaders in the industry, resulting from a century of testing in practice and in the courts.

The Conditions of the Contract (General, Supplementary and other) are said to form three of the six parts of any construction contract, the others being the Drawings, the Specifications, and the Owner–Contractor Agreement. "The general Conditions of the Contract are standardized contractual provisions describing the rights, responsibilities and relations of parties to the construction contract, as well as the related duties and responsibilities of the Architect, and are generally exclusive of procedural provisions. . . . For the most part, the General Conditions are suitable for both private or public work. . . . The Supplementary Conditions, drafted in collaboration with the Owner and the Owner's legal counsel for each project, modify or extend the General Conditions as the special details of each project may require. . . . "Other" Conditions refers to situations where a standard set of Supplementary conditions must be further complemented." Handbook, Chapter 13.

The Institute discourages any use of the General Conditions except in full, and in the printed form supplied by it. "The value of AIA Document A201 lies partly in the fact that its frequent users—architects, contractors, subcontractors and owners—become thoroughly familiar with its provisions, have confidence in their fairness, and recognize its format at a glance. . . . [I]ndividual practitioners are ill-advised to substitute their own provisions without expert advice since they may thereby unknowingly weaken the relationships among the document's provisions or between AIA Document A201 and the Agreements and other coordinated documents mentioned earlier." Ibid.

The Text of the General Conditions extends to some 19 pages.

1997 EDITION

AIA DOCUMENT | A107-1997

Abbreviated Standard Form of Agreement Between Owner and Contractor for Construction Projects of Limited Scope where the basis of payment is a STIPULATED SUM

This document includes abbreviated General Conditions and should not be used with other general conditions.

AGREEMENT made as of the   day of
in the year
(In words, indicate day, month and year)

This document has important legal consequences. Consultation with an attorney is encouraged with respect to its completion or modification.

BETWEEN the Owner:
(Name, address and other information)

and the Contractor:
(Name, address and other information)

This document has been approved and endorsed by The Associated General Contractors of America.

the Project is:
(Name and location)

the Architect is:
(Name, address and other information)

The Owner and Contractor agree as follows.

ARTICLE 1 THE WORK OF THIS CONTRACT

The Contractor shall fully execute the Work described in the Contract Documents, except to the extent specifically indicated in the Contract Documents to be the responsibility of others.

ARTICLE 2 DATE OF COMMENCEMENT AND SUBSTANTIAL COMPLETION

2.1 The date of commencement of the Work shall be the date of this Agreement unless a different date is stated below or provision is made for the date to be fixed in a notice to proceed issued by the Owner.

(Insert the date of commencement, if it differs from the date of this Agreement or, if applicable, state that the date will be fixed in a notice to proceed.)

2.2 The Contract Time shall be measured from the date of commencement.

2.3 The Contractor shall achieve Substantial Completion of the entire Work not later than
                    days from the date of commencement, or as follows:
(Insert number of calendar days. Alternatively, a calendar date may be used when coordinated with the date of commencement. Unless stated elsewhere in the Contract Documents, insert any requirements for earlier Substantial Completion of certain portions of the Work.)

, subject to adjustments of this Contract Time as provided in the Contract Documents.
(Insert provisions, if any, for liquidated damages relating to failure to complete on time or for bonus payments for early completion of the Work.)

ARTICLE 3 CONTRACT SUM

3.1 The Owner shall pay the Contractor the Contract Sum in current funds for the Contractor's performance of the Contract. The Contract Sum shall be
                                        Dollars ($),
subject to additions and deletions as provided in the Contract Documents.

©1997 AIA®
AIA DOCUMENT A107-1997
ABBREVIATED OWNER-
CONTRACTOR AGREEMENT

The American Institute
of Architects
1735 New York Avenue, N.W.
Washington, D.C. 20006-5292

3.2 The Contract Sum is based upon the following alternates, if any, which are described in the Contract Documents and are hereby accepted by the Owner:
(State the numbers or other identification of accepted alternates. If decisions on other alternates are to be made by the Owner subsequent to the execution of this Agreement, attach a schedule of such other alternates showing the amount for each and the date when that amount expires.)

3.3 Unit prices, if any, are as follows:

ARTICLE 4 PAYMENTS
4.1 **PROGRESS PAYMENTS**
4.1.1 Based upon Applications for Payment submitted to the Architect by the Contractor and Certificates for Payment issued by the Architect, the Owner shall make progress payments on account of the Contract Sum to the Contractor as provided below and elsewhere in the Contract Documents. The period covered by each Application for Payment shall be one calendar month ending on the last day of the month, or as follows:

4.1.2 Provided that an Application for Payment is received by the Architect not later than the day of a month, the Owner shall make payment to the Contractor not later than the   day of the   month. If an Application for Payment is received by the Architect after the date fixed above, payment shall be made by the Owner not later than   days after the Architect receives the Application for Payment.

© 1997 A I A ®
AIA DOCUMENT A107-1997
ABBREVIATED OWNER-
CONTRACTOR AGREEMENT

The American Institute
of Architects
1735 New York Avenue, N.W.
Washington, D.C. 20006-5292

4.1.3 Payments due and unpaid under the Contract shall bear interest from the date payment is due at the rate stated below, or in the absence thereof, at the legal rate prevailing from time to time at the place where the Project is located.

(Insert rate of interest agreed upon, if any.)

(Usury laws and requirements under the Federal Truth in Lending Act, similar state and local consumer credit laws and other regulations at the Owner's and Contractor's principal places of business, the location of the Project and elsewhere may affect the validity of this provision. Legal advice should be obtained with respect to deletions or modifications, and also regarding requirements such as written disclosures or waivers.)

4.2 FINAL PAYMENT

4.2.1 Final payment, constituting the entire unpaid balance of the Contract Sum, shall be made by the Owner to the Contractor when:

.1 the Contractor has fully performed the Contract except for the Contractor's responsibility to correct Work as provided in Paragraph 17.2, and to satisfy other requirements, if any, which extend beyond final payment; and

.2 a final Certificate for Payment has been issued by the Architect.

4.2.2 The Owner's final payment to the Contractor shall be made no later than 30 days after the issuance of the Architect's final Certificate for Payment, or as follows:

ARTICLE 5 ENUMERATION OF CONTRACT DOCUMENTS

5.1 The Contract Documents are listed in Article 6 and, except for Modifications issued after execution of this Agreement, are enumerated as follows:

5.1.1 The Agreement is this executed 1997 edition of the Abbreviated Standard Form of Agreement Between Owner and Contractor, AIA Document A107-1997.

5.1.2 The Supplementary and other Conditions of the Contract are those contained in the Project Manual dated   , and are as follows:

Document   Title   Pages

The remainder of Article 5
is omitted here. - eds.]

4

GENERAL CONDITIONS

ARTICLE 6 GENERAL PROVISIONS

6.1 THE CONTRACT DOCUMENTS

The Contract Documents consist of this Agreement with Conditions of the Contract (General, Supplementary and other Conditions), Drawings, Specifications, Addenda issued prior to the execution of this Agreement, other documents listed in this Agreement and Modifications issued after execution of this Agreement. A Modification is (1) a written amendment to the Contract signed by both parties, (2) a Change Order, (3) a Construction Change Directive or (4) a written order for a minor change in the Work issued by the Architect. The intent of the Contract Documents is to include all items necessary for the proper execution and completion of the Work by the Contractor. The Contract Documents are complementary, and what is required by one shall be as binding as if required by all; performance by the Contractor shall be required to the extent consistent with the Contract Documents and reasonably inferable from them as being necessary to produce the indicated results.

6.2 THE CONTRACT

The Contract Documents form the Contract for Construction. The Contract represents the entire and integrated agreement between the parties hereto and supersedes prior negotiations, representations or agreements, either written or oral. The Contract may be amended or modified only by a Modification. The Contract Documents shall not be construed to create a contractual relationship of any kind (1) between the Architect and Contractor, (2) between the Owner and a Subcontractor or sub-subcontractor, (3) between the Owner and Architect or (4) between any persons or entities other than the Owner and Contractor.

6.3 THE WORK

The term "Work" means the construction and services required by the Contract Documents, whether completed or partially completed, and includes all other labor, materials, equipment and services provided or to be provided by the Contractor to fulfill the Contractor's obligations. The Work may constitute the whole or a part of the Project.

6.4 EXECUTION OF THE CONTRACT

Execution of the Contract by the Contractor is a representation that the Contractor has visited the site, become generally familiar with local conditions under which the Work is to be performed and correlated personal observations with requirements of the Contract Documents.

6.5 OWNERSHIP AND USE OF ARCHITECT'S DRAWINGS, SPECIFICATIONS AND OTHER INSTRUMENTS OF SERVICE

The Drawings, Specifications and other documents, including those in electronic form, prepared by the Architect and the Architect's consultants are Instruments of Service through which the Work to be executed by the Contractor is described. The Contractor may retain one record set. Neither the Contractor nor any Subcontractor, sub-subcontractor or material or equipment supplier shall own or claim a copyright in the Drawings, Specifications and other documents prepared by the Architect or the Architect's consultants, and unless otherwise indicated the Architect and the Architect's consultants shall be deemed the authors of them and will retain all common law, statutory and other reserved rights, in addition to the copyrights. All copies of them, except the Contractor's record set, shall be returned or suitably accounted for to the Architect, on request, upon completion of the Work. The Drawings, Specifications and other documents prepared by the Architect and the Architect's consultants, and copies thereof furnished to the Contractor, are for use solely with respect to this Project. They are not to be used by the Contractor or any Subcontractor, sub-subcontractor or material or equipment supplier on other projects or for additions to this Project outside the scope of the Work without the specific written consent of the Owner, Architect and the Architect's consultants. The Contractor, Subcontractors,

© 1997 AIA®
AIA DOCUMENT A107-1997
ABBREVIATED OWNER-CONTRACTOR AGREEMENT

The American Institute
of Architects
1735 New York Avenue, N.W.
Washington, D.C. 20006-5292

sub-subcontractors and material or equipment suppliers are authorized to use and reproduce applicable portions of the Drawings, Specifications and other documents prepared by the Architect and the Architect's consultants appropriate to and for use in the execution of their Work under the Contract Documents. All copies made under this authorization shall bear the statutory copyright notice, if any, shown on the Drawings, Specifications and other documents prepared by the Architect and the Architect's consultants. Submittal or distribution to meet official regulatory requirements or for other purposes in connection with this Project is not to be construed as publication in derogation of the Architect's or Architect's consultants' copyrights or other reserved rights.

ARTICLE 7 OWNER

7.1 INFORMATION AND SERVICES REQUIRED OF THE OWNER

7.1.1   The Owner shall furnish and pay for surveys and a legal description of the site.

7.1.2   The Contractor shall be entitled to rely on the accuracy of information furnished by the Owner but shall exercise proper precautions relating to the safe performance of the Work.

7.1.3   Except for permits and fees which are the responsibility of the Contractor under the Contract Documents, the Owner shall secure and pay for other necessary approvals, easements, assessments and charges required for the construction, use or occupancy of permanent structures or permanent changes in existing facilities.

7.2 OWNER'S RIGHT TO STOP THE WORK

If the Contractor fails to correct Work which is not in accordance with the requirements of the Contract Documents, or persistently fails to carry out the Work in accordance with the Contract Documents, the Owner may issue a written order to the Contractor to stop the Work, or any portion thereof, until the cause for such order is eliminated; however, the right of the Owner to stop the Work shall not give rise to a duty on the part of the Owner to exercise this right for the benefit of the Contractor or any other person or entity.

7.3 OWNER'S RIGHT TO CARRY OUT THE WORK

If the Contractor defaults or persistently fails or neglects to carry out the Work in accordance with the Contract Documents, or fails to perform a provision of the Contract, the Owner, after 10 days' written notice to the Contractor and without prejudice to any other remedy the Owner may have, may make good such deficiencies and may deduct the reasonable cost thereof, including Owner's expenses and compensation for the Architect's services made necessary thereby, from the payment then or thereafter due the Contractor.

ARTICLE 8 CONTRACTOR

8.1 REVIEW OF CONTRACT DOCUMENTS AND FIELD CONDITIONS BY CONTRACTOR

8.1.1   Since the Contract Documents are complementary, before starting each portion of the Work, the Contractor shall carefully study and compare the various Drawings and other Contract Documents relative to that portion of the Work, as well as the information furnished by the Owner pursuant to Subparagraph 7.1.1, shall take field measurements of any existing conditions related to that portion of the Work and shall observe any conditions at the site affecting it. These obligations are for the purpose of facilitating construction by the Contractor and are not for the purpose of discovering errors, omissions or inconsistencies in the Contract Documents; however, any errors, omissions or inconsistencies discovered by the Contractor shall be reported promptly to the Architect as a request for information in such form as the Architect may require.

8.1.2 Any design errors or omissions noted by the Contractor during this review shall be reported promptly to the Architect, but it is recognized that the Contractor's review is made in the Contractor's capacity as a contractor and not as a licensed design professional unless otherwise specifically provided in the Contract Documents.

8.2 SUPERVISION AND CONSTRUCTION PROCEDURES

8.2.1 The Contractor shall supervise and direct the Work, using the Contractor's best skill and attention. The Contractor shall be solely responsible for and have control over construction means, methods, techniques, sequences and procedures, and for coordinating all portions of the Work under the Contract, unless the Contract Documents give other specific instructions concerning these matters. If the Contract Documents give specific instructions concerning construction means, methods, techniques, sequences or procedures, the Contractor shall be fully and solely responsible for the jobsite safety thereof unless the Contractor gives timely written notice to the Owner and Architect that such means, methods, techniques, sequences or procedures may not be safe.

8.2.2 The Contractor shall be responsible to the Owner for acts and omissions of the Contractor's employees, Subcontractors and their agents and employees, and other persons or entities performing portions of the Work for or on behalf of the Contractor or any of its Subcontractors.

8.3 LABOR AND MATERIALS

8.3.1 Unless otherwise provided in the Contract Documents, the Contractor shall provide and pay for labor, materials, equipment, tools, construction equipment and machinery, water, heat, utilities, transportation, and other facilities and services necessary for proper execution and completion of the Work whether temporary or permanent and whether or not incorporated or to be incorporated in the Work.

8.3.2 The Contractor shall enforce strict discipline and good order among the Contractor's employees and other persons carrying out the Contract. The Contractor shall not permit employment of unfit persons or persons not skilled in tasks assigned to them.

8.3.3 The Contractor shall deliver, handle, store and install materials in accordance with manufacturers' instructions.

8.3.4 The Contractor may make substitutions only with the consent of the Owner, after evaluation by the Architect and in accordance with a Change Order.

8.4 WARRANTY

The Contractor warrants to the Owner and Architect that materials and equipment furnished under the Contract will be of good quality and new unless otherwise required or permitted by the Contract Documents, that the Work will be free from defects not inherent in the quality required or permitted, and that the Work will conform with the requirements of the Contract Documents. Work not conforming to these requirements, including substitutions not properly approved and authorized, may be considered defective. The Contractor's warranty excludes remedy for damage or defect caused by abuse, modifications not executed by the Contractor, improper or insufficient maintenance, improper operation or normal wear and tear and normal usage.

8.5 TAXES

The Contractor shall pay sales, consumer, use and other similar taxes which are legally enacted when bids are received or negotiations concluded.

©1997 AIA®
AIA DOCUMENT A107-1997
ABBREVIATED OWNER-CONTRACTOR AGREEMENT

The American Institute
of Architects
1735 New York Avenue, N.W.
Washington, D.C. 20006-5292

8.6 PERMITS, FEES AND NOTICES

8.6.1 Unless otherwise provided in the Contract Documents, the Contractor shall secure and pay for the building permit and other permits and governmental fees, licenses and inspections necessary for proper execution and completion of the Work.

8.6.2 The Contractor shall comply with and give notices required by laws, ordinances, rules, regulations and lawful orders of public authorities applicable to performance of the Work. The Contractor shall promptly notify the Architect and Owner if the Drawings and Specifications are observed by the Contractor to be at variance therewith. If the Contractor performs Work knowing it to be contrary to laws, statutes, ordinances, building codes, and rules and regulations without such notice to the Architect and Owner, the Contractor shall assume appropriate responsibility for such Work and shall bear the costs attributable to correction.

8.7 SUBMITTALS

8.7.1 The Contractor shall review for compliance with the Contract Documents, approve in writing and submit to the Architect Shop Drawings, Product Data, Samples and similar submittals required by the Contract Documents with reasonable promptness. The Work shall be in accordance with approved submittals.

8.7.2 Shop Drawings, Product Data, Samples and similar submittals are not Contract Documents.

8.8 USE OF SITE

The Contractor shall confine operations at the site to areas permitted by law, ordinances, permits and the Contract Documents and shall not unreasonably encumber the site with materials or equipment.

8.9 CUTTING AND PATCHING

The Contractor shall be responsible for cutting, fitting or patching required to complete the Work or to make its parts fit together properly.

8.10 CLEANING UP

The Contractor shall keep the premises and surrounding area free from accumulation of waste materials or rubbish caused by operations under the Contract. At completion of the Work, the Contractor shall remove from and about the Project waste materials, rubbish, the Contractor's tools, construction equipment, machinery and surplus material.

8.11 ROYALTIES, PATENTS AND COPYRIGHTS

The Contractor shall pay all royalties and license fees; shall defend suits or claims for infringement of copyrights and patent rights and shall hold the Owner and Architect harmless from loss on account thereof, but shall not be responsible for such defense or loss when a particular design, process or product of a particular manufacturer or manufacturers is required by the Contract Documents, or where the copyright violations are contained in Drawings, Specifications or other documents prepared by the Owner or Architect, unless the Contractor has reason to believe that there is an infringement of patent or copyright and fails to promptly furnish such information to the Architect.

8.12 ACCESS TO WORK

The Contractor shall provide the Owner and Architect access to the Work in preparation and progress wherever located.

© 1997 AIA®
AIA DOCUMENT A107-1997
ABBREVIATED OWNER-
CONTRACTOR AGREEMENT

The American Institute
of Architects
1735 New York Avenue, N.W.
Washington, D.C. 20006-5292

9

362

8.13   INDEMNIFICATION

8.13.1   To the fullest extent permitted by law and to the extent claims, damages, losses or expenses are not covered by Project Management Protective Liability insurance purchased by the Contractor in accordance with Paragraph 16.3, the Contractor shall indemnify and hold harmless the Owner, Architect, Architect's consultants and agents and employees of any of them from and against claims, damages, losses and expenses, including but not limited to attorneys' fees, arising out of or resulting from performance of the Work, provided that such claim, damage, loss or expense is attributable to bodily injury, sickness, disease or death, or to injury to or destruction of tangible property (other than the Work itself), but only to the extent caused by the negligent acts or omissions of the Contractor, a Subcontractor, anyone directly or indirectly employed by them or anyone for whose acts they may be liable, regardless of whether or not such claim, damage, loss or expense is caused in part by a party indemnified hereunder. Such obligation shall not be construed to negate, abridge, or reduce other rights or obligations of indemnity which would otherwise exist as to a party or person described in this Paragraph 8.13.

8.13.2   In claims against any person or entity indemnified under this Paragraph 8.13 by an employee of the Contractor, a Subcontractor, anyone directly or indirectly employed by them or anyone for whose acts they may be liable, the indemnification obligation under Subparagraph 8.13.1 shall not be limited by a limitation on amount or type of damages, compensation or benefits payable by or for the Contractor or Subcontractor under workers' compensation acts, disability benefit acts or other employee benefit acts.

ARTICLE 9   ARCHITECT'S ADMINISTRATION OF THE CONTRACT

9.1   The Architect will provide administration of the Contract and will be an Owner's representative (1) during construction, (2) until final payment is due and (3) with the Owner's concurrence, from time to time during the one-year period for correction of Work described in Paragraph 17.2.

9.2   The Architect, as a representative of the Owner, will visit the site at intervals appropriate to the stage of the Contractor's operations (1) to become generally familiar with and to keep the Owner informed about the progress and quality of the portion of the Work completed, (2) to endeavor to guard the Owner against defects and deficiencies in the Work, and (3) to determine in general if the Work is being performed in a manner indicating that the Work, when fully completed, will be in accordance with the Contract Documents. However, the Architect will not be required to make exhaustive or continuous on-site inspections to check the quality or quantity of the Work. The Architect will neither have control over or charge of, nor be responsible for, the construction means, methods, techniques, sequences or procedures, or for safety precautions and programs in connection with the Work, since these are solely the Contractor's rights and responsibilities under the Contract Documents, except as provided in Subparagraph 8.2.1.

9.3   The Architect will not be responsible for the Contractor's failure to perform the Work in accordance with the requirements of the Contract Documents. The Architect will not have control over or charge of and will not be responsible for acts or omissions of the Contractor, Subcontractors, or their agents or employees, or any other persons or entities performing portions of the Work.

9.4   Based on the Architect's evaluations of the Work and of the Contractor's Applications for Payment, the Architect will review and certify the amounts due the Contractor and will issue Certificates for Payment in such amounts.

9.5   The Architect will have authority to reject Work that does not conform to the Contract Documents.

© 1997   AIA®
AIA DOCUMENT A107-1997
ABBREVIATED OWNER-
CONTRACTOR AGREEMENT

The American Institute
of Architects
1735 New York Avenue, N.W.
Washington, D.C. 20006-5292

10

9.6 The Architect will review and approve or take other appropriate action upon the Contractor's submittals such as Shop Drawings, Product Data and Samples, but only for the limited purpose of checking for conformance with information given and the design concept expressed in the Contract Documents.

9.7 The Architect will interpret and decide matters concerning performance under, and requirements of, the Contract Documents on written request of either the Owner or Contractor. The Architect will make initial decisions on all claims, disputes and other matters in question between the Owner and Contractor but will not be liable for results of any interpretations or decisions so rendered in good faith.

9.8 The Architect's decisions on matters relating to aesthetic effect will be final if consistent with the intent expressed in the Contract Documents.

9.9 Duties, responsibilities and limitations of authority of the Architect as set forth in the Contract Documents shall not be restricted, modified or extended without written consent of the Owner, Contractor and Architect. Consent shall not be unreasonably withheld.

9.10 CLAIMS AND DISPUTES
9.10.1 Claims, disputes and other matters in question arising out of or relating to this Contract, including those alleging an error or omission by the Architect but excluding those arising under Paragraph 15.2, shall be referred initially to the Architect for decision. Such matters, except those relating to aesthetic effect and except those waived as provided for in Paragraph 9.11 and Subparagraphs 14.5.3 and 14.5.4, shall, after initial decision by the Architect or 30 days after submission of the matter to the Architect, be subject to mediation as a condition precedent to arbitration or the institution of legal or equitable proceedings by either party.

9.10.2 If a claim, dispute or other matter in question relates to or is the subject of a mechanic's lien, the party asserting such matter may proceed in accordance with applicable law to comply with the lien notice or filing deadlines prior to resolution of the matter by the Architect, by mediation or by arbitration.

9.10.3 The parties shall endeavor to resolve their disputes by mediation which, unless the parties mutually agree otherwise, shall be in accordance with the Construction Industry Mediation Rules of the American Arbitration Association currently in effect. Request for mediation shall be filed in writing with the other party to this Agreement and with the American Arbitration Association. The request may be made concurrently with the filing of a demand for arbitration but, in such event, mediation shall proceed in advance of arbitration or legal or equitable proceedings, which shall be stayed pending mediation for a period of 60 days from the date of filing, unless stayed for a longer period by agreement of the parties or court order.

9.10.4 Claims, disputes and other matters in question arising out of or relating to the Contract that are not resolved by mediation, except matters relating to aesthetic effect and except those waived as provided for in Paragraph 9.11 and Subparagraphs 14.5.3 and 14.5.4, shall be decided by arbitration which, unless the parties mutually agree otherwise, shall be in accordance with the Construction Industry Arbitration Rules of the American Arbitration Association currently in effect. The demand for arbitration shall be filed in writing with the other party to this Agreement and with the American Arbitration Association and shall be made within a reasonable time after the dispute has arisen. The award rendered by the arbitrator or arbitrators shall be final, and judgment may be entered upon it in accordance with applicable law in any court having jurisdiction thereof. Except by written consent of the person or entity sought to be joined, no arbitration arising out of or relating to the Contract Documents shall include, by consolidation, joinder or in any other manner, any person or entity not a party to the Agreement under which

© 1997 AIA®
AIA DOCUMENT A107-1997
ABBREVIATED OWNER-
CONTRACTOR AGREEMENT

The American Institute
of Architects
1735 New York Avenue, N.W.
Washington, D.C. 20006-5292

such arbitration arises, unless it is shown at the time the demand for arbitration is filed that (1) such person or entity is substantially involved in a common question of fact or law, (2) the presence of such person or entity is required if complete relief is to be accorded in the arbitration, (3) the interest or responsibility of such person or entity in the matter is not insubstantial, and (4) such person or entity is not the Architect or any of the Architect's employees or consultants. The agreement herein among the parties to the Agreement and any other written agreement to arbitrate referred to herein shall be specifically enforceable under applicable law in any court having jurisdiction thereof.

9.11   CLAIMS FOR CONSEQUENTIAL DAMAGES
The Contractor and Owner waive claims against each other for consequential damages arising out of or relating to this Contract. This mutual waiver includes:

.1 damages incurred by the Owner for rental expenses, for losses of use, income, profit, financing, business and reputation, and for loss of management or employee productivity or of the services of such persons; and

.2 damages incurred by the Contractor for principal office expenses including the compensation of personnel stationed there, for losses of financing, business and reputation, and for loss of profit except anticipated profit arising directly from the Work.

This mutual waiver is applicable, without limitation, to all consequential damages due to either party's termination in accordance with Article 19. Nothing contained in this Paragraph 9.11 shall be deemed to preclude an award of liquidated direct damages, when applicable, in accordance with the requirements of the Contract Documents.

ARTICLE 10 SUBCONTRACTORS
10.1   A Subcontractor is a person or entity who has a direct contract with the Contractor to perform a portion of the Work at the site.

10.2   Unless otherwise stated in the Contract Documents or the bidding requirements, the Contractor, as soon as practicable after award of the Contract, shall furnish in writing to the Owner through the Architect the names of the Subcontractors for each of the principal portions of the Work. The Contractor shall not contract with any Subcontractor to whom the Owner or Architect has made reasonable and timely objection. If the proposed but rejected Subcontractor was reasonably capable of performing the Work, the Contract Sum and Contract Time shall be increased or decreased by the difference, if any, occasioned by such change, and an appropriate Change Order shall be issued before commencement of the substitute Subcontractor's Work. The Contractor shall not be required to contract with anyone to whom the Contractor has made reasonable objection.

10.3   Contracts between the Contractor and Subcontractors shall (1) require each Subcontractor, to the extent of the Work to be performed by the Subcontractor, to be bound to the Contractor by the terms of the Contract Documents, and to assume toward the Contractor all the obligations and responsibilities, including the responsibility for safety of the Subcontractor's Work, which the Contractor, by the Contract Documents, assumes toward the Owner and Architect, and (2) allow the Subcontractor the benefit of all rights, remedies and redress afforded to the Contractor by these Contract Documents.

ARTICLE 11 OWNER'S RIGHT TO PERFORM CONSTRUCTION AND TO AWARD SEPARATE CONTRACTS
11.1   The Owner reserves the right to perform construction or operations related to the Project with the Owner's own forces, and to award separate contracts in connection with other portions

© 1997 A I A ®
AIA DOCUMENT A107-1997
ABBREVIATED OWNER-
CONTRACTOR AGREEMENT

The American Institute
of Architects
1735 New York Avenue, N.W.
Washington, D.C. 20006-5292

12

of the Project or other construction or operations on the site under conditions of the contract identical or substantially similar to these, including those portions related to insurance and waiver of subrogation. If the Contractor claims that delay or additional cost is involved because of such action by the Owner, the Contractor shall make such claim as provided in Paragraph 9.10.

11.2 The Contractor shall afford the Owner and separate contractors reasonable opportunity for introduction and storage of their materials and equipment and performance of their activities, and shall connect and coordinate the Contractor's activities with theirs as required by the Contract Documents.

11.3 The Owner shall be reimbursed by the Contractor for costs incurred by the Owner which are payable to a separate contractor because of delays, improperly timed activities or defective construction of the Contractor. The Owner shall be responsible to the Contractor for costs incurred by the Contractor because of delays, improperly timed activities, damage to the Work or defective construction of a separate contractor.

ARTICLE 12 CHANGES IN THE WORK

12.1 The Owner, without invalidating the Contract, may order changes in the Work within the general scope of the Contract consisting of additions, deletions or other revisions, the Contract Sum and Contract Time being adjusted accordingly. Such changes in the Work shall be authorized by written Change Order signed by the Owner, Contractor and Architect, or by written Construction Change Directive signed by the Owner and Architect.

12.2 The cost or credit to the Owner from a Change in the Work shall be determined by mutual agreement of the parties or, in the case of a Construction Change Directive, by the Contractor's cost of labor, materials, equipment, and reasonable overhead and profit.

12.3 The Architect will have authority to order minor changes in the Work not involving adjustment in the Contract Sum or extension of the Contract Time and not inconsistent with the intent of the Contract Documents. Such changes shall be effected by written order and shall be binding on the Owner and Contractor. The Contractor shall carry out such written orders promptly.

12.4 If concealed or unknown physical conditions are encountered at the site that differ materially from those indicated in the Contract Documents or from those conditions ordinarily found to exist, the Contract Sum and Contract Time shall be equitably adjusted.

ARTICLE 13 TIME

13.1 Time limits stated in the Contract Documents are of the essence of the Contract. By executing the Agreement the Contractor confirms that the Contract Time is a reasonable period for performing the Work.

13.2 The date of Substantial Completion is the date certified by the Architect in accordance with Subparagraph 14.4.2.

13.3 If the Contractor is delayed at any time in the commencement or progress of the Work by changes ordered in the Work, by labor disputes, fire, unusual delay in deliveries, abnormal adverse weather conditions not reasonably anticipatable, unavoidable casualties or any causes beyond the Contractor's control, or by other causes which the Architect determines may justify delay, then the Contract Time shall be extended by Change Order for such reasonable time as the Architect may determine, subject to the provisions of Paragraph 9.10.

© 1997 AIA®
AIA DOCUMENT A107-1997
ABBREVIATED OWNER-
CONTRACTOR AGREEMENT

The American Institute
of Architects
1735 New York Avenue, N.W.
Washington, D.C. 20006-5292

13

ARTICLE 14 PAYMENTS AND COMPLETION

14.1 APPLICATIONS FOR PAYMENT

14.1.1 Payments shall be made as provided in Article 4 of this Agreement. Applications for Payment shall be in a form satisfactory to the Architect.

14.1.2 The Contractor warrants that title to all Work covered by an Application for Payment will pass to the Owner no later than the time of payment. The Contractor further warrants that upon submittal of an Application for Payment all Work for which Certificates for Payment have been previously issued and payments received from the Owner shall, to the best of the Contractor's knowledge, information and belief, be free and clear of liens, claims, security interests or other encumbrances adverse to the Owner's interests.

14.2 CERTIFICATES FOR PAYMENT

14.2.1 The Architect will, within seven days after receipt of the Contractor's Application for Payment, either issue to the Owner a Certificate for Payment, with a copy to the Contractor, for such amount as the Architect determines is properly due, or notify the Contractor and Owner in writing of the Architect's reasons for withholding certification in whole or in part as provided in Subparagraph 14.2.3.

14.2.2 The issuance of a Certificate for Payment will constitute a representation by the Architect to the Owner, based on the Architect's evaluations of the Work and the data comprising the Application for Payment, that the Work has progressed to the point indicated and that, to the best of the Architect's knowledge, information and belief, the quality of the Work is in accordance with the Contract Documents. The foregoing representations are subject to an evaluation of the Work for conformance with the Contract Documents upon Substantial Completion, to results of subsequent tests and inspections, to correction of minor deviations from the Contract Documents prior to completion and to specific qualifications expressed by the Architect. The issuance of a Certificate for Payment will further constitute a representation that the Contractor is entitled to payment in the amount certified. However, the issuance of a Certificate for Payment will not be a representation that the Architect has (1) made exhaustive or continuous on-site inspections to check the quality or quantity of the Work, (2) reviewed construction means, methods, techniques, sequences or procedures, (3) reviewed copies of requisitions received from Subcontractors and material suppliers and other data requested by the Owner to substantiate the Contractor's right to payment, or (4) made examination to ascertain how or for what purpose the Contractor has used money previously paid on account of the Contract Sum.

14.2.3 The Architect may withhold a Certificate for Payment in whole or in part, to the extent reasonably necessary to protect the Owner, if in the Architect's opinion the representations to the Owner required by Subparagraph 14.2.2 cannot be made. If the Architect is unable to certify payment in the amount of the Application, the Architect will notify the Contractor and Owner as provided in Subparagraph 14.2.1. The Architect may also withhold a Certificate for Payment or, because of subsequently discovered evidence, may nullify the whole or a part of a Certificate for Payment previously issued, to such extent as may be necessary in the Architect's opinion to protect the Owner from loss for which the Contractor is responsible, including loss resulting from acts and omissions described in Subparagraph 8.2.2, because of:

.1 defective Work not remedied;

.2 third party claims filed or reasonable evidence indicating probable filing of such claims unless security acceptable to the Owner is provided by the Contractor;

.3 failure of the Contractor to make payments properly to Subcontractors or for labor, materials or equipment;

.4 reasonable evidence that the Work cannot be completed for the unpaid balance of the Contract Sum;

.5 damage to the Owner or another contractor;

© 1997 AIA®
AIA DOCUMENT A107-1997
ABBREVIATED OWNER-
CONTRACTOR AGREEMENT

The American Institute
of Architects
1735 New York Avenue, N.W.
Washington, D.C. 20006-5292

.6 reasonable evidence that the Work will not be completed within the Contract Time and that the unpaid balance would not be adequate to cover actual or liquidated damages for the anticipated delay; or

.7 persistent failure to carry out the Work in accordance with the Contract Documents.

14.2.4 When the above reasons for withholding certification are removed, certification will be made for amounts previously withheld.

14.3   PAYMENTS TO THE CONTRACTOR

14.3.1   The Contractor shall promptly pay each Subcontractor, upon receipt of payment from the Owner, out of the amount paid to the Contractor on account of such Subcontractor's portion of the Work, the amount to which said Subcontractor is entitled, reflecting percentages actually retained from payments to the Contractor on account of such Subcontractor's portion of the Work. The Contractor shall, by appropriate agreement with each Subcontractor, require each Subcontractor to make payments to sub-subcontractors in similar manner.

14.3.2   Neither the Owner nor Architect shall have an obligation to pay or see to the payment of money to a Subcontractor except as may otherwise be required by law.

14.3.3   A Certificate for Payment, a progress payment, or partial or entire use or occupancy of the Project by the Owner shall not constitute acceptance of Work not in accordance with the Contract Documents.

14.4   SUBSTANTIAL COMPLETION

14.4.1   Substantial Completion is the stage in the progress of the Work when the Work or designated portion thereof is sufficiently complete in accordance with the Contract Documents so that the Owner can occupy or utilize the Work for its intended use.

14.4.2   When the Architect determines that the Work or designated portion thereof is substantially complete, the Architect will issue a Certificate of Substantial Completion which shall establish the date of Substantial Completion, establish responsibilities of the Owner and Contractor for security, maintenance, heat, utilities, damage to the Work and insurance, and fix the time within which the Contractor shall finish all items on the list accompanying the Certificate. Warranties required by the Contract Documents shall commence on the date of Substantial Completion of the Work or designated portion thereof unless otherwise provided in the Certificate of Substantial Completion. Upon the issuance of the Certificate of Substantial Completion, the Architect will submit it to the Owner and Contractor for their written acceptance of responsibilities assigned to them in such Certificate

14.5   FINAL COMPLETION AND FINAL PAYMENT

14.5.1   Upon receipt of written notice that the Work is ready for final inspection and acceptance and upon receipt of a final Application for Payment, the Architect will promptly make such inspection and, when the Architect finds the Work acceptable under the Contract Documents and the Contract fully performed, the Architect will promptly issue a final Certificate for Payment stating that to the best of the Architect's knowledge, information and belief, and on the basis of the Architect's on-site visits and inspections, the Work has been completed in accordance with terms and conditions of the Contract Documents and that the entire balance found to be due the Contractor and noted in the final Certificate is due and payable. The Architect's final Certificate for Payment will constitute a further representation that conditions stated in Subparagraph 14.5.2 as precedent to the Contractor's being entitled to final payment have been fulfilled.

14.5.2   Final payment shall not become due until the Contractor has delivered to the Owner a complete release of all liens arising out of this Contract or receipts in full covering all labor, materials and equipment for which a lien could be filed, or a bond satisfactory to the Owner to indemnify the Owner against such lien. If such lien remains unsatisfied after payments are made, the Contractor shall refund to the Owner all money that the Owner may be compelled to pay in discharging such lien, including costs and reasonable attorneys' fees.

14.5.3 The making of final payment shall constitute a waiver of claims by the Owner except those arising from:

 .1 liens, claims, security interests or encumbrances arising out of the Contract and unsettled;

 .2 failure of the Work to comply with the requirements of the Contract Documents; or

 .3 terms of special warranties required by the Contract Documents.

14.5.4 Acceptance of final payment by the Contractor, a Subcontractor or material supplier shall constitute a waiver of claims by that payee except those previously made in writing and identified by that payee as unsettled at the time of final Application for Payment.

ARTICLE 15 PROTECTION OF PERSONS AND PROPERTY
15.1 SAFETY PRECAUTIONS AND PROGRAMS
The Contractor shall be responsible for initiating, maintaining and supervising all safety precautions and programs in connection with the performance of the Contract. The Contractor shall take reasonable precautions for safety of, and shall provide reasonable protection to prevent damage, injury or loss to:

 .1 employees on the Work and other persons who may be affected thereby;

 .2 the Work and materials and equipment to be incorporated therein; and

 .3 other property at the site or adjacent thereto.

The Contractor shall give notices and comply with applicable laws, ordinances, rules, regulations and lawful orders of public authorities bearing on safety of persons and property and their protection from damage, injury or loss. The Contractor shall promptly remedy damage and loss to property caused in whole or in part by the Contractor, a Subcontractor, a sub-subcontractor, or anyone directly or indirectly employed by any of them, or by anyone for whose acts they may be liable and for which the Contractor is responsible under Subparagraphs 15.1.2 and 15.1.3, except for damage or loss attributable to acts or omissions of the Owner or Architect or by anyone for whose acts either of them may be liable, and not attributable to the fault or negligence of the Contractor. The foregoing obligations of the Contractor are in addition to the Contractor's obligations under Paragraph 8.13.

15.2 HAZARDOUS MATERIALS
15.2.1 If reasonable precautions will be inadequate to prevent foreseeable bodily injury or death to persons resulting from a material or substance, including but not limited to asbestos or polychlorinated biphenyl (PCB), encountered on the site by the Contractor, the Contractor shall, upon recognizing the condition, immediately stop Work in the affected area and report the condition to the Owner and Architect in writing. When the material or substance has been rendered harmless, Work in the affected area shall resume upon written agreement of the Owner and Contractor. The Contract Time shall be extended appropriately and the Contract Sum shall be increased in the amount of the Contractor's reasonable additional costs of shutdown, delay and start-up, which adjustments shall be accomplished as provided in Article 12 of this Agreement.

15.2.2 To the fullest extent permitted by law, the Owner shall indemnify and hold harmless the Contractor, Subcontractors, Architect, Architect's consultants and agents and employees of any of them from and against claims, damages, losses and expenses, including but not limited to attorneys' fees, arising out of or resulting from performance of the Work in the affected area if in fact the material or substance presents the risk of bodily injury or death as described in

© 1997 AIA®
AIA DOCUMENT A107-1997
ABBREVIATED OWNER-CONTRACTOR AGREEMENT

The American Institute
of Architects
1735 New York Avenue, N.W.
Washington, D.C. 20006-5292

16

Subparagraph 15.2.1 and has not been rendered harmless, provided that such claim, damage, loss or expense is attributable to bodily injury, sickness, disease or death, or to injury to or destruction of tangible property (other than the Work itself), and provided that such damage, loss or expense is not due to the sole negligence of a party seeking indemnity.

15.2.3 If, without negligence on the part of the Contractor, the Contractor is held liable for the cost of remediation of a hazardous material or substance solely by reason of performing Work as required by the Contract Documents, the Owner shall indemnify the Contractor for all cost and expense thereby incurred.

ARTICLE 16 INSURANCE

16.1 The Contractor shall purchase from and maintain in a company or companies lawfully authorized to do business in the jurisdiction in which the Project is located insurance for protection from claims under workers' compensation acts and other employee benefit acts which are applicable, claims for damages because of bodily injury, including death, and claims for damages, other than to the Work itself, to property which may arise out of or result from the Contractor's operations under the Contract, whether such operations be by the Contractor or by a Subcontractor or anyone directly or indirectly employed by any of them. This insurance shall be written for not less than limits of liability specified in the Contract Documents or required by law, whichever coverage is greater, and shall include contractual liability insurance applicable to the Contractor's obligations. Certificates of Insurance acceptable to the Owner shall be filed with the Owner prior to commencement of the Work. Each policy shall contain a provision that the policy will not be canceled or allowed to expire until at least 30 days' prior written notice has been given to the Owner.

16.2 OWNER'S LIABILITY INSURANCE
The Owner shall be responsible for purchasing and maintaining the Owner's usual liability insurance.

16.3 PROJECT MANAGEMENT PROTECTIVE LIABILITY INSURANCE
16.3.1 Optionally, the Owner may require the Contractor to purchase and maintain Project Management Protective Liability insurance from the Contractor's usual sources as primary coverage for the Owner's, Contractor's and Architect's vicarious liability for construction operations under the Contract. Unless otherwise required by the Contract Documents, the Owner shall reimburse the Contractor by increasing the Contract Sum to pay the cost of purchasing and maintaining such optional insurance coverage, and the Contractor shall not be responsible for purchasing any other liability insurance on behalf of the Owner. The minimum limits of liability purchased with such coverage shall be equal to the aggregate of the limits required for Contractor's Liability insurance under Paragraph 16.1.

16.3.2 To the extent damages are covered by Project Management Protective Liability insurance, the Owner, Contractor and Architect waive all rights against each other for damages, except such rights as they may have to the proceeds of such insurance. The policy shall provide for such waivers of subrogation by endorsement or otherwise.

16.3.3 The Owner shall not require the Contractor to include the Owner, Architect or other persons or entities as additional insureds on the Contractor's Liability insurance under Paragraph 16.1.

16.4 PROPERTY INSURANCE
16.4.1 Unless otherwise provided, the Owner shall purchase and maintain, in a company or companies lawfully authorized to do business in the jurisdiction in which the Project is located,

property insurance on an "all-risk" policy form, including builder's risk, in the amount of the initial Contract Sum, plus the value of subsequent modifications and cost of materials supplied and installed by others, comprising total value for the entire Project at the site on a replacement cost basis without optional deductibles. Such property insurance shall be maintained, unless otherwise provided in the Contract Documents or otherwise agreed in writing by all persons and entities who are beneficiaries of such insurance, until final payment has been made as provided in Paragraph 14.5 or until no person or entity other than the Owner has an insurable interest in the property required by this Paragraph 16.4 to be covered, whichever is later. This insurance shall include interests of the Owner, the Contractor, Subcontractors and sub-subcontractors in the Project.

16.4.2 The Owner shall file a copy of each policy with the Contractor before an exposure to loss may occur. Each policy shall contain a provision that the policy will not be canceled or allowed to expire, and that its limits will not be reduced, until at least 30 days' prior written notice has been given to the Contractor.

16.5 WAIVERS OF SUBROGATION

16.5.1 The Owner and Contractor waive all rights against (1) each other and any of their subcontractors, sub-subcontractors, agents and employees, each of the other, and (2) the Architect, Architect's consultants, separate contractors described in Article 11, if any, and any of their subcontractors, sub-subcontractors, agents and employees for damages caused by fire or other causes of loss to the extent covered by property insurance obtained pursuant to Paragraph 16.4 or other property insurance applicable to the Work, except such rights as they have to proceeds of such insurance held by the Owner as fiduciary. The Owner or Contractor, as appropriate, shall require of the Architect, Architect's consultants, separate contractors described in Article 11, if any, and the subcontractors, sub-subcontractors, agents and employees of any of them, by appropriate agreements, written where legally required for validity, similar waivers each in favor of other parties enumerated herein. The policies shall provide such waivers of subrogation by endorsement or otherwise. A waiver of subrogation shall be effective as to a person or entity even though that person or entity would otherwise have a duty of indemnification, contractual or otherwise, did not pay the insurance premium directly or indirectly, and whether or not the person or entity had an insurable interest in the property damaged.

16.5.2 A loss insured under the Owner's property insurance shall be adjusted by the Owner as fiduciary and made payable to the Owner as fiduciary for the insureds, as their interests may appear, subject to requirements of any applicable mortgages clause. The Contractor shall pay Subcontractors their just shares of insurance proceeds received by the Contractor, and by appropriate agreements, written where legally required for validity, shall require Subcontractors to make payments to their sub-subcontractors in similar manner.

ARTICLE 17 CORRECTION OF WORK

17.1 The Contractor shall promptly correct Work rejected by the Architect or failing to conform to the requirements of the Contract Documents, whether discovered before or after Substantial Completion and whether or not fabricated, installed or completed. Costs of correcting such rejected Work, including additional testing and inspections and compensation for the Architect's services and expenses made necessary thereby, shall be at the Contractor's expense.

17.2 In addition to the Contractor's obligations under Paragraph 8.4, if, within one year after the date of Substantial Completion of the Work or designated portion thereof or after the date for commencement of warranties established under Subparagraph 14.4.2, or by terms of an applicable special warranty required by the Contract Documents, any of the Work is found to be not in accordance with the requirements of the Contract Documents, the Contractor shall correct it

© 1997 AIA®
AIA DOCUMENT A107-1997
ABBREVIATED OWNER-
CONTRACTOR AGREEMENT

The American Institute
of Architects
1735 New York Avenue, N.W.
Washington, D.C. 20006-5292

18

promptly after receipt of written notice from the Owner to do so unless the Owner has previously given the Contractor a written acceptance of such condition. The Owner shall give such notice promptly after discovery of the condition. During the one-year period for correction of Work, if the Owner fails to notify the Contractor and give the Contractor an opportunity to make the correction, the Owner waives the rights to require correction by the Contractor and to make a claim for breach of warranty.

17.3 If the Contractor fails to correct nonconforming Work within a reasonable time, the Owner may correct it in accordance with Paragraph 7.3.

17.4 The one-year period for correction of Work shall be extended with respect to portions of Work first performed after Substantial Completion by the period of time between Substantial Completion and the actual performance of the Work.

17.5 The one-year period for correction of Work shall not be extended by corrective Work performed by the Contractor pursuant to this Article 17.

ARTICLE 18 MISCELLANEOUS PROVISIONS

18.1 **ASSIGNMENT OF CONTRACT**
Neither party to the Contract shall assign the Contract without written consent of the other.

18.2 **GOVERNING LAW**
The Contract shall be governed by the law of the place where the Project is located.

18.3 **TESTS AND INSPECTIONS**
Tests, inspections and approvals of portions of the Work required by the Contract Documents or by laws, ordinances, rules, regulations or orders of public authorities having jurisdiction shall be made at an appropriate time. Unless otherwise provided, the Contractor shall make arrangements for such tests, inspections and approvals with an independent testing laboratory or entity acceptable to the Owner, or with the appropriate public authority, and shall bear all related costs of tests, inspections and approvals. The Contractor shall give the Architect timely notice of when and where tests and inspections are to be made so that the Architect may be present for such procedures. The Owner shall bear costs of tests, inspections or approvals which do not become requirements until after bids are received or negotiations concluded.

18.4 **COMMENCEMENT OF STATUTORY LIMITATION PERIOD**
As between Owner and Contractor, any applicable statute of limitations shall commence to run and any alleged cause of action shall be deemed to have accrued:

    .1 not later than the date of Substantial Completion for acts or failures to act occurring prior to the relevant date of Substantial Completion;

    .2 not later than the date of issuance of the final Certificate for Payment for acts or failures to act occurring subsequent to the relevant date of Substantial Completion and prior to the issuance of the final Certificate for Payment; and

    .3 not later than the date of the relevant act or failure to act by the Contractor for acts or failures to act occurring after the date of the final Certificate for Payment.

ARTICLE 19 TERMINATION OF THE CONTRACT

19.1 **TERMINATION BY THE CONTRACTOR**
If the Architect fails to recommend payment for a period of 30 days through no fault of the Contractor, or if the Owner fails to make payment thereon for a period of 30 days, the Contractor may, upon seven additional days' written notice to the Owner and the Architect, terminate the

Contract and recover from the Owner payment for Work executed and for proven loss with respect to materials, equipment, tools, and construction equipment and machinery, including reasonable overhead, profit and damages applicable to the Project.

19.2 TERMINATION BY THE OWNER

19.2.1 The Owner may terminate the Contract if the Contractor:

.1 persistently or repeatedly refuses or fails to supply enough properly skilled workers or proper materials;

.2 fails to make payment to Subcontractors for materials or labor in accordance with the respective agreements between the Contractor and the Subcontractors;

.3 persistently disregards laws, ordinances, or rules, regulations or orders of a public authority having jurisdiction; or

.4 otherwise is guilty of substantial breach of a provision of the Contract Documents.

19.2.2 When any of the above reasons exists, the Owner, upon certification by the Architect that sufficient cause exists to justify such action, may, without prejudice to any other remedy the Owner may have and after giving the Contractor seven days' written notice, terminate the Contract and take possession of the site and of all materials, equipment, tools, and construction equipment and machinery thereon owned by the Contractor and may finish the Work by whatever reasonable method the Owner may deem expedient. Upon request of the Contractor, the Owner shall furnish to the Contractor a detailed accounting of the costs incurred by the Owner in finishing the Work.

19.2.3 When the Owner terminates the Contract for one of the reasons stated in Subparagraph 19.2.1, the Contractor shall not be entitled to receive further payment until the Work is finished.

19.2.4 If the unpaid balance of the Contract Sum exceeds costs of finishing the Work, including compensation for the Architect's services and expenses made necessary thereby, and other damages incurred by the Owner and not expressly waived, such excess shall be paid to the Contractor. If such costs and damages exceed the unpaid balance, the Contractor shall pay the difference to the Owner. The amount to be paid to the Contractor or Owner, as the case may be, shall be certified by the Architect, upon application, and this obligation for payment shall survive termination of the Contract.

© 1997   A I A ®
**AIA DOCUMENT A107-1997
ABBREVIATED OWNER-
CONTRACTOR AGREEMENT**

The American Institute
of Architects
1735 New York Avenue, N.W.
Washington, D.C. 20006-5292

20

ARTICLE 20 OTHER CONDITIONS OR PROVISIONS

This Agreement entered into as of the day and year first written above.

_____   _____
OWNER*(Signature)*   **CONTRACTOR***(Signature)*

_____   _____
(Printed name and title)   *(Printed name and title)*

© 1997 AIA®
AIA DOCUMENT A107-1997
ABBREVIATED OWNER-
CONTRACTOR AGREEMENT

The American Institute
of Architects
1735 New York Avenue, N.W.
Washington, D.C. 20006-5292

21

†